One Hundred Years

of

HARTFORD'S

Courant

From Colonial Times through
the Civil War

BY

J. EUGENE SMITH

Archon Books
1970

ISBN: 0-208-00962-0
Library of Congress Catalog Card Number: 74-121759
Printed in the United States of America

CONTENTS

PART I: 1764–1783

I.	COLONIAL NEWSPAPER	3
II.	POLITICS AND REVOLUTION	17
III.	CULTURAL REFLECTIONS	38

PART II: 1783–1815

IV.	FEDERALIST PRESS	59
V.	FIGHTING THE NEW ORDER	80
VI.	NEWSPAPER GLIMPSES OF EARLY HARTFORD	101
VII.	HUDSON & GOODWIN, PUBLISHERS	117

PART III: 1815–1836

VIII.	FROM FEDERALIST TO WHIG	139
IX.	BENEVOLENCE AND BUSINESS	158
X.	THE GOODWINS AND THE *Courant*	177

PART IV: 1836–1865

XI.	CITY NEWSPAPER	193
XII.	WHIG POLITICS	207
XIII.	REPUBLICANISM AND SLAVERY	222
XIV.	RAILROADS, INDUSTRY, AND CULTURE	234
XV.	THE *Courant* IN THE CIVIL WAR	256

NOTES	269
BIBLIOGRAPHY	328
INDEX	331

ACKNOWLEDGMENT

The manuscript of this history was originally prepared while studying at Harvard University. The author appreciates the encouragement and help received from Professor Arthur Meier Schlesinger. He appreciates also the cooperation and assistance given to him by the Hartford Courant Company and by the librarians of the Connecticut Historical Society.

PART ONE
1764–1783

CHAPTER I
COLONIAL NEWSPAPER

ONE day in 1764 Thomas Green installed his press and printing utensils in a little wooden building on Hartford's main street over James Mookler's barber shop.[1] Having once hung out the sign of the Heart & Crown, he apparently first printed an almanac,[2] and then, on October 29, issued the prospectus of a newspaper he hoped to print. It bore these words:

The Connecticut Courant, (a Specimen of which, the Publick are now presented with) will, on due Encouragement be continued every Monday, beginning on Monday, the 19th of November, next: Which Encouragement we hope to deserve, by a constant Endeavour to render this Paper useful, and entertaining, not only as a Channel for News, but assisting to all Those who may have Occasion to make use of it as an Advertiser.

Subscriptions to this Paper, will be taken in at the Printing-Office, near the North-Meeting-House, in Hartford.

For the previous four years Green had managed the New Haven office of James Parker & Co., New York printers. There he had turned out some 50 known publications—books, pamphlets, and broadsides. There he had edited and printed Parker's weekly *Connecticut Gazette,* the colony's oldest paper. There also he had managed the post office for John Holt, deputy postmaster and one-time boss at the printing shop. Holt had moved to New York in 1760, and one can imagine that four years of experience in printing, conducting the newspaper, and overseeing the post office had provided young Green with the necessary competence to make a success of his Hartford establishment.[3]

Printing was something of a family tradition with him and it may have been, in the course of planning his future, that some interesting thoughts of the past moved through his mind.[4] In 1649, under the patronage of Harvard College, great-grandfather Samuel Green assumed the management of the first press in the Massachusetts Bay Colony. Three of Samuel's sons were printers and one of these, grandfather Timothy Green of New London, became official printer for the colony of Connecticut in 1713, an office which he held for over 40 years. Five of Timothy's sons followed the trade, and one of them was young Thomas's father. Two of Thomas's brothers were printers, and the boys, just as their father before them, had probably learned to work at case and press in their grandfather's office. When old Timothy died in 1757, the New London shop remained in family hands, but Thomas Green had probably left for New Haven to work for Parker & Co. sometime before Holt placed him in charge of affairs in 1760.

Green may not have fancied being in Hartford at all except for a series of events quite beyond his choosing. The firm of Parker & Co. gave up the New Haven business to Benjamin Mecom, a nephew of Benjamin Franklin, and Franklin appointed Mecom postmaster of New Haven.[5] Since Green was 29 years of age, married, and the father of two children, his prospects there, in terms of income and independence, had probably seemed not very promising.[6] So he must have commenced scouting the merits of such towns as he knew with thoughts of plying his trade elsewhere.

Connecticut contained perhaps a dozen growing towns with populations of 3,000 or more.[7] Some 40 miles east of New Haven was New London, and within easy traveling distance, the thriving settlements at Stonington and Norwich. Twelve miles to the west lay Stratford at the mouth of the Housatonic, and a few miles beyond that, Fairfield; and of course there were the smaller shore-line towns all the way from Rhode Island to the New York boundary. For one hoping to publish a newspaper, a printing office in any of the communities bordering Long Island Sound offered certain newsgathering advantages because all of them rested on the old Boston Post Road. But in another and more practical sense, their promise was poor. Newspaper subscribers were far too few in any one or two small villages to support the expenses of printer and press, and the towns in this area were more or less pre-empted by other newspaper printers. Green's brother, Timothy, was already printing the *New London Gazette*,[8] presumably Mecom would continue publishing the *Gazette* at New Haven, and the educated gentlemen in the smaller places to the west of Fairfield could be accommodated either by Mecom's paper or by one of the weeklies published at the time in the city of New York.[9]

The settlements up the Connecticut River Valley gave Green much likelier prospects of success, for neither printing press nor newspaper had been established there. Hartford, in particular, had several advantages. It was a flourishing community of about 4,000 inhabitants. As one of the colony's capitals, the General Assembly met there each May. It was the seat of government of the most populous county, and within a radius of 15 miles were the relatively sizable towns of Wethersfield, Windsor, Farmington, and Middletown.[10] It lay near the head of river navigation and had traffic with the inland settlements to the east and west, and with the northern river communities in Massachusetts.[11] Not least of all, the New York and Boston posts met at Hartford near Saturday and postriders went forth with letters and packets to many of the colony's interior towns.[12]

Whatever Green's thoughts before going to Hartford, for the following three years he worked hard at his trade. In the spring of 1765 he moved from over the barber shop to the second floor of a store opposite the Court House and next door to Bull's Tavern.[13] At both locations he offered a variety of commodities for sale.[14] These included Dutch quills, ink powder, wafers in boxes, red and black sealing wax, leather inkpots, pewter and lead inkstands, slates, hornbooks, writing paper, and spectacles, as well as such printed materials as plain and gilt Bibles, common prayer books, catechisms, Watt's *Psalms,* reprinted sermons, Bible stories, almanacs, histories, political tracts, self-teaching music books, and record books for town clerks. Curious townsfolk, who stopped in at the sign of the Heart & Crown, could frequently have found Green setting type from the manuscript of a sermon or pulling a political tract from his cumbersome press. He published, among other works, funeral and election sermons, an agricultural tract, a petition to the king, official proclamations, pamphlets, and a politico-religious volume of about 250 pages.[15] Between times, perhaps most sedulously on Saturdays and Mondays, he performed the task of compiling and printing the *Connecticut Courant.*

Judged by later standards, Green's *Courant* presented a crude, makeshift appearance. The prospectus contained four pages of two columns each. The subsequent papers, which began publication on November 26, rather than on the 19th as intended,[16] carried the Heart & Crown emblem, the title, and the printer's imprint at the top of page one. Few issues were the same in size, for they varied between 11½″ and 14″ in length, and 6¾″ and 9″ in width. The print paper was thick, strong, and absorbent, rough in texture, and frequently deckle-edged. From several fonts of type, Green at first used mostly brevier, resulting in print that was small, sometimes blurred, often of varying impression, and certainly difficult to read by candlelight. Later on, he dropped the Heart & Crown symbol for several months, and used larger types.[17] He experimented with the number of columns to the page, sometimes printing three columns, sometimes two and one half, sometimes two, sometimes a half column so placed that it had to be read by turning the paper sideways; [18] but finally he generally used three. Occasionally the *Courant* appeared on half a sheet printed on both sides, and infrequently important news crowded the advertisements into a single-page supplement. [19]

The news which the *Courant* carried was presumably the sort that Green thought his subscribers wished to read. Little of it, oftentimes none, pertained to Hartford or the nearby towns—an occasional death notice of more than ordinary interest, the ordination of a minister, the convening or adjournment of the General Assembly, the commencement at New Haven, election results, a disastrous fire, storm damage, or a comment on unusual weather. [20] The prospectus, on the other hand, contained items not only from Boston, New York, the West Indies, and London, but from Naples, Cadiz, Genoa, Paris, Stockholm, Hamburg, Lisbon and Amsterdam. Later issues had much from areas even more distant. An interest in empire trade and politics gave point to the bulk of this news from the outside, while that which was local could probably sooner be heard at church, in the tavern, along the road, or from the postrider. Green seems to have selected the outside news for the information of his readers, but inserted local items mostly for the benefit of outsiders. Thus local events were seldom newsworthy.

The printer therefore leaned heavily upon other papers for news. The out-of-town journals, principally those from Boston and New York, reported events in their own localities and funneled the news from letters, from the southern and foreign papers, and from sea captains. The posts carrying them to Hartford reached Green on Saturday. In severe weather they were sometimes late, but the *Courant* went to press anyway with news from old papers already at hand. [21] The issue of December 31, 1764, noted: "As neither of the Posts are arrived, the Publication of this Paper will be deferred till To-Morrow"; and added a postscript under date of January 1: "VII o'clock Afternoon, the Posts not arrived."

Green assembled the news without headlines, without captions, and, with rare exceptions, without comment. What introduction there was often indicated the original source of the relayed news and offered the reader his clue to the time lapse. Thus, under a Boston date line of May 30, in the issue of June 3, 1765, appeared the following: "Since our last arrived here, Capt. Jacobsen, in 39

Days from London, who brought the Prints to the 15th ult." The issue of April 14, 1766, bore a letter from a "Gentleman of Character" in London dated March 1. Introductions of this type were common not only for news from beyond the seas but for news from other colonies and from the empire outposts in the western wilderness. Occasionally Green printed original news from the outside, but not often—a description of land in the West from Israel Putnam [22] or an excerpt from a letter received by someone in Hartford. He wrote no editorials and whatever news editing he did lay in this process of selection and rejection.

Green was indebted also to essay writers and to the merchants who advertised. Gentlemen who signed such pseudonyms as "Cato," "Eucrates," or "Alexander Windmill" were afforded a public screen for the projection of ideas on a variety of topics— the evils of tea drinking or how to make pot ashes or perhaps some political subject. Occasionally there were anecdotes and bits of verse. The paid advertisements increased in number during Green's years in Hartford until they occupied about a third of the *Courant*'s space. Here were listed, without much embellishment, whatever English and India goods the merchants in Hartford and towns close by were offering for small down payments in cash or country produce. Besides "vendue" or public auction cards, lost, found, and want ads, runaway slave, apprentice, tax, and bankruptcy notices, were the advertisements of companies concerned with land development in New York, Massachusetts, Vermont, and Pennsylvania. There were also the announcements of school teachers and doctors. In effect, the newspaper gave a degree of mobility and ubiquity to the town bulletin board not otherwise possible.

How widely the *Courant* circulated during Green's three years in Hartford or how many copies the printer pulled from his press each week or how much he worried over collecting his debts will probably never be known. The extant issues reveal none of his boasts and few complaints. When making ready to leave Hartford at the close of 1767, he mentioned the heavy expenses of business and requested immediate payment in cash or country produce.[23] He dunned subscribers again in the spring and came back to town to adjust accounts, some of which he was still trying to settle in 1771.[24] However, nothing indicates that the *Courant* was anything but a paying concern by the beginning of 1768. Green still retained a financial interest in its future and it undoubtedly offered his successor the promise of a respectable living.

Green went into partnership with Ebenezer Watson probably in December, 1767.[25] Sometime in the winter, he moved his family back to New Haven where the discontinuance of Mecom's paper had given him the chance to enter business with his brother Samuel.[26] *The Connecticut Journal and New-Haven Post-Boy,* which they published, made its appearance in October, 1767, and Green may have spent most of his time in New Haven from then on. At any rate, Watson had complete charge of the *Courant* for the next three years when it bore the Green & Watson imprint.[27] At the end of that time, in December, 1770, Green severed connections with the paper which he had founded and Watson remained its sole proprietor until his untimely death in 1777.

The *Courant*'s new printer, a native of Bethlehem, Connecticut, was in his twenty-fourth year when Green left Hartford. Green taught him the trade. He had likely worked in the Hartford office from the beginning, and before that, in New Haven.[28] As it developed later, Watson was a person of considerable enterprise, so one can suppose that he took hold with enthusiasm. He was destined, in the 10 years ahead, to see the paper through many difficulties.

In the second week of December, 1768, the *Courant*'s office was moved into more appropriate quarters in a building near the Great Bridge, later the Main Street bridge over Park River.[29] Here and in the shop next to Bull's Tavern, Watson carried the usual sermons, statutes, almanacs, music books, and blanks of all kinds, along with timely pamphlets by Dickinson and Paine.[30] He sold lottery tickets[31] and second-hand books—Greek, Latin, religious works, French grammars, volumes on mathematics and philosophy.[32] He issued *Watson's Register, and Connecticut Almanack* and published *Common Sense,* installments of *The Crisis,* and the proceedings, resolves, and addresses of the First Continental Congress.[33] The *Courant* advertised small quantities of articles he had probably taken in on barter—indigo, linseed oil, peas, and, at one time, a gold watch.[34] He was the agent, just as Green had been, for persons who wanted farm workers, journeymen, or apprentices,[35] and for those who had lost things[36] or had things to dispose of.[37] He had agents of his own in several towns who sold writing supplies and some of his published pamphlets.[38]

The routine of newsgathering went on as usual with the winter posts often late from Boston or New York and sometimes from both places.[39] In September, 1770, Watson changed the *Courant*'s publication date to Tuesday to circumvent these hazards, but four years later he changed back again to accommodate one of his riders.[40] For a brief time at the outbreak of the Revolution, all the posts were interrupted, but they started moving again under the direction of Congress [41] and special news came sometimes by express or by army postrider.[42] In these periods of crisis, interest was undoubtedly high and the failure to get news must occasionally have been exasperating. In April, 1775, under a Boston date line of March 30, was this report:

A gentleman from Newbury informs, that a Vessel arrived there last Thursday from the West-Indies, the master of which said, that ten days before, he spoke with a vessel bound to New-York from London, in ballast, who had been out only 28 days, and that the Captain of her told him there was glorious news for America, but the wind blowing very fresh he could hear nothing further.[43]

With the British occupying New York, Watson complained that "The southern Post did not bring a single Paper from that Quarter —and the Post from Boston NEVER arrives in town till after this Paper goes to Press." [44]

With Watson's management, the *Courant* underwent changes in content and size. The Heart & Crown gave way to the King's Arms which the paper bore until September, 1774, shortly to be replaced by the Connecticut seal.[45] For a time, the title became *Connecticut Courant, and Hartford Weekly Intelligencer,* with the familiar by-line, "Open to ALL PARTIES——not under the IN-FLUENCE OF ANY." [46] There appeared also, "Containing the Freshest ADVICES, both Foreign and Domestic," a phrase resurrected from the *Courant* of 1765.[47] In 1769 the *Courant* carried its first small commercial cut: a prancing steed advertising "Handsome Harry," the stud horse, and later used for strayed or stolen horses.[48] In December, 1770, the printer introduced a "Poet's Corner" which featured odes, elegies, parodies, lampoons—crude verses upon Tom Gage, tyranny, death, friendship, religion—

> If all Things succeed, as already decreed
> And immutable Impulses rule us,
> To Preach and to Pray, Is but time thrown away,
> And our Teachers do nothing but fool us.[49]

Death notices, heretofore scattered, became common for a period, and marriage announcements first appeared in the paper.[50] The print was oftentimes poor and the papers varied in color and tex-

ture, but finally, in the first month of 1776, the *Courant* attained
uniform size (10″ by 16½″) and a relative dignity of appearance.

For a number of reasons the *Courant* took on a more personal
tone. Watson apologized for worn-out types, for the poor quality
of his paper, for typographical errors, for mistakes in spelling.[51]
He insisted on knowing the names of the paper's correspondents
and sometimes rejected their letters or required the deletion of pro-
voking passages.[52] Personal disputes irked him and he wished that
those of his writers who aspersed their neighbors would learn to
extenuate human imperfections, at least in the public prints.[53]
Ardently patriotic on the eve of the Revolution, he used his press
to single out those whose sentiments or conduct invited public
reproach.[54] Perhaps more than anything else, he carried his business worries to the *Courant*'s readers, partly in the hopes of loosen-
ing their purses and partly, one supposes, because of the magnitude
of his troubles.

Each December the printer balanced his books, as numbers of
his subscribers had reason to know. At the end of the first year of
partnership, Watson reminded his public of the expenses of moving
the printing office in which he and Green were currently involved
and begged them to discharge their obligations in cash, wheat, rye,
Indian corn, oats, or wood.[55] The *Courant* was selling for six shillings a year or for eight shillings by special postrider.[56] One year
later he complained sharply of the persevering negligence of the
majority of his subscribers. If we believe what he printed, the firm
of Green & Watson had collected an average of less than two
shillings out of six since the beginning, not enough to pay for the
paper the *Courant* was printed on.[57] In view of this sorry situation,
he threatened to stop publication with the issue of December 11,
1769, unless the *Courant*'s readers appropriately voted its continuance. They might settle by cash, produce, or note; those who lived
near could bring wood, and even other methods of payment were
open to discussion; but settle they must if the *Courant* were to go
on.[58]

Whether because Watson was undecided, or too busy scurrying
after debtors, or simply prolonging a threat, no issue came from
his press for a fortnight after the 11th; but Christmas Day found
him printing his papers quite as usual. In the future, new customers
would lay down three shillings when they subscribed and three at
the end of the year. Those with advertisements would have them
in the office by Saturday noon with cash on the counter![59] At the

close of the next year, when the partnership ended, Watson enlarged the *Courant* and raised the price to seven shillings, or nine shillings by newsrider.[60] Thereafter he continued to press his subscribers, at one time sending out a collector, at another threatening suit.[61] In 1775, pleading a debt for types, he gave public thanks to 300 subscribers for the punctual settlement of accounts, but threatened about 400 more with a speedy stoppage of services unless they presently mended their habits. Some of them, according to his records, were in arrears six and seven years.[62] After the war started, rising prices created additional problems which the printer eased temporarily by boosting the *Courant*'s price to 12 shillings a year.[63] But by this time his prospects were happier, for he had achieved at least the partial solution of another harassing problem.

The difficulty of supplying his business with paper resulted in chronic embarrassment for Watson. For about the first year and a half of publication the *Courant* was necessarily printed on paper imported from outside Connecticut. After paper making began at Norwich, in 1766, both Green and Watson advertised for clean cotton and linen rags and old sail cloth which they traded for paper at the Norwich establishment.[64] The available stock of paper, however, was not consistently satisfactory, for sometimes, presumably when spring freshets, summer droughts, or prolonged freezing weather interrupted the water power at the mill, the *Courant* appeared in diminutive dress, on greyish blue paper, and even on blue wrapping paper. Watson, who lamented and was eventually disgusted with this state of affairs,[65] entered partnership with a young man named Austin Ledyard and set about erecting a paper mill across the river from Hartford.[66] This project, which was under way in the summer of 1775, took longer to finish than Watson estimated. In October, with stock running low, he hoped to be producing in five or six weeks.[67] Meantime, the papers were small, some of them half sheets, blue, and of inferior, rough texture. At the end of the business year, in December, came the decision to discontinue the *Courant* until the local mill began operations—a period of not over two weeks at the outside.[68] Despite this promise, no issue came from his press for over a month, and then, although of respectable size, the paper was soft and of extremely poor quality.[69] But finally, by March, 1776, it was as good as ever, and the uniform size of the issues until Watson's death indicated the abatement of some of his worries on this score.[70]

His subscribers, too, had increased in number. Some called for their papers in Hartford, some got them by mail, and others received them weekly or fortnightly by special delivery. *Courant* newsriders covered not only a wide sweep in Connecticut but traveled to towns in the four western counties of Massachusetts and to some in New York.[71] After the war started, Watson mentioned the great and unexpected encouragement which an increasing circulation had given him.[72] When British troops occupied Boston, one writer mentioned the general circulation of the *Courant* in Worcester County and another spoke of its readers in the province of New Hampshire.[73] In the winter of 1776 Watson requested those who called for their papers to get them on Tuesdays since the great number made it impossible for him to print them all in one day.[74] Since each paper required four impressions, issuing the *Courant* from a crude hand press was undoubtedly slow and tiring. According to Isaiah Thomas, who then published the *Massachusetts Spy,* the *Courant*'s circulation increased rapidly, after the British occupation of New York, until it equaled or surpassed that of any paper published on the continent.[75]

With the new mill operating and the circulation enlarged, Watson's troubles were not yet terminated. He now needed sizing and plenty of rags to keep the mill stocked. Accordingly, he advertised for calves' pates and especially for rags. "A little bag or basket, hung up in some convenient place, will receive the rags with the same trouble that will be necessary to sweep them into the fire." [76] Watson offered three pennies per pound and, the better to cultivate the institution of an American rag bag, hired collectors in a number of towns who worked on commission.[77] He appealed to the "Daughters of Liberty" to prevent the streams of intelligence from drying up, and threatened to sell no writing paper to towns careless about saving rags.[78] Besides this, getting new types was a matter of no small moment because they were expensive and hard to procure. By the end of 1772, subscribers were complaining of the *Courant*'s poor print but Watson lacked the funds to provide any remedy.[79] Later, through "unexpected assistance" from friends in Hartford, he hoped to have types from England by the following winter but they failed to appear until June, 1774.[80] And now, when the circulation swelled, they were once again badly worn. Watson decided to journey to a distant state, sometime in April, 1777, to buy new ones and for this reason he wanted those who owed to pay their bills.[81] In May, he apologized for not having gone. He had taken the smallpox and the rush of work attendant upon the spring meeting of the General Assembly had kept him busy subsequently, but he was determined to set out at the end of the session.[82] Unfortunately he never did.[83] The print was still poor in the black-bordered issue of September 22, 1777, which carried the following sorrowful announcement:

On Tuesday last departed this life after a distressing sickness, Mr. Ebenezer Watson, Printer, in the 34th year of his age. A gentleman of a most humane heart, and susceptable of the tenderest feelings for distress, in whatever manner discovered—Jealous of the rights of human nature, and anxious for the safety of his country, his press hath been devoted to the vindication of rational liberty. The Governor's company of Cadets, of which he was an Ensign, in token of respect for the deceased, attended the funeral in their uniforms. He has left a melancholy widow, with five young children, and a numerous circle of friends to lament his death.

The *Courant's* second owner died intestate with an involved but solvent estate. The appraisers left the following interesting inventory of the *Courant's* office.[84]

1 Printing Press	£ 20– 0–0
11 Pair Printing Cases @ 15/	8– 5–0
2 Large frame for Dº 20/ 7 Small Dº 35/	2–15–0
Half the Shop Belonging to Green & Watson	30– 0–0
The Printing Room Over Mʳ Doolittle's Shop	30– 0–0
Lye Trough 24/ Iron for Sign 10/	1–14–0
Large Iron Kittle 7/ Iron Pot 7/6	0–14–6
Iron Pounder 8/ Small Iron Kettle 2/	0–10–0
Blanks 3/10 Accompt Book 30/	5– 0–0
Old Wrighting Desk 8/ Iron Skillet 1/6	0– 9–6
37 Ream Printing Paper @ 10/	18–10–0
Saw 2/ 6 Small Gallies 9/0	
2 folio Dº 6/	0–17–0
1 Long Dº 2/ Salmons Gazetteer 4/	0– 6–0
3 Chairs 7/ 4 Composing sticks 48/	2–15–0
Twine 4/ Bank 4/ old Slice + Hand-	
irons 2/6	0–10–6
All the Old Printing Types Belonging to	
the Office	50– 0–0
New Types Lately Imported from Philadelphia	161– 0–0
	£ 333– 6–6

Watson's share in the paper mill was valued at £400 and his whole estate, against which there was an imposing array of claims, at £872 in silver money.

Watson's second wife, the former Hannah Bunce of Lebanon, Connecticut, inherited the *Courant* and owned the paper mill with Mrs. Ledyard whose husband had died the autumn before.[85] At the end of the year, Mrs. Watson entered partnership with George Goodwin of Hartford who had worked in the printing office since boyhood and upon whom the responsibility of compiling the *Courant* had devolved presumably when Watson took to his death-bed. Goodwin was only 20 years old at the time, but since he was competent, and, according to Isaiah Thomas, a better printer than Watson, the firm of Watson and Goodwin might have looked to the future with something less than discouragement.[86] This may have been the case when the partnership began on January 1, 1778, but within the month occurred an incident sufficient to disturb even the stoutest of philosophers, to say nothing of the widows Ledyard and Watson and young George Goodwin.

On the night of January 27, the paper mill took fire. All the machinery, 150 reams of writing paper, almost 100 reams of printing paper, and a large supply of rags and other stock were reduced to ashes. The loss was heavy and the cause of the fire not ascertained but suspected to have been of incendiary origin. Goodwin was perturbed:

Thronged as this town is with British and tory prisoners rambling with impunity at all hours of the night, and open to the secret malice of every hardned villain, Would it not be proper that a suitable guard should nightly patrol the streets not only for the security of private property, but for the safe keeping of what nearly and deeply concerns the public? [87]

In withstanding the gloom and discouragement of this particular fall and winter, the owners of the *Courant* had never again to encounter circumstances quite so trying. Watson had been active in Hartford, aside from his trade, both in church and military affairs,[88] and his widow undoubtedly received what sympathy and help the community could offer her at the time of his death. But when the mill burned, the expense of rebuilding it must have been additionally upsetting since the printing business depended upon it and Goodwin had doubts that the *Courant* could continue without interruption. The issue of subsequent events, however, was happier than expected. The General Assembly authorized agents of the widows Ledyard and Watson to raise £1,500 by public lottery,[89] and by the month of May, 1778, the owners of the new mill were advertising for calves' pates, deer's ears, and scraps of skin of any kind that might be used for sizing.[90] The *Courant,* moreover, had endured the crisis so that no suspension of publication proved to be necessary.

Goodwin was the first printer of the *Courant* to call himself an editor,[91] yet the paper had little personal flavor throughout the remaining years of the war. He injected almost none of his worries into the *Courant.* By 1778 the war had settled down to a contest of dreary endurance, the lively days of Tory hunting had passed, and the inducements for noisy patriotism were considerably less urgent than once they had been. Just as Watson had done, Goodwin sometimes rejected the offerings of would-be contributors and otherwise occasionally printed his opinions.[92] But only at the conclusion of the Revolution, with the joys of victory at hand, did Goodwin's *Courant* approach the spirited newspaper that reflected so plainly the ardent feelings of the patriotic Watson.

The routine affairs of the business went along much as usual with the posts late, rags wanted, bluish papers, a dearth of local news, and plenty of war intelligence from letters, loyalist and rebel newspapers, from prizes, and from ships of truce used in exchanging prisoners. Goodwin published the *Courant* on Tuesday rather than Monday, varied the seal when he entered the partnership and then shortly dropped it from the head, never to use one again.[93] With wartime inflation, the *Courant's* price was fixed at 18 shillings a year; then at one bushel and three pecks of wheat or equal value in rye, flour, wood, or cash; subsequently at 30 shillings, and finally at 10 silver shillings or the currency equivalent.[94] The number of subscribers was presumably gratifying in these years for over half a century later, when old George Goodwin was still puttering about the office, the *Courant* recalled a wartime circulation of about 8,000 copies per week—enough, one would suspect, to have kept the printer more than moderately busy.[95]

In March, 1779, the *Courant's* publishing firm underwent an important change when Goodwin acquired a partner in the person of Mrs. Watson's new husband, Barzillai Hudson of Hartford.[96] Hudson, a widower with two children, had lost his wife from smallpox early the year before.[97] The Hudsons had been neighbors and friends of the Watsons and it may even have been that Hudson, a mason by trade, had sometimes worked in the printing shop.[98] He appears also to have been a citizen of some importance since the governor and Council of Safety had appointed him commandant of the guards around the county jail at Hartford where numbers of war prisoners were incarcerated during the Revolution.[99] In the new member of the company, who was then 37 years of age, the firm probably got what it most needed—a responsible person to manage and expand its business interests while Goodwin gave full time to the printing.[100]

Whatever form the division of responsibility took, the *Courant*'s advertisements indicate that Hudson was soon tending store at the north door under the printing shop where he sold not only the usual line of printer's goods but sugar, chocolate, spices, tea, coffee, pocketbooks, hats, pigtail tobacco, and other items.[101] Before the end of the war, the firm sustained an interest in not one, but two paper mills across the river [102] and had published two works of considerable importance—Trumbull's much lauded *M'Fingal,* and Noah Webster's famous spelling book, long to remain a successful school text.[103]

This was the beginning of the prominent firm of Hudson & Goodwin, book printers, and for many years to come, prosperous publishers of Hartford's *Connecticut Courant.*

CHAPTER II

POLITICS AND REVOLUTION

IN the autumn of 1764, when Thomas Green assembled items from the Boston, New York, and Newport papers to compose the first issue of the *Courant,* he included the following paragraph:

It is now confidently affirmed by some, which however may not be true in fact, that the severity of the new a–t of p——t is to be imputed to letters, representations, NARRATIVES, &c., transmitted to the m——y about two years ago by persons of eminence this side of the water . . . To whatever cause these severities are owing, it behooves the colonies to represent their grievances in the strongest point of light, and to unite in such measures as *will be effectual* to obtain redress. The northern colonists have sense enough, at least, the sense of *feeling;* and can tell where the *shoe pinches.*[1]

The Revenue Act of 1764, to which this alluded, taxed imported English fabrics and Oriental goods, forbade the importation of French wines, and placed prohibitive rates on those from Spanish and Portuguese sources. It was the first of a series of parliamentary enactments between 1764 and 1775 which incurred appreciable displeasure in the colonies; and Green's inclusion of such criticism in the *Courant*'s prospectus introduced a motif which characterized the paper during the subsequent dozen years.

It is not difficult to suggest an analysis of the situation which gave tone to the *Courant*'s point of view. By and large, the *Courant* reflected the political prejudices of the dominant elements in the northern American colonies. Merchants and farmers were directly and indirectly involved in trading and financial transactions that played over wide areas to the east and the south. This complexity of activities and the imperial politics which affected their business prosperity gave men of affairs in Pennsylvania, New York, and the New England provinces a sustained interest in political and business tidings from England, the West Indies, and the port towns along the Atlantic. Embellished news reprints, rumors, lamentations, predictions, and other material relayed from these areas filled the pages of the *Courant* until the Revolution was well under way, all suggesting the deep-running disapproval of an imperial meddling with the prosperity of trading.

The economic position of the colony of Connecticut, moreover, was deemed to have been unfortunately unique.[2] Though Connecticut contemporaries lamented the economic vassalage of the colony, there was no gainsaying that its geographical location gave it a vital dependence upon the merchants of Massachusetts, New York, and in lesser degree, Rhode Island. Connecticut had scarcely any direct trade with England. The bulk of her exports went to the West Indies where horses, cattle, lumber, and provisions were exchanged for rum, sugar, molasses, cotton, coffee, cocoa, salt, money, and other commodities. Most of the molasses was converted into rum in Connecticut, and, with the surplus of West India goods, taken to New York and Boston. Connecticut boasted no wholesale mart, and the retailers who bought English dry goods, drugs, and other manufactured articles swelled the profits of New York and Boston importers. To this economic situation was laid the lamentable dearth of money, an object of complaint throughout this period.

The points of significance in this connection, however, were two. In the first place, Connecticut traders engaged directly in a valuable and necessary West India traffic that conditioned them to resent imperial regulations which adversely affected trading activities in the West Indies area. Secondly, the degree of their economic dependence on their brethren in Boston and New York forged strong bonds of sympathy with these centers of anti-imperial agitation. The *Courant* reported the news from those two thriving seaports with a thoroughness never accorded to towns anywhere inside the boundaries of its own colony.

The peculiar position of Hartford as a determinant of the *Courant*'s perspective is also worth noting. With a population of around 4,000 in 1763, Hartford was by no means the first town of Connecticut; [3] yet its location at the head of navigation on the Connecticut River gave it the promise of future expansion, especially as the upper valley areas were being populated. Hartford merchants bought and sold, mostly bartered with the merchants and farmers from western and up-river regions. They collected stock for the West India trade, selling what of their surpluses they could, trading with New York and Boston importers, retailing their English goods to all who would buy. In the warmer months, when river navigation was free, West India craft from New York and Boston, light enough to clear the Saybrook Bar at the mouth of the stream, docked at the Hartford landing to ply their business. When the river froze, the season opened for overland traffic to Boston and New York. Hartford, therefore, had some of the characteristics of both an inland and port town.

Its inland location sheltered it from some of the elements which provoked friction elsewhere. There were no tidewaiters, collectors, or other customs officials; there were none of those searches and seizures that occasionally excited some of the maritime settlements, and never did an informer incur the collective wrath of Hartford's good townsfolk.[4] No Court of Vice-Admiralty sat at Hartford, and no sloop of war lay off her landing intent upon impressing seamen for His Majesty's Navy. Hartford had none of these small dramas to stimulate the printer's indignation.

On the other hand, Hartford was one of the political capitals of a colony that had always enjoyed virtual independence and self-government. The force of this tradition, coupled with her trade connections, set the stage for a determined point of view on questions of parliamentary regulation. Her strategic position for news-gathering on the post road between Boston and New York, the contacts with travelers which this afforded and with the colony's leading figures who gathered there from time to time for sessions of the General Assembly, served not only to whet and to broaden the interests of local people but to keep them almost abreast of the prejudices of their fellow colonists.

It is not very surprising, therefore, that the opposition which greeted George Grenville's Stamp Act of 1765 found a ready mirror in Green's colonial paper. Readers learned that Grenville himself introduced the bill with some notably specious words; that those members of Parliament who opposed him were incomparably superior in point of argument; and that a combination of court favoritism and deceit enabled the ministerial hacks to carry the day by a small margin of votes. As for the colonies:

. . . it was hoped they would assert their rights, by resolves entered on the journals of their several houses of assembly, and remonstrate by petitions to his Majesty and the other branches of the legislature, and by every means in their power endeavour to frustrate the designs form'd to deprive them of one of the most valuable blessings that God has bestowed upon them, and reduce them to a level with abject slaves that groan under the tyranny of the most arbitrary monarchs in the universe.[5]

Incitement to colonial opposition, letters and essays, resolutions from lawyers, towns, and legislatures, the spirited activities of Sons of Liberty, stories of riots and effigy burnings glutted the *Courant*'s pages.[6] As delegates to the Stamp Act Congress wended their slow way to New York, readers winnowed the print for tidings of stamped paper [7] and for news and rumors from across the Atlantic, such as impending changes in the ministry,[8] Britain squirming under the boycott,[9] hard times, merchants petitioning for relief, unemployment and riot among the working people.[10] While stamp distributors were forced to resign in most of the colonies, Barbados was execrated for tamely taking her loss of rights.[11] As the crisis intensified, the paper reported that couples rushed into marriage,[12] debtors broke jail,[13] and at least one young lady preferred spinsterhood to prospects of the "illegal" act.[14] Green had personal reason, in common with other printers throughout the colonies, to disapprove a law that taxed newspapers and he composed his issues accordingly.

As incidents of Stamp Act agitation began occurring nearer home, Green's readers were already steeped in the ideology of opposition and appreciative of the spirit and dimensions of the movement. Meantime, Jared Ingersoll, London agent for the Connecticut merchants, had managed to capture the lucrative appointment of Stamp Distributor for His Majesty's Colony in Connecticut.[15] The act was designed to become effective on the first day of November, 1765. At the beginning of September, when stamp officers in some of the neighboring provinces had already resigned,[16] Green opined that Ingersoll's office would be about as popular with the people of Connecticut as was a publican with the Jews.[17] He had been paraded about, hanged, and burned in effigy at New London and towns to the eastward.[18] The *Courant* carried Governor Thomas Fitch's proclamation against rioting,[19] but little did it deter those determined colonials who rode over the hills to Hartford one mid-September day. Green, who had one of his few opportunities for first-hand reporting, printed the following temperate account:

Last Wednesday Afternoon, a large Company of able-bodied Men, came to Town (on Horseback) from the Eastern Part of this Government, and informed those who were willing to join them, that they were on their Way to New-Haven to demand the Stamp-Officer of this Colony to resign his Office—that a Number of their Companions, were gone on the lower Roads, and that they had all agreed to rendezvous at Branford, the next Day, (Thursday) and that they should tarry in Town that Night; they then dispersed to different Parts of the Town for lodging. In the

Evening, Advice was received, that Mr. Ingersoll was on the Road to this Place, that he would be in Town, the next Day, and that he intended to apply to the Assembly for their Protection; and it being conjectured, that he might come to Town in the Night, to shun the Mob, (Who he had heard were on their Way to pay him a Visit) it was agreed that a Watch should patrol the Streets all Night, to prevent his coming in unnoticed, but they made no Discoveries. On Thursday Morning, the whole Body, (including a considerable Number from this Town) set off, on their intended Expedition, and in about an Hour met Mr. Ingersoll, at the Lower End of Weathersfield, and let him know their Business,—he at first refused to comply, but it was insisted upon, that he should resign his Office of Stamp Master, so disagreeable to his Countrymen;—after many Proposals, he delivered the Resignation, mentioned below, which he read himself in the Hearing of the whole Company; he was then desired to pronounce the Words, *Liberty and Property,* three Times, which having done, the whole Body gave three Huzza's; Mr. Ingersoll, then went to a Tavern, and dined with several of the Company: After Dinner, the Company told Mr. Ingersoll, as he was bound to Hartford, they would escort him there, which they did, to the Number of almost Five Hundred Persons on Horseback. After they arrived in Town, Mr. Ingersoll again read his Resignation in Public, when three Huzza's more were given, and the whole Company immediately dispersed without making the least Disturbance.[20]

A fortnight earlier, Green reprinted a letter from the *Connecticut Gazette* inciting freemen to take action in their next town meetings. According to this, the Stamp Tax was unconstitutional, its method of collection wasteful, and people were debt-laden to boot. Moreover, the extended jurisdiction of Vice-Admiralty courts, a measure designed to diminish smuggling, infringed the right of trial by jury. Readers were advised to have their representatives present resolutions and petitions to the General Assembly.[21] After November 1, when the law became operative, Green suspended the *Courant* for five weeks.[22] To have published with stamps was unthinkable under the circumstances, and to have published without them was illegal. Fellow printers in New Hampshire, Massachusetts, Rhode Island, and Connecticut issued their unstamped papers without interruption.[23] Indeed, on the very first day of the month illegal copies of the *New London Gazette* and the *Connecticut Gazette* at New Haven bristled with patriotic defiance.[24]

It is not clear whether the *Courant*'s owner was simply circumspect or whether he disliked the radical turn of events.[25] Before and after the *Courant*'s suspension, the official resolves of Hartford

and a few other towns were printed.[26] Wallingford approved a
fine of 20 shillings for any who introduced stamped paper.[27] A
gathering of Litchfield County delegates declared the Stamp Act
unconstitutional and therefore void.[28] The *Courant* recorded the
activities of local Sons of Liberty who were busy composing resolves, appointing committees of correspondence, and scanning the
scene for trouble.[29] On the other hand, when a sizable convention
of them determined to unseat Governor Fitch next Election Day,
Green emerged from behind his press long enough to wonder how
they reconciled political meddling with the spirit of liberty they
professed, specifically, when presuming upon the liberty of freemen to elect candidates of their own choosing. Fitch, it may be
noted, had run afoul of the Stamp Act patriots.[30]

In April, 1766, conflicting reports of the repeal of the act began
filtering into the *Courant* [31] and, when finally the good news came,
it was roundly celebrated. At Hartford, May 23, 1766, bells rang,
ships displayed their colors, and 21 cannons fired a salvo. Green
reported that joy smiled in every face until a terrific powder explosion demolished the Brick School House, killing six persons and
wounding above a score more.[32] Nevertheless, in the next issue
readers found grounds for more optimism. The duty on molasses
would probably be reduced and Parliament was even pondering
the idea of free trade with the Spanish and French West Indies.[33]

As a matter of fact, complaints against the unpopular trade laws,
which attempted to divert traffic from the Spanish and French
Indies, had been largely elbowed aside by the Stamp Act excitement; but now again, an undertone of antitrade law feeling gave
point to newspaper complaints and fears like the following: New
England goods were glutting the market at Dominica;[34] the sag-
ging price of wheat would likely bankrupt prominent New York
and Philadelphia merchants;[35] the laws encouraged French colonials to manufacture their own rum and to engage in trade for
themselves.[36] Moreover, there was an alarming scarcity of money
hardly to be assuaged by hopes for a paper currency.[37] Connecticut, perhaps more than other colonies, was jeopardized by money
drainage.[38]

A related and equally significant line which Green had pushed
from the beginning now gained intensity. This was the propaganda
for an incipient Buy-American movement. As the spirit of these
years endorsed the desirability of getting along with less imports,
especially English and Oriental goods, frugality became the virtue

of the day. Times were hard, money scarce, and the *Courant*'s
readers were invited to economize, each according to his character
and circumstances.³⁹ The colony might have saved £10,000 per
annum had people but accustomed themselves to sage brew in place
of tea; ⁴⁰ coffee, made cheaply from rye, had more nutritive value
than the usual costly beverage; ⁴¹ inexpensiveness in clothes was
commendable, as when a wedding party to the eastward dressed in
homespun.⁴² Green endorsed the new mode for funerals which
sanctioned simplicity in dress and which disapproved gifts of gloves
and scarves to pallbearers.⁴³ Contributors censured the extrava-
gances of roistering students and of idle ladies.⁴⁴ In distant Virginia,
to believe the *Courant,* patches and patriotism were all but synony-
mous.⁴⁵

The encouragement of domestic agriculture and industry
matched the spirit of frugality. Public-minded people attempted to
stimulate the production of flax, hemp, silk, wool, and potash.⁴⁶
A Boston dispatch in the *Courant*'s first issue reminded readers that
many in neighboring colonies were clothed in colonial manufactures while at Hempstead, Long Island, an American woolen
factory awaited shopkeepers' orders. When stores for home manufactures were opened in New York and Philadelphia, Green hoped
that Connecticut might have one also.⁴⁷ As Watson succeeded
Green at the printing shop and the Townshend duties incurred
the boycott of colonial merchants, this emphasis was more pronounced. The best people of Boston were said to be drinking no
tea; ⁴⁸ young men of respectable families at Harvard, Yale, and
Princeton resolved in favor of homespun garb,⁴⁹ while gentlemen
of distinction, and even ladies, set laudable examples of sartorial
economy; ⁵⁰ and wives, daughters, and grandmothers were complimented for their sedulous spinning.⁵¹ Premiums encouraged the
raising of sheep and the making of shoes, cloth, paper, guns, glass,
and ironware.⁵² For Connecticut, the *Courant* printed letters urging economic self-sufficiency.⁵³

But meantime, more dramatic news. Soldiers of the regular army
came to America under authority of the Quartering Act; Charles
Townshend, Chancellor of the Exchequer, sponsored measures
affecting the customs administration and the Vice-Admiralty
courts; colonial imports of paper, paint, tea, and glass were taxed.
Once again the *Courant* articulated the sentiments of the opposition by assembling and digesting appropriate material from many
sources. Chief among a goodly number of political essays designed

to instruct and enlist opinions were the effectively written "Letters from a Farmer in Pennsylvania," in which it was argued that the Townshend duties were no whit less dangerous to colonial liberties than the late hated Stamp Tax.[54] Watson reprinted the famous Circular Letter in which the General Court of Massachusetts besought the concerted action of colonial legislatures on a number of imperial grievances.[55] There were affirmative responses from Connecticut and other colonies, and long, biased accounts of the ensuing squabble between governor and lawmakers in the Bay Colony.[56] From Virginia came the equally well-known Resolves of 1769 reaffirming the right of colonists to petition their king for redress of grievances, and avowing the sole right of taxation to have been, then as ever, in the general assembly with the consent of the king or his governor.[57]

As the nonimportation movement grew, readers noted the resolves of "patriotic" merchants and were invited to share their indignation against evaders.[58] Vigilance groups were formed, shipmasters quizzed, goods reshipped or stored, nonsubscribers publicized and defamed.[59] There were comforting accounts of the distress of merchants and manufacturers in England, where, according to one exaggeration, "The spirit of despotism shakes the constitution . . . the soberest men begin to be alarm'd: and ruminate upon the scenes of the last century." [60] Boston merchants warned their Connecticut brethren that proscribed tea was en route to Hartford, and down the river Middletown merchants were ready to confiscate it.[61] When traders from Rhode Island were less than cooperative, Hartford and Wethersfield merchants seized their bootleg commodities.[62] For the defense of their liberties, Connecticut's General Assembly lauded the merchants of Massachusetts, Connecticut, New York, and Pennsylvania.[63] Finally the *Courant* carried the call for an all-Connecticut meeting at Middletown, February 20, 1770.[64] There a newly formed central merchants' organization resolved to import necessities only, and to break relations with nonsubscribing colonies.[65] All this and much more about soldiers, informers, and customs officers [66] created a slow crescendo in the *Courant* until, by the time of the so-called "Massacre" in Boston, March 5, 1770, Watson printed one of the traitorous "Junius" letters which cast harsh reflections upon the person of the king himself.[67]

About this time it became known in the colonies that Parliament had removed all the Townshend duties except the one on tea, and the storm in the *Courant* as well as in the country began to subside. When merchants in Newport and New York resolved to modify their agreements, the *Courant* called upon New York importers to close out their accounts with Connecticut traders, who were resolved to have no business with them; [68] but this position was economically untenable for Connecticut so Watson became discreetly silent thereafter. As one cynical correspondent expressed it, "No sooner had N. York vessels by order of their owners returned home loaded with British goods, but the high blown resentment of Connecticut merchants had got to quite an ebb tide . . ." [69]

From the fall of 1770 until the *Courant* carried a write-up of the turbulent Tea Party of 1773, there was an occasional piece in derogation of tyranny, the corrupt ministry, or an overly zealous colonial official; [70] but, by and large, the problems of imperial administration were considerably less agitated than in any period since the beginning of the paper. This is not to say that Watson rested on his oars. The revenue laws as well as the tax on tea were genuinely unpopular features of the British colonial system, and traders attempted to evade them where it was possible and profitable to do so. To this practice of evasion, or smuggling, he printed a number of sympathetic references. In the summer of 1769, for example, appeared an enlightening admonition from New London:

There has lately appeared off this harbour, an ill-looking voracious Sea Monster; which has put all our Coasters upon a sharp look out, to steer clear of its devouring Jaws. It has been observed to devour whole vessells at once. . . . It is particularly fond of all sorts of West India produce; Rum, Molasses, Sugar, Cotton, Coffee, Cocoa, &c. [71]

Items in the spirit of this one increased notably after 1770. [72] Watson included references to searches, seizures, and informers, [73] and in one issue did what amounted to a bit of editorial worrying about the much hated Writs of Assistance. [74] When the *Gaspee,* a revenue vessel, was burned at Newport and a court of inquiry set up to ferret out the culprits, he promoted the flare of excitement by reprinting Virginia's invitation to the other legislatures to form committees of correspondence and inquiry on the matter; [75] but the trials fizzled and nothing much came of the whole affair. However, according to the *Courant*'s New London dispatch, a new revenue boat was being fitted out at Halifax

. . . for the base Purpose of going into every Harbour and Creek between that Place and this, which it is thought will be a more proper method to take the fair Trader in his honest Industry, and pilfer him of all he has in the World. . . . It is therefore hoped that every Person in the least Danger of being hurt in Circumstances, will take Warning by this, and be looking out most vigilantly for those pimping R——ls, those Locusts of America, and be ready to receive them in such a Manner as they shall think the Nature of their errand Demands.[76]

Invective of this tenor shortly became commoner in the *Courant* for the famous tea ships were soon preparing to sail for America. When first the *Courant*'s readers heard of it, they were apprised that this was not ordinary commercial business of the East India Company's but a scheme of Lord North's designed to trick them into tacitly acknowledging Parliament's right to impose taxes upon the colonies.[77]

Men who have the Disposal of large Sums, for the Purposes of Seduction, have many melancholy Proofs of human Frailty and are apt to conclude that true Virtue and Patriotism are mere Names without any real Existence; but it is hoped the Americans will convince Lord North that they are not yet ready to wear the Yoke of Slavery and suffer it to be rivetted about their Necks; but that they will send back the Teas from whence they came.[78]

To gauge the temper of the colonists from Watson's *Courant,* resentment on this score was born full-blown, for indignation glared from every issue. There were sentiments and resolutions from Boston, New York, and Philadelphia,[79] and the printer queried his public on the advisability of an immediate meeting at Hartford to resolve on measures similar to those adopted elsewhere.[80] Citizens read that tea harmed the health, that it bred fleas, that Chinese coolies tramped it with their "nasty feet and legs," that most public houses in England and France had discontinued serving it because of its pernicious effects.[81] Finally, when whooping "Indians" dumped the tea into Boston's harbor, Watson reported their provocative rampage in a single, ironical sentence:

We hear from Boston that last Thursday evening, between 300 and 400 Boxes of the celebrated East-India TEA, by some ACCIDENT! which happened in an attempt to get it on Shore, fell overboard— That the Boxes burst open and the Tea was swallowed up [by] the vast Abyss! [82]

Although it was not apparent for several months what reaction such an enormity would inspire in Parliament, the *Courant*'s readers might well have hoped that nothing punitive would result from the destruction of so much property. Watson, like Green before him, had inserted excerpts from partisan letters originating in England which purported to reveal the sympathetic state of English opinion and the genuine unpopularity of Parliament. Indeed, the first reference to what people abroad thought about the Tea Party professed to discover the universal applause with which they greeted it and their determination to have the East India Company shift for itself as best it could.[83] Once readers were disabused of this illusion and the *Courant* printed the Boston Port Act,[84] Watson continued to carry hand-picked sentiments of this sort to bolster the spirit of American opposition.[85]

About a week before the harbor of Boston was blocked, and under the caption, "JOIN OR DIE," Watson called upon all to co-operate against this attack upon liberty. Unity, strong resolution, and decided perseverance were needed to avoid slavery.[86] Freemen from near-by Farmington burned the unpopular Thomas Hutchinson's effigy and determined to support their unlucky brethren in Boston.[87] The day the act became effective, the muffled bells of Lebanon as well as of Philadelphia pealed sympathy and sorrow.[88] Thereafter the countryside seethed with meetings, rumors, and resolutions.[89]

Let us contribute something to relieve the Sufferers in Boston. Let us break off all Trade with Great-Britain, which will soon reduce them to the greatest Distress. I hope there is none in America, that is so sordid and stupid as to sell his Birth-Right for a Mess of Pottage, or that value Liberty at so small a Price as tamely to submit to the cruel Insults of a tyrannical Ministry.[90]

The *Courant* was now filled with more material of opposition than it had ever been before. Watson urged all the towns in Connecticut to pass measures of petition and protest.[91] A congress, he told them, was soon to be formed where action looking to the total suspension of commercial intercourse between the colonies and Great Britain would likely be taken.[92] Town resolves poured in condemning the despotic ministry, appointing committees of correspondence, arranging subscriptions for the relief of Boston's townsfolk.[93] Connecticut's delegates to the Continental Congress were elected,[94] and those from Massachusetts ceremoniously entertained in Hartford on their way south.[95] A deal of military spirit filled the air when, early one September Sunday, false rumors sent men from several Connecticut towns hustling toward Boston with muskets to shoot for their rights.[96] Plans were already afoot for a meeting of delegates from Litchfield, Hartford, New London, and Windham counties to approve in advance whatever nonimportation articles the Philadelphia Congress might recommend, and plans were soon laid for a larger assemblage.[97] In truth, by the autumn of 1774, the *Courant*'s fever of opposition had reached such a pitch that the day of exposure was about at hand for those individuals whose circumstances and sentiments impelled them to disapprove the extremities they observed.

Some Episcopal clergymen in Connecticut, whose temporal ties were closer to England than most peoples' and upon whom the odium against the Quebec Act spilled over,[98] were among the first to be visited with suspicion. Watson reported that on September 12, 1774, about 200 "patriotic" gentlemen awaited the Reverend Nichols of Farmington and elicited a lengthy statement from him, the gist of which follows:

I James Nichols of Farmington . . . do believe the principles and sentiments contained in the declaration of rights adopted and passed in the hon. house of representatives of this, colony . . . be fully vindicated by the laws of GOD and the English constitution. And I do hereby, without any equivocation, or mental reservation, adopt the same as containing the sum of my belief, on those important subjects.[99]

As regarded the recent governor's proclamation appointing a day of fasting and prayer for Boston, the reverend gentleman, whose scruples had then induced him to condemn it, professed now to discern the light, and accordingly asked forgiveness from all assembled. If we may believe Watson, sundry others, who offended in matters of a like pernicious tendency, duly humbled themselves and engaged to do better thereafter.[100] The same month, the Reverend Samuel Peters fled Hebron for Boston when his parishioners were roughly used by the townsmen.[101] Some of his intercepted letters were reprinted in the *Courant,* but Watson thought that his villainy, the prostitution of his sacred trust, and the gross violation of truth and decency which characterized him were too well known to need comment.[102]

The people of Ridgefield and Newtown, Connecticut, shortly registered protests against the proceedings of the Continental Congress. Watson reprinted this undesirable truth from *Rivington's New-York Gazetteer* as much to stigmatize the paper as to advertise the towns.[103] When two freemen from Ridgefield put in at a

Wethersfield tavern and noisily delivered themselves of sentiments which smacked of Toryism, it was thereupon decided, according to the *Courant,*

. . . that these Persons should be returned, the Way from whence they came, under safe Conduct, from Town to Town, *to the said Place lately known by the said Name of Ridgfield;* and . . . instantly to attend them as far as Farmington, on their Return; and there to acquaint the Inhabitants of their Behavior, and leave them, to their further Transportation, as is usual, and as by Law is provided, in Cases of stroling Ideots, Lunatics, &c.[104]

Rivington's *Gazetteer* not only approved places like Ridgefield, but took pains to goad the rest of the colony for its disloyal behavior. According to one of Rivington's extracts from a Hartford letter, nothing but a spirit of independence begot such military ardor as was exhibited throughout the colony. Watson reproached Rivington by reprinting this insult to Connecticut "patriots," [105] and subsequently expressed some notable observations of his own:

The infamous author of the above production might possibly in some part of his life, have passed this place, but never had any fixed abode in the town of Hartford. From my knowledge of the soil I will venture to assert, that this part of the country will not bear such noxious fruit: An ardent thirst for liberty, and a noble uniformity of sentiment reigns indeed among all ranks of people, and if occasion should require, we shall doubtless be ready to vindicate our rights at the risk of our lives; but no one even dreams of a state of independence, nor is there a noddle in Hortford, so crazy as to imagine our parchment justly endangered by the transactions of the people of this colony. The people of Connecticut to their immortal honour be it spoken, move forward in the cause of liberty with circumspection, firmness, dignity, and uniformity; there being but very few anomolous heads disposed to disturb the order of nature, and wrest our privileges from us.[106]

The loyalism of Rivington's press angered not only Watson, who inserted some vulgar allusions to it,[107] but also the leading spirits of Hartford County who took action against it in January, 1775.[108] Reproachfully disclaiming the remotest desire for independence, a group of delegates had words to print about the difference between a newspaper with which they agreed and one with which they disagreed. Watson carried their conclusions in full, from which one quotation throws light upon the theory of suppression:

While contending for the liberties of British America in general, we would by no means encourage or countenance any measure that may be construed in any degree to infringe that of the press . . . But when the conductor of a press labours incessantly, not to convince, but to vilify and abuse, not to insert every article of intelligence just as it was first published or related, but with such malicious insinuations, groundless hints and fictitious anecdotes, as tend to lead the unwary and unattentive into a wrong conception of the facts reported—when he labours to spread jealousies and fears among the people, to undermine and destroy that mutual confidence of the colonies in each other . . . A press thus conducted, ceases to be a blessing to mankind, becomes highly the reverse, and is not unlike fire-brands, arrows and death, in the hands of a madman, . . . we need but name James Rivington, Printer and Stationer in New-York. . . . Resolved, Therefore, that it is the opinion of this body, that every subscriber in this county, for his paper, called Rivinton's Gazeteer, ought forthwith to order him to send no more, and that no further dealing or correspondence ought to be had with him.[109]

In addition to committees of correspondence, towns had appointed committees of inspection whose members scrutinized the behavior of neighbors with reference to recommendations of the Continental Congress.[110] In Farmington, Martha and Solomon Cowles, who purchased and drank tea after March 1, publicly pledged to abstain forthwith;[111] while a fellow townsman of theirs, whose cupidity bested his patriotism, not only humbled himself for price raising, but donated the excess profits to Boston's needy.[112] Cases like these, which Watson publicized, were a mere drop in the bucket to what poured in when the war spirit developed.

After General Gage's force came into conflict with the colonials at Lexington and Concord in April, it scarcely behooved *Courant* readers to let their hands wax feeble or their hearts faint, for God was conceived to be in favor of their constitutional liberties.[113] The unchristian behavior of Britain's soldiers appeared from a Worcester report:

Americans! forever bear in mind the BATTLE OF LEXINGTON!—where British troops, unmolested and unprovoked, wantonly, and in a most inhuman manner fired upon and killed a number of our countrymen, then robbed them of their provisions, ransacked, plundered and burnt their houses! nor could the tears of defenceless women, some of whom were in the pains of child birth, the cries of helpless babes, nor the prayers of old age, confined to beds of sickness, appease their thirst for blood!—or divert them from the DESIGN of MURDER and ROBBERY![114]

Connecticut's proximity to the war areas, the enlistment and passage of troops through the colony, newspapers and letters, the tales of soldiers and postriders, the presence of British prisoners and the excitement of Tory hunting fostered a bristling spirit in the *Courant*'s precincts. Hatred throve with the persecution of loyalists, a practice which Watson zealously abetted. There were notices galore of those who confessed their false beliefs, and of those who refused to confess them. Some of the more recalcitrant were jailed, some fled, and many were held up to public view as worthy of detestation. Printed newspaper warnings solicited universal neglect for them, while the colony took steps to prevent their migration.[115] Watson pilloried them, called them "a Lousey Pack," "Vultures," "Vermin," "Animals";[116] and finally struck off a plan to merge profits with patriotism. All persons, whom committees of inspection exposed in the *Courant,* would thereafter have names and addresses published on page one, column one, until they repented; but let each penitent accompany his confession with a dollar for the printer's pains.[117] This went on for half a year until one reader complained that his paper was "eternally polluted with the hateful names of this stinking Race."[118] To add fuel to the fire, the *Courant* relayed some rumors and lies: at Lexington, 10 minutemen were murdered ere a single colonial musket discharged;[119] at Boston, Gage's doctors mixed arsenic with medicine;[120] in Virginia and among patriot troops, the enemy attempted to propagate smallpox;[121] at Halifax, American prisoners suffered barbarous treatment.[122] There were reports that Indians and Hessian mercenaries were going to be used;[123] patriot leaders were to be killed and their followers shipped to the East Indies to sweat for their courage.[124] As bitterness grew with the months, sentiments of political independence began to appear in the *Courant.*

On April 1, 1776, Watson printed an interesting letter from a correspondent who recorded these thoughts:

The depravity of human nature renders constitutional government necessary, for the maintaining the impartial administration of justice, and the security of person and property. Rebellion against good and constitutional government, against the Magna Charta of the British constitution, is . . . a transgression of an eternal law of nature. . . . Such an infernal rebellion has lately been set on foot at Westminster, by that deluded tyrant, who was once the lawful king of the British empire, and by the machinations of those bloodhounds, Bute, North and Mansfield.[125]

To whatever degree this theory may have been current earlier, it hewed close to the point, used later by the General Assembly, that the king's conduct had absolved his Connecticut subjects from their allegiance and subjection to the crown of Great Britain.[126] Wishful readers found support for this view in rumors that there was talk of another Cromwell in the streets of London, that civil war was imminent.[127] In the autumn issues of 1775 a single contributor considered the possible necessity of independence;[128] but after the beginning of 1776, Watson furnished his subscribers with the whole of Paine's *Common Sense* in order to have them peruse it, so he averred, as soon as possible.[129] To believe one correspondent, Paine's arguments dispelled prejudices with irresistible energy.[130] Watson reported that the town of Canterbury voted unanimously to support the adoption of Paine's principles of independence,[131] and other expressions of opinion to this end, public and private, subsequently found place in the *Courant*.[132] In the issue of July 15, 1776, less than a fortnight after its adoption by the Continental Congress, Watson inserted the American Declaration of Independence. The same issue, appropriately enough, carried news of New Yorkers melting a statue of their king for bullets.

By the time of Watson's decease in 1777 the *Courant,* so to speak, had solemnly entrenched itself for the tedious duration of the Revolution. The first shock of excitement had passed and noisy indignation deepened into a constant, less vociferous hatred which colored the tidings of much that the *Courant* recorded. Most Connecticut Tories either were squelched or had departed, and the Tory baiting in which many so joyously indulged had all but subsided. The controversy, now clarified by the issue of independence, had long moved from the plane of argument to the battlefield, and much of the lively polemic material with which Watson filled the *Courant* had given way to the motley literature of a society at war.

The *Courant* printed a great mass of material relevant to the conflict. Facts, falsehoods, rumors, reports, letters and documents, official and unofficial opinions, threats, warnings, and appeals, convey an impression of persistent devotion to the cause to which it is difficult to do justice in the telling. Since the obstacles to reporting, multitudinous according to later standards, were now appreciably increased by the hazards of sea travel and the occupation of New York, the time lapse between deed and account gave currency to myriad guesses and doubts. From the resultant hodgepodge of news readers were chiefly indebted to the official releases of Congress for dependable details of the fortunes of the conflict. All in all, Watson and his successors did a rounder job in relating the ebb and flow of the war when the northern and middle colonies provided the theater for conflict. When the main phases of combat moved to the south, the record seems faded, bereft of supplementary items, and shorn of the excitement which arises from propinquity.

Perhaps the *Courant*'s chief service to the struggle came from the partisan nature of its journalism. By persistently plying the approved prejudices, its printers bolstered the hopes and hates of their constituents. Comfort derived, for example, from rumors of riot and bloodshed in England, Scotland, and Ireland; [133] of bedlam in Europe supposed to necessitate the return of the Hessians; [134] of the decisive defeat of the British Navy, and even of the demolition of English port towns by French and Spanish enemies.[135] Conversely, the alleged propensity of the opposing soldiery for raping, butchering wounded patriots, wantonly destroying property, and abusing their captives gave play to wartime malevolence.[136]

Battle accounts were generally played up or down to fit predilections. When the colonial defenders abandoned New York, the *Courant* carried only a casual glossary of the whole affair with accent upon minor skirmishes in which Americans were reported to have been victorious.[137] Of the one serious disaster of the retreat, the loss of Fort Washington with its entire garrison and all its munitions, readers learned that their soldiers behaved with admirable resolution, that about 300 of them were killed and wounded, and that the enemy suffered a loss of 1,700, most of them mortally.[138] With Howe's occupation of Philadelphia, naïve folks were invited to believe that Washington accomplished a victory. The *Courant*'s initial news, an item reprinted from Fishkill, New York, gave them this slant:

Howe might have possessed himself of the city sooner, had this been his principal design. His aim was to get General Washington in the trap he is now in himself; where in case of a defeat, he has no safe way to retreat, or to receive succours. Howe's army, to human appearance, is in a worse situation than they have been since they entered Pennsylvania . . . and, in case Howe is defeated, of which there is the greatest probability it will be almost impossible for his army to escape.[139]

In 1780, after Lincoln surrendered Charleston to Clinton, the first truthful report was reprinted from Rivington's *Gazetteer*, but subsequent issues of the *Courant* denied this report, later doubted it, then finally confirmed it.[140] Quite in contrast to this shrinking from the truth was the exultant spirit of printer and press in falsely announcing the capture of Montreal [141] or in telling of Bennington, Saratoga, and Yorktown! [142]

Scores of printed communications augmented the effectiveness of such refracted accounts. Periods of adversity brought letters of encouragement, counseling unity and perseverance. Paine's *Crisis* was chief among these, and installments of it appeared from time to time in the *Courant*.[143] When British generals and commissioners made overtures of reconciliation, there were essays of hostility and indignation.[144] Glad tidings of recognition from France and Spain or of Clark's victories far to the west [145] or of almost any encouraging development begot a share of literary rejoicing. Letters published by order of Congress and a great number of Congressional addresses and resolutions, including the "Declaration setting forth the Causes and Necessity for taking up Arms," [146] imparted dignity and a sense of organized strength to the cause which the *Courant* supported.

Whatever the *Courant* contributed to the maintenance of war morale among its readers, it also provided a medium for the exposition of some of the accompanying internal difficulties. Contrary to the recommendations of Congress, prices began to rise precipitately in the first months of the Revolution. In 1775, when Connecticut merchants were generally believed to have advanced prices on imported goods anywhere from 25 per cent to 40 per cent, correspondents questioned the patriotism of this practice.[147] The committees of inspection of Hartford County published a set of "just prices" for molasses, rum, sugar, and salt, and resolved that none higher should be charged.[148] The committees were accordingly accused of exceeding their powers, of being composed of farmers, lawyers, and consumers who cared or knew little of the exigencies of trade.[149] As money continued to depreciate, some tavern keepers refused to buy rum, and merchants were said to be grinding the faces of the poor.[150] According to one writer, while almost everyone professed to be contending for the public good, almost everyone avidly pursued his own private interests.[151]

Early in 1777 the General Assembly believed that most wholesalers were taking profits of from 500 per cent to 600 per cent on imported goods.[152] Thereupon maximum retail prices were fixed for a long list of vendibles as well as for the wages of farm laborers and artisans.[153] Sentiments criticizing or commending this drastic exertion of the legislature appeared in the *Courant*.[154] If some towns resolved to support it, some merchants thought bitterly of the farmers who dominated the Assembly.[155] When Watson wrote with scorn of those responsible for depreciating the currency,[156] others argued the impracticability of regulating the "natural" price level.[157] Regulating acts were twice enacted and twice repealed by the General Assembly; colonial and intercolonial conferences were held to ponder the problem, but with little effect.[158] Currency speculation developed and merchants came frequently to advertise their wares for barter or hard money only.[159] Although contributors spoke accusingly of "extortioners," "engrossers," "sharpers," and "Tories," a few wrote of such factors as a lack of metal reserves, lack of confidence in the government, the abnormal state of trade, and the increased volume of the currency.[160]

In the later years of the Revolution, an illicit traffic in commodities, plied between Connecticut and New York, became both flourishing and notorious. According to Governor Trumbull:

Whereas notwithstanding the laws strictly forbidding any persons to carry provisions out of this State, (except for the army or navy) without a special permission for that purpose; I am given to understand that many persons regardless of the said laws, and instigated by the secret machinations of the enemy or excited by the most insatiable avarice, have not only transported provisions into other States contrary to law; but have furnished the enemy with very considerable supplies.[161]

Colonial craft allegedly frequented Long Island and even New York harbor to bring back their bootlegged British goods which were at one period more or less openly displayed in Connecticut shops.[162] As public indignation arose, the *Courant* printed accounts of seizures of boats and of illegal British and India goods from many towns in the state.[163] There were whispers of the implication of prominent names, and even the governor took steps to scotch rumors of his personal involvement in the trade.[164] As more goods and sloops were confiscated, the town of Farmington resolved that, although the laws already enacted were sufficient for the purpose, something had better be done to enforce them more strictly.[165] In response, delegates to a Hartford County meeting recommended to towns the more zealous detection and prosecution of violators;[166] but the printers inserted a letter from "Pacificus" wondering whether the Farmington resolutions were not better designed to encourage hotheads in the vulgar employment of tar and feathers.[167] It might have been wiser, according to a Philadelphia dispatch, to have allowed the export of lumber and provisions in exchange for the necessary "hard money" with which to prosecute the war.[168]

In printing a paper which sought throughout the war to give information and morale to its readers, Hudson & Goodwin continued the policies of their predecessor. The *Courant*'s issues from 1777 until 1781 differed in no appreciable respects from the last productions of Watson's press. If the stirring crises connected with the beginning of the Revolution had prompted Watson to vent some of his personal views, he later relapsed into the printer's practice of assembling, without comment, letters and communications from other papers. It was only toward the end of the war, when colonial success was in sight, that Hudson & Goodwin expressed their opinions in what amounted to bits of incipient editorializing.

When Cornwallis surrendered, the printers were gleeful:

All the late New-York papers have at length confessed the surrender of Lord Cornwallis to be real. They have even condescended to insert the articles of capitulation verbatim from the Philadelphia gazettes. The women are in tears, the soldiery in a panic, the merchants selling off their goods for much less than the first cost in Europe, the tories are in the utmost consternation, and Benedict Arnold himself, it is said trembles like an aspen leaf—in the midst of this scene of distress and wretchedness, with a superior French fleet on the coast ready to swallow them, the demagogues of that city are publishing in their gazettes contents of rebel mails and criticisms upon poems written by the king of Prussia; which conduct is full as ridiculous and stupid as if a criminal on his way to the gallows, and sitting on his coffin, should at the same time be amusing himself with Ben Johnson's jests, or writing strictures on the stile and language of the sheriff's warrant which condemns him to be hanged.[169]

As loyal colonists were fleeing, the *Courant* fired this caustic shot:

A second division of refugees, with their wives and other baggage, are embarking at New-York, and will shortly sail for Halifax. Their intermarriage with the spurious breed of Canadians, the aborigines of Penobscot, St. Francis, Lauret, Algonquin, Little Eskimaux, and the other northeastern tribes of Savages . . . will soon render Nova-Scotia a very populous colony; and, in a few years, extend the trade and dominion of Great-Britain so as to compensate for the loss of the *Thirteen States*.[170]

When rumors of peace and independence began to appear in the *Courant,* the printers exulted that heaven had showered its blessings upon a people, erstwhile so handicapped, who now counted among its friends the ancient House of Bourbon and the great

States of Holland—a people emerging gloriously triumphant over one of the most powerful, wealthy, and warlike nations ever to have darkened the pages of history.[171] They thought it inconsistent with the dignity of Congress to conclude a separate peace with the British commissioners, and upon receipt of the first allusion to the provisional treaty announced it a likely forgery.[172] The exciting report of a definitive and general cessation of hostilities reached Hartford the last week in March, 1783. As the *Courant* reported it:

Last Thursday morning, at 7 o'clock, Col. Wadsworth received a letter from John Carter, Esq. by express, dated at Philadelphia, the 23d of March, half after six o'clock P. M. informing that a Packet had arrived at Chester, with the news of a GENERAL PEACE, being signed the 20th of January. As this express came solely to bring the news, and we had no doubt of its being true, the inhabitants of this town manifested their extreme joy by the firing of cannon, ringing of bells, and in the evening fireworks and illuminations.[173]

On May Day, 1783, the sheriff of Hartford County formally proclaimed peace from an especially constructed stage in front of the State House. Soldiers attended upon parade, and between appropriate maneuvers and detonations, this worthy official invoked God's blessing upon the future of the people of the United States. "Every bosom glowed with joy and uttered their expressive plaudit in loud huzza's." The celebrants moved to the meetinghouse to sing psalms and receive an oration; dinner, sociability, and an evening of fireworks completed the day. About 11:30 o'clock that night, someone discovered a fire near the lantern atop the State House, but happily the citizens extinguished it. As Hudson & Goodwin explained:

After all, every candid mind will admit that demonstrations of joy and gratitude upon such great occasions, are practised and approved by all christian people, though at the same time Providence may direct unforeseen events contrary to human expectation, and the most careful attempts to avoid them.[174]

CHAPTER III

CULTURAL REFLECTIONS

THE Revolutionary generation was interested in more than farming, trading, and the slow progress of a struggle against British imperialism. The *Courant's* early issues were fraught with evidences of a preoccupation with family and community concerns. News items, advertisements, and letters to the printers all revealed glimpses of the social and intellectual fiber of the provincial culture in which the paper functioned.

Early marriages and sizable families were not then the economic liabilities that they have since become. Emphasizing the mark of social respectability which accompanied them, the *Courant* printed complimentary allusions to families of unusual number. On her seventy-ninth birthday, Mrs. Starkweather of Stonington had 152 living descendants scattered through four generations,[1] while an old lady from East Hartford lived to have 214.[2] In 1771 appeared the eulogy of one matriarch whose progeny numbered 410, 336 of whom were alive at the time of her funeral.[3] Since society gave the nod of approval to prodigious works of this sort, the social stigma which attached itself to unmarried young women comes as no surprise. Whereas their married sisters were not old until they reached their sixties, spinsters were definitely the objects of compassion at an early age.[4] Contrariwise, there was a deal of humorous frowning at the rare cases of late marriage:

On the Evening of the 8th Inst. was married, Mr. John Taylor of Johnson, to Mrs. Anne Kelton of this Town. This venerable Pair, whose Ages amount to 161 Years (i.e. 89 by 72) promise little Hope of Success in the more common Effects of the matrimonial State.[5]

Of the superiority of male over female, no question was raised. As one correspondent expressed it:

God has given to the man strength of body and intrepidity of mind, which qualifies him to undertake the greatest hardships, and face the most imminent dangers; whilst the woman is of a weak and delicate constitution, accompanied with a natural softness, and modest timidity, which seems to point out a sedentary life as most proper for her, and dispose her to keep within the precincts of the house.[6]

This supposedly innate state of affairs prescribed the passive subserviency with which women could best function to the advantages of society. If purity, patience, and resignation were desirable virtues for unmarried young ladies,[7] married women had best eschew gossip and argument, be pious and economical, affectionate mothers, and dutiful wives.[8] Conversely, good husbands were good providers, resolute and independent, models of Christian piety and frugality.[9]

Against this pattern of approved concepts, unlucky individuals were held up to public gaze. A husband advertised his wife:

Whereas Hannah, wife of Richard Smith in Glastenbury makes it her steady business to pass from house to house, with her buisey news, tattling and bawling and lying, and carrying out things out of my house, things contrary to my knowledge—these are therefore to forbid all persons of having any trade or commerce with the said Hannah.[10]

Accused wives sometimes retaliated by describing their husbands' vices.[11]

The printers themselves were prone to moralize when appropriate texts came to hand. This doleful reprint appeared in April, 1765:

On Sunday last the remains of the once prosperous, gay, beautiful, and almost irresistably engaging Miss Teresia Constantia Phillips, were interred in the Church-yard in this town, unattended by a single friend of either sex! While we hope no ungererous insult will be offered to her ashes, we cannot forbear adding our wishes, that a catastrophe so striking and melancholy may prove an advantageous lesson to many of the surviving fair [sex]; and convince them, however flattering appearances may be, on their first deviation from the paths of rectitude and honor, that no admiration will be lasting, no happiness secure, which is not founded on the basis of virtue.[12]

Occasional writers dipped their quills to lament the increasing extravagance of women especially with reference to dress. For the delectation of ladies, the Hartford and Middletown merchants loaded their shelves with a variety of temptations. There were gewgaws for the more fashionable: fans and head flowers, multi-colored ribbons, earrings, black and colored ostrich plumes, necklaces of coral, wax, and French paste, lockets, rings, fancy looking glasses, and even "essence of pearl" toothpaste. More substantial goods in dress materials, imported from abroad, could be taken away for small down payments in cash or country produce. Broadcloth, cambric, linens, taffetas, velvets, chintzes, serges, and calicoes are names still familiar; but the meanings of tammies, durants, shalloons, sagathees, and calimancoes have since faded. Woolen hats, silk mits, cotton and worsted hose, Barcelona handkerchiefs, and russel shoes were offerings in ready-made wearing apparel.[13]

Young women, to believe their critics, should have been taught to keep the tastes of their station in life. But instead, they imitated the styles of those higher up in the scale so that the fashions of St. James's Park were communicated by a chain of ridiculous mimicry to the streets of the meanest towns in Connecticut. Some women dressed in cambric, silk, and velvet for ordinary wear. They spent more than half their time in cards, visits, dances, talk, and tea, rather than at the distaff; and fashionable daughters polished their exteriors to the ruination of their poor fathers.[14] Reactions like these suggested the impingement of urban culture upon a traditional rural morality.

The Connecticut towns were growing, and the increasing community life which they fostered provoked changing patterns of social behavior. At one time it might have been easy to guess a man's station by the clothes he wore, but this was said no longer to be the case. People of the "meaner sort," according to their "betters," were living above their levels, and a stranger would do well to distinguish a wealthy master from his lowly apprentice.[15] Community living encouraged social emulation and competition.

Two advertisements from early issues of the *Courant* were interesting appeals to fashion-conscious townsfolk.

Sally Tripper

Hath newly imported from Europe, and to be sold at her Store in Draw-Lane in Hartford, opposite to the Sign of the Trowell, a Number of Female Aprons, most elegantly decorated, and suitable for Ladies of the finest Taste, from Eighteen Years old, to Fifty; where they may be supplied for less than the Prime Cost.—The said Sally also gives Directions when and how, in the most polite Manner, those Aprons ought to be worn. Whoever applys to purchase, or to take Directions either with, or without a Veil on, will be genteelly used, and have no Questions asked.[16]

Samuel Mattocks, Periwig Maker, Queen Street, Hartford:

Begs leave to acquaint the Public, That he has hired a compleat Workman from London, who not only makes all Sorts of Wiggs that are worn on the Continent; but also a new Fashion lately introduced in Boston, in Imitation of Hair: And also cuts and dresses Hair in the neatest and newest Fashion, for such as still continue to wear their Hair, notwithstanding it is so much out of Fashion, both in Europe and the fashionable

Parts of America. And . . . will make it his peculiar Care and Study to give universal Satisfaction to all who shall please to favour him with their Custom; and will take for pay, English and West-India Goods, Wood, and other Produce of the Country.

N. B. He also buys all Sorts of Hair, suitable for Wiggs.[17]

Town ways of living were probably becoming prescriptive, to some degree, in even the remoter rural areas of Connecticut. The *Courant* published an interesting letter in 1788, source unknown, which is remarkable for the insight it suggested on this point. An unidentified farmer wrote:

My parents were poor, and they put me at twelve years of age to a farmer with whom I lived till I was twenty-one. My master fitted me off with two stout suits of homespun, four pair of stockings, four woolen shirts, and two pair of shoes. At twenty-two I married me a wife, and a very good young woman she was. We took a farm of forty acres on rent. By industry we gained a-head fast. I paid my rent punctually, and laid by money. In ten years, I was able to buy me a farm of sixty acres, on which I became my own tenant. I then in a manner grew rich— and soon added another sixty acres with which I was content. My estate increased beyond all account. I bought several acres of outland for my children, who amounted to seven, when I was forty-five years old. About this time, I married my oldest daughter to a clever lad, to whom I gave one-hundred acres of my out-land. This daughter had been a working dutiful girl, and therefore I fitted her out well and to her mind: for I told her, to take of the best of my wool and flax, and to spin herself gowns, coats, stockings, and shifts:—nay, I suffered her to buy some cotton, and make into sheets, as I was determined to do well by her.

At this time, my farm gave me and my whole family a good living on the produce of it; and left me one year with another, 150 silver dollars, for I never spent more than ten dollars a year, which was for salt, nails and the like. Nothing to wear, eat, or drink was purchased, as my farm provided all—with this saving, I put money to interest, bought cattle fatted and sold them, and made great profit.

In two years after, my second daughter was courted. My wife says, "come, you are now rich,—you know Molly had nothing but what she spun—and no other cloathing has ever come into our house for any of us. Sarah must be fitted out a little,—she ought to fare as well as neighbour N-'s Betty. I must have some money and go to town." "Well, wife, it shall be as you think best. I have never been stingy: but it seems to me that what we spin at home would do." However, wife goes to town, and returns in a few days, with a calico gown, a calimanco petticoat, a set of stone tea-cups, half a dozen pewter tea-spoons, and a tea kettle, things that never were seen in my house before. They cost but little, I did not feel it—and I confess I was pleased to see them. Sarah was as well fitted out as any girl in the parish.

In three years more my third daughter had a spark—and wedding being concluded upon, wife comes again for the purse: but when she returned, what did I see! a silken gown, silk for a cloak, looking glass, china tea-gear, and a hundred other things, with the empty purse. But this is not the worst of it . . . Some time before the marriage of this last daughter, and ever since, this charge increased in my family, besides all sorts of household furniture unknown to us before—Cloathing of every sort is bought—and the wheel goes only for the purpose of exchanging our substantial cloth of flax and wool, for gauze ribbons, silk, tea, sugar, &c. My butter, which used to go to market, and brought money, is now expended at the tea-table. Breakfast, which used to take ten minutes, when we were satisfied with milk or pottage made of it, now takes my whole family an hour at tea or coffee. My lambs, which used also to bring cash, are now eaten at home—or, if sent to market, are brought back in things of no use—so that, instead of laying up 150 dollars every year, I find now all my loose money is gone. . . . and further what it costs me to live (though a less family than formerly, and all able to work) is fifty or sixty dollars a year more than all my farm brings me in. . . . I am not alone.Thirty in our parish have gone hand in hand with me—and they all say hard times.[18]

Although contemporary society imputed a dubious moral value to the unproductive employment of mind and muscle, the *Courant* printed a few references to amusements. Bull's Tavern in Hartford was a place where younger and older men sat, talked, drank, gambled, and occasionally scandalized the town by their carousals.[19] At one time, Westmoreland, a long-legged horse of fierceness and spirit, was expected to run a race with great "vehemence" in the Town of Hartford;[20] and there was card shuffling aplenty, to believe one traveled critic, while the exhibition of a few plays each year was winked at as productive of no apparent evil.[21] There were glimpses, entirely too brief, of other good times: hunting,[22] a fishing party,[23] a bear roast,[24] a naval ball at New London,[25] bowling on the Hartford Green for a "dinner and trimmings,"[26] games of cricket,[27] and free drinks on Election Day.[28] In the hard days of 1778, the *Courant* printed a resolution of the Continental Congress:[29]

That it be . . . earnestly recommended to the several states, to take the most effectual measures for the suppressing of theatrical entertainments, horse-racing, gaming and such other diversions as are productive of idleness, dissipation and a general depravity of principles and manners.

The paper printed more about the maladies which afflicted people than about the amusements which diverted them. One of the most dreaded diseases was smallpox and there were many allusions to its ravages in the 20 years before 1785. In 1771, when it was prevalent throughout the colony and especially at Middletown, a notice warned all people to unite in preventing its spread.[30] Probably ignorance and helplessness encouraged dark suspicions that ". . . some evil disposed persons with a view to their own private emolument, would willingly propagate that most dismal disease throughout the continent."[31] In the winter and summer of 1776, Hartford was in the throes of an epidemic;[32] during the first fortnight of December, 1779, 30 persons came down with it in the small village of Sharon.[33] Between occasional epidemic periods, scattered death notices indicated the almost constant presence of the disease. Until 1777, law-abiding Connecticut residents had to travel into the neighboring colonies to acquire immunity by the smallpox inoculation.[34] Advertisements inserted by doctors from Long Island, up the Connecticut Valley in Massachusetts, and just across the New York line, indicated some traffic of this sort,[35] but there is evidence that large numbers of people were illegally immunized in their own homes.[36]

It is a commonplace to think that disease made life more precarious in the past than it does now. The advertisements of doctors, testimonials of friends, prescriptions of laymen, merchants' medicines, and even the names of diseases culled from the *Courant*'s columns, tend to verify this impression. A noted Boston merchant died from a "mortification";[37] His Majesty suffered from an "Imposthume" in his breast;[38] the "Iliac Passion" killed a Yale tutor;[39] others were the victims of "inward inflammation," "bilious cholic," and "gout in the stomach"[40]—internal disorders vaguely understood.

To people suffering from ills the *Courant* carried many a suggestion, occasionally a prescription. For allaying the fever and ague, one amateur advised: "Take of Spider's webb sufficient for three pills, rolled well together, about the size of a large pea, drink them off in a gill of good old spirits, just as the chill commences."[41] Merchants offered a wide choice of pills and powders, many of them opiates and purgatives, "tent-wine" for consumptives, and such "genuine medicines" as candied orange peel and citron.[42] Grateful friends sometimes recommended doctors[43] and some doctors endorsed themselves. Dr. Skinner of Hartford had learned from a famous French medico how to cure cancers and wens.[44] Another physician, recently from London, could diagnose rheumatism, consumption, dropsy, and scurvy by the urine test.[45] "Wyantonomoo, the Disease-Killer," could cure them all by herbs some of which came from Patagonia.[46] One had bought a secret epilepsy cure; another carried pickled cancers about in testimony of successful practice; a third had discovered a syrup cure for dropsy.[47] As one person wrote:

> If you want health, consult our pages,
> You shall be well, and live for ages;
> Our empiricks, to get them bread,
> Do every thing but raise the dead.[48]

If the afflicted failed to take assurances of this type, he could purchase books on home medicine which the *Courant* advertised;[49] or, if the season permitted, he could set out over the hills on a health pilgrimage. The sulphurous spring water at Stafford, Connecticut, had a therapeutic reputation throughout New England.[50] Physicians traveled there to hold consultations with all who might apply.[51] President Thomas Clap of Yale College recommended the constant attendance of a doctor at the springs,[52] and the printer hoped that one of the visitors, Dr. Joseph Warren of Boston, might be induced to remain there in a professional capacity.[53] One physician prescribed mineral water for anemia, kidney stones, jaundice, rickets, ruptures, rheumatism, disorders of the stomach, spleen, kidneys, and lungs, as well as for pleurisy, ulcers, sores, and possibly cancers—a gill per dose to begin with and afterward never more than a pint.[54]

Contemporary critics complained in the *Courant* that Connecticut was infested with rambling quacks.[55] Although it would be impossible now to plot the line of division between quackery and reputable practice, the paper carried news of developments promising for the future. In order to combat fakers, one correspondent proposed a professorship of physic at Yale College,[56] and another sought public support for appropriate legislation.[57] In 1767, 31 doctors signed a letter to the *Courant* revealing the rules of a newly formed society with which all "reputable" doctors were invited to affiliate. To join the "Medical Corporation, in Litchfield County," members pledged themselves to professional study and cooperation, and they determined to issue certificates of endorsement to strangers and apprentices who wished to practice.[58] A group of New

London County physicians in 1774 called upon medical men from all the Connecticut counties to appoint representatives to an Election Day meeting in Hartford for the purpose of petitioning the legislature to pass medical police laws to curb quackery.[59] In 1779 a society composed of members from Connecticut and nearby areas in New York and Massachusetts was formed at Sharon to "unite its members in a cordial affection, to add life, and vigour to the healing art; to suppress quackerism; and encourage medical knowledge, and virtue." [60] They also intended to examine candidates, to boycott unethical doctors, and to summon county and state medical conventions to place the practice of physic on a more rational basis.[61] At the end of the Revolution, according to the *Courant,* medical societies existed in many parts of the state.[62]

Most of the *Courant*'s crime news, much of it in the advertisement columns, took cognizance of offenses against property in one form or another. Runaway slaves from New York and Connecticut frequently headed northward to Boston and their masters posted substantial rewards to get them back.[63] Chagrin occasionally inspired an amusing description. Wrote the master of an absconded apprentice:

He is about five feet ten inches high, square shoulder'd, and of a sallow Complection, some what pock mark'd, an *undertermined* cross, inconsistent, unpromising Countenance: very aukward in his Walk and Address!—speaks with a trembling Tone, and very inconnected in his Mode of Expression—When he tells a *Story* makes it very long, and never to the Purpose; is very fond of misquoting Acts of Parliament to shew his *Knowledge* where they have no Connection, and always looks very much *frighted*.[64]

Suggestive of the personal flavor of justice was the following typical notice:

Stolen out of the pasture of Ozias Pettibone, the night after the 2nd day of October instant, a sorril stallion horse, 3 years old last spring, upwards of 14 hands high, paces and trots: The supposed thief has stolen a number of calf skins out of a shop in Westfield. Whoever will take up said thief and horse, and convey them to me, shall have five dollars; and all necessary charges paid by me,

Ozias Pettibone.

Simsbury, 4th October, 1772 [65]

Counterfeiters and insolvent debtors were punished with a severity befitting the greatest of rogues,[66] but, to take the *Courant*'s testimony, the counterfeiter's trade throve heartily all the same, especially after 1776.[67] Descriptions of counterfeit dollar bills, French guineas, and Continental notes, made from the New York, New London, and Boston prints, were placed in the paper to put Connecticut merchants on guard.[68] There were accounts of culprits apprehended and jailed in many Connecticut towns, but the supply of them must have seemed inexhaustible. A belief, current about Boston, that a single gang included 500 members, suggested the existence of some extensive minting and printing, to say the least.[69] When times were hard the *Courant* carried insolvency notices, and many a poor fellow, unable to meet his obligations, took to his heels or else spun his philosophy in jail.[70]

The crime of burglary, although less common, provoked newsworthy castigation.[71] The sorry tale of one animated young man, whose name even the children must have known, ran in and out of the *Courant* for years. In 1771 the sheriff of Hartford County inserted this notice:

The notorious Burglarian, that called himself Richard Steel, that has been twice crop'd and branded, and was at March Court, at Hartford, again tried for the third Offence, but found not guilty, pursuing his old Trade, was again taken up and closely confined in Irons, but has found Means to get them off. His appearance is that of a likely young Man, of about 21 years of Age, about middling for Height somewhat slender, has a lively, keen, dark colour'd Eye, and is finely pitted with the Small Pox, wears his Hair, pretty dark Colour'd, but not unlikely he may soon get a wig to cover his Ears; he is pretty quick and lively in speaking, and has a little different Manner from persons born among us.[72]

There were allusions to such punishments as stocks and pillories, whipping, ear cropping, and branding,[73] and sometimes, as the paper reported, the chastening matched the crime with amusing literalness:

On Monday last Andrew Peter, who had been convicted of Horse-Stealing, was for the second time brought from the prison in this City, to be mounted on a *Wooden Horse* as a *Punishment* for his offence. It seems that the culprit had before suffered considerably by riding this bareboned animal, and had so far reflected on his *latter end* as to secure himself against a second scarification by stuffing a blanket in his breeches. The Sheriff who was very inquisitive into the cause of the apparent quiet and satisfaction of the prisoner, at length discovered the evasion, and directed the cavalier to unbutton and dislodge the blanket. As others may not have the same sagacity, it seems necessary to caution all sheriffs who may have the command of this new species of Cavalry, to observe the breeches of their recruits, and see that they are of no more than legal size and thickness, that the only salutary purposes of the law against horse-stealing may not be defeated.[74]

On those rare occasions when public executions occurred, great numbers of curious people attended.[75] Before Moses Dunbar was hanged in Hartford, the *Courant* recorded that a minister from Middletown preached him a last sermon in the jail, whereas the Reverend Nathan Strong of Hartford delivered the traditional sermon to the spectators warning them against all of the wages of sin.[76] In over 20 years, the *Courant* printed only isolated protests against any aspect of the current penal treatment of offenders.[77]

Jailers' and sheriffs' advertisements indicated that the Connecticut town and county jails were notoriously poor places for confinement, at least from society's point of view. The county jails at Hartford and Litchfield, for example, were broken over 20 times in five years.[78] After the first state prison was established in the deserted shafts of some old copper mines in Simsbury, the paper noted at least a dozen breaks within a decade.[79] On one occasion six inmates fled with the keeper's gun and keys.[80] Later, 28 of them broke out by killing one guard and wounding another.[81] Convicts twice burned down the prison house to escape.[82]

Much of the *Courant*'s picture of education likewise emerges from paid advertisements. According to the issue of April 10, 1775, a student wishing to enter the Hartford Grammar School must write legibly, read the Bible with propriety, and be disposed to make the study of Greek and Latin his leading activity. Once admitted, he would also study arithmetic, geometry, trigonometry, surveying, navigation, geography, writing, speaking, and perhaps other subjects. He could be boarded about three quarters of a mile from school for five shillings and six pence per week, washing and mending included.[83] Schoolmaster Wales assured the parents of his pupils that: "A watchful Eye is kept over the Morals of the Youth; and unwearied attempts made to enrich their Minds with virtuous Sentiments, and the Principles of the Christian Religion." [84]

Advertisements indicated the presence of a number of ephemeral private schools in the inland towns of Connecticut. In 1781 appeared the following:

The subscriber, desirous of promoting Education, so essential to the interest of a free people, proposes immediately to open a school at Sharon, in which young Gentlemen and Ladies may be instructed in Reading, Writing, Mathematicks, the English Language, and if desired, the Latin and Greek Languages—in Geography, Vocal Music, &c. at the moderate price of Six Dollars and two thirds per quarter per Scholar. The strictest attention will be paid to the studies, the manners and morals of youth, by the public's very humble servant,

Noah Webster, jun.

P. S. If any persons are desirous of acquainting themselves with the French Language, they may be under the instruction of an accomplished master in Sharon.

Sharon, June 1, 1781 [85]

The usual school was supported by tuition rather than by endowment. It was almost always owned and operated by a pedagogue whose classes met in his house, in a vacant shop, or beneath some other convenient roof. Out-of-town pupils who came from prosperous homes sometimes lived at the schoolmaster's house. School terms had no uniform length or season.[86]

In towns where there were no grammar schools, private schools were arising to offer a classical education. Like Webster, Timothy Dwight advertised a school at Northampton to teach advanced reading and writing, mathematics, grammar, geography, Latin, and Greek.[87] New Milford had a Yale preparatory school in 1782,[88] and other classical schools were set up at East Windsor, Enfield, Lebanon, and Windham.[89] Since tradition had well entrenched the old grammar school curriculum with its heavy Latin and Greek, the new schools offered changes in emphasis and content. The classical school in New Milford gave attention to the study of "physick." [90] In Hartford, John Miller set up a practical commercial school.[91] Fagan and Ballentine taught arithmetic in their school but specialized in instrumental music and composition.[92] Webster, who came to believe that there should be more English along with less Latin and Greek, later advertised a "Rhetorical School" in Hartford to "diffuse propriety and uniformity of speaking." [93] Other Hartford schools stressed French, a subject which acquired a sort of educational validity in the Revolutionary period.[94]

The *Courant's* columns, moreover, reflected the growing demand for a wider educational opportunity for girls.[95] The learned young men at Yale College debated the justice of this situation [96] at a time when occasional schools were already advertising. Schoolmaster Miller held a morning session from seven o'clock until eight-thirty for young ladies desirous of improving themselves in writing and keeping accounts.[97] Both Webster and Dwight were willing to teach the Classics to mixed classes;[98] and girls could get a good classical education at Windham.[99] Even the Hartford Grammar School began having both morning and night classes in which young men and women studied writing, arithmetic, geography, surveying, navigation, and probably other subjects.[100]

In several institutions of higher learning the *Courant* displayed a perennial news interest, perhaps chiefly in Dartmouth and Yale.[101] Commencement days, usually well attended, were roundly and sometimes excessively celebrated. At Dartmouth, in 1772:

His Excellency Governor Wentworth distributed to the vast Concourse of People assembled there, an Ox roasted, Bread, and a Hogshead of Liquor, which amply refreshed some hundreds who partook of his Bounty, with a decency and decorum that astonish'd most of the Gentlemen, who from the general Licentiousness of the times, conceiv'd it scarcely possible that so great a number could be so liberally entertain'd without an instance of Excess or Indecency.[102]

At the end of the Revolution, correspondents of the *Courant* noted that the passing years had brought changes to which Yale College had failed to adjust; that the curriculum remained narrowly theological despite the fact that a large majority of the graduates would never preach the Word of God; and that the government of the corporation, then a monopoly of the clergy, should be diffused and brought under state control.[103] In 1783 the printers ran a series of 12 critical letters elaborating these points,[104] and Hudson & Goodwin were later advertising a shilling pamphlet entitled "The Right of the General Assembly to inspect, regulate and reform the Corporation of Yale-College in New Haven." [105] As one of their writers expressed it: "The intent of the university is to bring up youth, of the most promising genius, for *orators* and *philosophers, statesmen, legislators, judges, councellors at law, physicians,* &c. as well as for the *pulpit.*" [106]

One of the lively learning interests of this generation involved the materials of "natural philosophy" or what would today be called "natural science." The *Courant*'s pages contained many allusions to unusual natural phenomena: severe storms, earthquakes, lightning, meteors, comets, northern lights, and eclipses. Some of these were of intimate significance to people whose profits, kin, and acquaintances were abroad on southern waters plying the West Indian trade. Moreover, there was an attitude of popular curiosity and speculation about the nature and mysterious purposes of some of these things which the findings of science have since allayed. Severe weather conditions at sea, especially in the Caribbean, received dozens of notices in the early papers. Matter-of-fact reports of shipwrecks and cargo losses, a common form of marine intelligence,[107] must occasionally have carried the sting of tragedy to Connecticut readers; but whatever the philosophy with which grief was assuaged the causes were all too ordinary to inspire speculation worth printing.

Earthquakes, more severe in the West Indies than to the north, were of course more unusual, and readers were frequently apprised of the damage they inflicted.[108] One year, the printers recounted the remarkably dense fogs in England, the "rising" of the Hebrides, and the many volcanic and seismic disturbances of unusual severity in several parts of the world. Some concluded that the earth was off its orbit, but the printers themselves were in doubt:

Whether this be a fact or not, we are not able to decide; but whether the convulsion, occasioned by the burning and eruption of vast bodies of sulphurous matter from the bowels of the earth, may not be sufficiently violent to impel the earth from its natural position with respect to the solar system in general; and whether the established laws of gravitation, would not, in such case, counteract the effect of such force and restore the earth to its original situation; are enquiries that may not be unworthy of philosophical curiosity.[109]

The electrical findings of the great Dr. Franklin had probably given people of this generation a keener interest in the whimsical works of lightning than ever before. Printers sometimes traced the zigzag path of the "fluid" with special reference to the composition of the materials which attracted it.[110] People disagreed as to whether the bolt came from the clouds to the earth or shot from the earth to the clouds in wreaking its havoc.[111] Apparently there were some, deserving to be called "anti-electricians," who regarded doing anything about it a presumptuous meddling with heaven's artillery; [112] but opposition to lightning rods got no encouragement from the printers, who readily made object lessons of the disasters which they reported.[113]

Meteors were sometimes described in the *Courant* by interested parties.[114] In the summer of 1765 a meteor, said to be nearly as big and bright as the sun or moon, was seen by numerous people to pass over Northampton, Hadley, Springfield, Litchfield, Kent, and Poughkeepsie. President Clap of Yale College wrote in to invite ministers and other gentlemen to collect and send him exact information concerning its transit.[115] He believed that meteors were solid bodies, at least one-half mile in diameter, traveling from 20 to 30 miles high at a speed of 500 miles per minute. Characterized by loud explosive noises, they swung about the earth in long ellipses and might be expected to reappear.[116] This was contrary to the common opinion that meteors always disintegrated by breaking into pieces.[117] Another person, who observed an unusually bright meteor, perhaps the one above described, noted that the next morning there was a hard frost which did much damage to the fruit.[118]

The Reverend Nehemiah Strong, once Professor of Natural Philosophy at Yale College, author of a book on astronomy, and the *Courant*'s authority on celestial mechanics, held that comets, unlike meteors, were not near the earth, but were distant, opaque bodies swinging about the sun. Whether they were good or evil influences, heralds of calamity, or hells for punishment, he was admittedly unable to say.[119] One comet, which appeared in 1769, attracted enough attention for the *Courant* to run a series of philosophical essays on the subject, and sometime later to print a good-sized diagram depicting the descent of the comet with respect to the positions of the heavenly bodies.[120] The Aurora Borealis was still more puzzling. It might have been the illumination from great fires to the north, or the reflection of the sun upon vast unexplored bodies of northern water, or perhaps it was simply "electrical effluvia." Nobody knew, but all these notions were ventilated in the paper.[121]

The *Courant* printed but few references to eclipses of the sun. A Boston item noted one such occurrence to the accompaniment of an unusually severe snowstorm which lasted several days.[122] A correspondent from Cornwall described what must have been a partial eclipse, and asked any informed person to tell him what it was.[123] In 1780 the printers of the *Courant* reported a "very singular darkness of the visible heavens" and requested their philosophical customers to give an account of the particular phenomena attending it, especially, exact data on the time of its beginning, continuance, and end, together with the appearance and color of the clouds and other perceptible objects.[124]

On the subject of inventions the *Courant* had less to say. In 1771 it carried what purported to be a list of American inventions made between 1740 and 1766.[125] This compilation included but four items: mercurial inoculation, by a doctor from Long Island; lightning rods, by Benjamin Franklin; the process of making iron from black sand, by Jared Eliot of Connecticut; and the theory of investigating the quantity of matter in comets, by John Winthrop of Harvard College. This was obviously no age of crackpot gadgets, yet the General Assembly granted Benjamin Hanks of Litchfield a fourteen-year patent on a clock that wound itself by air and apparently promised to do so until its parts wore out.[126] A person from the distant Kentucky country wrote to stake his life on the perfection of a perpetual-motion mechanism which some genius from those parts had allegedly contrived to devise.[127] In 1784 the printers described a somewhat more significant attempt at labor saving:

There has lately been invented and made upon an entirely new construction, by a Gentleman in this state, a Float, or Water-Craft, rowed by two horses. It arrived last Friday at the Landing in this city. . . . The movement of this machine will be always certain, as it goes against wind and tide; it is expeditious, there being no loss of time in motion, as in the interrupted impetus of oars; it is cheap, as one horse will perform the service of six or eight men.[128]

As it appeared to bystanders, the craft consisted of two scows hitched together, a water wheel on each side, and the horses walking in circular motion on an elevated treadway. It could move three miles per hour.

The same year, customers of the *Courant* must have read the following account from New York City with considerable interest:

Letters from Avignon, dated Oct. 24, brought by the Packet Le Courier de L'Amerique, mention, that Mr. Joseph Montgolfiere has made several ingenious and useful experiments on the resisting power of the air. After having thrown a sheep six times from the top of a tower in that neighbourhood, upwards of 100 feet high, by the aid of a machine called a Parachute, without the animal receiving any damage, he prevailed on a man condemned to suffer a long imprisonment, to try the experiment, which was performed with the utmost safety, to the satisfaction of many thousand spectators; in consequence of which the Magistrates remitted the adventurer's punishment. The machine, we hear, is in many respects similar to an umbrella.[129]

There were thrilling items about French balloon experiments, too. In one instance, men met death trying to fly the English Channel.[130] In another, two intrepid flyers supposedly ascended nevermore to return to earth.[131] Finally, the *Courant* reprinted this exciting piece of news from the *Maryland Journal:*

Will be exhibited, in a field near Baltimore, on Thursday the 24th instant, if fair, if not, the next fair day, at eight o'clock in the morning, or at five in the evening . . . an Aerostatic Balloon, nearly 35 feet diameter, with a splendid Chariot suspended at the bottom, fixed for the reception of two persons, in which the subscriber proposes to ascend above the clouds, after a short lecture on the great uses to which this important discovery may be applied.[132]

The war years inevitably produced conditions which affected the daily lives of the people. Inhabitants of the maritime settlements were generally fearful of the pillaging expeditions of the enemy. In New London especially, colonial war boats lay at anchor, privateers hauled in their prizes, or traders awaited opportune times to sail.[133] New Londoners were now and again excited by the appearance, off harbor, of enemy sails before Arnold's troops finally landed to capture Fort Griswold, burn parts of their town and of Groton, and lay low a number of colonial defenders.[134] Earlier in the war, Tryon marched inland to Danbury with a goodly accompaniment of soldiers, seized and destroyed some of the army stores which were kept there, and safely effected a retreat.[135] His attacks upon New Haven, Fairfield, and Norwalk, and several lesser "Tory raids" at other points served to maintain the expectancy of disaster.[136]

In these and other communities new avenues of employment and adventure opened up. The *Courant* advertised for gunsmiths, coppersmiths, blacksmiths, wheelwrights, armorers, carpenters, shoemakers, saddlers, and harness makers.[137] Aside from joining the fighting forces, young men could sign up with privateers which were periodically setting out for booty.[138] Young women were wanted at one time for hospital service at $1.00 a week.[139] People were called upon to furnish shoes, shirts, stockings, and mittens for soldiers.[140] Strangers came to town. In the beginning merchants from Boston established themselves in Hartford and elsewhere.[141] Local jails housed Tories and British prisoners.[142] The latter were sometimes placed with families, worked on farms or at trades, and took a limited part in the life of the neighborhood.[143] Not only did the Revolution bring mounting prices and shortages in such important household commodities as sugar, molasses, rum, salt, and tea, but it placed a premium upon cereals and dairy products.[144] In 1780 the General Assembly levied a grain tax upon the towns.[145]

If all kinds of English goods were more difficult to get and painful to pay for, they were nevertheless obtainable. Before the Netherlands and England were at war, sloops from Connecticut traded with England by way of Amsterdam.[146] Such goods were later received through the illicit trade with New York.[147] Prize ships laden with British wares were sold frequently and it was suspected that some of these seizures were prearranged.[148]

Although much that was printed in the *Courant* concerning manners and morals, crime, education, disease, and "natural philosophy" bore the flavor of prevalent religious concepts, nothing approaching an intimate view of the religious beliefs and practices of this generation came to light in the paper. Alongside the churches of the Puritan forefathers, congregations of the Anglican faith had come to function within the accepted scheme of things; and at a time when all good people were rending the heavens with cries against unjust taxation, one writer wondered why Episcopalians should be taxed to support the traditional meetinghouses, especially when they enjoyed no voice in the matter.[149] The General Assembly received enough of their petitions for tax relief to attract newspaper comment,[150] but events were already working against them. The *Courant* invited the inference that some of the Anglican clergymen were exercising an independence not quite in line with popular approbation.[151] Did the law require them to read from their pulpits the governors' proclamations setting days for fasting and prayer? Apparently not; but in one instance which the *Courant* recorded, eight members of the Anglican Church in Hebron were fined for breach of public fast during the Easter holidays.[152] Prominent persons to the southward, moreover, were reported to be agitating the question of an Anglican bishop for the colonies,[153] but Watson assured his readers "that the petition lately presented to his Majesty for an American Bishop was rejected, it having been considered in its true light, as the desire of a few meddling priests, and not of the people." [154] Shortly after the close of the Revolution, Connecticut achieved the distinction of having the first American Episcopal Bishop in the person of the Reverend Samuel Seabury of New London, and with the abatement of the wartime odium against Anglicanism, Hudson & Goodwin expressed more liberal sentiments:

The Episcopalians are a respectable body of men, who are tolerated and countenanced by the laws of this State, and their mode of worship ought not therefore to be the subject of private ridicule. . . . As the

Deity has not directed that any particular forms of worship shall be observed, every body of men have a right to establish such forms as they judge decent and proper and consequently to alter them at any time, to accomodate them to their local and political condition.[155]

News items indicate that on Sundays, on Election Days, at public hangings, and at the New Haven commencement anniversaries, preachers harangued their listeners from appropriate texts. Sermons delivered on special occasions were often printed and sold. Innumerable references to the need for propitiating the Divine Will in all the departments of human conduct suggested the social pervasion of religious thinking reminiscent of an earlier New England. Perhaps this was nowhere more aptly summarized than in the obituary remarks which the paper published. There was still visible the Puritan emphasis upon the immanence of death:

> Short is the Date, and narrow is the Span,
> Which bounds the little life of foolish Man.[156]

The *Courant* reminded its readers that youth, wealth, mental accomplishments—none was security against the inexorable hand of the Grim Reaper:

Her Curtains that were made of the Gold and Silver Thread, to adorn her Lodgings, are furled up, being changed for a Napkin and a Winding Sheet, spun by the Spider and the Worm—the Marriage and festal Days were begun and carried on with proper Joy and Solemnity; but—their End is Death, without Dancing, or a merry Mood.[157]

Often did the printers pass on that venerable piece of advice perhaps best expressed in the words: "Be ye also ready." [158]

PART TWO
1783–1815

CHAPTER IV

FEDERALIST PRESS

ONCE the muskets of the Revolution were stacked, Hudson & Goodwin hoisted the flag for "law and order." Amidst the social unrest in the 1780's and the mounting political agitation in the decade following, they dedicated the *Courant* to the interests of the socially and politically dominant. This was first apparent in their stand on the "Commutation Act" in which Congress promised the officers of the late Continental Army full pay for five years.

In the beginning the paper presented the arguments of "the people." What justice was there in this measure, especially when Congress granted no such boon to the common soldiers? And what about the citizens who served in the militia at Bennington and Saratoga? The depreciated pay of the officers had already been made up to them; and some of them, moreover, by trading and by even more dubious practices connected with provisioning the army, had come out of the war richer than when they entered it. Already they had formed themselves into the elite, hereditary Order of the Cincinnati wearing the badges of peerage and awaiting bounty from the purses of the people. The act of Congress, worse than an odious discrimination repugnant to a free people, was an unwarranted invasion of state sovereignty. By what constitutional right did that body set up a select circle of pensioners? [1]

As the popular movement gained ground, however, the *Courant* shifted position. The resolutions of several towns, including Hartford, condemned "Commutation." [2] Delegates from 28 Connecticut communities convened at Middletown in September, 1783, to score the iniquity of pensioners and placemen with reference to both state and federal governments. [3] But when the lower house of the General Assembly favored a remonstrance to Congress, the *Courant's* editors emerged with a theme which they elaborated until the issue died down. What salutary effect, they asked, could be expected from such a protest?

The Assembly of Massachusetts remonstrated last spring upon the same subject. . . . But when a people, so much enlightened as the inhabitants of this state, suffer themselves to be duped out of their senses by the foes of our independence and British emissaries, who are scattering the seeds of discord in the regions of tranquillity, it seems the design of heaven to punish their blindness by some fated catastrophe.[4]

The lower branch of the Assembly dispatched its protest to Congress and delegates met again in Middletown to pass resolutions derogatory to the Cincinnati and to such Connecticut papers as were espousing the cause of the officers.[5] But meantime the *Courant* carried the resolves of towns which determined to withdraw support from the Convention.[6] The printers and their correspondents poured ridicule upon the Middletown assemblage and its leaders, upon the resolutions of towns supporting it, and upon the *Freeman's Chronicle,* a short-lived Hartford newspaper which endorsed the Convention sentiments.[7]

So obvious were the *Courant's* leanings that the Middletown delegates were urged to get their constituents to boycott the paper. The printers retorted with a letter to the public:

It has been repeatedly reported in the state, especially in remote towns, where such reports would be most likely to pass uncontradicted, that we have been partial—that we have published every thing in favour of commutation, and either delayed or suppressed essays and resolves against the act of Congress. . . . But if such suggestions have obtained any credit . . . we solemnly declare, that every thing in favour of the people against commutation, has been published in turn as soon as it could be admitted. . . . Neither officers nor people shall find us partial to their particular interests. If either party wants a tool to answer its particular purpose, they must apply to some other Printer. . . . As we ever have, so we ever shall conduct ourselves with the strictest impartiality, and sooner than deviate from this resolution, we will suffer every misfortune that slander can produce, and submit to any honest employment for daily subsistence.[8]

These remarks may be interpreted as meaning that Hudson & Goodwin had printed before and would print thereafter occasional letters from those who applauded the views of the Convention.[9] But aside from this, the disavowal meant nothing because they were soon again squirting sarcasm upon the persons of the opposition.[10] In March, 1784, when the Convention formulated a public letter against the Commutation Act, the subsequent three issues were replete with letters of ridicule and significantly devoid of a single pro-Convention sentiment.[11] According to the *Courant's* writers, a few demagogues with Tory inclinations were seeking to glide into office on the disaffection of the mob; the Cincinnati were certainly a harmless group; [12] and, at any rate, the Act had been passed and nothing could now be done about it.[13]

Although the controversy soon subsided, conflicting considerations on the more fundamental but related problem of public indebtedness and taxation had already come to the fore.[14] Since the Confederation had emerged from the war saddled with a foreign and domestic debt, the desirability of funding its obligations became a pressing concern. Inasmuch as Congress had never been very successful in requisitioning money from the states, it sought their permission to lay a duty of 5 per cent upon imports. Those who opposed this "impost amendment" contended that the exercise of taxation ought to remain, *in toto,* with the state legislatures. Far from being the "Tories" which the *Courant* dubbed them, they seemed to have retained too well the patriotic prejudices they had learned in the days before the war. According to their arguments, which appeared in the paper, the adoption of the amendment would probably usher in, under federal auspices, searches, seizures, ransacked homes, and the whole paraphernalia of British tyranny.[15] The American people were therefore admonished to proceed with circumspection after the late, bitter experiences of the Revolution.[16]

This point of view, Hudson & Goodwin contested. In the fall of 1783, shortly after the General Assembly rejected the request of Congress, they featured a series of letters by Noah Webster.[17] He held that the union of the States was necessary for war, for the regulation of commerce, for the conduct of foreign relations, and, above all, for taxation. As in all sovereign states, a supreme authority was a *sine qua non.* What sort of arrangement was it for Congress to possess the right to make contracts but not the authority to fulfill them? Specifically, if congressmen had been granted the authority to borrow money for the United States, "they have or ought to have power to compel their constituents to discharge the debt." The 5 per cent impost, far from overburdening the Connecticut farmers and workers who were so strongly opposing it, would fall principally upon the wealthier consumers in the state. It would be an "equitable" tax. The mere fact that Connecticut, Rhode Island, and some other states refused to ratify it indicated the need for federal authority to compel recalcitrant states to comply with their common obligations.

Much to the gratification of the printers, the Assembly reconsidered and ratified the amendment in the spring of 1784,[18] but the general outlook was pregnant with pessimism. As Webster had expressed it:

During the late war our foes often foretold the consequences of our independence. They told us that we should be without order, law and government – – – that we should be distracted into parties – – – that jealousies would arise between the States – – – that the confederation would not have energy sufficient to manage the numerous and discordant interests of such a body as the Thirteen States – – – that our taxes would be heavy and produce uneasiness, if not insurrections, among the people – – – – that our trade would be laid under such restrictions by foreigners as to deprive us of every advantage. These and many other evils . . . are already in part taking place.[19]

Hudson & Goodwin felt that the refusal of the states, from motives of local interest, to cooperate with each other, would probably end in the creation of some compulsory power which would oblige them to act in concert. More to be dreaded, the whole situation might terminate in a total breakdown of the Confederation.[20]

The *Courant* carried scornful allusions to the cheap-money movements in Rhode Island and elsewhere.[21] The printers pursued Shays into the hills of Vermont without a penny's worth of sympathy for his cause and even detected some slight symptoms of "anarchy" in Connecticut.[22] His followers were said to have labored under the intolerable grievance of paying their honest debts.[23]

Let us run in debt less, spend less, and pay more, be more frugal and industrious and we shall soon find our affairs mending; our debts both public and private lessening, and money become plenty. For the scarcity of money, is a disease that will work its own remedy, and make a plenty as in other merchandize. But it must be in a way of industry and frugality—and whenever money becomes plenty in any other way, it does more hurt than good, and it creates idleness and wickedness among a people, of which we have already too much.[24]

Conflicting land grants generated disputes between the states and Webster again wrote a series of letters on Connecticut's claim to the Wyoming settlement in Pennsylvania.[25] Connecticut speculators wanted their rights confirmed or their investments returned, but Webster went on to pose several fundamental questions. If all the states rushed in to claim such lands as lay within the limits of their overlapping, carelessly defined grants, would not a civil war ensue, more terrible than that which had occurred in the Wyoming country? If the larger states undertook campaigns to extend their boundaries, what power would put a stop to their aggressions? Congress was debating its answer to the controversy between Connecticut and Pennsylvania, but what would happen if the several disputes became acute? It seemed to him, finally, that all the states should cede their claims to the federal government for their mutual benefit. A part of the lands might be sold to sink the domestic debt, and a part reserved to defray the future expenses of the national government.[26] This arrangement, he thought, would form a strong and permanent bond of union.

As conditions refused to mend, the *Courant* ran the heavy, satirical *Anarchiad* of the Hartford Wits [27] and Hudson & Goodwin lamented the rumblings from the social substratum which the Revolution had produced:

Most people may be honest, because life and property depend on the principle; but most people are very ill qualified to govern. The reason why the New-England states are worse governed than heretofore, is, that men of sense and property have lost much of their influence by the popular spirit of the war. People once respected their governors, their senators, their judges and their clergy . . . their laws were obeyed, and, the states were happy in tranquillity.[28]

One of the *Courant*'s writers inquired whether the situation and circumstances of the United States might not require some important additions to be made to the federal system of government.[29]

From the time when news of the coming Philadelphia Convention appeared, the arguments for a firmer union became more and more insistent in the pages of Hudson & Goodwin's paper. A stronger government was needed to keep the domestic peace. There may have been a time-and-place validity for "revolution," but none even theoretically existed within a republic where freemen settled their problems by ballot. The objective of the late Revolution was to effect a separation from Great Britain and nothing more. A stronger government was needed to protect property and to enforce the punctual fulfillment of contracts. Promises to individuals by the government were sacred. Faith in the government had been sorely wounded; widows, orphans, and patriotic citizens had suffered grievous wrongs. With foreigners monopolizing American trade, ships rotting at the wharves, unemployed workers in the cities, farmers bent under taxes, creditors complaining to the heavens, bankruptcies, and paper money, a stronger government was obviously wanted to regulate commerce.[30] Without such a government, according to Hudson & Goodwin, the northern states might soon be impoverished and the southern ones mere vassals of Europe.[31]

When the Convention met, whether repairs were to strengthen the fabric of the old government or a new and more vigorous one was to be erected in its place, were but matters of form to the owners of the *Courant:*

Various opinions are propagated respecting the probable result of the foederal convention; but, whatever means are pursued, it seems, to be unanimously agreed, that a strong and efficient executive power must be somewhere established. How widely different would have been the character of the union, if in Congress had resided a power to controul the selfish interests of a single state . . . in order to promote the common weal. . . . In considering then, what form of government is best calculated to promote the principles of universal justice . . . fatal experience will instruct us that little can be left to the voluntary disposition of the people.[32]

As soon as the *Courant* published the Constitution, the printers admonished their readers to shun all sham patriots, appearances notwithstanding, who counseled them to reject the new federal government.[33] The alleged enemies of the commerce, respectability, and independence of the United States—Elbridge Gerry, George Mason, Richard H. Lee—had their motives and characters impugned in the *Courant.* The smaller fry in Connecticut was almost beneath respectable mention.[34] Some of the old Middletown group were again accused of fomenting discontent, but their numbers and influence had greatly dwindled since the days of the Commutation fight.[35] According to dispatches, the Constitution provided for the wisest, most free, and most efficient government that ancient or modern times had produced.[36] As plans got afoot for the ratification meeting at Hartford, the printers felt confident that righteousness would out: "The Convention, notwithstanding some Judasses, will be composed of the most respectable men in the state—men venerable for their age and abilities, and possessed of the public confidence." [37]

After the vote at Hartford had given a lop-sided victory to the friends of the Constitution, it was alleged by the dissidents that the people had been asked to elect delegates to the convention at a time when they could scarcely have read the Constitution, and that the Connecticut newspapers had subsequently been muffled to prevent their obtaining much enlightenment.[38] Whatever the truth of these charges, Hudson & Goodwin made no secret of their views. Until the Constitution was published, the *Courant* carried a single letter in opposition to a strengthened federal government and this one was uniquely labeled "Paid." [39] In a period of 15 weeks between the time the *Courant* published the Constitution and the time the printers announced its ratification by Connecticut, the paper displayed not a letter opposing it.[40] Twice in this period, conceding repeated criticism, the partners entered vigorous and lengthy denials of "partiality"—once in conjunction with the printer of the *American Mercury,* another Hartford paper.[41] According to these statements, in a period of 12 weeks not a single essay containing the slightest objection to the Constitution had been received by the local papers. While noting that heated opposition arguments from other states might have been reprinted, Hudson & Goodwin found them one-sided and expressed a preference, in any case, for "original talent":

It is true that we make no secret of our private opinions respecting the questions now under consideration; but we pledge ourselves to the public that we ever have and ever mean to maintain the liberty of the press, and to publish any pieces which we judge will not disgrace our paper, uninfluenced by our private opinions of the merits of any question, or the wishes of any party whatever.[42]

Once the fight had terminated at home, the *Courant* followed the results elsewhere and its optimism swelled with the weeks.[43] When finally the ratification by New Hampshire converted hope into happiness, the printers humorously advertised the old, well-worn Articles of Confederation for sale and offered to throw Rhode Island into the bargain.[44] Their joy expanded to embrace the whole wide world and they found it good:

The year 1788 has begun with events of the most interesting nature. The African slave trade is likely to receive a deadly blow in Great-Britain. The parliaments of France have claimed, and will probably recover, their ancient privileges. The Russians have begun a war, which may end in the destruction of Turkish power, and of the Mohomitan impostures in religion. The United States have formed, and perhaps (by this time) *adopted* a government, which will secure and perpetuate her liberties, we hope, to the end of time. And lastly, the king of France has not only extended the blessings of a free toleration to all religious sects, in every part of his dominions, but opened the door of power and office to them.—Happy aera in human affairs!—when reason and religion unite their influence in the government of the different nations of the world! [45]

As competent hands launched the new government and the years of Washington's first administration glided by, the *Courant* and its editors were complacent and contented. The old officers of government were good; religious toleration was good; town-supported free education was good; Hamilton and the fiscal policies of the federal fathers were good.[46] The only jarring note came from what Hudson & Goodwin called the rum-drinking Irishmen who inhabited the hills of western Pennsylvania, but even the early disaffection there created no great editorial stir.[47] Although the ancient order of affairs was crumbling in Europe and the papers were heavy with news of the French Revolution, this downfall of despotism also gave cause for rejoicing.[48] Perhaps no sin, the editors thought, surpassed that of complaint, especially since the republic enjoyed peace, plenty, and religious liberty: "Let us look at the old world—see famine, war, commotion and destruction pervading a great part of it: Then view our own country, and let reason and justice draw the distinction." [49]

Before the end of the quadrennium, however, the complexion of world events appeared to be changing. When the *Courant* reported Edmund Burke as noting only six men of property among the 700 members of the French National Assembly, the editors wonderingly called it a "curious description." [50] Only a few weeks later, their concern became pronounced:

The deplorable state of France, at this moment, must excite the compassion of every feeling man. The King deposed by a decree of the National Assembly —— and both King and Queen, with their family, obliged to shelter themselves in this very Assembly, from the lawless fury of the Parisian populace. The guards of the palace butchered before the threshold, and the palace rifled by the mob —— an army of 200,000 Austrians and Prussians, headed by the brave and warlike, but implacable Duke of Brunswick, determined at all events, to penetrate to Paris and restore the King to his throne and his prerogatives —— disunion, suspicion and treachery among the national councils —— fierce animosity between the Jacobins and the generals of their armies, and distraction throughout the whole nation. A scene so gloomy and terrible is seldom unfolded on the theatre of this earth! As men, as philosophers, and as good citizens, let us pause —— let us withold a part of our admiration of the French Constitution, which places legislative power in a *single body* of men, *unchecked* and *uncontrolled*.[51]

Coming to think of the French Revolution as the apotheosis of the forces of evil and destruction, Hudson & Goodwin heartily embraced Washington's proclamation of peace and neutrality following the British declaration of war against France. The governor of Connecticut seconded the President's pronouncement and citizens of Hartford and the other Connecticut towns were urged to endorse it.[52] Favorable resolutions from papers outside the state were placed in the *Courant*.[53] The French-American commitments of 1778 were only implicitly refuted by a lone correspondent who scornfully deprecated the "altruistic" motives of the French Government in assisting the colonies to establish their independence.[54] When Minister Edmond Charles Genêt, arriving from France in April, 1793, proceeded to invoke the hostility of those who supported Washington's position, the columns of the *Courant* carried nothing but rebuke for this "uninformed foreigner" who came here to convert the citizens of a free country.[55] "Influenced by the example of blood thirsty and blasphemous leaders, the [French] nation has forgotten every ornament of rational, and civilized life, and is rapidly retreating toward a savageness and barbarity." [56]

Unfortunately, to believe the *Courant,* not all the forces that threatened the established values of society were operating on the other side of the Atlantic. Here in the States, what had hitherto been scantily reported as a purely domestic political faction, appeared to assume more sinister significance. The opposition to Hamilton's financial program and to earlier federal measures may have seemed the work of visionary theorists with fallacious, antifederal ideas of government,[57] but now came suggestions of an ominous, "revolutionary" strain. The beam of suspicion was leveled upon Jefferson:

The gentleman, at the head of the party, who acquire their consequence by opposing all the measures of our government, who rail at every article in the system of finance . . . who pour forth the torrent of their invectives against the Secretary of the Treasury, who abuse the Vice-President by perpetual and wilful misrepresentations of his political opinions, and whenever they dare, aim their secret arrows against the just popularity of the President—is the avowed patron of scepticism in religion, and of the levelling system of Mr. Paine in politics.[58]

When an assemblage of Bostonians feted the accomplishments of the French Revolution, the *Courant*'s editorial comment was scathing:

We are told that at the mighty *civic feast,* the feast of *equality* in Boston, some little *distinction* was observed, by placing citizens *such a one* and *such a one* at the *head* of the *table* in the hall and spreading a table *out of doors, sub dio,* for *fellow citizens* of the rabble. Bostonians . . . are full of notions: But to be consistent let citizen Hancock and citizen Adams be seated at the table cheek by joul with their citizen butcher and citizen oyster-man. Untill this is done, their practice will burlesque their professions and expose them to ridicule.[59]

As the so-called "Jacobin" or "Democratic" clubs emerged in New York, Philadelphia, and elsewhere, the *Courant's* readers were invited to recognize a co-ordinated attempt to undermine the structure of republican government: [60] "In the bosom of America we have a faction, the unrelenting enemies of the national government, and now devoted tools of French emissaries, who after having vented all the abuse and insult possible . . . are eagerly impatient to proceed from words to blows." [61]

Some of the newspapers were showing the symptoms of sedition, too. The *Courant,* accused of having "aristocratic leanings," waxed indignant. The pro-Jeffersonian *National Gazette* of Philadelphia published a letter allegedly from Hartford:

We have been highly favoured here (through mercy) in having generally escaped the contagious Philadelphia fever, considering the many travellers from that city that were daily passing through from thence, and even sojourning here during the months of August and September. It is with much pleasure I can assure you that only three persons in this city are certainly known to be down with the so much dreaded yellow fever, viz. Messrs. Hudson and Goodwin, Editors of the Connecticut Courant, and a correspondent of theirs, who dwells a few doors distant. All three of these poor gentlemen took the infection from a certain southern newspaper, which they happened to peep into without previously fumigating their nostrils with hot vinegar. . . . They are frequently delirious, and it is remarkable that in the paroxysms of the fever they yelp exactly like puppies; often, in their frenzy, *snapping* at the Gazette that was the innocent cause of their calamity.[62]

Nor was the *Gazette* alone. Even in Hartford, some local citizens collaborated to produce the "anti-federal" *Hartford Gazette,* a sheet quite beneath the notice of the *Courant's* editors. But as one of their correspondents put it, certainly no other printers in Connecticut were depraved enough as to allow foreign gold to induce them to molest the peace of their countrymen.[63]

All in all, bits of evidence accumulated: the disgraceful conduct of John Hancock, Samuel Adams, and the Bostonians, the partisans of Genêt, the Jacobin clubs, the brawling behavior of New London's "democrats," demagogues haranguing the barflies in Vermont's taverns, pro-French newspapers, the rabble, Tom Paine's *Age of Reason*.[64] George Clinton and the Jefferson faction, enemies of the federal government, were known to be plotting for power. Certainly by the years of Washington's second administration, the attentive reader of the *Courant* must have known that all was not well in the best of all possible societies.

For some weeks the marine intelligence from various quarters was deemed to have been of the most melancholy nature.[65] The *Courant* carried news of depredations committed upon American shipping by the French, the Spanish, the Algerine pirates, and especially by the British authorities in the West Indies and elsewhere —vessels seized, seamen impressed, cargoes condemned. The administration's enemies played upon the ensuing public resentment to demand action from the federal government. Some news items spoke of the "inevitability" of a war with England.[66] Others made a point of demanding patience with preparedness, arguing that whatever injuries we sustained from the British were aimed at the French; that whatever hostility the British displayed resulted from the ill will of our own domestic "democratic" faction.[67] As the Jay mission sailed forth to negotiate with the British Government, this honorable gesture of peace was credited to the true friends of law and order rather than to the legislators from south of the Potomac.[68] Yet the editors of the *Courant* were no Anglophiles. The agents of the Crown, they believed, were still inspiring the Indians with hostility:

While a hope of peace remains, it is the duty of all good citizens to restrain their passions and wait the event of pending negociations. It is possible than an amicable adjustment may take place; but should the agressions and hostile appearances be removed, without bloodshed, they will still create a most rancorous enmity between the American and British nations, and this will be among the means of accelerating the loss of the British possessions in America—an event that seems to be rapidly approaching. The unjustifiable conduct of Great Britain may therefore prove a fortunate circumstance ultimately, in ridding these States of disagreeable neighbors.[69]

When publication of the Jay Treaty evoked a widespread public reaction against it, all the prejudices of the *Courant* rallied to its support. The efforts of its opponents were attributed to low, personal motives of a political or financial nature, or else to a hope of overthrowing republican government.[70] The Whiskey Rebellion, then in the news, was linked by innuendoes to the opposition as well as to Paris.[71] The "rejection" of the treaty by town meetings in Boston, New York, Philadelphia, and Charleston was described as the cut and dried work of democratic demagogues, the rabble, and "deluded mechanicks." [72] On the other hand, Hudson & Goodwin paraded the resolutions of towns, of "respectable citizens," of merchants' groups favoring the treaty, and cluttered their issues with a mass of items and essays designed to persuade the uninformed.[73] They thought it unlikely that the great body of Americans would be induced by a few factious inhabitants of some of the state capitals to exchange their present blessings for the horrors of anarchy and confusion.[74] They observed with especial satisfaction that the citizens of Connecticut were busy harvesting their grain rather than heaving stones and brickbats. As long as these good people were free from debts and taxes, had bountiful crops, high prices, and good markets, they would not easily become the dupes of frenzied mobs in Boston and New York.[75]

Once the treaty was ratified the agitation subsided, but the task of maintaining peace and neutrality remained. The editors thought that the problems involving American commercial rights were about as besetting as ever:

The situation of our country is extremely critical. To pursue a line of policy that shall maintain our peace and neutrality, consistent with national honour and independence, will be found more difficult at present than at any former period of the European conflict. The West Indies is about becoming the theatre of active operations. The maritime strength of England, Holland, and France, will be displayed in the neighbourhood of the American continent. The politics of the Islands will experience revolutions embarrassing for the present to our commercial intercourse, but eventually improve our mercantile relations. The restrictions and prohibitions, which the jealousy of despotism has imposed, will give way to a more natural and liberal policy. The future condition of this country, however, as it respects its commercial relations with the West-Indies, will in a great measure depend on the event of war. To cultivate a pacific disposition, is certainly the true and substantial interest of the United States. But irritating circumstances must be anticipated.

The commercial rights of nations cannot escape violation when so great a proportion of Europe is involved in the evils of war. France, as well as England, has commenced the capture of our merchantmen. This unfriendly disposition is said to have been fostered by the late Treaty of Amity and Commerce with Great-Britain. It is hoped the government of this country will take such measures against the two powers, as shall manifest a desire of remaining at peace and a resolute determination of protecting the rights and interests of its citizens.[76]

Not frequently in the future would Hudson & Goodwin write so dispassionately about anything capable of partisan, political interpretation, for the temper of the times was changing. The popular commotions, lately exhibited on the occasion of the treaty, sounded the tocsin. The waxing organization and strength of what appeared to be the subversive forces of "democracy" produced a reaction in the *Courant* ever more vituperative and vindictive during the last years of the eighteenth century. It reached an intensity hitherto unattained on the eve of Jefferson's election to the presidency in 1800.

Men's motives were impugned. For many a moon to come those who were identified, either by vote or by spirit, as opponents of the Jay Treaty were hounded in the *Courant*. John Randolph, Edward Livingston, John Rutledge, Samuel Adams, and Albert Gallatin were only a few of the greater personages accused of dotage, duplicity, or seditious French involvements.[77] As the election of 1796 approached and Jefferson was known to be aspiring to office, the *Courant* spoke of him as having imbibed French philosophy and exalting Thomas Paine above Christ. He was the French Government's candidate for president of the United States. Genêt had planted the Democratic Clubs; Joseph Fauchet, his successor, and leaders of antifederalism had made the whiskey excise a pretext for stirring revolution; and now Pierre Adet, the incumbent French minister, was sponsoring Jefferson's candidacy. Not an elector north of the Delaware but would rather be shot than vote for this partisan of Paris![78] As the years of Adams' administration went by, the names of James Monroe, James Madison, W. C. Nicholas, Gerry, and a host of lesser lights were impounded in the *Courant* for whatever abuse could be given them, almost always with treasonable French implications.[79]

Franco-American relations, never satisfactory since the Proclamation of Neutrality and the Jay Treaty, were rapidly becoming worse. Hudson & Goodwin told more and more of the injuries sustained by American ships at the hands of French privateers.[80] Monroe, minister to France, had been recalled by Washington; the French Government recalled its own minister and then declined to accept

Monroe's successor, Charles C. Pinckney. When Adams dispatched Pinckney, John Marshall, and Gerry to effect a settlement of the differences existing between the two governments, the famous XYZ affair ensued; and soon the Americans and French were engaged in the naval warfare of 1798–1799. With these events, the editors developed an increasingly hostile attitude toward the French, a circumstance with direct bearing upon their interpretation of the antifederalist opposition nearer home.

The Jeffersonian "democrats" were held responsible for this sorry state of foreign affairs. According to the *Courant*'s interpretation, the domestic French faction, ever since the organization of the federal government, had been consciously plotting its destruction. Jefferson, whose duties as Secretary of State had compelled him to vindicate the independence of the United States in the Genêt correspondence, had probably resigned because of his pro-French sympathies.[81] Since then, a number of treasonable Americans in France, activated by the faction in America, had been fomenting the hostility of the French. Monroe had abetted it while in Paris; the French envoys had cooperated over here; and Jefferson, along with some other high officials, had consistently been privy to the plans of the French Government.[82] A few years earlier, some of these elements made it necessary either to fight or to come to terms with Great Britain. They had opposed the Jay Treaty.[83] Failing in this, they had urged the French to seize unlawful tribute by plundering American ships.[84] Meanwhile, French partisans in Congress tended the fires at home and were suspected of deriving motivation from Parisian gold.[85] Gallatin himself, according to the editors, was generally believed to have been nothing less than a French agent.[86]

When the official XYZ correspondence was being published at length in the *Courant,* the editors reprinted a letter from the *Gazette of the United States* blaming the failure of the mission upon the American renegades in Paris.[87] They had explained to French officials beforehand, it was alleged, that Pinckney was an aristocrat, Marshall an Anglophile, and that Gerry, whose principles were republican, had been sent along merely to be outvoted by his colleagues. The editors were wroth, at any rate, over the whole affair, especially since Americans were threatened with the same evils which the countries of Europe had already experienced:

Let Americans read, let them reflect, and they will unite in defending their country and their independence, and in execrating every thing that bears the name of Frenchman, Jacobin, or Illuminatus; whether engaged in spreading misery and bloodshed in Europe, or in plotting the same things in America; whether hearing the infamous name of Executive Director, or the more respectable title of Vice-President.[88]

As Governor Trumbull said in a speech to the General Assembly, a total separation from a nation of infidels and atheists, with whom there could be no foundation for faith or confidence, was an event devoutly to be wished for.[89]

In view of the *Courant*'s analysis, it occasions no surprise that Hudson & Goodwin wholly endorsed the suppressive Alien and Sedition Laws of 1798. In their opinion, the Sedition Law, so obnoxious to the printers of the opposition, could hardly have been an abridgment of the freedom of the press. They had declared their principles sometime before:

As men, as freemen, having a common stake at hazard, with the rest of our countrymen, and believing that all our dearest interests depend upon the support of our present government, we shall always take the liberty to refuse to publish any thing, we hold to be inconsistent with the support of that government, and destructive of the peace of our country.[90]

The implication was plain. They believed, with Washington, that a republic had no place for political factions; and consequently, that disloyalty to the administration was inseparable from disloyalty to the country. Accordingly, at a time when the laws had already made the Adams administration unpopular, the editors thought that the only thing wanting was their stricter and prompter enforcement. If several hundred mischief-making foreigners had been deported, and a few more editors incarcerated for their sedition, there would have been fewer falsehoods, slanders, and factions in the country. The Virginia and Kentucky resolutions, they thought, were designed to embarrass the government and to promote disunion.[91]

Meantime, the tenets of Federalism were not standing unchallenged in the *Courant*'s home territory. According to Jeffersonian critics, Hudson & Goodwin's paper, in conjunction with other organs of the "aristocracy," had long been hoodwinking the great body of the people.[92] The colorful Matthew Lyon, then a member of Congress from Vermont, accused all the Connecticut printers of a uniformly jaundiced and one-sided handling of political news.[93] But scarcely had Hudson & Goodwin lampooned the author of this taunt before one "Diogenes" offered the editors a piece of interesting information:

In Porcupine's Gazette of the 21st of February [1798], he has re-published a paragraph, from a Newspaper printed at New-London in this state, called "The Bee" . . . I presume, the Bee never was heard of by ten men in the state, except now and then a democrat, fifteen miles from New-London. . . . Who the printers are, I do not know. I dare say they do not wish that many enquiries should be made about them. . . . As for its forwarding the schemes of the French, it is the idlest whim in the world. They may as well lean upon Matthew Lyon, or Tom Jefferson.[94]

For the readers of the *Bee,* some of whose names they professed to have discovered, the editors of the *Courant* subsequently threatened public exposure, as for some great scandal.[95] For Charles Holt, the printer, and for the paper itself, they reserved the crudest sort of invective.[96] Holt's eventual indictment for a libel under the Sedition Law may easily have been the occasion for gloating; but by this time, Elisha Babcock's *American Mercury,* the *Courant*'s Hartford competitor, had begun to display some of the symptoms of political apostasy.

The *Mercury*'s conversion to Jeffersonian principles was gradual and also, if one may believe the *Courant,* a little puzzling to the staunch partisans of Federalism.[97] At the time of Holt's arrest in 1799, the *Courant* accused Babcock of harboring "democratic" principles, partly on the grounds that he visited the New London editor in jail.[98] Babcock's evasive rejoinder was an interesting in-dication of the hostility engendered by the growing conflict of po-litical schools of thought even in Hartford:

That the *Connecticut Courant* and *American Mercury,* are conducted on different principles, can never be doubted,—that those principles are *essentially* different, is equally true:—For while the former displays the villainy of *France* the latter exposes the knavery both of *France* and *England*—and indeed it is not easy to determine from which of these governments we receive the most abuse. But how doth it happen that the *Courant* is so partial to *Great Britain?* This is not difficult to be under-stood: The fact is, we have so long and patiently endured the insults and depredations of *George the 3rd,* that the remnant of his *loyal subjects here,* as well as some of our *home-bred cowards,* consider his conduct *now* as perfectly *just.* The silence of the *Courant* on *British depredations* &c. can be justified on no other ground, unless the Editors claim the merit of participating in the *Loaves* and *Fishes.*—Money will always go a great way in hard times.[99]

Despite this feeling, which was reciprocal, it was only after Jefferson's election that the *Courant* could at last accuse Babcock of running a forthright Jeffersonian newspaper.[100] As the *Courant*'s commentators saw it, the *Mercury* had some of the characteristics of a weathercock, pleasing neither the partisans of Jefferson, as did the *Bee,* nor the firm supporters of Federalism, as did the *Courant.*[101]

Hudson & Goodwin not only bore down upon the newspapers of the opposition but they despised the personnel and the methods of the Connecticut "Jacobins." Gideon Granger of Suffield, whom Jefferson later appointed Postmaster General, and Abraham Baldwin of New Haven, were singled out as the arch fomenters of faction within the state, and were accordingly the victims of bitter derogation.[102] These gentlemen and their followers were accused of introducing, into the annual state elections, ways which were new to the traditional modes of Connecticut. They "electioneered," sending forth rhetorical missionaries to harangue the people in clubs and taverns. They exhibited themselves publicly as candidates for election. They distributed printed lists of candidates to serve as voters' guides at the annual freemen's meetings.[103] The *Courant* admitted that the opposition organized well and voted efficiently.[104] But unhappily, as one commentator observed, they had already effected changes in the ancient order of things, and other corruptions were all but rolling in upon Connecticut from the south.[105]

In self-defense, the *Courant* itself campaigned vigorously in the annual state elections of the late 1790's. Its columns conveyed the censures, the appeals, the warnings, the predictions, the lamentations, and the congratulations, always of those who professed to guard the tried and true ways of old Connecticut. Before 1800 Hudson & Goodwin's writers were chronically gratified that only a few avowed "democrats" had succeeded in gaining seats in the state assembly, and that none from Connecticut were on the governor's council or in Congress.[106] But as Jefferson's supporters the country over were fired with the prospects of placing their chief in the presidency, the editors of the *Courant* looked into an ominous future.

As they portrayed Thomas Jefferson in 1800, he was a Virginia slaveholder, devoted to French philosophical ideas, who favored no government strong enough to assure the security of persons or property. It was he who maligned the fathers of the Constitution of the United States as timid persons preferring the calm of despotism to the tempestuous sea of liberty. It was he who had written that "it does me no injury for my neighbour to say there are *twenty gods,* or *no god."* It was he who had been the enemy of the federal government in all its works, and the leader of that faction sympathetic with the theory and practice of the French revolutionaries. He was no friend of the commerce of the United States, or of the American Navy which was designed to enforce the rights of commerce on the high seas. He and his followers were the foul calumniators of Jay, Hamilton, Oliver Ellsworth, Timothy Pickering, John Adams, and even the late great father of the country. They were the cause of "French depredations." They were venal.[107]

The consequences of allowing such a man and such a party to accede to power in the United States were conceived to be catastrophic. There would ensue a planned breakdown of government, a ruination of the economic life of the people, an assault upon the moral and religious aspects of society, anarchy, civil war, or secession.[108] Beginning late in June, the *Courant* featured a series of lurid campaign letters, by "Burleigh," calculated to stir the resistance of all people everywhere who feared the threatened and lugubrious "new order of things." Federalist printers throughout the country were urged to copy them.[109]

According to "Burleigh," 10 years of carping opposition to the measures of the federal government had revealed the Jeffersonians to be devoid of a constructive political program. Theirs was a destructive philosophy. If they were placed in high office, their control over the federal executive departments would enable them to accomplish a fundamental purpose, to effectively destroy the form and substance of the American Government. The president would undoubtedly replace incumbent federal employees with creatures of his own choice. The Department of the Treasury would be expected, by anyone familiar with "democratic" ideas of finance, to bring reproach upon the public credit. With the federal navy laid up, commerce would again be plundered, ships would rot at the wharves, agricultural produce would perish, farmers would be impoverished, and merchants ruined. The possibilities of manipulating the Post Office Department to poison the channels of public opinion were especially sinister. One of the "jacobinical" methods of preparing thoroughgoing revolution consisted of undermining the morals and the religion of the people. Philip Freneau's *National Gazette* had reviled, lied, and slandered before its mantle fell upon the *Aurora.* In conjunction with these fountainheads, Greenleaf's

Argus (New York), Adams' *Chronicle* (Boston), and other newspapers about the country, sometimes distributed *gratis,* had already
effected the swift rise of Jacobin influence. If this much could be
accomplished with Federalism in the saddle, what could be done
when Jefferson's party controlled the post offices? What if from
seven to eight hundred Jacobin postmasters, all of whom enjoyed
franking privileges, dispersed the *Aurora,* Callender's *Prospect Before Us,* Paine's *Age of Reason,* the letters of Joel Barlow, and other
literary instruments of sedition and atheism? [110]

It would be a solemn thing, wrote "Burleigh," for the American
people to affront God by electing an infidel to lead a Christian
nation. Jefferson's followers, as destitute of religion and morality
as the French Jacobins, only awaited the opportunity to inflict the
miseries of France upon the country.[111] Then, indeed, might God
say, as He said of the Israelites, "They have rejected me, that I
should not reign over them." [112]

Unrestrained by law, or the fear of punishment, every deadly passion
will have full scope, private quarrels will be revenged, and public feuds
and rivalships will call forth the bitterest hate and vengeance. Neighbours will become the enemies of neighbours, brothers of brothers, fathers
of their sons, and sons of their fathers. Murder, robbery, rape, adultery,
and incest, will be openly taught and practised, the air will be rent with
the cries of distress, the soil soaked with blood, and the nation black with
crimes.[113]

Where was the man who contemplated such scenes with equa-
nimity? If things reached this dolorous pass, what could the
Federalist states do? "Pelham" had written, four years before:

The northern states *can* subsist as a nation, a republic, without any connection with the southern. It cannot be contested . . . a union would
still be more desirable than a separation. But, when it becomes a serious
question, whether we shall give up our government, or part with the
states south of the Potowmack, no man north of that river, whose heart
is not thoroughly Democratic, can hesitate what decision to make. That
this question is nearly ripe for decision, there can be but little doubt.[114]

In 1797 "Gustavus" presented similar and stronger sentiments in
a series of letters which Hudson & Goodwin published.[115] In 1798
they reprinted the letters of "Pelham." [116] Therefore it was no new
thought for the *Courant's* readers when "Burleigh" averred that
the northern states would probably be disposed to separate the
federal union to avoid sharing these dire calamities.[117]

On September 22, 1800, the editors were more than happy to report that Federalism had won the day in Connecticut. The base arts, innumerable falsehoods, and incredible diligence of the "democrats," with which they hoped to carry the state for Jefferson, had come to naught:

. . . we congratulate the friends of Federalism, order, virtue, and religion, on the steady firmness of this state—that the Freemen of Connecticut still love their country, its laws, and Government; and will not yet agree to Elect an unbeliever to be their Chief Magistrate.[118]

By October, "Burleigh's" passionate appeals to the American electorate reflected the imagined imminence of national disaster:

Look at your houses, your parents, your wives, and your children. Are you prepared to see your dwellings in flames, hoary hairs bathed in blood, female chastity violated, or children writhing on the pike and the halbert? If not, prepare for the task of protecting your Government. Look at every leading Jacobin, as at a ravening wolf, preparing to enter your peaceful fold, and glut his deadly appetite on the vitals of your country. Already do their hearts leap at the prospect. Having long brooded over these scenes of death and despair, they now wake as from a trance, and in imagination, seizing the dagger, and the musket, prepare for the work of slaughter. GREAT GOD OF COMPASSION AND JUSTICE, SHIELD MY COUNTRY FROM DESTRUCTION.[119]

Hoping doggedly until the last bad piece of election news reached Hartford, the *Courant*'s owners continued to load their columns with the partisan pleas, predictions, and news of politics. In the issue of December 22, they passed to their readers the unpleasant intelligence that the Jefferson-Burr ticket had completely succeeded in South Carolina, and that therefore they might consider the new order of things as about to commence. The final wish remained that the House of Representatives would choose Aaron Burr for president in preference to Jefferson; [120] but of little avail anyway, for the friends of Washington were passing from power and the old order waned.

According to letters which appeared in the *Courant,* the elections had demonstrated, beyond a doubt, that the people of New England were unwilling to exchange their long-tried institutions for the visionary projects of "democratic" reformers.[121] The Federalists had always supported as much liberty and equality as was good for the people anyway; it was indeed not easy to conceive of a greater measure being compatible with human nature and society. True Federalists would now seek to preserve government by their upright private conduct, by shunning the mean struggles for power, the calumny and falsehood which were currently so prevalent.[122] Verily, the days of adversity were at hand:

> Almighty God, still let us lie,
> Safe as the apple of thine Eye,
> Still, still protect this happy land,
> Within the hollow of thine Hand.[123]

CHAPTER V

FIGHTING THE NEW ORDER

FOR a generation after 1800, the *Courant* continued to express the feelings of the class in Connecticut to which some of the evolving modes and values of the Jeffersonian era were anathema. As institutional readjustments became more and more insistent, those persons whose comforts and allegiances bound them to the old social arrangements—the group for whom Hudson & Goodwin spoke—generally resisted the innovating forces and lamented their effects as more or less degenerate. This point of view led them to regard the abettors of these innovations as foreigners either by philosophy or birth, as Southerners whose ways were not those of New England, and as rabble-rousers whose motives were offensive to an upright and God-fearing Connecticut people.[1] The changes that were developing and the newer concepts which both reflected and anticipated them, were some day to achieve a cultural reputability; but that day had not yet come for Connecticut, and the *Courant* stoutly resisted its arrival.

Thomas Jefferson's first inaugural address on March 4, 1801, drew no editorial fire. It was conciliatory in tone, for he had said: "We are all Republicans, we are all Federalists." But as the President began making his appointments, replacing some of the Federalist officeholders with men from his own following, he was accused bitterly of belying the spirit of his words. From far and near came stories of honorable men and old war heroes turned out of office for none but factional purposes.[2] Elizur Goodrich's removal from the customs office at New Haven, a post to which Adams had given him a midnight appointment, created pronounced indignation.[3] When Gideon Granger of Connecticut became Postmaster General, the *Courant* seemed to find the news all but incredible.[4] Gallatin was presented as a foreigner scarcely able to speak the language, whose assignment to the Treasury insulted the American public.[5] Dozens of letters poured into the *Courant* laying strictures upon Jefferson and some of his officers. Gallatin was suspected of having secretly sold the government's shares in the United States Bank;[6] Granger allegedly distributed postmasterships to his personal friends and manipulated deliveries to embarrass the *Courant;*[7] lesser figures were charged with having perpetrated shady financial deals,[8] and almost all of them with being incapable, parasitic, or profligate.[9] The *Courant* averred that the people were governed by foreigners from England, Ireland, and Geneva.[10] In all this, some writers detected the shameless scheming of Burr to discredit Jefferson, and some reported Madison as threatening to resign his post in protest against an administration so flagrantly unjust.[11]

At his inauguration the President had mentioned the need for economy in public expenditures in order to ease the burden on labor. When Congress now abolished the internal revenue taxes and pared the army and navy appropriations, the *Courant*'s editors registered resolute opposition. The repeal of internal taxes on whiskey and carriages was made to appear as a piece of sectional and class hypocrisy: at the expense of the New England working people, the Virginia aristocrats had reduced taxes for themselves and for Gallatin's whiskey-drinking constituents in western Pennsylvania.[12] If Jefferson and his party cherished the welfare of "the people" as they pretended, why had they not reduced the customs duties on salt and molasses, on tea, coffee, and brown sugar? It seemed that "the people" were not New Englanders.[13] Hudson & Goodwin printed misspelled letters from some of the alleged poor who resented this invidious and counterfeit economy,[14] and the names of some of Jefferson's appointees with their salaries appeared repeatedly in the paper.[15] The President himself, characterized as inimical to the Constitution, was charged with sabotaging the Union in the interests of the state of Virginia.[16]

The so-called attack upon the courts, which was said to be a part of the same sectional conspiracy, created even greater misgivings among the *Courant*'s contributors. The Republican leaders in Congress proposed to repeal the Circuit Court Act of 1801 which had enabled President Adams to appoint a number of Federalist judges on the eve of his retirement from office. The repeal was construed to be an assault upon the Constitution.[17] Hudson & Goodwin gave their subscribers the reprint of a lengthy speech by James A. Bayard of Delaware which they hoped had made Jefferson's ears tingle; [18] and they urged readers to study a number of Federalist speeches currently inserted in the paper.[19] When the Senate passed the repeal bill, they framed the announcement in black. When the House concurred, they believed that the Constitution had suffered a wound from which it might never recover.[20] Other writers recorded that intelligent men despaired of the Republic and, indeed, the *Courant* carried references to sentiments for disunion.[21] The limits to which the *Courant*'s views extended and the political sectionalism which characterized the paper are illustrated by an editorial communication which appeared during the first Republican Congress:

The Northern States will see thro' this *when it is too late*. But let them remember, that when this Constitution is gone, another will never be voluntarily made. FIFTY-FOUR of the present House of Representatives, are NATIVE VIRGINIANS. *This is a majority of the whole*. Let New-England keep a steady eye on Congress. The *present* Constitution is good enough, when well administered, for us. But, WE WERE NEVER BORN TO BELONG TO PROVINCES OF VIRGINIA.[22]

These implications continued and expanded in the *Courant* for years to come, inviting what plausibility developing circumstances could give them. The impeachment and trial of Justice Samuel Chase of the Supreme Court, whom the editors described as an aged pillar of the American Revolution, took shape as a wanton assault upon the American form of government.[23] The innocent-sounding Twelfth Amendment to the Constitution seemed entirely sinister as it emerged from the editorial matrix:

When the present ruling party destroyed the Judiciary of the Nation, the measure was beheld with alarm, by the wise and good of our country. It was considered as a bold, and dangerous step, in the administration, to lop away one essential branch of the Constitution. It was not, however, conjectured, that in three years from the time the affairs of government came into their hands, they would deliberately take off the masque, and go to work to mould the Constitution into an engine, calculated to perpetuate the power of the nation in their hands. We have lived to see even this attempted—and not only attempted, but well-nigh carried into effect. An Amendment to the Constitution, has been proposed in Congress, and has been ratified by several of the Legislatures of the States, the object of which is, *to secure to Mr. Jefferson his Presidential dignity, as long as he shall choose to wear it; and to place it forever in the power of Virginia, and two or three other large states, to share among themselves the two highest offices of the Government.*[24]

Perhaps more than any previous Jefferson measure, the purchase of Louisiana upset the *Courant*. Fifteen million dollars for bogs, mountains, and Indians! Fifteen million dollars for uninhabited wasteland and a refuge for criminals! [25] And for what purposes? To enhance the power of Virginia's politicians. To pour millions into the coffers of Napoleon on the eve of war with England.[26]

As much as the acquisition of vast outlands might dazzle romantic visionaries and swaggering partisans in Connecticut, Hudson & Goodwin prophesied that the transaction would eventually be execrated even by Republicans, and for a number of reasons. It would drain population from the southern and western states. It would depress land prices, devaluating the uncultivated property of individuals and decreasing government revenue from the sale of the public domain. It would saddle an inequitable burden upon the Atlantic states and especially upon New England, whose influence in the councils of the nation would decline as western settlement developed. It would commit the people to Indian wars, to costly and difficult defense measures, to an unprecedented expansion of the slave traffic. If incorporated into the Union, it would insure, to believe many wise and patriotic men, the eventual disintegration of the federal government.[27] The *Courant* printed the apprehensions of others who foresaw a prospective scarcity of labor and of money, and an involvement in the vortex of European politics.[28]

In contrast to the *American Mercury,* which reported the Hartford celebration of those who observed the national jubilee on the occasion of the annexation of Louisiana,[29] the *Courant* carried no account of it. The outlook seemed gloomy, even foreboding:

In Greece, and in Rome, and in modern revolutionary France, *the people* were amused, and dazzled with games, shews, and festivals, whilst the chains of slavery were forging for them—chains, which in the two former countries were never broken, and under which in the latter, they are now groaning in the most abject, and insufferable bondage. Here is the secret of this festival. *Fetters are forging for the United States.* Our necks are now basely bending to receive them—they already clank in the hands of our Virginia Masters—and ere a few short years are run, our freedom, our independence, and our Union will be with the years beyond the flood. Let the warning be listened to before it is too late.[30]

Hudson & Goodwin might have shown less apprehension as to federal events if certain local developments had been less disquieting. During the week of Jefferson's first inauguration, Governor Trumbull lamented what he deemed a prevalent drift toward infidelity.[31] According to one writer, the ancient institutions of New England had become subjects for ridicule in all the Jeffersonian papers, and the "steady habits" of Connecticut had been for some months the butt of the *American Mercury;* vice, irreligion, sedition, and calumny were surging into view and everywhere asserting their claims upon people.[32] The editors themselves noted signs of quickening moral laxity in the docket of the county court—bigamy, forgery, assault with attempt to rape, manslaughter, counterfeiting —and found none but murky prospects ahead.[33]

At least some of this moral obliquity, according to the *Courant,* characterized the rank and file of Jefferson's party in Connecticut. His followers in Wallingford listened to profane oratory, danced in the meetinghouse to strains of "Yankee Doodle," and ignominiously avoided the payment of bills.[34] A number of homeless itinerants attended a Jefferson convention at New Haven, where the expected ball was canceled for want of respectable female partners.[35] At Stafford, at Tolland, and elsewhere, Republicans were addicted to the vice of alcoholic stimulation, their morals were dubious, they were self-seeking and antireligious.[36] Nor was the plausibility of such allegations weakened for readers who believed Thomas Callender's circulating calumnies against the president,[37] who disapproved his consorting with Thomas Paine,[38] or who noticed the lapse of traditional proclamations summoning national gratitude to God for the continued prosperity of the nation.[39]

Those whom the editors credited with condoning these matters were engaged in belittling the political eminence of the Connecticut clergy and especially "Pope Dwight" of Yale College who inveighed lustily against the rise of Connecticut Jacobinism.[40] But the *Courant*'s writers defended Timothy Dwight, defended the clergy, defended their time-worn privilege to an annual Election Day dinner at state expense, defended the orthodox ecclesiastical polity against all moves for legal disestablishment.[41] The *Mercury* twitted the *Courant* for its "priestcraft" and reflected upon its integrity:

The exclusive *"friends of order"* have held up the Connecticut Courant to be an oracle of truth, pure, pious and immaculate. Whatever appears in this vehicle of public intelligence was neither to be controverted nor doubted. To question the authenticity of a paragraph in the Courant would be deemed an offence against religion, morality and good order.—Happily, time is making daily discoveries how far the pretensions of this paper to superior correctness, impartiality and truth, are well founded.[42]

Other Republican practices likewise offended the *Courant*'s standards of seemliness. It charged Jefferson's followers with ensnaring voters by free drinks, transferring property deeds, and false swearing.[43] At one session of the General Assembly, a Republican bloc issued a "minority protest" against a piece of legislation;[44] at the opening of another they scattered printed petitions among the members of the legislature.[45] All these deviations from custom emerged from methods deemed still more dishonorable. Now, more openly than before, Republicans were issuing circular letters, summoning conventions, making out party tickets, and "electioneering."[46] Granger himself took election furloughs from his federal employment and was said, at one time, to have traveled about the state displaying Jefferson's picture in all the lowly taverns and barber shops along the road.[47] Through their state, county, and town committees, the *Courant*'s editors admitted that the Republicans had created an organization worthy of better purposes.[48] The Federalists themselves were conceded to have been handicapped by the effective, though vicious, tactics of their opponents.[49]

The Connecticut Republicans agitated for universal manhood suffrage. As the law then stood, the franchise belonged to male citizens attaining the age of twenty-one years, who possessed, in addition to approved morals, a freehold estate of at least seven dollars per annum, or a personal estate of 134 dollars.[50] The *Mercury* affirmed that, though there were 50,000 adult males in Connecticut, only about 19,000 votes were cast in hotly contested state elections.[51] The Republicans proposed to cure as much of this disparity as might be attributable to property qualifications, and, to implement their plans, urged the holding of a state constitutional convention. Hudson & Goodwin disapproved the whole program for constitutional change. It would be, they wrote, "the entering wedge to perpetual change and confusion."[52]

Why universal suffrage, anyway? The women of Connecticut had no vote, yet existing political arrangements adequately guarded their interests.[53] The editors, accusing the *Mercury* of flirting with certain dangerous French ideas on the "equalization of property,"[54] maintained that the "security of elections" was at stake; that is to say, the landholders might no longer be able to control them, a situation subversive of the approved structure of society.[55] As other writers explained, the only way to insure the safety of property was to lodge the power of state in the mass of independent, landed proprietors. The want of property generally evidenced a lack of intelligence or integrity, even though the deed of possession did not invariably attest the presence of these attributes.[56] How long would it take any young man worth half his salt to lay up 134 dollars? Hudson & Goodwin admitted that some estimable citizens in the state lacked the franchise, but nevertheless the great majority of nonvoters were "idle, dissolute, and worthless characters." [57] It seemed to them that wherever universal suffrage had been advocated in America, it had arisen from unwholesome party motives rather than from those of the public interest.[58]

The case for the constitutional convention came off no better in the views of the *Courant*'s supporters.[59] Since the state still operated under the old colonial charter, the Republicans claimed that Connecticut really had no legal constitution, hence that the current government derived from an illegal conspiracy of the Federalist ruling party.[60] Pierpont Edwards and a number of fellow Republicans, whom the editors charged with sedition, met at New Haven to lay plans for the convention campaign.[61] Nothing substantial came from their efforts except that the Federalist legislature added a *coup de grace* by revoking the commissions of certain Republican justices of the peace who were thereby relieved of the paradox of serving a government which they alleged to be illegal and unconstitutional.[62] Hudson & Goodwin applauded these Federalist expedients, observing that Montesquieu himself could hardly have endorsed this particular revolutionary clamor for a new state government with checks, balances, separation of powers, and universal suffrage.[63]

After the spring of 1806 the *Courant*'s fears of internal "revolution" noticeably abated. Connecticut indeed, of all the states in New England, consistently maintained Federalist administrations for a generation after the beginning of the nineteenth century. This is not to say that the *Courant* remained unscathed by the newer methods of the Jeffersonian school, for nowadays, albeit with distaste for the necessary compromise, the editors endorsed the findings of Federalist conventions, displayed the names of Federalist nominees, and copiously advised the freemen how to vote on Election Day.[64] They explained, sometime in 1806, that the New England people were slow to adopt the ways of the new order for a variety of reasons: most of them were native Americans of marked religious propensities and superior education; they exhibited deep veneration for the habits of their provident forbears; and therefore they were capable of preserving more stable social and political arrangements than the populations organized in governments to the south of them.[65] All might have been well, they thought, except for the persistence of "democratic" intrigue.[66]

Hudson & Goodwin were wroth at what they termed the "pusillanimity" of the administration in maintaining American "rights" on the high seas.[67] According to them, commerce constituted the mainstay of the nation; ships were being boarded, seamen impressed, cargoes seized, and the flag consistently insulted by British, French, and even Spanish men-of-war; the nation suffered greater losses through reduced revenue, increased marine insurance, and higher prices than it would have cost to equip a navy to prevent such losses; and certainly the leaders of government could never expect to exact satisfactory treatment for American bottoms unless they were fully predisposed to enforce it.[68] These observations not only disparaged Jefferson's "gunboat" or small-navy policy, but decried as well the psychology of the country's leaders. Southern aristocrats, as the editors had already observed, tended to look down their noses at the honest pursuits of trade and commerce.[69]

In December, 1807, following the failure of protracted negotiations with Britain and the issuance of the British Orders in Council, Jefferson's government enacted the famous Embargo Act. The weak nonimportation scheme of 1806 had not been well received in the *Courant* [70] and neither had the war talk over the exciting *Chesapeake* affair of the last summer,[71] but these were the very trivia of human annoyances compared to the drastic retaliatory policy upon which the country now embarked:

The Jeffersonian administration, have led us blindfold into the most perilous situation—they have brought us to the brink of ruin, by their weak, or worse than weak measures—they have destroyed our trade, beggared our seamen, cut off the farmer from his market, and the mechanic from his trade—our merchants are ruined because their business is broken up, credit is annihilated—and to crown the whole we are madly rushing into a destructive war with Great-Britain, because Mr. Jefferson and Mr. Madison insist upon it that they will protect deserters from British vessels.[72]

Following the publication and praise of a letter by Timothy Pickering setting forth a strong Federalist view on the imminence of unnecessary war with Britain,[73] the editors began to suggest Napoleon's crafty concern in this lamentable business.[74] What the people wanted, according to them, was the official correspondence with the French Government. To what degree did the administration's pretensions to neutral rights comply with some imperial mandate emanating from Paris? [75] Only 10 years ago, with Federalists at the helm of the Republic, the countryside had resounded with the cry, "Millions for defence, not a cent for tribute," but now—! [76]

The unpopular embargo promoted political repercussions which pleased the editors. The Republicans had carried the municipal elections at Hartford in 1807, but in the spring of 1808 the city offices were again turned over to Federalists.[77] With Federalist victories in New Hampshire, Vermont, Massachusetts, and Rhode Island, the *Courant* gathered hopes that the end might be drawing nigh for "democracy." After six months of experiment, far from languishing from the loss of trade, the British provinces were observed to be increasing their wealth, and no country had yet suffered except the United States.[78] As the federal elections of 1808 approached, Hudson & Goodwin warned their public against placing credence in the assertion, currently circulated, that the next session of Congress might repeal this degrading means of defending the nation. Jefferson had determined to prevent the country from ever recovering its foreign trade.[79] As for domestic manufacturing, which the government's policy was said to encourage, the economy had from the earliest times been based upon agriculture and commerce:

And who that has seen the happy state of society throughout our villages, can wish it to be exchanged for the dissipated and effeminate manners and habits, which extensive establishments of manufactures, never fail to bring in their train? [80]

Indeed, little hope remained for repealing the law until the members of the present administration found their political seats denied to them, and only by the election of Federalists could this desirable embarrassment be accomplished.[81]

Before and after the election of Madison, Hudson & Goodwin printed letters, addresses, memorials, resolutions, and petitions against the embargo,[82] always decrying in editorials the alleged motives which inspired it and advertising its destructive consequences. In January, 1809, when Congress passed the Force Bill the better to cope with violators, the paper's spirit of resistance reached a climax.[83] Governor Trumbull, following the lead of Massachusetts, refused to furnish the state militia requested for enforcement work, and the General Assembly met to confirm the governor's noncompliance, declaring the Embargo Act to be unconstitutional.[84] Averring that resolutions were coming in daily, the editors assured their brethren in other states that the people of New England had not withstood "democracy" all these years for nothing, nor would they tamely yield up their rights to any military force at the present juncture of affairs.[85]

With the repeal of the embargo and Jefferson's retirement, the *Courant* relaxed somewhat, hoping that Madison might shun the temporizing and popularity-seeking tactics of his predecessor.[86] They claimed to see also the growth of free and independent thinking in Congress, a pleasing phenomenon which they called the breakup of factionalism and the resurgence of Federalism.[87] In 1809, when the Erskine negotiations failed to conclude an amicable accord with England, they were roundly disappointed but they cast no aspersions upon the president. They believed emphatically that Madison wanted no war, at the same time recognizing factors that might make it difficult for him to avoid one.[88] When the Smith-Jackson discussions likewise failed, the *Courant*'s tune began to change, for Madison was then thought to be showing considerable animus toward England along with a remarkable suavity toward France.[89] Soon thereafter and for the remaining years of his administration, the *Courant* held Jefferson's friend in habitual disesteem, at one time or another comparing him with Burr or Cromwell, impeaching his integrity, or questioning his personal fitness for the high office he filled.[90]

During the prewar years the *Courant* advanced arguments to show that, however admirable an ideal "freedom of the seas" might have been, hopes for its achievement were unrealistic.[91] Under the Tyrians, the Carthagenians, and the Romans, such sought-for freedom, once gained, had ineluctably degenerated into a sort of sovereignty of the seas. Pirates had one time infested the sea lanes, but the freedom from piracy, implemented by numbers of national armed ships, had left something again to be desired. The nation which gained ascendency of sea power never failed to exercise a practical sovereignty, assuming unequal privileges for itself and withholding from others a share of their rights. At present, human nature being what it was, the great British Navy made Englishmen haughty and insolent, but since Napoleon himself strove for "freedom of the seas," what constituted the alternative to British sovereignty? What kind of sovereignty would Napoleon wield and what kind of "freedom" might he be expected to grant, having already interdicted neutral commerce, burned neutral vessels, and sequestered neutral cargoes? To take a practical view, three choices lay open to Americans: to protect their trade, to abandon it, or to carry it on under some degree of abridgment of rights. The first of these choices bore the endorsement of Washington and Adams, and the latter's little fleet proved better than a thousand proclamations and all the diplomatic logic in the world. Had Jefferson preserved and expanded it since 1800—and at less than one tenth the cost of losses by capture, embargo, and nonintercourse—neither the French nor the English Navy would have given the stars and stripes the treatment they habitually received. As nations respected one another more from fear than from affection, the only way to escape insult was to be prepared to punish it. In a period of unprecedented world war, a great commercial nation with its ships sailing the seas unprotected was something new under the sun, and persons of good sense might have surmised the consequences.

Hudson & Goodwin claimed that the impasse in Anglo-American relations had developed, in the first instance, from the refusal of the federal government to adopt vigorous measures against Napoleon's Berlin Decree of 1806.[92] Jefferson should have resisted immediately, for as little as a protest would have exempted American ships from the prohibitions which the tyrant of France sought to impose upon trade to the British Empire. Subsequently, the British Orders in Council might have granted a similar exemption, or indeed might never have been issued.[93] Above all, the government in Washington had no right, in the conduct of neutral relations, to become neither more nor less than the tool of one of the belligerent nations.[94] Nor would this have been the American position except for the anti-British prejudices of Jefferson and Madison.[95] The former condemned the Monroe-Pinckney agreement with England in 1807, and from then on, matters had been so ingeniously contrived that every ostensible attempt to negotiate had tended to widen the breach. When George Rose came over to settle the *Chesapeake* claims, all possible prejudices were stirred against him. The inexperienced David Erskine was cunningly wheedled into contravening his orders. Francis J. Jackson, arriving with full powers, was dismissed for an alleged insult. Finally, after Augustus Foster reached the country, the United States frigate *President* attacked the British *Little Belt* and killed 30 of her men, a convenient coincidence to say the least.[96] The Orders in Council, to boot, were rather more theoretical than practical because the British Navy had shown its good intentions by refraining from clearing American ships off the seas which it might easily have done.[97] On the other hand, although Napoleon had repeatedly insulted the government, Madison declared the renewal of commercial intercourse with France, a move he could never have been induced to make with respect to Britain.[98]

Our violent patriots, our pretended sticklers for national honour, kiss the hand that scourges them, and cringe to the foot that spurns them. It seems to be a fixed maxim with them, that Napoleon can do no wrong. Whether this system of violence and rapacity be carried on openly, or by secret stratagem and treachery, as in the instance of Spain; whether, contrary to express treaty, he hold the American property in a state of sequestration only, or actually confiscates it; whether he merely plunder our vessels, or sinks or burns them; whether he merely strip our sailors of their all, or crowd them together into noisome prisons and dungeons; whether he snubs our Ambassador, or scornfully refuses him an answer —he is always in the right. His conduct, if not openly justified, is openly palliated, by the same men who would make the nation believe that all the wrongs done us by England call for immediate war.[99]

These same men, the *Courant* contended, had continued to contrive the policy of the federal government so as to ruin the political and commercial power of the northern and eastern states. A résumé of the Republican position since the days of the Jay Treaty revealed a consistent drive to these ends.[100] When Jefferson took the president's oath, the country was at peace in the full tide of commercial prosperity and connected by treaties with the great nations of Europe; but every Republican measure of the decade following had exhibited the baneful consequences so seasonably predicted by Federalist leaders.[101] The greater part of the millions of dollars needed to support the national government had come from the commerce of New England and the middle states, yet probably four fifths of the total proceeds had gone into areas to the south and west of the Potomac to feed and fatten men who had all along viewed commerce with jealousy and hatred—into Louisiana where clusters of new states would someday reduce the northern and eastern delegations to Congress to a status comparable to that of the Irish contingent in Britain's House of Commons.[102] The state of Virginia had continuously supplied presidents or vice-presidents for the federal government. Her overweening influence increased with the years and might be expected in the end completely to destroy the economic nerves of the commercial states. These states now suffered tenfold more from restrictions and oppressions than when they were British dependencies.[103] Never had there been so much insolvency in the country. Many useful citizens—ship carpenters, tradesmen, and mechanics—were seeking asylum in Canada.[104] Harsh and unjust laws begot evasions, infractions, and perjury; but who taught the merchants to smuggle, and who set them an example by political knavery?[105] Hudson & Goodwin prophesied that the hard results of the embargo would be felt by the country for 20 or perhaps 30 years to come.[106]

As for the view that benefits might emerge from the period, Adam Smith and the editors were incredulous. Madison, like Jefferson, may have indicated the merits of encouraging American industrial establishments, but the forcing of such enterprises by law tended to impoverish the nation by enriching manufacturers at the expense of consumers.[107]

Common sense teaches that it is for the interest of individuals to carry the productions of their industry to the highest markets, and to purchase the necessaries for their own consumption, at the lowest. And as this is for the interest of individuals generally, so, of course, it is for the interest of the nation at large. . . .

Whenever our country is ripe for any particular manufacture, that manufacture will naturally grow up and flourish of itself. It will need no other encouragement than the profits arising from it. Individuals, with a view to profit, will carry it on with eagerness, and to a sufficient extent.[108]

Some of the editorials took on a nostalgic flavor. In the years of Washington and Adams, the affairs of the nation had been in good repute; but subsequently, the vexations attending both foreign relations and internal concerns, the loss of countless millions in property, the ruin of trade, the bankruptcies of merchants and shippers, perplexities at home and disgrace abroad, stemmed, in great measure, from a departure from the wise, honest, and dignified policy of Washington.[109] We of the *Courant* were accused of being schismatics covered with the dust of antiquity, but we were satisfied with the Washington system. We were told that we were unhappy and that we needed something new, but we failed to be convinced. The mountain labored to bring forth the mouse, and for a number of years now, our country has been in the ebb tide of unsuccessful experiment.[110] We were promised "economy" and we see an expensive, ill-provided, and ill-governed army along with a multitude of paltry gunboats, built at vast expense, and hitherto employed for the heroic purpose of imprisoning our own commerce. We see the various corruptions of the new order of things accompanied by an unexampled decline in public morality. We see an exhausted treasury.[111]

Ten years ago, congress, and most of the state legislatures, were conspicuous for their talents. And there are now men enough in this country of talents, and integrity too, for all the purposes of legislation, and for all departments of government. But, with few exceptions, they have been proscribed, and hunted down, and have very little more to do with the direction of public affairs than though they lived in China or Japan; save only that they have the privilege of voting at elections, which is equally enjoyed by hundreds, if not thousands, of culprits and miscreants vomited out upon our shores from the jails of Europe.[112]

Hudson & Goodwin claimed to offer such representations with no degree of pleasure, or to give them with any other purpose in mind than that of animating their fellow countrymen in strictly constitutional efforts to provide better government.[113] But it was yet to be determined, according to them, whether American independence would prove to be a blessing or a curse.[114]

Inasmuch as the federal government continuously maintained commercial restrictions of one kind or another during Madison's first term, and since also Anglo-American relations were continuously precarious, considerable speculation arose on the possibilities of an eventual war with Great Britain.[115] Hudson & Goodwin feared such an outcome weeks before it occurred. They thought a war with Britain would be next to impossible to win.[116] Aside from crushing taxation and the destruction of trade, it might bring about the loss of the Republic.[117] Or supposing victory, what could the Americans gain? More land? [118] Because of the failure of nonintercourse, was the government drifting into war as an alternative to a sound naval defense program? This might have suited the southerners who had little commerce to lose, but not those who lived in the middle and New England states.[119] Despite the fact that the chances of capturing Canada or of damaging British commerce were slight, the good people of the country could rise to the occasion if war were really necessary; but not for the mere purpose of combating the principles of the British blockade, and not to the end that Napoleon might enjoy sovereignty of the seas as well as the mastery of all Europe.[120]

In 1811, more or less counter to the drift of current events, the editors advanced arguments for declaring war against France.[121] According to them, since British citizens were the only foreigners now possessing political freedom, the continuance of their independence, their civil rights, and their national power was essential to the freedom and safety of the American republic. Britain's control of the seas might have been evil in theory, but in fact it was the only effective obstacle to Napoleon's subjugation of the entire civilized world. For the Americans to take up arms against England would be to promote destruction; but

In case of a war with France, and during that war, an immense commerce would be opened to our citizens; a free-trade with Great Britain, and all its dependencies on the American continent, in the West Indies, upon the coasts of Africa, and in the East Indies; a trade, not only to Spain and Portugal, but to all the Spanish and Portuguese settlements, both in the islands and upon the continent of America. Nor would it be in the power of Bonaparte to hinder this trade, or to interrupt it in any considerable degree.[122]

The *Courant* maintained that the threats of war against England, now reaching high pitch in Congress, were at first invented to sell additional commercial restrictions to the gullible public, but that the President's "submission-men" had somehow exceeded his control.[123] When hostilities looked inevitable, the paper proclaimed that this, unlike the Revolution, was not a people's war but rather a face-saving arrangement for Madison & Co.; and that the people were in effect saying to their Congress: "Declare war at your peril; we the people are not with you."[124] It is not surprising, therefore, that the editors wrote, in the issue announcing the "dreadful tidings," that they were unable to express the sensations excited in the minds of all classes—dissatisfaction, disgust, and apprehensions of the most alarming nature.[125] But the die was cast:

We would ask one question—with everything to lose, what have we to gain? Let this be answered at the conclusion of the war. . . . We cannot, will not predict the consequences. We can only say, the crisis is big with events. What will result from heavy taxes, a cumbersome national debt, the divided sentiment of our citizens, must be left to time to unfold.[126]

From the outset of hostilities the War of 1812 was strictly Madison's affair as far as Hudson & Goodwin were concerned. The vast majority of the people in the North and many in the South were allegedly opposed to this folly of the federal administration.[127] Why especially should the inhabitants of New England support an unnecessary war which could be counted upon to ruin their commerce and their prosperity? [128] The army grafters, Madison's political sycophants, and the money-changers might come out of it with princely fortunes, for thousands of them were sucking the lifeblood of the nation; but the common people would bend their backs beneath an onerous tax burden.[129] At the end of the war the *Courant*

asserted that more than two thirds of the people north of the Potomac had loathed it from the beginning and almost all of them at
the end.[130]

It seemed remarkable to the *Courant*'s owners that the authorities of the United States should declare war upon the government
best equipped to destroy the commerce they were professing to
protect, and even more because of the defenseless American sea-
coast, the government's empty treasury, and its weak national
credit.[131] They could scarcely muster scorn enough for administration leaders who spoke of fighting to preserve commercial rights—
they who for five years back had done almost everything in their
power to destroy commercial prosperity and who now had taken
steps whereby numbers of American-born seamen pined in cap-
tivity and in prison.[132] Inasmuch as the Orders in Council were repealed, what were we fighting for? Apparently over the abstract
matter of impressment, the right to employ foreign deserters at
higher wages, a point which the British could never grant except
at the peril of their navy.[133]

While intermittently disposing of the *casus belli* in this manner,
the *Courant* advanced other explanations for our involvement.[134]
Editorials attributed it to Madison's thirst for political power and
patronage; to a national Anglophobia which the Republicans had
generated in their struggle for political eminence; to the administration's long-standing partisanship for France; to a Virginian
contempt for the pursuits of commerce which some other states
had come to accept; to a pronounced jealousy of the growing wealth
of the maritime states and a desire to keep them poor; to a lust for
Indian lands, for Canada and the Floridas; to a gigantic hope of
diverting the streams of western trade from the eastern seaboard
via the Great Lakes and the St. Lawrence or down the Mississippi;
and to a strong conviction that Bonaparte would eventually master
Europe and defeat Britain.

Before and after the national political campaign of 1812, much
was made of the argument that war had been declared to keep
Madison in the presidency.[135] An editorial appeal of October 6,
elaborated this contention:

It is beyond the power of charity itself to believe, that Madison and his
minions in congress declared war out of pure regard to the country.
They well knew, unprepared for it as they were, that the war would expose the country to immense losses, and bring upon it most grievous suf-
ferings; and that there was very little chance, if any, for its successful

termination. But they hoped to keep themselves in power by it; which, in their estimation, was a thousand times better than the country's welfare. In pursuance of this darling object, they had settled among themselves the following plan of operations. It was determined that with the commencement of the war there should commence a reign of terror, in so far as to abolish freedom of speech and of the press. . . . No man in the realm was to be suffered to call in question the justice or expedience of the war, but at the peril of incurring the wrath and becoming the victim of King Mob. On the other hand, the placemen and pensioners, the sycophants of the court, and the profligate printers, from Maine to New Orleans, were to raise the war-yell, the cry of blood and vengeance, and to waken in the people, if possible, the enthusiasm of '76. The President was to be presented from all parts of the country, with memorials extolling his wisdom and firmness; and under these toward circumstances his re-election was to be made sure. This is neither a dream, nor a fiction.[136]

The pro-French implications of the administration's war position were likewise played up in a number of issues.[137] On January 5, 1813, appeared the following editorial:

An awful spectacle—By one man the earth is filled with violence. In the form of man, there is beheld a monster, whose eye pitieth none, whose bloody footsteps are traced from the sunny climes of the south to the frozen regions of the north; a monster gorged with blood, but not satisfied, trampling upon all law divine and human, uprooting every principle that binds man to man, breaking down the venerable pillars of society, scattering at his feet, crowns, diadems, and the insignia of republics, with the same relentless ferocity. We see three nations, the last hope of the continent of Europe, struggling for existence, struggling for every thing that is dear and sacred; we see their plains crimsoned with blood, and covered with the corpses of their slain; we see them ready to perish, and calling aloud for help. Extending our view, we behold the powerful mistress of the sea, pouring forth her armies to succour and save those falling nations, and by her fleets, limiting the power and curbing the fury of the fell destroyer of man. We see her stand, as the only remaining bulwark against the universal domination of the bloodiest tyrant the world was ever cursed with. We see her stand, firm and unappalled, though sorely pressed on every side, and menaced with destruction. Calling home our attention, we behold our infant republic, the only republic that the gory despot has not yet annihilated, we behold it, *at his instigation,* and entangled in his "knot," plunged into war—not in defence of the bleeding nations of Europe, but . . . on the side of the foe of the human race. We behold the American republic, volunteering in his cause, and cooperating with him in war with a nation, whose overthrow would be the sure precursor of its own thraldom. We see the rulers of our confederate republic, obstinately persisting in this ominous war, though the alleged cause of it has ceased, and although the voice of the people is against it. Finally, we see, or we seem to see, a covenant with death, an express and open alliance with Napoleon Bonaparte, who, without a single exception, has made the nations, first his allies, and then his vassals.

Napoleon's Russian reverses of 1812, his abdication in 1814, and his decisive defeat at Waterloo were subsequently the grounds for excited rejoicing.[138] On one occasion, over 70 gentlemen celebrated his eclipse by a banquet at Bennett's Coffee House in Hartford where they applauded the words of Timothy Dwight.[139] As the *Courant* observed, the idol of the "democrats" had fallen, and the days of his followers were surely numbered.[140]

Nor did the editors neglect to give the war a strong sectional interpretation,[141] writing at one time that neither embargoes, high customs duties, direct taxes, nor war would have afflicted New England except for the agency of Ohio, Kentucky, and Tennessee.[142] The anticommercialism of the South and the West was traced from the days of George Washington, and the restrictions which formerly galled the colonies of Britain were declared to be beneath comparison with those which New England now sustained.[143] In a message to the General Assembly in 1813, Governor John Cotton Smith drew consolation from the remarkable and extensive growth of manufacturing establishments in Connecticut, but the editors only lamented that people who were once independent had now to let themselves out as spinners or weavers in factories, or migrate into the wilderness, or else starve.[144] Other causes aside, Hudson & Goodwin felt that the war had been projected upon the nation by southern and western interests for sectional purposes, and that the government at Washington, now dominated by those sections, was as foreign to the vital interests of New England as if it were operating in London.[145] The people of New England were strong for the federal union when administered impartially, and their cordial attachment would return under favorable circumstances, but had they foreseen the measures now oppressing them they would have rejected the Constitution by a vote of at least 50 to one.[146] They were suffering from what the *Courant* called "elective despotism." [147]

In view of all this, the paper did what it could to encourage those who would obstruct the government's war program. Editorial arguments and exhortations supported Connecticut's refusal to furnish militia for wartime services.[148] They alleged that the requisition, made by the Secretary of War under pretence of imminent danger of invasion, was deceptive and unconstitutional. The Constitution authorized the federal use of militia to suppress insurrections, repel invasions, and execute the laws of the United States, none of which needs existed. Therefore the militia should rally 'round the state government rather than be dragged away to fight Indians or to die under the walls of Quebec. Let those who wished, including post-masters, collectors, and other civil servants, enlist in the regular army to prove the sincerity of their convictions. The costs of the war were also decried,[149] the editors hoping at one time that Congress might decline to appropriate funds, suggesting at another that capitalists might be unwilling or unable to buy government bonds, and at still another time prophesying national bankruptcy.[150] The friends of peace, according to the *Courant,* would obey the law to the letter, but in the present situation they intended to volunteer nothing and do nothing, unless under compulsion, to encourage the war either directly or indirectly.[151]

The government's plans to invade Canada were consistently disapproved. American generals were ridiculed for their failures and charged with conducting campaigns of conquest and plunder against peaceful neighbors.[152] The Canadians were held to be defending certain sacred rights against the threatened imposition of a French commercial system and an American military dictatorship.[153] The editors called William Hull's surrender of Detroit the work of "democracy" from beginning to end, and suggested, in his reverses, some divine plan for bringing justice upon those westerners who viewed with indifference the prospective destruction of New England's commerce.[154] Providence, so they wrote, would see the Canadians through.[155]

The successes of American naval commanders begot no editorial praise until Decatur's squadron took refuge in the harbor of New London. The *Courant* had remarked before that our sea victories might only provoke retaliation upon our defenseless ports,[156] but in 1813:

We lament that Commodore Decatur's squadron was driven into N. London, as none of us before that event felt the least alarm from the enemy. But is there a citizen in the state, who would willingly see the brave fellows on board those ships suffer? . . . These are the men who maintain the honor of our nation. Washington founded our navy, and its officers are his sons. Deep indeed would be our disgrace, but for such men as *Decatur, Jones, Biddle,* and the other officers of this squadron.[157]

Despite brilliant American exploits, the British blocked the Atlantic seaboard, coastwise traffic lay at their mercy, and it seemed to the editors that American ships must inevitably be wiped out should hostilities continue for another year or two.[158] Nevertheless, they underscored the point that the American Navy, originally the product of Federalist policy, had at last acquired the plaudits of its erstwhile enemies.[159]

In a number of issues the war was pronounced to be an unmitigated failure.[160] Millions in money, thousands in lives, and altogether too much time had gone into the futile Canadian campaigns.[161] Commerce and fisheries had been destroyed, merchant ships captured, and seaports impoverished. Privateering was unprofitable, people were saddled with tremendous debts, and many of them had been ruined financially. No valuable object had been gained, nor would the war procure better peace terms than the country might have had without it.[162] In the summer of 1814, Hudson & Goodwin extended Madison an editorial invitation to emulate Napoleon Bonaparte and to "abdicate." Should the price of his abdication be an annuity of $25,000, he should have it if only the councils of the nation might be filled with "sound practical men." [163]

The bitter antiwar feeling, which characterized many of New England's leading lights, culminated in the Hartford Convention of December and January, 1814–1815.[164] During this long-remembered congress of Federalist dignitaries, the *Courant* printed a few inflammatory letters advocating a withholding of federal taxes, a declaration of New England neutrality, and something a little resembling the spirit that moved the men of '75.[165] But the editors themselves were relatively restrained. They taunted their southern colleagues for accusing some of the New England papers of wishing to dissolve the Union. They thought subsequently that the Convention report would refute those who slandered and maligned the able and distinguished men who composed it.[166]

In the wake of this climax of disaffection came the news of PEACE.[167] The citizens of Hartford celebrated it:

In the evening a splendid and universal illumination took place throughout the City. Night seemed to be transformed to Day. Every house, in all the principal streets, sent forth irradiations of artificial light, seeming to betoken the lively joy which reigned within. Every where was seen the smile of congratulation. Every where was heard the voice of joy. The streets were crowded with ladies, with carriages, and company of every description, and age, enjoying the beautiful scene. The night was clear and serene. A complete band of martial and other music paraded the streets, to add to the delight, and festivity of the occasion. As for party spirit, which has so often before unhappily infused bitterness into the cup of our public pleasures, it seemed now to have followed after "the shades of departed Time," and was no where to be found. All were united. All were happy.

About the sober hour of nine, the bells, which had continued to ring all the evening stop'd their "tuneful voice." In half an hour more the Illumination was generally extinguished. And our fellow-citizens, with their characteristic love of order, observing sobriety even in the midst of pleasure, quietly returned to their homes, satisfied, and grateful for the multiplied instances of the Mercy and unmerited Goodness of the Gracious Ruler of the Universe, who has once again permitted Peace to smile upon our land.[168]

Hudson & Goodwin were withal a little sad. An indifferent peace, to be sure, had been preferable to even a successful war,[169] but the golden opportunities for cultivating a bountiful harvest had come and gone, probably never to return. A surplus of English imports, speculation, and bankruptcies might now be expected, and the people of the postwar generation would of necessity return to the hard and frugal ways of their industrious ancestors.[170]

CHAPTER VI

NEWSPAPER GLIMPSES OF EARLY HARTFORD

WHEN Green established the *Courant,* Hartford was an old country town with a concentration of shops and dwelling houses near the river front. One day in 1766, citizens chased a bear along the main street,[1] and the paper was wont to print items on such subjects as big pumpkins, remarkably large hogs, and oversized cucumbers.[2] It is assumed that the inhabitants attended their individual, family, and community interests and that these were expressed in a variety of approved forms. At the same time, since the *Courant* accorded distant developments an almost exclusive patronage before the Revolution, it revealed little of what happened locally.[3] Hartford was not new, there was nothing spectacular about its behavior or growth, and the common aspirations of its leading people had designated no program for accomplishment contagious enough to have left traces in the paper. It exhibited none of that civic consciousness which in later years gave rise to a phenomenon known as "community boosting." [4]

After 1783 certain widespread maladjustments prompted newspaper speculation as to the future of Connecticut and provoked, on the part of some of Hartford's citizens, tangible tokens of organized effort. Economic dislocation followed the war. For a while His Majesty's laws precluded American trade with the British West Indies; interstate tariffs hampered the domestic exchange of commodities; money became scarcer; and any expectations of immediately resuming the approximate practices of prewar trade were forthwith frustrated.[5] The merchants of Hartford and of other Connecticut towns organized to discuss the means of facilitating business and to induce the General Assembly to support measures to stimulate commercial prosperity.[6] As a result, the commercial settlement in the town of Hartford became an incorporated city in 1784.[7] Thomas Seymour was elected mayor, and Hudson of the *Courant,* among others, became a councilman.[8] Officials were appointed for the inspection of beef, flour, fish, tobacco, hoops, staves, casks, clapboards, shingles, rum, brandy, wines, grain, and other articles. Exporters were forbidden to transport specified commodities from Hartford without certificates indicating quantity and quality.[9] The paper had previously explained that economic advantages might flow from such arrangements. Hudson & Goodwin thought the incorporation of Hartford and of other trading towns could hardly fail to render the state both wealthy and populous.[10]

For a decade following, the *Courant* printed occasional letters concerned with Connecticut's commercial future. It was pointed out that the state's imports habitually exceeded her exports;[11] that seven eighths of the imported consumer's goods came from New York, Massachusetts, and Rhode Island in retail quantities;[12] and that local merchants paid an advance of at least 12½ per cent upon them.[13] It appeared also that a combination of topography, bad roads, and multiple waterways divided the capital resources of Connecticut's merchants. Some traded on the Thames, Connecticut, Housatonic, or Hudson rivers, and others directly to Rhode Island or onto the Sound. This facilitated transportation to New York and Boston, but it likewise promoted Connecticut's dependence and inhibited commercial expansion.[14] The lack of a capital trading town had hitherto prevented the direct shipment of goods from England, and even when rum from the West Indies came in by the cargo, it had to be bartered by the hogshead and the surplus shipped to New York.[15] As for Hartford, a wholesale import trade with Europe had never been tried. Most Hartford merchants dealt directly with New York whence their commodities came up the river in relatively small orders.[16] The paper carried some discussion of canals and channel dredging to cultivate the northern river trade, and some reference to the potential utility of the thinning pine forests which once covered the Connecticut Valley.[17]

The *Courant*'s writers argued that banks were needed for better business and that the establishment of one in Hartford would encourage a local wholesale trade.[18] Since farmers conveyed more goods to town between September and March than could be locally absorbed, it might become their agent of disposal, giving them a needed cash market. It might also eliminate the shortage of specie and do away with bartering, hitherto a necessary practice of questionable moral value.[19] All Hartford citizens interested in petitioning the legislature for a bank charter were invited, in the *Courant* of February 27, 1792, to meet at David Bull's tavern at six o'clock that evening. In August, the Hartford Bank opened for business, capitalized at $100,000.[20] Along with the Union Bank of New London it was the first state bank in Connecticut.[21] Some of its rules were printed in the *Courant*. Notes for discount were received on Wednesdays and cashed on Thursdays. Drawers or endorsers had to be local residents. People might deposit money and valuables without charge.[22]

The editors and others stressed the desirability of supporting manufactures as well as commerce.[23] Connecticut was said, in great measure, to have populated Vermont. Useful citizens were moving westward into New York, Pennsylvania, and Ohio. Employment should be furnished them at home if local interests were to prosper.[24] The need for cultivating mulberry trees and for sundry industries was noted.[25] Attention was called to Enos Doolittle's local foundry where bells and clocks could be supplied for public buildings.[26] A short-lived woolen factory was erected at Hartford in 1788.[27] George Washington visited it, ordered cloth for his servants' outfits, and appeared before Congress in a crow-colored suit made from material purchased there.[28] According to a correspondent, the local mill could supply the clergy, the lawmakers, the justices, and the gentry of the country with clothes appropriate to their stations in society.[29] In the first issue of 1790, the *Courant* reported that 10,287 yards of cloth had been turned out since September, 1788:

It is with pleasure we add that this Manufactory is in a flourishing state—four thousand weight of fine Wool has just come to hand from Spain, which with what was before on hand makes a large stock—A number of good workmen are employed, and broad and narrow cloths of various colours, superfine, midling and low prized, are sold on as reasonable terms as they can be imported.[30]

In 1791 an editorial discussed the inadequacies of food marketing in Hartford.[31] Sufficient amounts of grain and meats but seldom enough fowl and fruits were available. Poultry usually appeared in quantities around Thanksgiving and Election Day, but the city folks were beginning to demand it weekly. Farmers were accordingly urged to turn from grains to poultry, to produce more cherries, apples, plums, strawberries, pears, and melons, and to carry these into the city by wagon. Five years later local enterprisers erected Hartford's first market house and invited the patronage of farmers and housewives.[32] The desire for vegetables was said to be increasing daily and the proprietors, by centralizing the market and discouraging peddling, hoped that the citizens might be profitably afforded a greater variety of provisions at cheaper prices. City authorities imposed market regulations to guarantee cleanliness and the accuracy of weights and measures.[33]

Most of the roads, by which farmers jogged into town, lay over a soil of clay or loam.[34] Since the traveling was difficult, especially in wet weather during the spring and fall seasons, the *Courant's* letters and advertisements reflected an interested stake in hard-road construction.[35] By 1810 the turnpike movement was observed to have effected improvement in highways all over the state, with relatively good care then being given to even secondary arteries.[36] But the legislature, according to one critic, had chartered too many competing companies and some of the building in the 1790's had been poor and cheap. The roads were allegedly in need of constant repairs and some of them still too narrow. The leveling and grading left something to be desired, and in some cases stumps and rocks, once buried in the foundations, were reappearing as the roads wore down.[37]

The *Courant* noted also the insurance business for which Hartford one day would become famous. Marine insurance could be bought at Hartford; [38] and in 1794 Sanford & Wadsworth advertised the underwriting of houses, furniture, and merchandise against damage by fire.[39] In 1810 the legislature incorporated the Hartford Fire Insurance Company with a permissive capital of $250,000. The *Courant* carried the largest advertisements for this company that it had yet printed.[40] In 1811, on the occasion of the burning of an uninsured distillery, the editors offered the following good advice:

The numerous accidents of this kind within a few months past, place in a striking point of view the prudence of resorting to INSURANCE for security. The premium paid is in no instance greater, and in many instances not equal to the hazard. In England it has become almost universal to insure against fire. The security to creditors and the family distress which is thereby prevented, powerfully recommend this precautionary measure to the merchant, the farmer and the landlord.[41]

The old ways of meeting these emergencies were changing. As one letter pointed out, the traditional practice of taking up collections to re-establish the victims of fire loss ought no longer to be countenanced since property could now be insured by a comparatively slight investment.[42]

The whole problem of fire, fire prevention, and fire fighting became a major concern as Hartford grew. In the issue of November 17, 1788, the editors wrote:

Last Tuesday, at about 11 o'clock A.M. while the wind blew with extreme violence, this town was alarmed by the cry of FIRE. Anxiety and terror were excited in the highest degree among the inhabitants; as they well know how unprepared they were to oppose the raging of this destructive element. Happily, the fire was soon extinguished: But will not this occurrence serve to show the owners of houses and other property which is exposed to the ravages of fire, how exceedingly important it is to have proper regulations for extinguishing fires? This town is now so large and compact, that without such regulations, property is exceedingly precarious. A couple of good *tight* engines, with men properly appointed for working them, together with some other regulations, would be a great security against the destructive violence of this element.

Shortly afterward the city government appointed a chief engineer and raised three volunteer companies to cooperate with the several city fire wardens.[43] Money rewards were arranged to encourage their alacrity, the number of volunteer units later increased, and ordinances imposed precautionary measures upon the public.[44] To regulations concerning chimneys, fireplaces, stoves, bonfires, and the storage of powder,[45] certain prohibitions were added: all persons were forbidden to enter barns, stables, or haylofts with exposed candles or lamps, and citizens were enjoined not to smoke pipes or cigars within city limits except in stores, houses, or shops— not even on the streets.[46] In 1810, the Assembly enabled the common council to make such building regulations as were thought advisable.[47]

In cases of fire, besides the organized companies, male residents between certain ages, at one time 15 to 60, were expected to rush to the scene with buckets of designated size and to take orders from the authorities.[48] Certain citizens were appointed to appear with sacks in which to deposit such domestic appurtenances as might be retrieved.[49] At a night alarm, all householders placed candles in the front windows of their homes and those in charge at the fire, the better to be seen, wore white hats and carried white wands five feet in length.[50] The *Courant* complained repeatedly of the confusion and the lack of discipline on these exciting occasions.[51] Some of the citizens were lax in keeping their leather buckets in good repair[52] and, to quote one writer: "Every Booby in the city makes it his business to smoke Segars incessantly in the streets."[53]

Perhaps as frightening as fire were the epidemics of yellow fever which threatened the city. The paper reported recurring visitations of the scourge in Baltimore, Philadelphia, New York, Boston, and some of the lesser port cities nearer home.[54] In 1795 rumors of the prevalence of the disease in Hartford elicited editorial deprecations which appeared to regret their effect upon local business. It was said that the dysentery had prevailed, but, except for the usual "autumnal remitting fever," little other sickness had occurred.[55] In the summer of 1799, the *Courant* conceded some deaths, recording that the area from Front Street to the river had been vacated; but by mid-September business had recommenced with the city again wearing its usual appearance of cheerfulness and industry.[56] Upon the threat of such calamities, the editors at different times counseled attendance at prayer meetings and the collection of funds for the families of victims elsewhere.[57] A health committee sponsored clean-up activities and examined incoming ships from foreign and domestic ports.[58] It was understood that the disease afflicted populous cities in hot, dry seasons, arising in filthy, "unnatural" neighborhoods along waterfronts.[59]

The disposal of refuse, the keeping of pigs, the cleaning of shad, salmon, and alewives, leather tanning, and soap boiling were subjected to community control.[60] Local slaughterhouses were at first moderately regulated and then effectively curtailed, none being allowed except for animals raised in the city or for strictly personal use.[61] Officers were charged to see that the streets were free from the cattle, geese, swine, and sheep which occasionally roamed at large, at least in the 1780's and 1790's.[62] In 1801 local enterprisers were seeking contractors "to conduct water into the City of Hartford, by means of subterraneous pipes, from the mountain lying about 5 miles West of said City";[63] and in December, 1815, the shopkeepers along Main Street were meeting to consider the desirability of a common sewerage for that particular area.

The prevention of smallpox was likewise a concern of the community. In the 1790's town authorities maintained an isolated house where people might be inoculated.[64] At the turn of the century, when vaccinations came into vogue,[65] arrangements were made for treatment at town expense and all residents were urged to avail themselves of the opportunity.[66]

The care and cure of most diseases and ailments, however, were primarily private responsibilities. The doctors were organized into county and state associations which examined medical candidates, awarded M.D.'s, recommended students for the Yale Medical School which opened in 1810, and at times exerted pressure upon the state legislature.[67] Except for announcing inoculation and vaccination services, they no longer commonly advertised in the *Courant*.[68] Itinerant dentists began to proclaim their skills at cleaning and extracting teeth, supplying false ones, caring for gums, and plugging cavities with gold, silver, or tinfoil.[69] They sold pastes and powders and some of them were oculists as well, skilled in the craft of fitting artificial eyes.[70] The paper printed occasional "cures" for diseases, a few letters on the efficacy of the mineral waters at Suffield and Stafford, and a testimonial or two for Dr. Perkins' metal "tractors" which were alleged to draw excess "animal electricity" from the bodies of patients.[71] The most copious medical advice came now from the patent medicine advertisements which appeared after the Revolution. According to these, "Jaundice Bitters," "Vegetable Drops," "Antispasmodic Elixir," "Antiscorbutic Tincture," and a host of others were effective for everything from bladder stones to dull-looking teeth.[72] The *Courant*'s owners themselves joined in the trade and at one time were selling, by special appointment and at three dollars a bottle, "The Cordial Balm of Gilead," a "remedy" for all persons who were in any way undersexed.[73] As the years went on, the claims of such nostrums took up considerable space in the paper.

Local civil disputes and criminal cases came to focus in the county court which sat at Hartford. Before and after the war, writers remarked the extremely litigious propensities of Connecticut Yankees, most of the actions apparently involving neglected promises to pay.[74] In the 1790's notices of suits for divorce, on grounds of adultery and desertion, began to appear in the paper.[75] Instances of local criminal behavior—mostly horse stealing, burglary, and counterfeiting—were reported; and servants and apprentices sometimes ran away.[76] An offender was hanged in 1797 amidst what the editors estimated to be six to ten thousand spectators.[77] The city was divided into "watch wards" and all citizens called upon to do so were expected to stand night watch and to pick up wandering individuals after certain hours.[78] The town selectmen were instructed to approve strangers or transients who took up abodes in Hartford and townspeople were warned not to hire or harbor such persons without reporting them for inspection.[79] The *Courant*'s inclusion of crime news from outside points indicated a more or less prevalent degree of interest in the grosser forms of antisocial conduct.

The advertisements of an increasing variety of tutors and schools in Hartford reflected the desires of parents who wished for their

children some of the elements of socially esteemed "background."
Among these were morning and evening schools, schools for young
ladies, schools for boys, and mixed schools.[80] In addition to the
three R's, geography, surveying, navigation, bookkeeping, English
literature, Greek and Latin, there were teachers of French and of
music, both vocal and instrumental, and those who instructed in
drawing, painting, and elocution.[81] Self-styled European masters
taught fencing and dancing—minuets and cotillions, jigs, reels,
hornpipes, and country dances—and played upon the prestige their
Old World connections gave them.[82] The announcement of one
of them follows:

Le Bal de Quarter de Mons. VALUE will be on Friday evening, the 3rd
of September. The parents and relatives of his Elives will confer great
honour and happiness on him by attending. Young gentlemen are respectfully informed that the room will be at their service at 9 o'clock.
   Mr. Value begs leave to arrest the public attention for a moment, on
the important topic of education. His *Nouvelle et permanente Academie
pour les enfans et la jeunesse,* will be opened the 15th of September.—
Should there be a sufficient number of applicants, his son, a young
gentleman of talents, who was educated in the best university in France,
will assist him.[83]

   For those who liked to read books and cared to spend money to
do so, the *Courant* printed accounts of circulating libraries in Hartford. One cooperative arrangement began in 1774 when a group of
subscribers contributed books, chose a librarian, and adopted rules
for borrowing.[84] The proprietors, among whom the books circulated, housed their library in the Hartford grammar school and
paid annual sums with which to enlarge it.[85] After the war it came
to be called the "City Library" and one of the *Courant*'s writers
considered it a sufficient inducement for permanently locating the
state capital at Hartford.[86] A similar project was apparently under
way in 1794 and still others, owned by individuals, invited public
patronage through the *Courant* at rates ranging from fees for single
volumes to membership at six dollars a year.[87]
   Before and after the Revolution, good music was commonly considered the handmaiden of religion. Most newspaper references to
local music concerned psalmody, and collections of hymns and
anthems were frequently advertised by booksellers.[88] The earliest
commercial concert which the *Courant* recorded took place in
Hartford's new theater in 1796 where orchestral compositions by

Haydn and Pleyel were performed along with a variety of songs, instrumental solos, and quartet numbers;[89] but this was altogether unique and nothing like it occurred for a long time to come. The advertisements of teachers of piano and stringed instruments became a feature of the paper in the 1790's[90] and the number of public dances or balls increased,[91] implying the wider social usage of secular tunes as the years passed by.

Itinerant artists came to Hartford to paint portraits, cut profiles, and make miniatures.[92] Silhouettes might be gilded on glass and then framed, or the cheaper ones were cut from paper, and relatively inexpensive miniatures were made with colored crayons.[93] Traveling waxwork exhibits and paintings enabled people to see the likenesses of the great of their generation and to view depictions of the death of Lord Nelson, the Hamilton-Burr duel, George Washington's tomb, or some stirring naval battle.[94] In 1797 Joseph Steward established in the State House what was known later as the Hartford Museum.[95] Here were displayed not only historical paintings and waxworks, but Peruvian pottery, stuffed birds and animals, meteor fragments, Indian relics, snake skins, costumes and weapons from the Orient, Africa, and the South Seas, and even an East Indian pagoda. The curator himself cut profiles for 12½ cents and did large and small portraits.[96] Hudson & Goodwin thought his collection ranked well with similar exhibits anywhere in the United States.[97]

A company of Boston actors played in Hartford for five seasons in the 1790's. Among the many advertised plays with such titles as *No Song No Supper* and *Love A-la-Mode,* were a few by Shakespeare, Sheridan, Goldsmith, and Garrick.[98] The city's first theater house, replete with boxes, pit, and gallery, opened in 1795.[99] Shows ran three nights a week that summer beginning at 6:30 o'clock. Tickets were bought at the door or at Hudson & Goodwin's. Ladies and gentlemen were requested to have their servants at the theater by five o'clock, at the latest, to hold their seats for them.[100]

When the new building was being erected, one of the *Courant*'s writers recorded this view:

A frequent attendance at a theatre, leads youth of both sexes to read plays. Experience has shewn, that the reading of plays at an early age, more especially of comedies, has a very injurious effect. It is much like the reading of novels. They are both, generally fabricated on some imaginary love-tale; and being read at the time of life, when the passions begin to expand; and when, to inexperience, the world appears in the most lively and fascinating colours, they rarely fail to beget in the youthful mind, wild and romantic ideas of purity and sincerity.[101]

After the opening night, the editors took issue with such sentiments:

The NEW THEATRE in this City was opened on Monday evening last, with a celebrated Comedy entitled, The DRAMATIST. . . . From the specimen that has been given of the abilities of the performers, and the assurance of the Managers that they will so conduct the Theatre, that it may be justly stiled a *School of Morality,* it is presumed, that it will be a great source of instruction and amusement to those who visit it; and we will hazard the assertion, notwithstanding the prejudices that some have entertained against it, that as an amusement, it is the most innocent, and as a source of instruction it is the most amusing of any that we have ever yet experienced. While the Theatre is well conducted on chaste principles—when Vice is drawn in colours that will disgust, and Virtue painted with all its alluring charms, it is hoped it will meet the approbation and encouragement of the citizens, and of the neighboring towns.[102]

As long as the theater continued, the *Courant* supported it in editorials, letters and advertisements. Its good spirit and order, the professional capacity of the actors, the patronage of "respectable" people, and the waning of erstwhile prejudices were all objects of comment.[103] According to the editors, several informed individuals believed the local productions to be nowise inferior to those of the British and French theaters. As far as they knew, all persons who attended in Hartford had been highly gratified by the plays they had seen.[104] However, among the laws enacted by the General Assembly in 1800, was one entitled "An Act to prevent Theatrical Shows and Exhibitions."[105] This came at a time when many Federalists, perceiving the spread of Jeffersonian liberalism, had rising fears for the security of law, order, and good morals. It was evident that the sentiments of some of the people in Hartford were no longer representative of the beliefs of the Connecticut farm folks. For many years after 1799, Hartford had no similar enterprise.[106]

Some of the elements which were later institutionalized in the American circus began to advertise in the paper. At different times people were urged to see trained horses and expert equestrians, a juggler, a tumbler and slack-rope performer, a dog-and-monkey show, entertaining clowns, and something called "Archimideal Phaetons, Vertical Aerial Coaches, or Patent Federal Balloons," in which parties of two, four, or eight might be accommodated.[107] Miss Sally Rogers painted flowers and landscapes, threaded needles, and cut paper and cloth without the use of hands or feet. Don Cesar Cossa, lately from Italy, walked on live coals, rang bells and fired pistols with electricity. An African horse added, subtracted, multiplied, divided, told time, and counted the buttons on gentlemen's coats.[108] Animals were sometimes exhibited at the taverns [109] —an elephant, a lion, a leopard, a moose, a bison, and camels. The last named were perhaps the least familiar to Hartford's citizens:

These stupendous Animals are most deserving the Attention of the Curious, being the greatest natural Curiosity ever exhibited to the Public on this Continent. They are Nineteen Hands high; have Necks near Four Feet long; have a large high Bunch on their Backs, and another under their Breasts, in the form of a Pedestal, on which they support themselves when lying down; they have Four Joints in their hind legs, and will travel Twelve or Fourteen Days without drinking.[110]

Each year, on the Fourth of July and on Election Day in May, the city gave way to unusual festivity with dignitaries on parade, military escorts, sermons, banquets, and balls.[111] A similar pomp of circumstance greeted famous men—Washington, Lafayette, and John Adams—on such occasions as they visited or passed through Hartford.[112] The *Courant* sometimes recorded these events in interesting and happy language.

Less casual than some of these forms of recreation were the few business, humanitarian, and fraternal organizations of which the paper took notice. Aside from the local doctors and merchants, there were probably no other well-organized vocational groups.[113] In 1792 the mechanics were invited to unite in resisting certain alleged impositions of their employers,[114] but as far as the *Courant* reveals, nothing came of it. Believing it to be less easy for poor workers than for farmers to keep their large families together, about 60 local citizens formed the "Charitable Society" which hoped to provide for people not adequately covered by the existing poor laws.[115] The Connecticut Bible Society distributed religious information to the indigent. The ladies, through the "Hartford Female Beneficent Society," concerned themselves with "the amelioration of female indigence together with moral decency in various ways." [116] These organizations had a religious flavor as did the St. John's Masonic lodge which convened from time to time.[117] Occasionally the state Order of the Cincinnati met in Hartford to celebrate the Fourth of July, to parade, to feast, and to listen to sermons.[118] The *Courant* reflected a bit of antislavery feeling before the Revolution and some of Hartford's citizens belonged to the state society for the advancement of freedom which was established afterward.[119] A few also were members of "The Connecticut Society of Arts and Sciences," formed in 1786.[120] Some of the antiliquor sentiment associated with the name of Benjamin Rush of Philadelphia appeared in the paper, but no local organization arose to promote it.[121]

Institutionalized religion in Hartford was becoming diversified. Besides Episcopalians and members of the orthodox church, the *Courant* alluded to Methodists, Universalists, and Baptists.[122] An established belief in the allowance of doctrines at variance with those of the forefathers had become a part of the working pattern of the community, and the editors undoubtedly endorsed the opinions of many when they scored the absurdity of the old religious intolerance.[123]

The complete separation of church and state, however, was quite another issue. The Connecticut Toleration Act of 1791 excused dissenters from paying church taxes provided they belonged to other churches, provided they proved it by depositing certificates with the clerks of the established church societies, and provided they paid taxes to support the churches in which they worshiped.[124] Dissenting groups, in the way of correcting this prescribed inferior status, now demanded the withdrawal of state support from any and all denominations.[125] Although their efforts bore no fruit until 1818, the agitation was too much in the air for people in Hartford not to have entertained thoughts concerning it.

Some people might have argued for legal disestablishment on grounds that a man's religion was his private concern, but not the editors or their supporters. To them, the legislature had as much right to lay taxes for churches as it had for schools. Every man might be free to worship as he pleased, but if he refrained from worshiping he should certainly contribute to support the worship of others. Religion produced the good observance of civil law and order of which every man shared the benefits.[126] "Religious knowledge hath a beneficial influence on our outward circumstances as well as our internal peace. While it is infinitely more valuable than riches or power, it hath a tendency to increase our temporal prosperity."[127]

Aside from these contentions, the *Courant* had isolated references to a decline in churchgoing and in Sabbath observance.[128] Some of the barber shops were said to have opened on Sundays and some of the young people rode about on horseback or in carriages.[129] Sermons were shorter than of yore, and as Federalists came to lament the French Revolution and the rise of Jeffersonian ideas, deism and immorality were thought to be taking their toll, pervading especially the lower classes of people.[130] "Justinian," looking back 30 years from 1800, perceived a lessening reverence for the attributes of the Deity, the atonement, and the final state of rewards and punishment.[131]

The more immediate or workaday preoccupations came to focus in the many little stores, shops, and "manufactories" in Hartford. Merchants, traders, and artisans advertised a diversity of vendibles. The stock of Amos Bull's "general store" near the South Church indicated some of the purchases, mostly of English goods, that might have been made in 1789:

. . . A QUANTITY of low priced Irish Linens, Callicoes, Muslins, Shawls, Handkerchiefs; Cambricks, Lawns, Gauzes, &c.—Sattins, Modes, Sarsenets, Diapers, Drawboys, Dimities, Merseilles Quilting; Cotton Denims, Royal Ribs, Velvets, &c.—Superfine Florentine; Sattinets, Lastings, Durants, Calmancoes, Moreens, Tabbyretts, Rattinets, Shalloons, Camlets, Corduretts, Flannels, Hosiery, Gloves, Leghorn, and Felt Hats, Ladies Stuff Shoes, warranted, Muffs and Tippets, Morocco Leather, Green and Mahogany Oil-cloths—Ribbands, Tastes, Tapes, Laces, Cap and Ribband wire, Silk-Twist, Thread, Bobbins, Paper, Quills, Ink powder, Sealing wax, Wafers; Buckles, elegantly gilt, and suited to the present season of festivity, with plated Buckles, and more common ones; Federal and other elegant, and common Buttons; Knives and Forks in abundance; Cuttoes, Penknives, Rasors, Scissors, Shears, Strops, Shaving boxes, Ivory Combs; almost Every Kind of Brushes; Sconces, Candlesticks, Snuffers, Brass knockers, Cabinet and Coffin Furniture, Brass Nails and Ecutcheon pins, Chimney and other Hooks, Brass Knobs and Rings, Looking-glass pins, Brasswire, Knitting pins, Brass-Cocks, White chapel Needles, Thimbles, Shoe and Knee chapes, Fishhooks, Cork-screws, Spectacles, Spoons, Hinges, Locks, Bolts, Tapborers, Gimblets, Hammers, Compasses, Rules, Chalklines; Chisels, Gauges, Plane-Irons, Bits, Brads, Handsaw files; Wood-screws in plenty; Spades, Shovels, Awls, Tacks, Shovels and Tongs, Jewsharps; Trowels, Currycombs, Bridle-Bits, Stirrups, Setts, Spurs, Switch-Whips; Powder of excellent quality; Shot, Bar lead, Indigo, Loaf and Lump Sugar, and good Hyson Tea; with several articles not enumerated.[132]

The following list of advertisers suggests the variety of craftsmen who plied their trades in Hartford:

goldsmith	chaise and harness maker
bell-maker	weaver
silversmith and jeweler	flax miller
distiller	soap boiler and tallow chandler
fanlight manufacturer	glovemaker
rope-maker	currier
caulker	comb manufacturer
glassmaker	snuff manufacturer
coppersmith and brazier	wall paper manufacturer
nailor	stoneware manufacturer
looking-glass manufacturer	tinsmith
milliner	stonecutter
dyer	shoemaker
watchmaker	printer
saddler	button manufacturer
cabinet and chair maker	baker
maker of musical instruments	scythemaker
blacksmith	hatter and clothier

The Connecticut River played a vital role in the lives of the business people. Sometimes it raged, destroying their quays, mills, and bridges.[133] Commodities were loaded and unloaded at the waterfront, and boats, carrying passengers and freight, plied seasonally between Hartford and the outside world.[134] "Viator" wrote in 1792 that the public landings, once adequate, were no longer suited to the city's increased and growing commerce.[135] Traders sometimes sold goods at the wharves and sometimes their sloops lay up for the season as the river froze over.[136] Although the day of the steamboat had not quite arrived, one supposes that its potentialities had already begun to capture the imaginations of local enterprisers. One day in 1815, the *Fulton,* regularly running between New York and New Haven, steamed up the river: "The novelty and elegance of this vessel, attracted universal attention, and it is supposed, that on that day and the next morning, not less than seven or eight thousand persons were on board of her." [137]

Tavern keepers and merchants, among others, were undoubtedly interested in the development of stage travel. A few years before the Revolution, Nicholas Brown, local chaise and chair maker, and his brother Jonathan, were running advertisements for fortnightly stages to New York and Boston.[138] To either place, the trip took three days. In the 1780's travelers were accommodated twice a week in the winter and three times in the summer at 4 *d.* per mile with a baggage allowance of 14 pounds. The journey took two days only on summer schedule.[139] Stages thereafter ran to Springfield, Hanover, Hudson, Albany, and Providence. By the time of the War of 1812, stages were moving daily, Sundays excepted, to Boston and New York.[140] Those that rode at high speed, changing horses each 10 miles of the way, were leaving Hartford at 3 or 4 A.M. and arriving at either city by 9 P.M. the same day.[141] Passenger rates were six cents per mile.

One wonders, finally, what the people themselves thought of the appearance of their community with its river front, its dwelling houses, its streets, shops, stores, taverns, schools, churches, and other visible features. To the stranger at the tavern, casual conversation may have indicated a degree of pride in the new Statehouse built in the 1790's, in the first local bridge across the Connecticut, or in the new meetinghouses which were erected the following decade;[142] but the *Courant* gives little insight on this point. A traveler, writing in 1808, thought that the looks of the principal buildings had appreciably changed; that the Gothic and clumsy appearance of 30 years before had almost entirely disappeared; and that the houses and stores had taken on something of an air of "elegance." Although the streets, too, were observed to have been in better condition than formerly, they were all but intolerable at certain seasons. The sidewalks afforded relief as far as they extended, but in many places, especially in February, March, and April, a person noticed such mud as to astonish him in a city so flourishing. Ladies were seen hopping about as if in a trackless swamp, and gentlemen's boots were heavy with mire.[143]

The *Courant* gave far more space and discussion to the chartering of the Phoenix Bank in 1814 with its million-dollar capitalization.[144] Perhaps this was indicative of the scheme of values by which Hartford's citizens judged their community's worth. A long time afterward, Samuel G. Goodrich of "Peter Parley" fame recalled the later years of this period in the following passage:

. . . Hartford was then a small commercial town, of four thousand inhabitants, dealing in lumber, and smelling of molasses and Old Jamaica —for it had still some trade with the West Indies. Though the semi-capital of the State . . . it was strongly impressed with a plodding, mercantile, and mechanical character. There was a high tone of general intelligence and social respectability about the place, but it had not a single institution, a single monument, that marked it as even a provincial metropolis of taste, in literature, art, or refinement. The leading men were thrifty mechanics, with a few merchants, and many shopkeepers, society of course taking its hue from these dominant classes. There were lawyers, judges, and public functionaries—men of mark—but their spirit did not govern the town.[145]

CHAPTER VII

HUDSON & GOODWIN, PUBLISHERS

AMIDST the worries and triumphs of years of political campaigning, Hudson & Goodwin performed the various work of composing, printing, and distributing the *Courant*. At the close of the Revolution they were faced at once with certain general problems pertaining to this phase of the business. In the first place, as the war news abated, it seemed necessary to have on hand interesting and instructive peacetime reading material which they could assuredly use to fill out the content of the paper. Secondly, they needed to gird for local competition. Bavil Webster took a cue from the *Courant's* postwar political conservatism and began the publication of an opposition weekly, the *Freeman's Chronicle*.[1] The following summer Barlow & Babcock distributed the first issue of the *American Mercury,* for many years similar to the *Courant* in format and political appeal.[2] Partly for the needs suggested [3] and partly because a coterie of clever young writers were living in the neighborhood, Hudson & Goodwin wrote as follows in December, 1783:

By the return of commerce into a regular channel, they [the editors] are enabled to reduce the price of this paper, which, though much larger than formerly, will be afforded at the same price, it was before the war. Care will be taken to publish the most interesting articles of intelligence, foreign and domestic——and in order to render the paper beneficial to the community, during the tranquility of peace, several gentlemen have engaged to furnish occasional essays, moral, political, historical and entertaining, which will add the advantage of instruction to the pleasure of novelty.[4]

Contained in the *Courant* of the next decade were the usual news reprints, speeches of political dignitaries, state and federal laws, proclamations, and resolutions. For the first time the editors reported the debates of the lower house of the state legislature. Before the war only the titles of acts of Assembly had been offered to readers; during the war years numbers of the laws had been printed; and now, at the end of the sessions, appeared partial synopses of the discussions of the representatives.[5] Having been criticized for this innovation, Hudson & Goodwin wrote heatedly of the right of the people to know the conduct of their lawmakers. Especially were they irked that the doors of the upper house remained closed to the public.[6] In the fall of 1784 they advanced the whole distance:

The Editors of this paper, encouraged by the patronage of several of the most liberal, ingenious, and spirited members of the legislature, propose to give their readers a concise history of the business and debates which shall come before the present session of the Assembly. They are no party, and wish to be considered simply as the narrators of facts; of facts interesting to the well-being of every individual. The attempt, they are conscious is laudable; but as it is new in this state, they claim, in this public manner, the indulgence of the members of that honourable body individually; hope for such information as may prevent them from being betrayed into misrepresentation, or unintentional errors; and declare they will most chearfully stand corrected, if such should find their way into their publications.—Should these sketches, however deficient or imperfect they may be, have any tendency to enlighten or inform the citizens of this state, respecting their true political interests, and the great concerns of our national government, it will be an ample compensation for the extraordinary trouble of paying a minute attention to the proceedings of the legislature during their actual progress; and will, at the same time, supersede the necessity of giving any crude paragraphs at the close of the session, unsatisfactory on account of their brevity, or indistinctness to the public; or ungrateful, on any other account, to individuals.[7]

In addition, readers were treated to an increasing number of letters and essays on morals, politics, and trade. Copied from the *London Magazine* were lengthy extracts on the last voyage of Captain Cook and "Lectures on Modern History" sweeping the period from the beginning of the Christian Era.[8] For almost two years the papers were clogged with the details of the military transactions of the late war as recorded in the *British Annual Register*.[9] In addition to advertisements, beginning in 1785 a "Marine List" covered the port of New London, sometimes quoting commodity prices.[10] Tempering the general stodginess of the paper, principally in the middle 1780's, were bits of political satire in verse and prose.

Of the many anonymous essayists writing for Hudson & Goodwin, Noah Webster, whose contributions ranged over a ten-year period, was probably the most impressive and prolific.[11] He argued the need for banks,[12] for legislative and penal reforms,[13] for commercial improvements,[14] for federal union,[15] and expanded such various topics as the evils of excessive litigation,[16] apple worms,[17] the French Revolution,[18] western lands,[19] United States coins,[20] and the site for the nation's capitol.[21] His "Honorius Letters," a series on the commutation and impost controversies, were probably his most influential political production.[22] Commenting upon them afterward, he supposed that his zeal and perseverance had more than made up for his lack of years and knowledge. One of Governor Trumbull's councilors credited him with having decisively affected Connecticut opinion, and the Governor himself thanked Webster for his timely services to the state.[23] He wrote also the *Courant*'s most popular series of didactic essays, later published in nearly 100 editions, some of them in England.[24] Homely sayings were elaborated with good humor and good-natured satire:

I often say to myself, as I ride about the country, what a pity it is our farmers *do not work it right*. When I see a man turn his cattle into the street to run at large and waste their dung, during a winter's day, I say, this man does not work it right. Ten loads of good manure at least, is lost in a season by this slovenly practice—and all for what? For nothing indeed, but to ruin a farm. . . .

Whether in Congress or a kitchen, the person who *talks much* is *little regarded*. Some members of Congress then certainly *do not work it right*. A hint to the *wise* is sufficient; but twenty hints have not been sufficient to silence the clamorous tongues of some Congressional spouters. . . .

I once knew a young man of excellent hopes, who was deeply in love with a lady—The first time he had an opportunity to whisper in her ear, and before he had made any impression on her heart in his favor, he sighed out his sorrowful tale to her, in full explanation: The lady was frightened—she soon rid herself of the distressed lover; she said, *he did not work it right*.[25]

A number of Hudson & Goodwin's writers, Webster included, sought by political prose and doggerel to heap ridicule, refutation, and appeasement upon the heads of the dissident elements in post-Revolutionary Connecticut. Joel Barlow wrote letters, one of them "To the Bad People of the State of Connecticut." [26] John Trumbull defended the interests of the ex-officers of the army by "The Curious SOLILOQUY of one of the Thirteen Sisters . . . on the great Question, whether it were best to marry a wise Man, or a Fool." [27] As resolutions were adopted against the proposed federal impost, Oliver Wolcott, Jr., satirized them by resolving:

That Government is one of those evils brought upon men by the fall, and ought always to be opposed by a free people; that we are free and are determined never to be governed. . . .

That it is contrary to the articles of confederation for these states to comply with any recommendations of Congress, particularly for payment of the public debts; and that such *recommendations are strong proofs of the lust of power.*[28]

When the *Courant* and other papers were charged with being implements of the governing class, Webster mimicked the opposition:

> And if one Printer dare refuse
> To second our seditious views,
> And spread from Beersheba to Dan,
> The secret factious schemes we plan,
> Our grave committee of report
> Will tell us on't at our next court;
> And send by herald's, if they please,
> Th' important news of our decrees.[29]

In 1786 occurred an entertaining episode which gave vent to abounding satire in the *Courant* and led more or less directly to the publication of the once-famous "Anarchiad." [30] William Williams, signer of the Declaration of Independence, son-in-law of the late Governor Trumbull, and a member of the Governor's Council, wrote a letter to Joseph Hopkins, member of the state legislature from Waterbury. In some unexplained way Williams's letter fell into the hands of political enemies.[31] On October 9, it appeared in the *Courant* along with a lilting take-off in Hudibrastic rhyme.[32] Williams had decried the political connivings of the Cincinnati:

> You see, Sir, by the last Gazette,
> The Cincinnati are to meet;
> Their fair pretence is but a blind;
> There must be roguery in the wind,
> If from the schemes that we are brewing,
> We guess what other folks are doing.

He had mentioned Oliver Wolcott who was sympathetic with the Cincinnati:

> That W—— is a dangerous man,
> He's *honest,* and dislikes our plan,
> And since he's stubborn yet and stout,
> We must find means to turn him out.
> The U—— H——, which makes me sad,
> Have some few more almost as bad.

• • • • •

Hoping to see you in October
With face full long, and cant full sober;
So pray be cautious, sly and nimble,
Your loving servant, WILLIAM WIMBLE.

Two weeks later appeared the satirical version of an alleged reply from Hopkins to Williams which concluded:

I wish I could as safely say,
That you'd be in beyond next May.
And so remain with duty proper
Your Humble servant JOSEPH COPPER.[33]

These were the opening shots in the so-called Wimble War.[34] Meantime the internal crisis intensified and conservatives feared for the safety of government. Webster confessed to have lost faith in republicanism.[35] David Humphreys, Lemuel Hopkins, Trumbull, and Barlow collaborated to produce the "Anarchiad," originally published in the *New Haven Gazette*. Hudson & Goodwin copied it into the *Courant*.[36] The money and credit situation was out of hand in neighboring Rhode Island:

Hail! Realm of Rogues, renown'd for fraud and guile,
All hail, ye knav'ries of yon little Isle,
There prowls the rascal, cloth'd with legal pow'r,
To snare the orphan and the poor devour,
The crafty knave his creditor besets,
And advertising paper pays his debts:
Bankrupts their creditors with rage pursue,
No stop—no mercy from the debtor crew.
Arm'd with new tests, the licens'd villain bold,
Presents his bills and robs them of their gold;
Their ears, though rogues and counterfeiters lose,
No legal robber fears the gallow noose.[37]

In Massachusetts—insurrection!

In visions fair the scenes of fate unroll,
And Massachusetts opens on my soul.
There Chaos, Anarch old, asserts his sway,
And mobs in myriads blacken all the way:
See *Day*'s stern port, behold the martial frame
Of *Shays'* and *Shattuck*'s mob compelling name:
See the bold Hampshirites on Springfield pour.
The fierce Tauntonians crowd the alewife shore.
O'er *Concord* fields the bands of *discord* spread,

And Wor'ster trembles at their thundering tread:
See from proud Egremont the woodchuck train,
Sweep their dark files, and shade with rags the plain.
LO, THE COURT FALLS; th' affrighted judges run,
Clerks, Lawyers, Sheriffs, every mother's son.
The stocks, the gallows lose th' expected prize.
See the jails open and the thieves arise.
Thy constitution, Chaos, is restor'd;
Law sinks before thy uncreating word;
Thy hand unbars th' unfathom'd gulph of fate,
And deep in darkness whelms the new born state.[38]

During the course of events here alluded to, Wimble came to be associated with the unwelcome and the unsound. He had been smeared with "anarchy" and took his pen to deny sympathy for Shays or his ilk.[39] Humphreys answered him with a fable entitled "The MONKEY, who shaved Himself and his Friends." It concluded:

Who cannot write, yet handle pens,
Are apt to hurt themselves and friends,
Though others use them well, yet fools
Should never meddle with edge-tools.[40]

The very next month the authors of the "Anarchiad" had Wimble hanged and his elegy appeared in the *Courant:*

Mine be the task to celebrate
This hero sly and nimble;
Whose praise shall last, in spite of fate—
Who knows not *William Wimble?*

To fellow-creatures he was kind,
To brethren staunch and hearty;
He help'd the *weak,* and led the *blind,*
Whene'er he led his party.

Yet shall the foolish folks, *for aye,*
Whose brains would fill a thimble,
Striking their pensive bosoms, say,
"Here lies poor William Wimble." [41]

Such characteristic verses of the 1780's endured past the turn of the century in the *Courant's* annual New Year's poems. Old-timers recollected only two lines of the first of these, composed by John Ledyard, the traveler, presumably before the Revolution:

> As is man's life, so is the first of January,
> Short, fleeting, and completely momentary.[42]

The earlier rhymes were on separate sheets requesting a tip for the boy who distributed the papers in Hartford. In 1786:

> I intend to relate (and as fast as I can)
> That your rates are collected and new taxes laid,
> Your public debt funded, your private debts paid;
> That your Congress has power as becomes their high station,
> The rights of your commerce to fix with each nation;
> And many more things in the bosom of fate,
> Too dark to forsee and too strange to relate;
> But, till time shall unfold them, we there let them rest;
> Pray give me a shilling and hope for the best.[43]

In the 1790's they appeared as rhythmic news reviews always satirizing the foes of Federalism:

> Come sing again! since Ninety-Five,
> Has left some *Antis* still alive;
> Some Jacobins as pert as ever,
> Tho' much was hoped from Yellow-fever.[44]

In 1798:

> Raise now the song, and sing how France,
> Led down her first regen'rate dance;
> The dance of sage-inspiring mobs,
> Flush'd with th' atheist lore of Hobbes;
> When *Loyalty* was chang'd to *treason,*
> And GOD *depos'd* for *human reason.*[45]

Theodore Dwight wrote "The Triumph of Democracy" in 1801:

> Let every voice with triumph sing—
> JEFFERSON is chosen king!
> Ring every bell in every steeple,
> T'announce the "Monarch of the People!"
> Stop—ere your civic feasts begin,
> Wait 'till the votes are all come in;
> Perchance, amid this mighty stir,
> Your Monarch may be Col. BURR! [46]

Webster, Barlow, and others were among the *Courant*'s New Year's bards.[47] Several of the poems were incorporated in *The Echo,* published for the Hartford Wits in 1807.[48]

After 1790, year in and year out, Hudson & Goodwin continued to fill the paper with material that now seems heavy and dull. In addition to that mentioned, briefs of Congressional debates appeared intermittently,[49] and, during the last of the Adams administration, all the federal laws that were passed.[50] Returned prosperity and the assurances of sound government induced a sort of pleasant complacency in the early nineties; and if less political satire salted the reader's pabulum, the partners no longer reprinted from the *London Magazine* or otherwise offered the elements of classical education. As time went on, the course of events became more exciting and more momentous. Jefferson's opposition party took form. The drama of the French Revolution, European wars, and the tortuous path of American foreign policy focused attention on national and world affairs. The *Courant's* scope became broader and its general character less provincial.

Perhaps the most notable development of the period was the slow and unheralded arrival of the editorial. Ever since 1764 the printers had composed, under a Hartford date line, a short column made up of death notices and brief bits of original reporting. If they sometimes wished to emphasize a sentence or short paragraph from another paper, they reprinted it here. Occasionally they paraphrased a short letter or communication. By 1790 the Hartford column had become a little longer than formerly, but it remained essentially the same. The following was typical:

Hartford, May 9. [1791]
Last week was brought into this city to market, by Col. Joseph Abbot, of Ellington, a Hog which weighed six hundred weight after dressed.

At Northford, in the County of New-Haven, twelve-hundred runs of Silk were raised last year, which at three runs to one yard will make four hundred yards of Silk.—It is not more than seven or eight years since the first Mulberry Trees for this purpose were set out in that place.

In this paper of the 25th ult. was published under the Middletown head, an account of the murder of an infant child, by Solomon Foster and his wife, of Guilford. The following particulars of that affair are copied from the New-Haven Gazette of Wednesday last: . . .

DIED, at Middletown, the Hon. Jabez Hamlin, Esq. aged 82 years.

To make room for the List of Prizes in this paper, a number of Advertisements are omitted, which will have a place in our next.

On rare occasions before 1790, when the *Courant's* owners were especially stirred by the turn of events or felt impelled to defend themselves against charges of partiality, they had expressed their sentiments in this column.[51] Both Watson and Hudson & Goodwin had done so during the Revolution. After the war, the same column had spoken up in behalf of the Constitution and the need for a stronger federal government. As the partisanship of Hudson & Goodwin intensified, such expressions of opinion came oftener without being more than an exception to the rule. After 1800 they commented still more frequently; and on the eve of the elections of 1804, when "democracy" was deemed to be threatening the government of Connecticut, their paper blossomed with regular and lengthy editorials.

For 600 dollars a year, they hired Ezra Sampson, clergyman by training and late co-editor of the Hudson *Balance,* to be their editorial assistant.[52] Sampson, politically well informed, wrote on a variety of topics in a vigorous and bouncing style. Part of his work was to maintain a running fire with the papers of the opposition, as was customary in those days, and many of his remarks were especially uncomplimentary to the editor and writers of the Jeffersonian *Mercury.*[53] Although his full-time services terminated after 12 months,[54] the one-, two-, and three-column editorial continued, with lapses, to be a feature of the *Courant,* always under the Hartford date line.

When Hudson & Goodwin employed Sampson, they also established a weekly agricultural column entitled the "Farmer's Repository."[55] A number of gentlemen, presumably prosperous Federalist farmers, had urged them to do so, and having undertaken it, the *Courant* asked all who cared to help out to send in their pieces.[56] Oliver Ellsworth, retired Chief Justice of the Supreme Court, wrote most of the articles during the first year and may have selected those from other sources which appeared after his own pen ran dry.[57] At the head of the column appeared a motto from Dean Swift: "Whoever can make two Ears of Corn, or two Blades of Grass grow upon a spot of ground where only one grew before, deserves better of mankind and does a more essential service to his Country, than the whole race of Politicians put together."[58]

Many of Ellsworth's ideas came from the agricultural writings of Arthur Young.[59] He discussed old and new ways of growing the crops that throve best in Connecticut, old and new styles of implements, the treatment of cattle, and the newer means of restoring worn-out soils. He dwelt longest on the subject of fertilizers and may have been one of the first New England writers to explain the value of gypsum and to treat somewhat scientifically of the food of plants.[60] Probably to enliven his column, he gave two or three brief accounts of agriculture in early ages and strange lands.[61] Now and then he enforced his contentions with illustrations drawn from his own observations in other parts of the country or in Europe.[62] Still less frequently he indulged in terse political remarks as when he wrote: "Happy would it be if other good qualities could be as easily renovated as those of land.—Would to God, there were some kind of tillage also by which a republic that once loses its *virtue,* could be restored to virtue again!" [63]

Hudson & Goodwin were expected to assume responsibility for every statement of opinion that appeared in the *Courant,* and out of their years of experience certain standards of selection emerged. They had always been unwilling to publish material which might involve either the writers or themselves in religious controversies or in disputes of a strictly personal nature.[64] In politics, before 1800, they had claimed time and again that they spoke for no party, that their columns were open to the truth from any and all sources.[65] It was sometimes difficult to surmise exactly what they meant by these assertions. In the first place, by a process of selective editing, they had filled their columns with articles from other papers written by persons whose political convictions matched their own. Secondly, the letters and resolutions which they published had just as consistently presented a strong and one-sided Federalist view. They had been accused repeatedly in the 1780's and 1790's of being grossly "partial," a charge which they countered by extolling the patriotic and unbiased nature of their press.[66] The conclusion is inescapable that before 1800, at the earliest, they had been unable to think of the critics of Federalism as other than self-seeking demagogues, adept at truth distorting, and disloyally intent upon ruining the Republic. Such creatures were conceivably unworthy of space in a respectable newspaper.

As the *Courant* in fact became an organ of the national minority party in 1801, and as the development of editorial writing afforded the means of direct political expression, Hudson & Goodwin did not again deny the partisan nature of their journalism. Perforce they had grasped the emerging concept of the role of political parties in the Republic. This was suggested by an announcement in 1804:

The Connecticut Courant is among the oldest establishments of this nature in the country. . . . It was among the foremost, and not the least strenuous, in advocating the cause and independence of our country, in the revolutionary war. On the return of peace, it espoused the interests of a free, and efficient Federal Government, and zealously urged the adoption of the Constitution of the United States. Since that event took place, it has pursued the system of policy developed in the administration, and solemnly recommended in the farewell address of our beloved and venerable WASHINGTON; and has uniformly lent its aid in support of our State Government and Institutions.

Believing, that with those principles, are intimately connected the interests of morals, religion, science, and those of our republican government, and the Union of the States, we shall still hold them forth as the strong hold of our safety, and happiness. In the management of our paper, facts shall be fully and correctly stated; and political discussions conducted with candour, temperance, and decency.[67]

Although their partisanship became self-conscious and they promised that facts would be "fully and correctly stated," the more modern pretension of including the publisher's political philosophy within editorial confines was not then conceivable. The same practice of selective editing continued without abatement and the *Courant,* in news articles, letters, and editorials, presented a uniformly consistent point of view. All writing with any bearing upon politics was chosen or rejected in accordance with the party line.

Hudson & Goodwin were one time even sued for libeling the President and Congress of the United States in an article reprinted from the *Utica Patriot*. On February 13, 1806, Jefferson's Congress secretly appropriated $2,000,000 for the intended acquisition of West Florida. Inasmuch as the prospective purchase was to be effected under the auspices of the French Government, the *Courant*'s writers interpreted the transaction as a sort of homage to the great Napoleon to induce him to stop seizing American merchantmen.[68] In the piece referred to, the government was charged with bribery.[69] Accordingly, in September, 1806, a federal grand jury indicted the owners of the *Courant* for criminal libel under the common law.[70] After sessions of the Circuit Court in 1807 and 1808, their case was advanced to the Supreme Court for final adjudication. The important decision handed down in February, 1812, established that the United States courts have no criminal jurisdiction in common law cases and thus dismissed the suit.[71] The indictment produced no perceptible lull in the *Courant*'s partisanship.

Through all the years after 1783, Hudson & Goodwin improved the *Courant* in appearance and increased its size and cost. Although many issues of the eighteenth century were blue-grey in color, the quality of paper gradually bettered.[72] In 1791 *The Connecticut Courant, and Weekly Intelligencer* became simply *The Connecticut Courant,* published on different days of the week in different periods.[73] By 1810 its dimensions were 13 by 19½ inches, five columns to the page and four pages.[74] The printers issued several single-page "Extras," first to announce the XYZ Affair, and later to cover tidings of the conviction of Matthew Lyon under the Sedition Law, the Battle of the Nile, the declaration of war in 1812, and the Hartford Convention.[75] It became necessary to print a great number of supplements or additional single sheets to accommodate the advertisers.[76] In 1815 single-column advertisements not exceeding a square cost $1.00 for three weeks and $.20 per issue thereafter.[77] Such insertions usually occupied from one third to one half the newspaper space. Subscribers paid 7 *s.* annually for their papers in Hartford, then 9 *s., $1.75* and finally, in 1814, $2.00 per year.[78] Those distributed over the countryside by stage or carrier cost more.[79] In January, 1795, Hudson & Goodwin boasted of 3,500 customers, accounting for a circulation they thought unrivaled in the state.[80] The list numbered almost 5,000 in 1799 and five years later they were claiming, probably with exaggeration, a more extensive patronage than any paper in the country.[81] In 1808 about 4,600 copies were printed each week.[82]

Ebenezer Watson's successors had less reason to be vexed by poor types, lack of paper, or scarcity of news. After the Revolution neither presses nor types had to be imported from abroad.[83] Fire and floodwaters destroyed two of their mills but dearth of paper never again suspended the *Courant.*[84] Issues were never postponed by delay of the news. Stages operated from Savannah to Portsmouth in the 1780's and the northern and southern mails came twice each week by winter, three times in the summer.[85] Connecticut's roads were improved, running time decreased, and additional lines fanned out from Hartford.[86]

For over a third of a century the firm of Hudson & Goodwin not only issued the *Courant* and continued the paper-making enterprises in East Hartford, but expanded the wholesale and retail merchandising of books and stationery supplies and engaged in the printing, binding, and publishing of books and pamphlets. Clerks, apprentices, and journeymen were hired.[87] About 1782 they erected a shop near the site of the old Green & Watson building and in 1796 moved to final quarters in a new brick building opposite the North Meeting House.[88] As the years passed the partnership prospered and eventually achieved the kind of institutional reputation accorded to old, conservative, and stable business establishments.

Gentlemen of the period who browsed among the books at Hudson & Goodwin's could have thumbed through a variety of works on law, history, theology, medicine, surgery, travel, philosophy, biography, and poetry. Perched on the shelves were the standard productions of Blackstone, Coke, Bunyan, Milton, Gibbons, Hume, Boswell, Burke, Chesterfield, Rousseau, Sterne, Smollet, Goldsmith, Addison, and Adam Smith. Schoolmasters might have scanned the spelling books of Dilworth and Webster, Cheever's *Accidence,* Morse's *American Geography,* school dictionaries, testaments and psalters, primers, picture books for children, books on arithmetic, surveying, and French. Included also were timely pamphlets, collections of sermons, statutes of the General Assembly, cookbooks for the housewife, and always the indispensable Bibles and almanacs.[89] The title page of Noah Webster's first dictionary bore the words "For Hudson & Goodwin, Book-Sellers, Hartford, and Increase Cook & Co. Book-Sellers, New Haven." [90] The book business was an important aspect of the Hudson & Goodwin enterprises.

Besides books, the partners took subscriptions for the New York newspapers, for copies of the *Journal* of the House of Representatives, for the printed laws of Congress, and for magazines, both British and American.[91] Lottery tickets, razor strops, traveler's kits, hair trunks, and patent medicines were occasionally offered to purchasers; [92] but the perennial stock consisted of what was then the usual stationer's line:

Imperial, Royal, Medium, Demy, and Fools Cap superfine writing Paper, by the Ream or Quire—Letter Paper, Demy and Fools Cap Marble Paper, Blotting Paper, Wafers, Sealing Wax, warranted Ink-powder—Scales and Dividers, Money Scales and Weights, Dutch Quills from 6 s. to 12 s. per hundred—large, midling, and small Morocco Pocket Books—Etwes and Thread Cases for Ladies and Children, Ass-skin Memorandum Books—Ivory Folders, Red Tape, Press and Bonnet Papers by the gross or dozen, Account Books of various sizes, Wrapping Paper by the Ream, Slates and Pencils, Copy Slips by the dozen or single, Morocco Skins.[93]

In payment for goods, Hudson & Goodwin were generally glad to accept commodities useful in the several branches of their business. Recurrent newspaper notices asked for wood, tanned sheepskins, cattle's feet, horsehair, beeswax, calves' pates, hog bristles, flannel cloth, cotton, linen, and woolen rags, fishnets, old sail cloth, and rope.[94] The general practice of barter was on the wane, but presumably other items also were received when the owners knew where to pass them on with profit.[95]

Since the *Courant*'s publishers were at one time or another engaged to print the productions of such authors as John Trumbull, Noah Webster, Joel Barlow, Timothy and Theodore Dwight, David Humphreys, Richard Alsop, and Lemuel Hopkins, these gentlemen and their friends must have rubbed elbows at the store with persons of lesser talent who had rags, calves' pates, or hog bristles to sell. Many of the offerings on the shelves were issued from the Hudson & Goodwin press; and since the partners were publishers as well as printers, entirely in order were conversations pertinent to the business arrangements of publishing. Until the last months of the Revolution neither Congress nor the state legislatures had passed copyright laws, a fact about which some of the discussions likely turned in the winter of 1782–1783.

In the late summer of 1782 Hudson & Goodwin published John Trumbull's *M'Fingal* in a large duodecimo volume of 100 pages. Advertised as a modern epic poem, this satire on the Tories was probably the most popular American poem of its length before Longfellow's *Evangeline*.[96] It went through more than 30 subsequent editions and still reflects in its cracked and distorted mirror of caricature the turbulent town meetings, the liberty poles and bonfires, the secret gatherings of Loyalists, and the tar and feathers of the stormy days of the independence movement. It was almost immediately pirated. Trumbull wrote long afterward:

As no author, at that period, was entitled by law to the copyright of his productions, the work soon became the prey of every bookseller and printer, who chose to appropriate it to his own benefit. Among more than thirty different impressions, one only, at any subsequent time, was published with the permission, or even the knowledge of the writer; and the poem remained the property of newsmongers, hawkers, pedlars and petty chapmen.[97]

When the first edition went on sale in September the *Courant*'s publishers no longer enjoyed the security that came from a local printing monopoly. Bavil Webster and Nathaniel Patten, rival printers and booksellers, had hung out their signs in Hartford.[98] The *Courant* of the day before Christmas bore their joint announcement that they were printing their own editions of *M'Fingal* and that the public might expect copies at a price more reasonable than that which had been charged by Hudson & Goodwin.[99] Both unauthorized editions were issued before New Year's Day, and both were identical except for the imprints.[100] Trumbull and Hudson & Goodwin were naturally wroth at being robbed of the fruits of their labor. The *Courant* printed Trumbull's bitter, anonymous letter:

. . . The moment his work has gained the public attention, he finds it reprinted by another, and all efforts, of slander, advertisement, subscription, and every other ungenerous method taken to prevent the sale of his edition. Even his own subscribers forget their obligation, and suffer many hundred copies printed perhaps only to satisfy their subscriptions, to lie on hand as waste paper, while they wholly neglect their engagements and perhaps purchase the meaner and therefore cheaper edition of the mercenary invader of his property.[101]

Trumbull contended for a statutory prohibition of such larceny. It seemed to him that the scholar's hard years of study deserved reward as did the willingness of a poet to hazard his personal reputation by satirizing others. As if in response to his arguments, the General Assembly on the very next day passed "An Act for the encouragement of Literature and Genius" which secured to authors the sole right of publication of their works for 14 years.[102] This was too late to protect the author and publishers of *M'Fingal,* but the injustice they endured contributed to the security of those who would write and publish in the future.

The content of Nehemiah Strong's almanac, which Hudson & Goodwin published annually in the 1780's, was likewise appropriated by fellow printers.[103] Added to the number of local rivals were now Joel Barlow and Elisha Babcock who formed a printing partnership just after the close of the war.[104] One of the popular almanacs of the time was Bickerstaff's. In the *Courant* of November 9, 1784, Strong flatly accused Barlow & Babcock of having published an edition of Bickerstaff which had been compounded of his own and of one by Eben W. Judd of Waterbury. Nathaniel Patten, he said, had printed another under the same title which was entirely his own except for the poetry at the head. Patten ventured no answer, but Barlow & Babcock attributed Strong's actions to an inordinate desire to increase the sales of his own work.[105] The dispute ended when Judd corroborated Strong's charges and related that the accused partners, with whom he had contracted to publish, had delayed printing his almanac in order to issue their private Bickerstaff.[106] Since the annuals were not copyrighted, the courts offered no justice. Strong insisted that all concerned should henceforth avail themselves of legal protection.[107]

In September, 1783, Hudson & Goodwin published the first edition of Noah Webster's *American Spelling Book,* then known as the first part of *A Grammatical Institute of the English Language* and certainly one of the bestsellers in American history.[108] Webster reputedly incurred the whole risk except for a little help from Barlow.[109] Hudson & Goodwin agreed to accept the author's note for the printing bill provided they might issue any succeeding editions.[110] Dilworth's speller, then the standard, was of English authorship, and fortunately the times were propitious for an American text. The original edition of 5,000 copies was exhausted during the course of the winter.[111] As an increasing demand convinced Webster of the prospects of unusual success, he traveled about the country lecturing, proclaiming his book, urging copyright legislation where none existed, talking to booksellers, clergymen, educators, and writing Hudson & Goodwin to send copies to Philadelphia, Baltimore, New York, Boston, or wherever agents were willing to handle them.[112] Newspaper advertisements bore the endorsements of the presidents of Harvard and Yale and of other worthies whose names were used to conjure the sales which author and publishers desired.[113]

As the text grew in popularity, the publishers could hardly have hoped, in justice to their client or themselves, to have retained a national printing and selling monopoly. Transportation costs were not negligible and Webster feared the appearance of imitation spellers designed to evade the copyright laws, especially in areas remote from Hartford.[114] On November 1, 1786, Hudson & Goodwin purchased, for a "good and valuable consideration," the exclusive rights to print and sell the speller in Connecticut, Rhode Island, Massachusetts, and New Hampshire for the term of the copyrights in the states named. A concern in Philadelphia bought the sole rights to print and sell for three years in Pennsylvania, Delaware, Maryland, and Virginia, and to sell concurrently in New York, New Jersey, and the states south of Virginia. To Samuel Campbell, New York bookseller, went the right to print in New York for five years along with selling privileges in certain states outside New England.[115] Hence Hudson & Goodwin retained the New England monopoly; but even this was eventually unsatisfactory. Around Boston and in northern New England, the demand exceeded the supply.[116] Sometime in 1788 the partners resold to Webster their rights in Rhode Island, Massachusetts, and New Hampshire, retaining the Connecticut market and the legal chance to compete elsewhere if they chose to do so.[117] For several years they paid Webster a one cent royalty on each copy of the speller and finally made a lump sum settlement for the duration of the Connecticut copyright.[118]

Despite such arrangements Nathaniel Patten imported and sold hundreds of Webster's spellers in his Hartford bookstore. Early in 1788 Samuel Campbell hired Hudson & Goodwin to print 5,000 copies, requesting the delivery of 2,000 of them to Patten with whom he had contracted for binding. Trusting neither Campbell nor Patten, the partners refused to accommodate the latter without his pledge to refrain from selling the books anywhere in New England. Failing to receive assurances, the sheets were shipped to New York much to the chagrin of Campbell who returned 1,500 copies to Patten. Patten bound them forthwith and placed them on the Hartford market at 10 *d.* each, undercutting the established Connecticut price of 14 *d.* per copy.[119] For this assault upon their profits and privileges Hudson & Goodwin hailed their neighbor into court and for several years incurred his active acrimony.

In court, in newspaper letters and handbills, Patten charged Hudson & Goodwin with gross profiteering arising from the maintenance of a monopoly not consonant with the public interest.[120] The spellers, he said, could be bought in New York or Philadelphia and resold in Hartford at a 40 per cent profit at 6 *s.* per dozen or 8 *d.* apiece. Hudson & Goodwin charged 10 *s.* a dozen. Assuming an annual sale of 20,000 spellers, Patten proclaimed the possibility of saving the inhabitants of the state of Connecticut over £330 a year were he but permitted to do the printing and binding. He demanded an amendment to the copyright act allowing the importation of any book from outside the state and he called for the statutory lowering of the prices at which Hudson & Goodwin sold.[121] Although Webster's publishers denied profiteering, denied having sold more than 8,000 copies a year, denied that their accuser could match his boasts in practice, it was true that their spellers sold in Massachusetts for less than they were offered to the people of Connecticut.[122] They charged Patten publicly with having tried to arrange a price-fixing conspiracy with them, but were generally satisfied to rest their case with the law rather than with the newspapers.[123] They went to court several times, Webster supported them, and in all they received more than £100 damages.[124] Having lost his cause, Patten ran off a huge impression of Dilworth's texts and placed them for sale at 10 *d.*, 4 *d.* cheaper than the now well-advertised cost of Webster's little books.[125]

The Hudson & Goodwin press issued other works which were fortunately devoid of copyright complications. Among them were numerous editions of Webster's grammar and reader, which were parts two and three of the *Institute*.[126] His *Sketches of American Policy* came out in 1785; in the 1790's, his two-volume history of epidemic diseases, an essay on the effects of slavery, and the book of homilies entitled *The Prompter*.[127] Barlow's ambitious undertaking, the grandiose *Vision of Columbus,* went to press in 1787 and numbered Washington, Lafayette, and Louis XVI among its subscribers.[128] Hudson & Goodwin had the volume "bound, gilt and lettered by an Artist equal to any in America, and perhaps not inferior to any workman in London." [129] The partners inherited connections with Ethan Allen whose strictures on the state of New York had been first published by Watson.[130] They published two of his pamphlets, but when Allen galloped to Hartford to proffer the manuscript of his famous "Bible," the relationship terminated.[131] They had been willing to defy the government of New York, but when it came to affronting the church of the fathers they balked. Benjamin Trumbull's *History of Connecticut* went on sale in 1797 and other publications included the poetry or prose of Nathan Strong, some of the Hartford Wits, and lesser authors whose names were soon forgotten.[132]

In 1789 the partners undertook to publish *The Children's Magazine.* Although the project failed, it was noteworthy as the first attempt in America to issue periodical literature for young people: [133]

This work is designed to furnish children, from seven to twelve years of age, with a variety of lessons on various subjects, written in a plain, neat, familiar style, and proper to lead them from the easy language of Spelling-Books up to the more difficult style of the best writers. Teachers of Schools have long complained of the want of such a work, and the Publishers are happy that they are now enabled to furnish it at a small expense.[134]

From time to time Hudson & Goodwin also published works of a religious purpose designed to correct the misinformed or console the saved.[135] After 1800 they enhanced their reputation with the clergy and the pious folk generally; for five years they published and distributed monthly the *Connecticut Evangelical Magazine,* a product of the Connecticut Missionary Society. The profits were used to form a permanent fund, the annual interest of which went to support missions in the West and among the heathen. The number of copies for the period averaged 3,730 annually from which the society received over 11,000 dollars.[136] They published Timothy Dwight's *Psalms,* which were widely adopted in the Congregational churches, replacing Barlow's revision of *Watt's Psalms.*[137] They printed thousands of Testaments.[138] Beginning in 1809 large editions of the attractive Hudson & Goodwin Bible were printed from imported English types which were locked in iron chases ready to be placed on the press.[139] These bore the H & G monogram on the title page and were the first Bibles printed in Connecticut.[140]

During the long life of their partnership, the *Courant's* owners achieved the esteem given to successful business men and good family providers. They had been stockholders in the old Hartford Theater and were among the founders of the Hartford Library and the Hartford Fire Insurance Company.[141] Hudson had been honored by a seat in the first city council and had helped promote the Hartford Woolen Mill.[142] Goodwin had worked on the council for many years,[143] had contributed heavily to the support of the First Church, and held directorships in the Hartford Bank and the Hartford-New Haven Turnpike Company.[144] The firm had made room for the oldest boys, Hudson's son, Henry, and Richard Goodwin, and had financed two younger sons in the mercantile establishments of B. Hudson, Jr. & Co. and Sheldon & Goodwin.[145] Henry Hudson was a director of the fire insurance company [146] and secretary of the Connecticut Bible Society,[147] and still other sons of Goodwin were advertising businesses in the *Courant.*[148]

To provide yet more assuredly for the security of all concerned, Hudson & Goodwin dissolved their partnership on November 15, 1815.[149] The inventory accounted for over $120,000 in sound and productive assets and the division of properties was amicably arranged. The Goodwins took the *Courant,* the Testaments, the store building of Sheldon & Goodwin, the mills at the upper falls in East Hartford, and an undisclosed sum of money. The Hudsons took the Bible, Webster's spelling book, one of the paper mills, and the bookstore with its entire stock of goods. George Goodwin & Sons opened for business on the corner of Pratt and Main Streets. Hudson & Co. remained in the old store opposite the First Meeting House which had been patronized so long by the friends of the firm.

Over 40 years later, Samuel Goodrich recalled the firm's reputation and recorded his memory of Barzillai Hudson and George Goodwin:

I formed an acquaintance with . . . a clerk in the establishment of Hudson & Goodwin, a firm then known all over this hemisphere, as publishers of the Bible, Webster's Spelling-book, and the Connecticut Courant. They were, in the popular mind, regarded as the bulwarks of religion, education, and federalism—three pretty staunch supporters of the New England platform, in that epoch of the world. It is very seldom that plodding industry rises so high. Mr. Hudson was a homespun old respectability, of plain, strong sense, sturdy principles, and rather dry harsh manners, having also a limp in the leg. He took charge of the financial department of the concern. Mr. Goodwin was a large, hale, comely old gentleman, of lively mind and cheerful manners. There was always sunshine in his bosom and wit upon his lip. He turned his hand to various things, though chiefly to the newspaper, which was his pet. His heaven was the upper loft in the composition room; setting type had for him the sedative charms of knitting-work to a country dame. I have often seen him, cheerfully swinging back and forth, as is the wont of compositors, and tossing the type merrily over his thumb into the stick, as if he were at work by the thousand ems, and had a wife and nine small children dependent upon his labors! [150]

PART THREE
1815–1836

CHAPTER VIII

FROM FEDERALIST TO WHIG

IN contemplating events at the close of the War of 1812, it was unlikely that the Goodwins appreciated the extent to which the spirit of Federalism had waned. It seemed to them that Jefferson's system had been the offspring of the French Revolution and that "democracy" could linger but a few years longer in America.[1] Yet, in April, 1816, the Republicans elected a number of state officers and carried the town of Hartford.[2] In 1817 they placed Oliver Wolcott in the governorship and gained control of both branches of the legislature.[3] By the spring of the year following, so hopeless were the Federalists that they presented no ticket and made no campaign.[4] A good many old supporters had deserted the party, but the Goodwins stood their ground with the uncompromising, adhering to the "principles of Washington," and feeling respect and attachment for others who had remained equally staunch.[5]

Reminiscent of the agitation of 1806, the opposition campaigned on a "Toleration" or "American" platform calling for "union" with the federal government, for an end to state support of the established church, for a "legal" constitution, and for "universal suffrage."[6] As the legislature and the constitutional convention of 1818 proceeded to effect the Connecticut revolution, the *Courant* made a last general defense of the old Federalist order.

The idea of universal manhood suffrage was just as unpalatable as ever. According to the *Courant*'s writers, the desirable qualification for voters was good character. Every person with the essentials —honesty, prudence, and industry—could have acquired the property requisite for the franchise. Since government functioned principally for the protection of property, it followed that assessments against property financed government. It seemed especially unjust that improvident men, who were liable to the bribes of interested parties, should be placed in a position to vote away the possessions of others. The best government was not that which rested in the hands of the greatest number of voters but rather that which rested with the greatest number of "independent" voters. In short, the extension of the franchise to all men was inconsistent with genuine principles of civil liberty and the stability of society.[7] As to Jeffersonian cries of "We, the People!": *"The People* are that respectable and all-important middle class that stands between the great ones and the rabble, and checks the ambition of the one, and the licentiousness of the other." [8] The Goodwins thought that the people had done a good job of ruling themselves for the last 200 years.[9]

Although the movement for repeal of the religious laws, which the Methodists and Baptists endorsed, amounted to a demand that the support of all denominations should henceforth be voluntary, the *Courant*'s correspondents feared for the future of public worship itself.[10] Most of their letters accordingly argued society's need for religion. One of them wrote typically as follows:

Such is the state of human nature, that the sanctions of religion are necessary to give energy to law. Mankind are held back from wrong, by the commanding awe of a power infinitely superior to the power of their own creating; and are excited to the practice of the moral and social virtues, by the animating hope and assurance of future approbation and reward.[11]

The legislature's decision that the orthodox clergy should no longer have Election Day dinners at the state's expense, their removal from the list of tax-exempt individuals, and the shuffling and coughing with which members of the Convention greeted those who spoke in support of the Gospel, elicited resentful comments from the editors.[12]

Not all the arguments against the changes of 1818 were drawn from the two major issues. In providing that annual sessions of the legislature be held alternately at New Haven and Hartford, the new constitution deprived Hartford of her exclusive right to the traditional Election Days. The *Courant* alleged that this would depreciate real estate values and lose trade for hatters, goldsmiths, taverners, shoemakers, drygoods merchants, and other local business men. Eventually the entire government might be established at New Haven.[13] The motives of the "reformers" were frequently attacked, their zeal for change being attributed to the hope of lucrative posts for themselves rather than anything nobler.[14] The *Courant* bandied petty charges of fraud, corruption, and insincerity with the recently established *Hartford Times,* the *Mercury,* the *New Haven Register,* and other papers of the opposition.[15] The Goodwins' comment in one of the November issues of 1818 summarized a number of these charges and suggested the spirit in which they accepted defeat:

By the return of votes it appears that the good people of this state have ratified a Constitution, which was got up for party purposes, at a time when the two great political parties were nearly equal—which was proposed by a Convention, scarcely a member of which approved it, but voted for it for fear of a worse and which the citizens in general dislike. Only three weeks were allowed to print, circulate, read and understand it—the consequences of this unreasonable haste has been, that thousands in the state never saw it till it was read in town-meeting—In many towns debating on its merits was not allowed—and finally ratified, with all its defects, by a very small majority. How long the people will remain quiet under such a constitution remains to be seen.[16]

Although Federalism became practically untenable in Connecticut thereafter, deep and long-held convictions lingered on in the *Courant*'s columns for years to come.[17] An air of political nostalgia settled over the paper as illustrated by the following excerpt from a communication of 1821:

I repaired to Hartford in season to be present at the opening of the session, and not having much business to occupy my attention at home, I contented myself during the greater part of the session, in hearing the debates in the House of Representatives, and occasionally mixing amongst the members abroad, to observe what was going on both in and out of doors. My principal object in doing this was, to satisfy my own mind as to the truth or falshood of the numerous reports abroad, respecting the character and conduct of those to whose care the people have committed the management of their public concerns. I have returned home fully impressed with a belief that what I had previously heard was founded in truth.

Placing myself in a situation from which I could have a fair view of most of the members of the House, I was surprised on looking down amongst the members, to observe only a very few of those respectable characters, who a few years since adorned the seats of that honorable House. The complexion of every thing appeared to have changed from what it formerly was. The faces I saw were new; the rules of the house and the mode of transacting business was new—indeed, the whole order of things appeared to be changed, all which has given to the legislative proceedings the semblance of a foreign government, more than that of the old government of Connecticut, which, for nearly two centuries has rendered this community prosperous and happy.[18]

One of the newer political devices which the Goodwins could not countenance was the legislative nominating caucus. It seemed to them simply a case of the politicians telling the people for whom to vote.[19] They wrote, in 1825, that for many years the great body of the people had wielded little influence in elections.[20] Often they spoke of the caucuses as "midnight orgies" and of the nomination lists, quite disdainfully, as "caucus tickets." [21] The whole procedure, in their view, amounted to a violation of the election privileges of the citizens to whom the constitution guaranteed the right to vote for persons of their own choice.[22]

Partly from an abiding dissatisfaction with the trend in Connecticut politics and partly from the good feeling which characterized Monroe's two administrations, the Goodwins more or less washed their hands of politics for a while in the 1820's.[23] They noted the President's "affable, unaffected, and dignified deportment" and contrasted the independence of his Congresses with the servile assemblies of Jefferson and Madison.[24] They approved the tenor of national politics, endorsing especially the declaration of foreign policy expressed in the Monroe Doctrine.[25] They criticized Andrew Jackson's conduct in Florida and the extension of slavery into Missouri,[26] but neither of these created a furor of which the *Courant* made capital. The waning of "parties" accorded with Federalist ideas of propriety and from time to time the *Courant* remarked the pleasing signs of such abatement.[27] Only the Connecticut "democrats" were objectionable,[28] but the paper was listless in supporting local "anti-Caucus" tickets, speaking sometimes of the desirable union of "honest men," of Federalists and old Republicans who were alike opposed to the newer practices.[29] There was scarcely a suggestion of the excitement which formerly characterized the paper.

As the approach of the election of 1824 revived political rivalries throughout the country, the editors professed an indifference over the matter of candidates.[30] The *Courant* thought that John Quincy Adams, William H. Crawford, Henry Clay, and De Witt Clinton (Andrew Jackson was not mentioned) were all qualified for the presidency. The election of any of them would effect no appreciable change in the nation's affairs,[31] so there was little point in quarreling over who should have the president's $25,000 salary.[32] The paper consequently offered no election advice until caucus tickets appeared in Connecticut, one pledged to Adams and the other understood to be for Crawford. Readers were then urged to stay away from the polls: [33] "Let those vote who can—but those who are not willing to yield up the privilege of self-government will stay at home rather than sacrifice it on the altar of party and faction."[34] Old Federalists were subsequently congratulated for having generally failed to take part.[35]

As with the principles of the Monroe government, the Goodwins generally agreed with the administration of John Quincy Adams. But while they conceded the chief magistrate to have been a man of excellent talents and experience, they never forgave him for being a Federalist renegade.[36] It seemed to them, at that time and later, that Adams had certain traits which precluded him from the sincere respect of virtuous men—ambition, jealousy, suspicion, inconsistency, and even questionable integrity.[37] As late as the middle of July, 1827, the Goodwins announced that they were neither disposed to crowd their columns with Adams and Jackson material nor to enlist under the political banners of either.[38] And yet, as the autumn and winter months moved on, they began to take part in the long campaign of 1828, showing sympathy for Clay,[39] attacking the reputation of Jackson,[40] finally defending the Adams administration,[41] and generally endorsing what came to be known as the American System.

The Goodwins' attachment to the American System was grounded in an adherence to the principles of the protective tariff. This, in turn, had come about with the changing nature of New England's enterprise. After the late war, when Congress passed the tariff of 1816, no responsive words came from the *Courant*'s editors. They believed in those days that Providence had marked the destiny of the United States, with its many bays, harbors, inlets, and navigable rivers, for the pursuits of agriculture and commerce; and that continued and extensive manufacturing, while capable of enriching the few, invariably impoverished the masses of the people.[42] By the fall of 1823 they had adopted other views. They were then hoping that the time might come when Americans could get government encouragement to supply themselves with all varieties of manufactured commodities which were currently imported from abroad.[43]

According to the *Courant,* the iron and textile interests which were clamoring for protection, were squeezed by British competition, and several well-managed woolen concerns about Hartford had recently quit business.[44] Although the objection to the tariff had been that it merely enriched the capitalists, the Goodwins denied this by discussing recent price reductions in coarse cotton fabrics which had been covered in the tariff of 1816.[45] In finally advocating the tariff bill of 1824, they urged attendance at meetings in Middletown and Hartford to memorialize Congress on the subject, at the same time giving generous publicity to the "Society for the Promotion of Manufactures, Mechanic Arts, and National Industry." [46] The opposition to the bill was attributed to the big city commercial and foreign interests. Its passage, they thought, would promote more prosperity in the country than anything since the beginning of the government.[47]

If the Goodwins had already begun to feel strongly on the tariff question,[48] it was small wonder that the *Courant* took up cudgels to dispute the presidential claims of a westerner whose views on the important issues of the day were nebulous. Nor was it surprising that readers were asked to recognize, at last, the relative merits of Adams' New England birthplace and his proven friendship for domestic manufactures and internal improvements.[49] In the person of Jackson himself, the *Courant*'s publishers sensed a determined enemy of protective principles, a feeling in no way dispelled by the political maneuvers of the tariff of 1828 which the paper correctly analyzed for its readers.[50] As the *Courant* came to look at the election of 1828, it lay between the advocates of that policy on which depended the success and prosperity of the manufactures, the progress of internal improvements, and the dignity and welfare of the country, on the one side; and on the other, a motley combination composed of the bitter foes of the tariff and internal improvements, Adams' personal enemies, and a generous assortment of unhorsed politicians and demagogues itching for public office.[51]

Rather than deal primarily with issues, the *Courant* followed the fashion of the campaign and laid before its readers an extended examination of Jackson's military record on the southern border— a scrutiny that revealed him to have been not only deficient in forbearance and gentlemanly conduct, but to have been also a pretty dangerous prospect for the country. From the Goodwin editorials, his chief claim to fame, aside from the postwar victory at New Orleans and certain triumphs over the savages, consisted of repeated instances of headstrong insubordination and misused authority in Louisiana and Florida. He had disobeyed the Secretary of War, insulted the governor of Georgia, arrested a legislator, imprisoned a federal judge, stopped the deliberations of a legislative assembly, violated the writ of *habeas corpus,* and generally oppressed the people, to say nothing of the needless bloodshed attached to his professional operations. In his more private intercourse, he had shown a ferocious and ungovernable temper that had led him to avenge insults at the expense of the laws of decency.[52] In a campaign characterized by a notable amount of billingsgate, the Goodwins claimed to refrain from personal and abusive attacks and preferred, as they declared, to let the well-authenticated facts of the public record speak for themselves.[53] As the *Courant* reiterated, one who would lead should first learn to obey; and certainly, on these grounds, the doughty westerner had shown himself totally unfit to preside over the destinies of the Republic.[54]

In its appeals to Connecticut voters, the *Courant* at times recovered its old political vitality. Zest was added to the campaign by the appearance of local Jackson groups in the spring of 1828.[55] Candidates were being nominated for state office by county conventions rather than by legislative caucus. Two complete state tickets were placed in the field, one favoring Jackson and the other against him.[56] John M. Niles, Noah A. Phelps, and Gideon Welles were not only whipping up Jackson sentiment in the *Hartford Times,* but were taking a fling at the spadework of party organization.[57] The *Times* smeared the Adams men with taunts of "Federalism" and the Goodwins resented it, making light of Jackson meetings about the state and showing no serious concern over the possible outcome in Connecticut.[58] Two months before the election, the *Courant* professed to discern a favorable swing in the national sentiment as the facts of Jackson's record had gained exposure and circulation. The editors were reasonably assured of the good results of the November balloting, especially since they saw indications that the votes of New York, Pennsylvania, Virginia, Indiana, Kentucky, and Louisiana would be cast for Adams.[59] Concerning the final decision of the people, which probably displeased George Goodwin as had none other since 1800, the *Courant* printed the following postelection statement:

We have advocated the re-election of Mr. Adams, not from any partiality to the man, but from a sense of duty, and an honest conviction that in the present crisis, the honor and welfare of the country depended on his success. We most sincerely regret his defeat, and feel the deepest solicitude for the consequences. The elevation of a man like General Jackson to the first office in the Government, we can regard in no other light than a national calamity—a foul stain on the character of our country—a comment on our republican institutions which cannot fail to degrade us in the eyes of other nations, and damp the hopes of the friends of freedom and good government throughout the world.[60]

The Goodwins thought that the reader of Jackson's inaugural address would have been puzzled to discover anything sufficiently definite to be inconsistent with the most opposite courses of policy; [61] but when the first tangible fruits of the new administration reached Hartford, they were not calculated to appease the supporters of Adams. Noah A. Phelps of the *Times* became the customs collector at Middletown; Benjamin H. Norton, recently a *Times* publisher, displaced an old-school Republican at the Hartford Post Office; Norton was in turn almost immediately removed in favor of John M. Niles, also of the *Times*.[62] This last maneuver, which was attributed to Gideon Welles, the *Courant* deemed an outrage upon the community, asserting that Niles was in the highest degree odious to more than nine tenths of the local citizens.[63] The Goodwins recorded a sizable protest meeting composed of 300 of the city's leading citizens (Welles reported an attendance of 140, mostly boys) and wrote that the scandal produced a pitch of excitement which they had rarely witnessed.[64] As to conditions elsewhere, the *Courant* claimed that it lacked the space to print the long lists of faithful government servants who were ousted to accommodate Jackson's henchmen.[65]

The Goodwins' greatest solicitude during Jackson's first term was for the preservation of the tariff of 1828. Their arguments were repetitious and general. Although particular rates were in some respects objectionable, they thought that every effort should be made to prevent repeal or emasculation.[66] They capitalized the issue in the state election of 1829. They decried the appointment to the Cabinet of men whose sentiments were unfavorable to the development of domestic manufactures. They looked ahead uncomfortably to the convening of the first Democratic Congress.[67] Jackson's equivocal public utterances were written off as so much political appeasement, evidences of a temporizing policy calculated to break down the whole tariff system.[68] As time went on, the *Courant* noted and encouraged public meetings to support the American System, always with dominant reference to the tariff.[69] According to the editors, New England had the employment of laborers, the prosperity of farmers, and tremendous investments in manufacturing establishments at stake in this particularly urgent issue: [70]

The importance of manufactures to New England must be acknowledged by all. Our commerce has long been declining, and is now too limited to prove a source of general prosperity. In the circumstances of our situation there are insuperable obstacles to agricultural enterprise with reference to a distant market. The low price of lands in the west, the richness and fertility of the soil, with the constantly increasing facilities for transportation, render it impossible for our farmers to compete with that section of the country, in their agricultural productions. With their habits of industry and frugality they may obtain from their farms sufficient to support their families—but without a market for their produce at home, they can do little more than this. Our only source is manufactures, and on them chiefly must the future wealth and prosperity of New England depend. In the encouragement of this branch of industry, therefore, the citizens of this state may be expected to feel a deep interest. It is a cause in which all classes in the community are concerned. Its success will benefit not merely a separate and distinct portion of the inhabitants, but the whole mass of our population. Thriving manufacturing establishments in our villages, will create a market at home for the produce of the neighboring farmers; they will furnish employment for the industrious mechanic, and give life and activity to the business of our cities.[71]

If the waning of commerce and the rise of manufactures explained the Goodwins' postwar conversion to the principles of protection, it also accounted for their warm endorsement of nationalism, an equally far cry from the *Courant*'s views during the sessions of the Hartford Convention. In the earlier years, Connecticut's merchants had desired the government to leave them alone, but nowadays her industrialists demanded the government's fostering care.[72] Consequently the tariff nullification movement in South Carolina was not only disapproved but was made in some sense to discredit the advocates of "free trade." [73] The Goodwins thought that Daniel Webster's principles, enunciated in the famous debates with Robert Y. Hayne, lay at the foundations of our civil institutions and would prove as enduring as the very structure of American government.[74] The past was not so much forgotten as forgiven.

The stability and permanence of the Union, is a subject of deep and solemn import to every sincere lover of his country. . . . The throes, which ushered our present constitution into being, the angry storms of party violence which rocked its infant cradle, and the austere scrutiny which it has endured from its friends as well as enemies during the whole stage of its existence, are sufficient to endear the sacred instrument to the American people.[75]

The Bank question was important also. In a discussion of Jackson's first message to Congress, the *Courant* prophesied the doom of the Second United States Bank if means lay within the President's power to accomplish it.[76] The Goodwins considered the issue pressing enough in the summer of 1830 to print a four-page supplement of the bank report of the House Ways and Means Committee.[77] When the Bank's directors applied for a new charter in 1832, the *Courant's* editorials thought that the whole question was one of the highest moment to the people of the entire country. The continued existence of the Bank was so vital to the financial operations of the government and to the preservation of a sound national currency that there could be little doubt as to the favorable sentiment of the people of Hartford.[78] The editors pushed other material aside to publish the President's veto message and Webster's speech in defense of the institution.[79] Allegations of the Democratic papers as to any improper political influence of the Bank's officials were simply brushed away as absurd.[80] The motivation of Jackson's behavior, as it was set forth in the *Courant,* lay in his unquenchable thirst for power. It was not sufficient that he controlled all the executive departments and the land and Indian agencies with more than 20,000 appointive positions, including 9,000 post offices and salaries totaling more than $20,000,000; but now the monetary institutions must be brought to bay, the present one abolished, and new Jackson banks set up under the aegis of presidential sovereignty.[81]

The internal improvements issue failed to take very much of the *Courant's* attention except to be mentioned incidentally, mostly during campaigns. No serious attempt was made to exploit Jackson's enmity for public works except in a rather minor way when he vetoed bills for removing obstructions from the Connecticut and Thames rivers.[82] The policy endorsing government appropriations for the increase of facilities of travel and transportation had significant connections not only with the tariff and Bank questions, but also with questions of westward migration and western land prices—connections which were probably well enough recognized by the Connecticut politicians, land speculators, and business men. But the Goodwins apparently never felt called upon, in the course of political agitation, to offer a rounded discussion of the implications of any of these issues. An earlier lack of enthusiasm for westward road and canal construction might have been imputed to them from an editorial of October, 1817. Having mentioned the great numbers of people moving westward, the fall in eastern real estate values, and the rising prices of western land, they continued:

As to the thousands and tens of thousands who, with their families, go on destitute, or with little or nothing more than to carry them to their journey's end, they will fall into two divisions. One part, and probably the greater part, must be labourers, by the month or day, in the service of such men as are willing or able to employ them. And will their labour maintain them better there than it would at home? It is doubtful, and more than doubtful. For these excessive emigrations occasion scarceness and dearness of labour in the old settlements, and a corresponding plenty and cheapness of it in the new. Not to mention that they must be in the employ of utter strangers, of whom a great proportion will be found fair in speech, but of knavish intentions; and that they will have a small chance, if any, of redressing the wrongs they suffer, in places where Law is less scarce than dear. The other division is properly termed, the Forlorn Hope. Finding grace in the eyes of the landlords, they purchase of them acres of wilderness on long credit, with the written promise of a title when the money is paid. At it they go. They build, they clear up, they plant and sow; but after their utmost exertions accompanied with distressing privations, the most they can do is barely to keep themselves and their families from starvation and nakedness. Payday comes, and they are utterly unprepared. Of course they are turned off penniless, to seek their fortunes amidst the deeper shades of the dismal forest. If it be not always so, we have reason to believe it is often so, and even in a great majority of instances.[83]

In 1829 and 1830 the Goodwins displayed extensive interest in the drawn-out dispute between the Cherokees and the state of Georgia. At that time they published a series of twenty-four long articles from the *National Intelligencer* along with additional material bearing upon the controversy.[84] Whether or not such a barrage of publicity stirred the citizens of Hartford, they convened one evening in January, 1830, to memorialize Congress to adopt all necessary measures to protect the Indians in the possession of their lands and government against intrusions of Georgia's sovereignty.[85] No matter how accurately Jackson's attitude reflected the views of western Americans or of the people of Georgia, the *Courant* had nothing but wholehearted sympathy for the position of the Indians, and nothing but criticism for the chief executive and his congressional supporters.[86] According to the Goodwins, it was easy for the Jacksonians to ascribe a sincere interest in behalf of the Indians to political prejudices, mawkish sensibility, or even hypocritical pretensions, but such criticism could hardly alter the facts of history or erase from its pages the violation of national faith.[87] When finally the governor of Georgia defied the Supreme Court and the Jackson prints applauded him for doing so, the *Courant* more or less trembled with editorial anxiety. Southerners were declaring the tariff unconstitutional, the Bank was being assailed, internal improvements were denounced, and now the authority of the Supreme Court of the United States was set at naught, all under the banner of "Liberty and Reform." If this new variant of nullification were sustained, so it was said, the federal government had indeed come to the end of the road.[88]

All this disapproval of what the *Courant* called Jacksonism became the rallying point of the conservative party in Connecticut. Jackson's election in 1828 had stimulated local politics. The Goodwins themselves, now thoroughly revived, thought that the people had been long enough disgraced by relatively incompetent representatives while men of known talent and dignity sat at home.[89] They therefore proposed, before the spring election of 1829, to make inquiries about the state in order to draw up and print a list of candidates tuned to the people's tastes. Such a list, called the "Independent Ticket," and supposedly composed of tried men from the old Federalist and Jeffersonian parties, later carried the state.[90] The Connecticut Jacksonians, to believe the *Courant,* were under the personal control of the *Times* "junto," and, although efficiently organized on a state-wide basis, were generally viewed with distaste for their avowed hostility to northern institutions and northern prosperity.[91] Asserting that old party lines had disappeared, that old political enemies had united in defense of good government, the *Courant* rebuked the *Times* for its frequent employment of such resurrected battle phrases as "priestcraft," "Hartford Convention," "bigotry," "Church and State," "aristocracy," and "federalism." [92] Much to the sorrow of the Goodwins, the Jacksonians carried Hartford County and even the town of Hartford in the election of 1830; but Jackson's enemies continued to hold the state under various party names in 1830, 1831, and 1832, always claiming to defend New England's workingmen and farmers against the protagonists of British manufacturers, and always busily supported in the *Courant's* partisan columns.[93]

The rise of the Antimasonic party introduced a new but minor note into the state politics of these years. The *Courant* respectfully noticed the activities and even solicited the votes of those who argued the social menace of secret fraternities, but had little real sympathy for their contentions.[94] The Goodwins expressed themselves unequivocally:

We have no inclination to engage in the prevailing controversy between masonry and anti-masonry. With our present views, we shall not deviate from the course we have hitherto pursued. Facts and documents which we may deem important and interesting to the public generally, we shall continue to publish; and in the selection of them we shall be governed by the exercise of our own judgment, and not by the dictation of our neighbors. The writer of this article is not a mason, and has no partiality for masonry. He is perfectly willing that those who consider it their duty should expose its evils, and use all fair and honorable means to enlighten and direct public sentiment in regard to it. But knowing as he does that some of the most worthy and valuable men in the country have been and still are members of the fraternity, he can never approve of that spirit which proscribes and denounces as enemies to their country and unworthy of public confidence, all who happen to be connected with this institution.[95]

By the election of 1832, the believing reader of the *Courant* had gained certain general impressions of the two leading candidates for the presidency. Henry Clay had been long ago presented as a man of splendid talents and unimpeached integrity whose faithful services to the nation had been viciously attacked by his political opponents.[96] His sponsorship of the broad, national program for which the *Courant* contended was a matter of common knowledge; and in recent months the many notices of "Clay meetings" about the country attested the national proportions of his popularity.[97] Andrew Jackson, on the contrary, was said to have come to the nation by means of a sectional conspiracy. He was the head of a party signally devoid of a constructive national program. The Goodwins had on occasions regarded Jackson with condescension as the tool of unprincipled counselors who had arranged to foist the Calhoun controversy upon him and who had betrayed him into an embarrassing and disgraceful quarrel with the members of his Cabinet.[98] They had spoken of his administration as "weak," profligate, declining in popularity, and had professed to believe that Jackson could not again seek an office which he had filled with such willful incompetence.[99]

It mattered not, they wrote, whether the will of Jackson were guided by ignorance or by design; it mattered not whether internal improvements were to be abandoned, or whether manufacturing, employment, and capital were to be annihilated. Men long known to the public for their wisdom, men who had studied the principles of government and the conduct of national rulers, were said to be raising their voices as they had never raised them before. They were not warning of petty encroachments of power or of trifling peculations from the public treasury, but they were staking their integrity upon the assertion that the confederation of the states was in jeopardy. The issue of the hour was nothing less than the preservation of the Union! The Goodwins declared that the contest between Jackson and Clay was more important than any since the formation of the national government.[100]

The *Courant* claimed to have no fears for the outcome in Connecticut, and certainly the editors did about as well as anyone could have expected. They encouraged their friends and beset their enemies. They urged the Antimasons to desert their own nominee in favor of Clay and the National Republicans. They crowded the *Courant* with so much of the stuff of politics as to make them apologize to those readers who became annoyed. They printed a lengthy series of letters from the *National Intelligencer* exposing the alleged usurpations, profligacy, and dangerous principles of the Jackson administration. In conclusion, they inserted what they deemed to have been one of Webster's masterly addresses upon the present state of the Union.[101]

The following forecast, giving Clay a majority of the electoral votes, they thought to be a fair estimate of the national picture: [102]

Certain for Clay:		*Probably for Clay:*
Connecticut	Maryland	Maine
Delaware	Massachusetts	Missouri
Indiana	New Jersey	
Kentucky	Ohio	
Louisiana	Rhode Island	

Certain for Jackson:		*Probably for Jackson:*
Alabama	New York	Illinois
Georgia	North Carolina	
Mississippi	Virginia	
New Hampshire	Tennessee	

Certain for Wirt [Antimason]:

Pennsylvania
Vermont   [South Carolina not mentioned]

Clay's victory in Connecticut was as overwhelming as his defeat in the nation. The *Courant* had swallowed bitter disappointment before without appreciable grace, and the present proved no exception to the past. The prospect of another four years with Old Hero was all but intolerable:

> The hopes entertained a short time since, that the present incumbent would be compelled to retire from a station for which he is so poorly qualified and which he has so unworthily filled, have been wholly disappointed. The people have decided, and so it must be, that Andrew Jackson shall administer the affairs of this government for another term. We have no disposition to disguise our regret and mortification at such a result. The line of conduct pursued by the present administration, as we have believed, and do still believe, has been marked with corruption unparalleled in the history of our republic. The doctrines and principles which have been put forth by its authority are at war with the constitution, and calculated, if carried out in their practical results, to subvert our government, and dissolve the Union of the States. With these views we cannot but lament the issue of the election. We fear the consequences of again entrusting the great interests of this nation to one whose official conduct furnishes so little to inspire confidence and so much to excite apprehension and distrust; whose whole life testifies to his incompetency and unfitness for any important civil station.[103]

After the election, the tariff and nullification disputes were compromised. The Goodwins applauded Jackson the only time in their newspaper career for his proclamation to the people of South Carolina. They hoped it might scotch nullification by appealing, if not to the leaders, at least to the deluded followers of that movement.[104] But more and more, letters, resolutions, and debates, including the philippics of Calhoun, Clay, Webster, and Adams, pointed up the crisis.[105] The *Courant* feared for the Union. The momentous question could not longer be avoided. Whether it lay in the power of a single state to prostrate the government and dissolve the federation would now be decided.[106] The *Courant* likewise feared for the tariff. Rich merchants from the seaports and the great planters from the South would add to their ships and slaves, but workers might soon have dark bread and exist after the mode of the underfed creatures of Manchester and Birmingham.[107] As a result of such apprehensions, Clay's compromise tariff of 1833, which provided for a gradual reduction of duties, proved to be moderately acceptable.[108] It had originated, thought the Goodwins, from sincerely patriotic motives. It was about the best that the manufacturers could have expected. It had disposed of the nullification crisis; it would give adequate protection for some years to come; and if, in the future, it should bring hardship to any one section of the country, it might then be modified in view of existing circumstances. It seemed very probable to them that later modification would be necessary.[109]

In the autumn of 1833, as rumors of the impending removal of government funds from the Bank were circulating the country, the *Courant's* publishers hoped that the President would act quickly and definitely in order to end the uncertainty and "lack of confidence" allegedly pervading the currency market.[110] When Jackson acted, the *Courant* placed its initial phrases of disapprobation on the high plane of constitutionality. Jackson's attempt to cripple the Bank was accordingly a defiance of law, contempt for Congress, the transgression of delegated power, a dangerous precedent, and injurious to republican principles.[111] In publishing the President's address and Secretary Roger B. Taney's report to Congress, the Goodwins thought that the latter's solemn discussion of the removal of the funds as a studied exercise of his own responsibility smacked of the ludicrous.[112] The *Courant* printed the report of the directors of the Bank along with lengthy speeches by Clay and by James K. Polk.[113] The directors, according to the Goodwins, ably exposed the sophistry and calumny of the arguments employed by Jackson, Taney, and the administration supporters.[114] All this was discouraging for the friends of Clay, but the people would eventually make known whether they preferred broken banks and depreciated notes to a system of uniform currency, especially when they discovered, amidst conditions likely to ensue, that if moneyed men suffered losses, the laboring class would suffer more.[115]

Within a month of writing this lugubrious forecast, the *Courant* carried reports of a derangement of business which was easily interpreted as the natural outcome of Jackson's misdirected persistence:[116]

Every day brings with it melancholy evidence of the disastrous consequences which the policy of the administration is producing in our country. The cry of distress is borne on every breeze—it comes from every quarter. In the larger cities, it is witnessed in the general prostration of business, the destruction of confidence and credit, constantly occurring failures, want of employment and want of the means of subsistence. The manufacturing villages, which have sprung up within a few years on every stream in New England and with their active and busy population opened new sources of wealth to the surrounding country, already feel the blighting influence of the President's rash and oppressive measures. The products of manufacturing labor no longer find a ready market—the owners are consequently compelled to suspend or curtail their operations; machinery is stopped, wages are reduced, workmen dismissed, industry paralyzed, and both owners and operatives threatened with bankruptcy and poverty. The agricultural classes also, who are generally more independent of the fluctuations of business than any other portion of the community, are seriously affected by the shock— the price of produce is greatly reduced, and purchases at any price are with difficulty obtained. The farmers are beginning to feel, and feel sensibly, the effects of President Jackson's experiment with the currency. They are undoubtedly destined to feel them still more sensibly. Some of the most prosperous and thriving agricultural sections of the country, are sending their memorials to Congress for relief. Mechanics too, must, and do already share in the general calamity. No portion of the community unless it be the office holders, speculators, and moneyed capitalists, are exempted. All who depend on their industry and credit for support, must, and do suffer.[117]

Such disaster, wrote the Goodwins, had sprung from the mere will and passion of a solitary human being bent upon self-gratification and the promotion of the political fortunes of his confidential cronies.[118]

The prolonged and blighting depression with which the Goodwins threatened their readers failed to develop in the year 1834. The employment of hyperbole had long been an American habit and it may have been that the *Courant,* which was as prone as other papers to exaggerate for political effect, was calculating in terms of the spring election of that year. In the previous spring, the Democrats had carried the state and the town of Hartford in what the paper called an apathetic contest.[119] Whatever the accuracy of this characterization, it was apparent that Jackson's final thrust at the Bank and the subsequently reported depression of business activity had stimulated action among the local opponents of the administration. The *Courant* now called them "Whigs" and under the new party designation, was glad to report, both in the spring and in the fall Congressional elections, that they had ousted the "Tories" from office.[120] But from the time of the spring election of 1835, the aspect of affairs changed.

Ever since the close of the War of 1812 the *Courant* had failed to display the sustained political spirit which had filled it during the administrations of Jefferson and Madison. The course of events which now ensued fairly dissipated whatever zeal the hostility to

Jackson had since stirred up. It seemed that nothing more, under the circumstances, could be done about either the tariff or the Bank issue. Jackson's followers took credit for the extinguishing of the national debt; [121] pleasing arrangements were made to distribute the government's surplus funds to the states; [122] a railroad mania seized New England; [123] and the economic consequences of Jackson's misdeeds were therefore not convincingly demonstrable in Connecticut. The local Democrats had presently achieved a fresh rallying point in the person of Martin Van Buren and the Whigs had little choice but to assume a defensive position. The state campaign of 1835 was vigorously conducted with the *Courant* training its guns on the alleged corruption of Van Buren and the Albany Regency, and denying all the while that banks or monopolies had a thing to do with the contest. [124] But to no avail, for the completeness of the Democratic victory left the Goodwins bemoaning Connecticut's "degradation" and commenting ruefully, when Governor-elect Henry W. Edwards entered Hartford, that "The Carmen and Butchers, in uniform and appropriate dresses, also joined the cavalcade in Wethersfield." [125] John M. Niles, Hartford's erstwhile postmaster, became a United States senator. [126] The spring elections of 1836 produced no general changes and the *Courant* seemed appreciably discouraged. [127]

Whatever hope the Goodwins might have had for a revival of major issues lay in the presidential elections in the fall of that year. They hoped that the Whigs would support Daniel Webster whose broad statesmanship and whose allegiance to the Constitution and the Union they had long admired. [128] But the Connecticut party endorsed William H. Harrison, a nomination which apparently left the *Courant* cold. [129] The Goodwins continued to treat Jackson with occasional venom, but never got around to nailing the names of Harrison and Granger or of any other pair of Whig candidates to the *Courant*'s editorial head. [130] The nation's Whigs were failing to achieve unity anyway, so the prospects for November were quite thoroughly dull.

At this point in the ebb of political fortunes the Goodwins chose to terminate their newspaper business by disposing of the ownership of the *Courant* to John L. Boswell. [131] The *Courant*'s new proprietor supported Harrison, but even the votes of Connecticut contributed to the election of Van Buren. [132] None of this pleased the Whigs, but at least the country would have no more of Jackson. Boswell's editorial of March 4, 1837, must have reminded the

Courant's readers of the familiar sentiments of old George Goodwin and his sons:

Yesterday the administration of Andrew Jackson came to an end. During the period in which he has presided over the United States, more frequent inroads have been made, by executive influence and example, upon the principles and provisions of the constitution, than had occurred since the organization of the government; and at the same time, a system of corruption has been introduced into the political concerns of the Union, which bids fair to destroy what the bolder strokes of despotic authority have left remaining.

CHAPTER IX

BENEVOLENCE AND BUSINESS

CONCOMITANT with the decline of the old order in Connecticut, the *Courant* became marked with a strong spirit of religion and humanitarianism. About the beginning of this period, four state societies were established whose works accounted for some of the activities in which the *Courant* took considerable interest. The Connecticut Bible Society, among whose directors were the leaders of the clergy and of the Federalist party, gave Bibles to the poor and to the western emigrants and frontiersmen.[1] The Connecticut Society for the Promotion of Good Morals furthered the preaching of "moral" sermons and campaigned against intemperance.[2] The Domestic Missionary Society for Connecticut and Vicinity was chartered in 1816, and the New England Tract Society established a branch about the same time.[3] The *Courant* bore the notices of local units of some of these groups and of organizations whose general aims were similar. Included among the latter were the Foreign Missionary Society,[4] the Evangelical Tract Society,[5] The Young Men's Auxiliary Missionary and Auxiliary Bible Societies,[6] the Marine Bible Society,[7] the Young Men's Benevolent Society,[8] the Young Ladies' Charitable Society,[9] the Female Tract Society,[10] and the Society for the Education of Indigent Young Men for the Ministry.[11] There were a good many notices of parishioners who made their pastors life members in one or another of the Bible societies;[12] and, on one occasion, of the inmates of the state prison who presented the warden with a permanent membership in the Connecticut Society.[13] Young women were urged to spin for the heathen. In one of the *Courant*'s issues, a group of young men advertised for farm land, the proceeds from which they intended to donate to missions.[14] The *Courant* gave publicity to the Cornwall Mission School and to the labors of missionaries in the Sandwich Islands. On the whole it reflected a notable amount of religious enthusiasm and interest among Hartford people.[15]

Emerging from the same spirit of uplift were a variety of engagements in behalf of the oppressed and the poor both abroad and at home. Appeals, concerts, fairs, lectures, societies, or rallies were advertised for the benefit of the Mohicans,[16] the Cherokees,[17] the

Jews,[18] the Greeks, and the Negroes. Aid for the last two, the *Courant* especially solicited. It heartily encouraged local efforts to support the cause of Greek independence with money, clothes, and missionaries,[19] and gave a great deal of publicity to the American Colonization Society whose program was to settle Negroes in Liberia.[20] The Hartford Sunday School Society took shape as a means of educating local underprivileged and uninstructed youngsters.[21] The Hartford Female Beneficent Society used donations from lectures, exhibitions, fairs, and church collections, to care for homeless and indigent girls.[22] The *Courant* carried begging editorials for the Orphan Asylum for Boys, established in 1832.[23] Sentiment arose against the imprisonment of debtors [24] and citizens were urged to inspect the new poor farm and jail which it was hoped would be self-supporting: "The building is spacious, one wing of wood, the other of brick, and must be pleasant to its tenants who are disposed to peace and order; while there are suitable apartments, well bolted and ironed for the refractory." [25] Charitable deeds toward the poor, wrote the Goodwins, were admirably adapted to give success to measures designed for their moral and spiritual improvement. Without their confidence, nobody could expect to exercise a salutary influence over their habits and character.[26]

The Goodwins were interested in the American Asylum for the Deaf and Dumb, established at Hartford in 1816. It was the first school of its kind in America:

Why should not these unfortunate beings be educated? Why are they not to be taught how to be useful and happy? Why are they not to be taught concerning God and their own souls, and how to read the word of life? Why are not these unfortunate beings more immediately and imperatively objects of our charity, than the heathen of Asia or the idolators of the Southern Ocean? [27]

The people of Hartford supported this institution generously, financing the travels of Thomas H. Gallaudet who brought Laurent Clerc back from Paris.[28] Gallaudet and Clerc conducted public exhibitions of their work. The Asylum drew pupils from a number of states and became one of the show places of Hartford.[29] The *Courant,* always warm in its praise, rejoiced in the emergence of some of the students from darkness and ignorance into the enjoyment of intellectual day and the "glorious light of gospel truth." [30]

This was eminently an age, wrote a committee of the Connecticut Medical Society, for religious, charitable, and humane institutions.[31] The doctors reported a state population of between five and six hundred "insane" persons in 1821 and forthwith formed plans to build the first Connecticut hospital for the mentally diseased.[32] The contributions of local citizens established the Retreat for the Insane at Hartford, which opened for the reception of patients on April 1, 1824.[33] According to the *Courant,* it was situated on high ground about a mile and a quarter from the State House and commanded a delightful view of the Connecticut River. The building, which was equipped with modern basement furnaces, accommodated about 50 patients and a like number of staff members. The Goodwins spoke of the whole project as a great piece of Christian benevolence, averring that the afflicted would get the kindliness, the moral, and the medical regimen which would likely restore them to sanity.[34] For many years the *Courant* apprised the public of the accomplishments and needs of the institution.[35]

Connecticut's first savings bank, established at Hartford in 1819, likewise attracted sentiments of benevolence. Economy and morality were customarily coupled in the *Courant*'s phraseology. The Goodwins accordingly recognized the virtue of institutionalizing the poor man's thrift. The office of The Society for Savings, accepting small deposits at 6½ per cent interest each six months, functioned with the stated design "to aid and assist the poorer and middling classes of society, in putting their money out to advantage." [36] Repeating Franklin's famous advice, the *Courant*'s owners urged them to accumulate their pennies and reported the patronage of children, widows, and "laboring females." One of the last saved the commendable sum of $55.00 in less than three years.[37] The attitude which the bank inspired might have been inferred, if from nothing else, from a part of the report which the *Courant* printed at the end of the Society's first two months of operation. According to this, the depositors were noted to have been 112 minors, 15 domestics, 16 females, 4 widows, 4 married women, 2 nurses, 2 dressmakers, 6 laborers, 2 clerks, 2 apprentices, 1 barber, 1 printer, 1 bank clerk, 1 grocer, 1 potter, 1 cabinetmaker, and 1 farmer.[38]

Having long regarded seminaries of learning as adjuncts of public morality, the *Courant* devoted an increasingly broad attention to the education of young people. Washington College, established by the Episcopalians at Hartford in 1824, was for years admired as one of the city's bright ornaments.[39] The Hartford Female Seminary (1829) likewise received the perennial compliments of publicity.[40] The Goodwins were not alone interested in higher education and in education for girls, but in manual training for boys,[41] schools for "infants," [42] instruction for the blind,[43] and, most of all, in public elementary schools. They hoped the day to be near when common schools, under improved regulations and in connection with the Sabbath schools, could be supported by every village in the United States.[44]

In 1827, when Gallaudet, Chauncey A. Goodrich, and other residents of Hartford County sponsored "The Society for the Improvement of Common Schools," the *Courant* noted a growing concern for education about the country.[45] Later, when teachers in Massachusetts were organizing to promote desirable reforms, the paper contended that Connecticut had fallen behind and that many of her schools, manned by underpaid and incompetent teachers, were closed for most of the months of the year. This condition might not have worried the wealthy, the Goodwins thought, but no really considerate person could regard it with complete indifference.[46] The *Courant*'s arguments advocated more taxes and less apathy.[47] The first state convention of teachers met at Hartford in 1830 under the chairmanship of Noah Webster, and the *Courant* supported it heartily.[48]

The paper also depicted and abetted the strivings of the adults of Hartford for art, music, books, history, science, and literature. The Natural History Society, the Connecticut Historical Society, and the Horticultural Society were organized.[49] The Hartford Museum, occasional exhibits of paintings, a proliferation of musical societies, concerts, libraries, and numbers of public lectures were some of the signs of a popular cultural awakening which marked the growing community of these years.

The museum, founded by the Reverend Joseph Steward and now enlarged, was claimed to be as extensive as any in New England. Its natural history paintings, particularly those of the North American birds, were believed to be unsurpassed anywhere on the continent. Citizens could see Biblical and historical canvases, copies of Benjamin West, and portraits of the Connecticut forefathers. They might examine stuffed animals and a variety of crystals, ores, stalactites, and shells. There was an accumulating number of wax figures, examples of lithographic art, a small steam engine, a modern organ, a miniature railroad with engine and cars, and doubtless an additional miscellany of objects for the intellectually curious.[50] Those who were especially fond of art could view temporary exhibits of miniatures, engravings, or oils at the State House, or at one or another of the taverns or "hotels" as they were coming to be called.[51]

The Goodwins, who regarded singing as an art well calculated to beget moral improvement, frequently boosted local musical events. Itinerant vocalists, the Hartford Handelian Society, and the several church choruses featured the compositions of Handel, Haydn, Mozart, and Beethoven.[52] A children's choir was organized,[53] the Hartford Band was formed,[54] the Hartford Glee Club sang English glees,[55] and the Hartford Musical Society played overtures, marches, waltzes, and, on one occasion, Haydn's "Turkish Symphony." [56] The "Misses Gillingham," possessing a repertoire of both sacred and secular songs, were the favorites of this generation of music lovers.[57] Whatever the direction of popular taste, one of the *Courant*'s correspondents noted a commendable improvement in choir singing, having listened in former years to strains that were productive of anything but feelings of devotion.[58]

Readers found many references to opportunities for intellectual improvement. The *Courant* still carried notices of the old Hartford Library Company [59] and of several new commercial ones.[60] The members of the Hartford Atheneum maintained a reading room as did some other groups.[61] The Mechanics Society, an organization of journeymen and apprentices, boasted a library of 700 books and sponsored lectures on subjects appropriate to the interests of its membership.[62] It became the mode for men of learning to give lectures to which tickets were sold for individuals and for families. A great many were advertised on astronomy, geology, chemistry, mineralogy, geography, disease, history, literature, business, temperance, phrenology, and other subjects.[63] In 1832 a number of local gentlemen, forming the Goodrich Association, determined to lecture to one another each Friday evening, opening their meetings to the public.[64] The *Courant,* believing that the diffusion of a taste for intellectual pursuits also improved public morals, had urged this kind of arrangement some time before.[65]

The Lyceum attracted especial notice because it seemed to offer an organized plan for the promotion of some of these means of popular education.[66] In 1829 the *Courant* editorialized as follows:

We have already observed that Lyceums have been formed in a few towns in Connecticut. As a general remark, however, they are but little known in this State—and on this account we have thought it our duty to invite the attention of our readers to the subject at this time. On the benefits of such institutions it is unnecessary to remark, as they must be obvious to every reflecting man. Their salutary tendency in affording a substitute for vicious amusements, exciting a spirit for intellectual improvement, diffusing useful information, and thus elevating the standard of intellect and morals in the community, cannot be too highly appreciated. A well conducted Lyceum in the different towns in our State, connected with the advantages of lectures and libraries, would give a new tone to society. . . . Let professional men, ministers of the Gospel, teachers, and all who feel an interest in enlarging and extending the means of improvement, unite their influence, and devote that attention to the subject which it deserves, and the most beneficial effects would follow.[67]

Lyceums were subsequently formed in Hartford. Citizens listened to speeches, debates, and held discussions on controversial topics of current interest.[68] Recognizing the deficiency of trained teachers, the Goodwins hoped that the spread of such organizations, the establishment of libraries in connection with them, lectures on the theory of instruction and other appropriate topics, might all contribute to improvement of the schools. It was impossible in that day to have an adequate supply of trained teachers, as they observed, and so many of them spent so much of their time in engagements of a nonintellectual sort.[69]

A number of means and occasions for enjoyment, some of them of the nonintellectual sort, were mentioned by editorial, letter, or advertisement. The city might have suffered from the invasion of elephants, baboons, and other wild beasts, as one contributor suggested, but the editors apparently enjoyed a good menagerie.[70] The Siamese twins aroused their interest and no objections were voiced to the Yankee fire-eater or to the hoax of the ancient Joice Heth, George Washington's 161-year-old nurse.[71] There were traveling elocutionists and ventriloquists.[72] An orrery and a "solar microscope" were exhibited.[73] Large crowds watched the ascension of illuminated balloons from State House Square.[74] Gentlemen arranged winter dancing assemblies and Election and New Year cotillions provided good times at Morgan's Coffee House.[75] Fashionable citizens who formerly traveled to Saratoga and Ballston began patronizing establishments along the Connecticut seashore.[76]

Since some of the local churches were beginning to celebrate Christmas, the *Courant* suggested the desirability of suspending ordinary secular activities at least for the duration of divine services.[77] As religious exercises and Sunday school parades became usual features of the Independence Day celebrations, the *Courant* objected to the firing of squibs and guns, referring to fire hazards, frightened horses, and jeopardy to life and limb.[78] People still derived whatever fun came from the purchase of lottery tickets, but the moral worth of permitting their sale began to be questioned.[79] Although many an honorable institution had received funds from these sources, the *Courant* noted the growth of public disapprobation and believed that such opportunities for waste and for gambling eventually ought to be suppressed.[80]

The *Courant*'s strongest dislike was reserved for the "circus." One appeared at different times in Hartford in the middle years of the 1820's and sizable crowds witnessed, among other things, horseback acrobatics, slack-rope stunts, and hornpipe dancing.[81] The management, despite gifts to charity and free tickets for members of the legislature, was eventually hailed into court.[82] The Goodwins had now no liking for theaters or kindred institutions, and, believing the state law expressly prohibited them, summoned the authorities to take action.[83] It had been said that if the people in populous areas were provided with this type of entertainment they might be diverted from that which was more vicious, but the *Courant* failed to see that the argument applied locally.[84] As the legislature proceeded to clarify the law, the Goodwins, opposing even local option,[85] laid bare the basis of their antipathy:

The ordinary exhibitions of the circus are justly classed with the lowest and most vulgar of all theatrical performances. There is nothing, connected with them, which is calculated to exalt the mind or purify the morals; on the contrary the supreme object of them seems to be, to show off feats of uncommon dexterity of body, coupled with the most debasing buffoonery. That such exhibitions were incompatible with the institutions of a free, intelligent, and virtuous community; that their existence ought not to be tolerated in a land of schools, where thousands in the giddy season of youth are entrusted to us to be educated, was foreseen by those, who have gone before us. Some doubts had latterly been entertained, whether the exhibitions of the circus came within the former statute, and, to prevent any misapprehension on the subject in future, the present bill was enacted, which we hope and trust will render it inexpedient for these strolling actors, with their horses, dogs, and *other cattle,* to be seen wandering about the country.[86]

The *Courant* became disturbed also about the liquor evil. The family heads of Hartford, summoned to a general meeting at the State House on August 5, 1823, took under consideration what was termed the alarming prevalence of intemperance.[87] From motives religious, moral, and financial, they regretted the local victualing shops as not only injurious to regularly licensed taverns, but also as the incubators of drunkenness and vice. Asserting that licenses for retailing wines and liquor should be given to none but men of good principle, and proclaiming the need for organized temperance promotion, they proceeded to form the Hartford Society for the Suppression of Intemperance. The *Courant,* which spoke of funerals, graveyards, poorhouses, jails, blasphemy, robbery, and murder as results of liquor, thought that the time had about come for society to extend sympathy to the weeping wives, widows, and children of habitual inebriates. The citizens of Hartford, it contended, could do much by setting an example for other Connecticut towns to follow.[88]

Within a few years, the vending and consumption of ardent spirits and the agitation of those who disapproved it figured as major topics in the *Courant.* The Goodwins were especially disgusted with the traditional militia musters, reporting on one occasion that upwards of 40 tables and booths accommodated the appetites of noisy crowds, and that the gambling, fighting, and general disorder thoroughly disgraced the city.[89] The temperance movement had so grown by 1828 that the *Courant* ran the following editorial endorsing total abstinence:

The numerous associations formed and measures adopted in various parts of the country for the promotion of temperance, indicate a great and decided change in public sentiment in regard to the use of ardent spirits. These associations are also exerting a reciprocal influence on public sentiment, and bid fair to prove a formidable barrier to the mighty evil which has so long desolated the land, and cast reproach on our national character. The principle of total abstinence, except for medicinal purposes, as the only sure remedy for intemperance, is fast gaining ground, and the idea of staying the ravages of this destructive vice, and effecting any important reformation by any process short of this, is exploded as false and fallacious. It is gratifying to trace the progress of public opinion on this subject, and to notice the great change which has taken place within a few years. To a great extent among the respectable part of the community, ardent spirits are now banished from the social circle, and it is considered as a mark of indelicacy and rudeness, rather than politeness, to place a decanter before a friend. The stage and steam boat passenger now scarcely ventures to call for a glass of spirits without assigning some special cause, or offering some apology for the use of it. Farms are cultivated, manufactures prosecuted, buildings erected, public meetings held, national events celebrated, without resort to intoxicating liquors. In every profession and department of life the subject is exciting unusual interest. The note of alarm has long been sounded from the pulpit—the medical faculty are awake to the danger, and exerting their combined influence to expose the fatal effects of ardent spirits on the health and constitution of their patients—mechanic associations are adopting energetic measures to discourage the use of the fatal poison among their respective trades—merchants are excluding it from their stores, and even the lawyers are uniting in the good cause. In short, a strong determination seems to prevail among all classes of society to banish this destroyer of human happiness from their ranks; and the time, we believe, is not far distant, when even the moderate use of ardent spirits will be considered not only dangerous, but disreputable.[90]

The Hartford and Hartford County temperance societies held propaganda meetings,[91] some of the county doctors entertained ideas of an asylum for the cure of drunkards,[92] and the *Courant* urged the payment of wages on Mondays rather than Saturdays as a preventive of "criminal indulgence."[93] In 1821 George Goodwin himself had taken a fling at the brewing business and as late as 1827 the *Courant* advised Connecticut farmers to go in for barley crops in order to supply the growing number of breweries.[94] By 1832 it seemed to the *Courant*'s proprietors that, if the traffic in spirits were morally wrong, so likewise was an indirect participation in it. The cause of temperance, they thought, was the cause of humanity; and from that day on, the *Courant* would accept no liquor advertisements.[95]

In the 1820's it became customary in Hartford to take Fourth of July collections for the Liberian project of the Colonization Society.[96] The Goodwins asserted that none of the numerous benevolent societies promised more for the human race or for the salvation of the desolate continent of Africa.[97] But as the northern abolitionist movement developed political and social complications, the *Courant*'s position required additional explaining. In 1833 a Democratic General Assembly displayed feeling against abolitionism by forbidding any town, without permission of the selectmen, to educate out-of-state Negroes.[98] The arrest and trials of Prudence Crandall of Canterbury on this account attracted widespread attention and were extensively reported in the *Courant*.[99] The Goodwins vigorously criticized the statute as discriminatory.[100] When local hoodlums despoiled the Hartford African Church and demolished some Negro dwellings, the issue became apparently too hot to handle;[101] but when rioters in Charlestown, New York, Philadelphia, and elsewhere broke up abolitionist meetings, the *Courant* reprobated the authorities and the mobs rather than the friends of the slave.[102] It held also that southern postmasters had no right to stop the delivery of abolitionist tracts and that the government had no right to suppress abolitionist organizations. The abstract principles of abolitionism, thought the Goodwins, were in the main correct.[103]

Yet the *Courant*'s owners were no abolitionists, a point on which their editorial record was consistently clear. It was summarized in July, 1834:

The subject of slavery and of our colored population generally, is one of vast interest. We wish their condition improved, as we do that of large masses of white people, some in our own, but far more in foreign countries. But we would not violate the faith pledged in forming our Constitution. We would not dissolve the Union, because the powers of regulating slavery are left with those who had the sole power before it was formed, and who would possess the sole power after such dissolution. We would not take measures which are likely to result either in deeper suffering to the slave, and more serious privations to the free colored race—or else will turn the Southern States into . . . a scene of insurrection and extermination, such as would bring ceaseless tears from every eye among us, and from none more freely than most of the very persons who think they can benefit the colored race by combining to produce immediate emancipation.[104]

The *Courant* thought that William Lloyd Garrison and his kind were men of intemperate spirit, faulty judgment, and misdirected zeal.[105] In Hartford, as in other cities, citizens convened to denounce the abolitionists for their troublesome agitation, and the paper hoped they might refrain from flooding the southern mails with their literature.[106] The Goodwins berated the southern "ultras" as well for their alleged want of intellectual moderation.[107] The solution lay, they believed, in a broader endorsement of the benevolent aims of the Colonization Society. This would keep the subject of emancipation in the public mind, especially in the South, in the safest and most practical form. It would afford a means to people, who favored emancipation, to register their views in a way not contravening the spirit of the Constitution. It offered the only ground on which northern and southern opinion could meet under prevailing circumstances. It could be made to embrace all other efforts and programs for the alleviation of conditions oppressing the Negro race.[108]

During these years the imperatives of newer modes of business and transportation, along with the waning authority of the orthodox church, produced changes in Sabbath observance. Some steamboats were beginning to operate on Sundays, stages traveled, the mails moved, and it was pointed out that an increasing amount of business and diversion had come to disturb the tranquillity of the customary days of rest.[109] It was said that the scrupulous regard of the early magistrates for the sacredness of the Sabbath had begun to incur the ridicule of some men of modern times.[110] The *Courant*'s readers were apprised of the Sunday celebrating and parading attendant upon Lafayette's grand tour of 1824, and of Monroe's profanation of the Sabbath when he and some of his friends inspected a government warship.[111] The *Courant* thought poorly of Adams for riding from Providence to Walpole, despite his presence at divine services that day.[112] These were regarded as bad examples in high places.

The issue came home impressively in 1826 when changed plans for the *Oliver Ellsworth,* a steamer running between Hartford and New York, provided for Sunday landings at the local waterfront.[113] The Goodwins got the news from the New York papers and with all due deference to the friends, the proprietors, and the captain of the boat, printed their surprise and regret at such an arrangement. Everybody, said the *Courant,* who had witnessed the noise and confusion occasioned by the arrival of a boat laden with passengers, baggage, and freight, would see at once that such occurrences on the Sabbath could hardly fail to introduce still greater encroachments on the good order of the day.[114] The proprietors bowed to the criticism and the boat resumed its old schedule,[115] but the concern of the friends of the Sabbath continued. Members of the clergy and layfolk from various denominations in Hartford County met in April, 1828, to express sentiments against the Sunday navigation of steam and canal boats anywhere, condemning Sunday stages and livery stables, condemning all Sunday travel and all "unnecessary" labor on the Sabbath.[116] The *Courant* printed reports and arguments which protested the overland conveyance of goods between Hartford and New Haven on winter Sundays and which decried the government's allowance of Sunday mails.[117] The Goodwins doled out to their readers the lengthy address and constitution of the "General Union for promoting the observance of the Christian Sabbath." [118] The arguments by which the Sabbath was defended were simply that its proper observance was indispensable to religion and morality. Only as the nation kept a high moral character could it hope to protect the cherished civil privileges of the American people.[119] The *Courant* ridiculed the idea that the outlawing of abuses would constitute religious legislation, or that the stopping of the Sunday mails could possibly offend any man's conscience. It believed that the proper observance of the Sabbath ought to be legally enforced.[120]

Jostling in type with the strongest sentiments of reform and beneficence were allusions to such varied items as corsets, hot and cold baths, an oyster house, a "soda fountain," uses for anthracite coal, steamboats, railroads, improved methods of road making, insurance, banking, and manufacturing establishments.[121] From among the newer productions of a changing material culture, the development of steamboat transportation, coupled with a high contemporary interest in canal construction, did more than anything else to focus the aspirations of Hartford's business men.

The *Courant* printed its first steamboat advertisements under a sailboat cut.[122] In 1818 a steam towboat, owned by Hartford merchants and designed to ply between the city and the mouth of the river, was launched at the local shipyard.[123] The emerging possibilities of defying wind, weather, and adverse river currents produced a growing enthusiasm, not only for steam travel between Hartford and outside points, but especially for the development of the up-river trade. Not content with what the *Courant* called the paltry, peddling commerce of yore, visions of the future pictured Hartford a thriving river port commanding the resources of the entire Connecticut Valley and with rich stakes in the exhaustless wealth lately opened to commerce by the new republics of South America.[124] Such dreams haunted the *Courant* during the years of the 1820's and indeed were only placed beyond redemption by the railroad fever which settled over the city in the following decade.

Before the establishment of a line of steamers between Hartford and New York, the Goodwins averred that such a project might capture much of the valley commerce with that city. A ride by stage through the pleasant country to Hartford, succeeded by passage along one of the most delightful rivers on the continent, might moreover induce those from Boston, who customarily journeyed through Providence, to turn their attention and their business to the Hartford route.[125] The *Courant* accordingly seconded the efforts of local promoters in whipping up investment sentiment to this end. It later described the *Oliver Ellsworth,* launched in 1824, in terms altogether glowing and elegant.[126] Other boats, propelled by steam, were subsequently engaged in the same run, and at one time the traveler could have gone to New York for the modest price of $1.50, paying extra for meals.[127] The Goodwins thought that the accommodations and the running time—17 to 18 hours from Hartford—were quite remarkable, but the cutthroat competition between lines depressed the returns of investors. By 1830 stock in the Connecticut River Steam Boat Company was selling for one fourth its original value.[128] The *Courant,* denying pecuniary involvement, appealed to the public to divert patronage from boats owned by outside capitalists. A $5.00 fare, it contended, might have brought reasonable profits to the local company, but very much less would simply destroy the business of all concerned.[129]

As people inhabiting the riverside towns to the north became increasingly desirous that their navigation be improved, none sympathized more with their aspirations than the citizens of Hartford or the busy writers of the *Courant.* In 1824 and 1825 crowded meetings were held in Hartford, in Greenfield, Massachusetts, and in Windsor, Vermont. Representatives from numbers of towns in Connecticut, Massachusetts, New Hampshire, and Vermont, appointed committees, adopted resolutions, and took other measures to instigate surveys for canal and river projects that might permit navigation all the way from Long Island Sound to the Canadian shores of Lake Memphremagog.[130]

The business men of New Haven, meanwhile, were supporting a canal project through Farmington and Southwick to Northampton on the Connecticut. They hoped to divert the trade of the upper valley into their own city. This scheme the *Courant* deemed to be quixotic and came to argue at length the superior feasibility of a river improvement program as against the Farmington Canal.[131] Agents representing both the New Haven and Hartford capitalists were said to have traversed the valley procuring petitions, memorials, and remonstrances for purposes of pushing their respective plans.[132]

According to the *Courant,* schemes were afoot even to connect the upper Connecticut with Lake Champlain on the west and with Boston on the east.[133] The Goodwins were convinced from the start that nothing had more importance for Hartford than clearing the bars, building the required canals and locks, and in other necessary ways facilitating the northern river navigation. It seemed to them that by this means a great deal of the overland commerce, which ordinarily went to Boston, might flow down the river to enhance the business and profits of Hartford enterprisers.[134]

In the meantime, the directors of the Connecticut River Company, unwilling to await the outcome of events, determined to place a small steamer on the waters above Hartford.[135] The *Barnet,* built in New York, arrived at the city on November 15, 1826. On the first attempt to ascend the river, she failed to pass the falls at Enfield, only a few miles to the north.[136] This apparently drew derisive comments from the friends of the Farmington Canal.[137] On a subsequent try, the boat not only made the rapids in Connecticut but her appearance was celebrated by people in towns as far north as Bellows Falls, Vermont, and especially by those in Hartford who cheered her return, discharged cannons, and banqueted at one of the local hotels.[138] On this occasion, the *Courant* paid its respects to New Haven:

The friends to an improved navigation of Connecticut River, cannot fail to be highly gratified with the result of the late experiment with the Steam-Boat Barnet. . . . The circumstance of her meeting with difficulty in passing Enfield Falls, which by the way was not greater than was anticipated, has occasioned some attempts at wit by the editor of the New-Haven Herald and others, who, while they know better themselves, would fain have it believed that the boat was intended and expected to navigate the falls in their present state. Our readers however need not be informed that such is not the fact, and that the lockage of Enfield Falls is included in the proposed improvements. And when it is recollected that three locks at Enfield with the six already at S. Hadley will afford uninterrupted steam-boat navigation from Hartford to Northampton, and far beyond—while the number of locks on the Farmington Canal between Northampton and New Haven is not less than sixty-one—some of those who have possibly invested more money in the canal than the editor of the Herald, may be disposed to think there is no great cause for exultation in the late excursion of the Barnet—but this is none of our affair.[139]

The upshot of the whole Connecticut Valley project, which the *Courant* followed closely, fell something short of the high hopes which had been earlier entertained. Interested citizens subscribed more than $15,000 for surveys of the river from Hartford to Lake Connecticut in northern New Hampshire, and also for surveys of three canal routes from Barnet, Vermont, north to Memphremagog. The river distance from Hartford to Barnet was over 200 miles along which it was purposed to build 17 miles of canal and 41 locks at estimated costs exceeding a million dollars. The Connecticut, New Hampshire, and Vermont legislatures passed acts enabling the Hartford-Barnet project, but the Massachusetts law-makers finally favored extending the Farmington Canal. At the same time they incorporated a company to undertake river improve-ments within the borders of their state.[140] By 1829 the *Courant* noted that public opinion, once united on improving the river, had become plainly divided.[141] The completion of the Enfield Canal was celebrated that year.[142] In 1830 a Vermont corporation, design-ing to clear the Connecticut between Hartford and Wells River, south of Barnet, sold stock in Hartford and up the valley.[143] Early in 1831 Vermont and New Hampshire delegates resolved to extend improvements almost to the Canadian border, and the *Courant* hoped that by spring five or six steam towboats might be operating far up the river.[144] This, however, was the final wave of enthusi-asm and never afterward did the paper display much excitement or interest. By 1835, when the *Courant* carried the story of the com-pletion of the canal from New Haven to Northampton,[145] rail-roads were decidedly the talk of the town and one supposes that Hartford's citizens had no more than memories of the threat which the Farmington Canal had once been.

The *Courant's* subscribers had read about English "steam coaches" as early as 1825.[146] In 1832 the General Assembly received application to charter a New Haven-Middletown-Hartford rail-road. The citizens of New Haven, according to a correspondent, were greatly excited over the idea; and why, he inquired, were the citizens of Hartford so strangely apathetic?[147] Two years later a second writer called attention to the projected Boston-Worcester road as a threat to Hartford's Connecticut Valley trade line. Would it not be wiser, he implied, for Hartford to make a direct rail con-nection with Worcester rather than to allow it to go through Springfield by default? Would it not be smart to take some action upon the New Haven and Hartford proposition?[148]

In January, 1835, a letter by "W." admitted the fear, which some of the citizens harbored, that a railroad to New Haven would de-press their investments in steamboat, stage, and turnpike compa-nies, and that it would diminish their investments in commerce and real estate. But on the other hand, what if a line were built from New York to Boston through New Haven and Providence, enabling the entire run to be made in less than 12 hours? What if the Boston and Worcester road were extended through Springfield to Albany? It seemed to the writer that people in Hartford ought immediately to consider whether they chose to allow their friends in Springfield to outmaneuver them. The big New York stockholders of the Farmington Company were allegedly angling to have a Springfield-New Haven extension utilize one of the banks of their canal; and the Springfield papers were hoping that a Boston-Springfield road might turn along the river and pass through Hartford on the way south.[149]

Local capitalists were again urged to see the wisdom of getting behind the New Haven project and pushing it from Hartford directly to Worcester. Having accomplished this, a line might then extend from Hartford up the valley into Canada, and thousands of tons of merchandise from Massachusetts, Vermont, and New Hampshire might subsequently enrich the Hartford market. "W." regretted Hartford's attitude, and the Goodwins, for their part, recommended the subject to the especial attention of Hartford's business men and merchants. Other projects were being agitated, they warned, and negligence at that time could well preclude local interests from entering the field in the future on equal terms with competitors.[150]

The city was apparently ready for railroad enthusiasm. Within a week of the Goodwins' admonition, the first of a series of popular conventions took place.[151] Accounts of the usual proceedings, reports, and resolutions of such meetings were jammed into the *Courant*'s issues, and the conventions of other towns in Connecticut, Massachusetts, and Vermont were followed with marked interest.[152] The business men of Norwich as well as those of Springfield were anxious to have the road from Boston to New York pass through their cities.[153] In March, 1835, a meeting in Hartford of delegates from several towns resolved as follows:

That we consider rail-roads as the greatest improvement in the means of communication, both as respects rapidity and facility, and that from the constantly increasing wealth, industry and populousness of this section of the country, they are here peculiarly important, and promise, sooner or later, amply to reward those who shall engage, in their construction. . . . That in the opinion of this convention, a rail-road through New-England, connecting Boston and New York, is of the highest importance to the community generally, and that it cannot but lead to a rapid improvement of all the great interests of society. . . . That from the facts communicated to this convention we consider the construction of a rail-road connecting New Haven and Hartford, with the Boston and Worcester rail-road by the most feasible rout as an object of high importance; and that immediate and efficient measures should be taken to accomplish it.[154]

Shares in the New Haven and Hartford railroad were placed on sale in June. In two days subscriptions in Hartford totaled over a quarter of a million dollars, and by the next week, about a million and a half.[155] With the stock taken up, the Goodwins announced that attention could now be focused upon other enterprises—the railroad to Worcester, a line northward to Canada, and one through West Stockbridge to Albany.[156] Meetings working up support for all of these projects were held in Hartford and were attended in other towns by Hartford delegates.[157] The *Courant,* always promoting the general excitement, carried a great deal of railroad propaganda until the onset of the depression of 1837.

Meanwhile, the paper took cognizance of certain city problems and of changing ways of coping with them. From time to time, wooden buildings, containing shops or dwelling apartments, were razed by fire.[158] Some of the conflagrations were serious.[159] While occasionally attributed to incendiary malice, the usual causes were thought to have been defective chimneys and stovepipes, wooden fireboards, and the careless disposal of ashes.[160] An unsatisfactory relationship existed between the citizens and the volunteer fire companies. Heedless of traditional duties, some people stayed home from fires and some who attended refused to cooperate. Some of the firebuckets leaked and owners sometimes came without them or locked them in their stores at night.[161] Although the city fathers purchased a hose engine in 1827, the *Courant* warned that the day of buckets had not yet passed.[162] The paper contained little crime news but now and again appeared references to gangs of thieves and the deeds they perpetrated.[163] As precaution against nocturnal fires and prowlers, property owners were urged to undertake voluntary watch and were lauded for doing so.[164]

In 1819 and in the early 1820's the paper reflected more or less apprehension from seasonal visitations of yellow fever in Boston and some seaports to the south.[165] The greatest fear of this sort came from the Asiatic cholera of 1832. The *Courant* plotted its spread from Europe to Quebec and into the American cities.[166] Reporting that the afflicted were mostly *bon vivants* and intemperates, the Goodwins nevertheless urged all proper means of prevention ranging from the free use of chloride of lime to some good old-fashioned praying.[167] The city was divided into "health districts." The "Board of Health" directed precautionary activities, quarantining ships, urging clean-ups, and advising citizens on matters of diet and clothing.[168]

As Hartford grew in population, new buildings replaced old ones and the *Courant* noted an unprecedented amount of construction—the Retreat, the College, a city hall, churches, business blocks, and dwelling houses.[169] Dogs wandering about the city, the trundling of barrows along the walks, playing fireball and handball, kicking bladders, hoop rolling, and fast driving in the streets became subjects for complaint.[170] In the winter, sleighs were sometimes driven without bells and an increasing number of women were riding about in carriages.[171] The city sidewalks were at many places irregular and narrow and pedestrians had to walk about piles of snow, doorsteps, and obtruding fences.[172] When the Council took measures to straighten the walks and curbs along Main Street, the *Courant* hoped that Hartford might have a promenade unsurpassed in elegance and comfort by that of any comparable city in the Union.[173]

The Goodwins thought that the new toll bridge across the river, erected in 1818, was an excellent example of the evils of monopoly,[174] but nobody could blame private investors for what was said to have been the lamentable condition of Hartford's streets. In wet weather, vehicles sometimes became fast in the mud, and in the summer there was an annoying accumulation of dust.[175] Citizens were beginning to take an interest in watering the streets,[176] and the *Courant,* printing information on the McAdam process of paving, prayed that some consistent plan might be adopted to make them passable at all seasons of the year.[177] Since Hartford was no longer a small rural community, one of the *Courant*'s correspondents called for the authorities to place numbers upon the buildings along the principal streets.[178]

In 1835 the *Courant* printed a more general description of the city from the pen of a flattering traveler:

Strangers who enter Hartford at one end, and go out at the other amidst clouds of dust, are disposed . . . to be anything but eulogistic of the place. But those who remain long enough to walk about the town, and ride around its beautiful suburbs, depart with very different impressions. Perhaps the city itself is not more beautiful than the central part of New Haven, although neither that town nor any other in the Union affords a vista at all comparable to that which opens to view in the spacious

Main street of Hartford, looking from the State House Square towards the South.

It is the environs, however, which form at once the pride and the attraction of this town. In the vicinity are numerous beautiful country seats, and for many more, sites, which, for rich land, comprising smooth lawns and pieces of woodland like the parks of England . . . are altogether unequalled in this country. Those who prefer a more distant ramble, can visit the range of hills which rise a few miles west of the city, where they will find a boundless view, replete with the gorgeous scenery of a fertile and long settled region.[179]

In this generation the *Courant* recorded pleasantly a number of gala days, among them the annual fair days of the County Agricultural Society and the celebration of Hartford's two-hundredth anniversary in 1835.[180] Perhaps none became better lodged in the reminiscences of old men than the exciting occasion of Lafayette's reception in the early fall of 1824. Arches were erected and buildings festooned. The distinguished Frenchman entered a crowded city where thousands had gathered to see him. The *Courant* spoke of the aged veterans of the Revolution, for indeed almost half a century had passed since the firing at Lexington Green.[181]

CHAPTER X

THE GOODWINS AND THE COURANT

IN November, 1815, when George Goodwin & Sons opened for business "10 rods north of the Court house," the prospects of profitably expanding their several trades probably seemed excellent.[1] Goodwin, though nearing his sixties, was in good health and had a long record of successful publishing experience behind him. Richard and George, Jr., were vigorous and personable young men in the prime of physical life, Yale graduates, and responsible heads of families.[2] Henry was in his early twenties. None of the boys were novices in the world of business. Richard had worked with Hudson & Goodwin and had likely written many of the *Courant*'s substantial editorials during the embargo and war period.[3] George had been in the grocery and hardware business under one name or another since 1806.[4] Henry had learned the printing trade at his father's side and for a year or two had been in the publishing and bookselling business with George Sheldon, a former Hudson & Goodwin employee of fine character.[5] The new firm was suitably located in a three-story brick building in the center of town.[6] Hartford was growing, the dislocating years of war had passed, and New England men of business looked hopefully to an era of peace and resumed commercial activity.

Except for binding books, the Goodwins intended to exploit the departments of business which had brought wealth and prestige to the late firm of Hudson & Goodwin.[7] According to the boys, their father was the sort who dried hay a day longer than his neighbors and always kept two or three less cows on a given acreage of pasture than anyone else.[8] He would be the firm's general manager, giving special attention to the newspaper work which he had done since childhood.[9] On the editorial end of the *Courant* he would have the help of Richard, who had received the best classical education of any of his sons.[10] Henry, a thorough and neat workman, would set up the weekly advertisements, make up the *Courant,* keep the printing office as clean as a milliner's shop, and serve as foreman of the press.[11] Young George, who ranked first among the boys in merchandising experience, would oversee the paper manufacturing and promote the business interests of the East Hartford mills.[12] Sometime later, Charles and Edward would join the firm, the former to be the storekeeper and tend to the stationery and bookselling enterprises, the latter to relieve Richard at the editor's desk.[13]

Through the postwar depression, through the ups and downs of the life of the firm, the forces which were then emerging to produce the more modern order of specialized business made it impossible for the Goodwins to conduct their affairs with the profit they might have hoped for at the outset. When the father had been a boy, he had worked in the only establishment in Hartford where books could be printed and bound, broadsides and pamphlets issued, or a weekly newspaper published. Books and stationery might have been bought elsewhere but for several years only the *Courant*'s owners made paper in and about Hartford.[14] Since then, rivals had set up in all the branches of business. Other papermakers, printers, binders, stationers, booksellers, and newspaper concerns were vying for local trade. In the two decades after 1815, such competition intensified. City booksellers and printers increased in number, local newspapers and literary magazines cropped up, and East Hartford throve as a center of the paper manufacturing industry.[15] Business no longer came in as a matter of necessity, and, in the years ahead, fortune shone upon the Goodwin enterprises with unequal favor.

Almost from the beginning the bookselling underwent restriction and specialization. As in former years, the *Courant*'s store carried standard works in law, theology, medicine, science, history, and literature, along with Bibles, almanacs, psalters, and textbooks.[16] But now the market was glutted with Bibles, the neighboring firm of Oliver D. Cooke captured most of the law trade, and competitors annoyed and undersold the Goodwins by the newer practice of quoting prices on books not at hand.[17] Prices on works of established merit fell far below the prewar level and the abundance of dealers in Hartford made it unlikely that old conditions would soon return.[18] Hence the Goodwins gradually sold out their law books and generally diminished their inventory, confining their sales by 1824 chiefly to school texts and works of religious instruction.[19] They made no pretense at keeping abreast the popular works of the day. By the close of the decade they were referring most prospective buyers to one or another of their local competitors.[20] By this time also they were refusing to handle magazines or to accept subscriptions for them.[21] Aside from a very few old standards and an extensive layout of school texts, a visitor to the store in the 1830's would have seen the usual assortment of writing articles and copious supplies of Goodwin paper, ranging from the finest letter sheets to the coarse stuff used for cartridges.[22]

Whatever publishing the Goodwins did depended upon the state of retail bookselling in Hartford.[23] Before 1824 they published almanacs, editions of Webster's school dictionary, Dwight's *Psalms,* Testaments, Bible lessons for Sunday schools, and works on surgery, biography, and philosophy.[24] Their books were bound in New Haven and exchanged with traders elsewhere, but even as early as 1816 they were speaking of curtailing publishing in view of the dullness of the local business.[25] By 1823, it seemed to them that books were not worth printing. The costs were about as high as formerly and their publications brought next to nothing when sold. Seven or eight local firms were trying to support themselves with work which Goodwin deemed insufficient for half that number; and he and his sons would have discharged their single journeyman printer had it not been for the *Courant.*[26] After that time the Goodwins did occasional job printing, but those who wished to submit manuscripts for separate publication were turned away.[27]

Also in the newspaper field the *Courant*'s owners were beset by competent local rivals. The *Connecticut Mirror,* first issued in 1809 and conducted by Theodore Dwight until after the war, had sought patronage from the same political elements as did the *Courant.* Indeed the secret journal of the Hartford Convention had been printed in the *Mirror* office.[28] Political opponents, still vigorously abetted by the *Mercury,* acquired additional support when Frederick D. Bolles founded the *Hartford Times* in 1817. The Goodwins were not so certain that Hartford would support four papers but Bolles thought otherwise, especially since seven of the ten state weeklies were then described as "federal." [29] After the *New England Weekly Review* in 1828, the *Jeffersonian,* the *Independent Press,* and the *Patriot & Democrat* were established. Religious weeklies, Congregationalist, Baptist, and Roman Catholic, were locally published and at least four literary magazines appeared in the early 1830's.[30]

Some of these journals were ably edited. John G. C. Brainard displayed his poetical ability in the *Mirror.* George D. Prentice, afterward famous as founder and editor of the Louisville *Journal,* attracted a group of correspondents whose literary contributions gave the *Review* a distinction rarely equaled in country weeklies. John Greenleaf Whittier succeeded him at the editor's desk. John M. Niles, one-time United States Senator and Postmaster General, and

Gideon Welles, later in Lincoln's Cabinet, wrote editorials for the *Times*. Thomas H. Seymour, who conducted the *Jeffersonian,* was afterward a member of the House of Representatives, thrice governor of Connecticut, and United States minister to Russia.[31] Whatever the financial success of the several enterprises, Hartford's papers suffered from no dearth of political and literary talent. Among them all, the *Courant* maintained an eminent position.

Running in the paper for three years after the war were Ezra Sampson's essays, which were reprinted in many other newspapers.[32] These "Brief Remarker" letters, later published in book form and used in the schools,[33] aimed to enhance the attractiveness of the *Courant* by treating didactic themes. For example:

It greatly behoves young men to form fixed resolutions at the outset of life, never to swerve from the *perpendicular,* in a single instance—no, not even in the most trivial one; for one trespass against the laws of honesty leads to another, as it were by a sort of natural and necessary connection. So that, though there may be many who in their intercourse with the world have never been guilty of one dishonest act, yet there are few who have been guilty of one, and *but one;* because the first, by corrupting the moral principle, weakens the power of resisting the next temptation; because one knavish deed often requires another, and sometimes several others, to cover it; and, lastly, because rooted knavishness of heart is harder to cure than any other moral malady, inasmuch as the corruption of the principle of integrity, is the corruption of the very source of all moral virtue.[34]

Beginning in these years also, the *Courant* stressed religion as well as morals. From English and domestic religious journals it copied reports of revivals, missions, church attendance, Sunday schools, Bible and tract societies. In the special interest of converting the heathen, it reported missionary activities in the American wilderness, in Palestine, Ceylon, the Sandwich Islands, and elsewhere. It gave particular attention to the foreign mission school at Cornwall. By 1821 such reading, captioned "Religious Intelligence," often filled from three to five columns each week.[35] But in the years following, as the prevailing evangelical spirit poured into humanitarian channels and political animosities revived on a nationwide scale, the *Courant* gave less room to this sort of news. By 1824 someone implied that the Goodwins were not all that they might be as Christian journalists; but the paper correctly maintained that none had more uniformly and generously supported the cause of religion.[36]

An "agricultural column" under an appropriate cut appeared regularly from 1817 to 1822, and thereafter the *Courant* featured such information from time to time. With county agricultural societies being formed in many parts of the country, reports of their annual exhibits and contests were deemed to be worthwhile reading. Current quotations on farm commodities in the New York and Boston markets, household hints from almanacs and other sources, letters from farmers, essays on coal, conservation of woodlands, and butter and cheese making were added to the expected advice on soil, plants, and animals.[37] During the spring and fall seasons when advertisements crowded the paper, and after the early 1820's when politics, reform movements, and canal and railroad building demanded more space, the Goodwins sometimes apologized for printing less of this information than they wished.[38]

Even in the decade before 1825, readers were treated always to a great deal of news pertaining to government. Beside detailed reports of the federal departments, the *Courant* as formerly carried long orations of state and national officials and recorded the deliberations of local and federal legislative bodies. The Connecticut revolution of 1818 was closely scanned and later, as Jackson's followers stirred the pot, the number of editorials, speeches, letters, and copied news items proliferated. Postmasters and town clerks were requested to show speed in forwarding the election returns [39] and the Goodwins, in conjunction with other publishers, maintained correspondents at Washington, Hartford, and New Haven.[40] Most of the legislative reporting was now factual and any remarks on the proceedings were confined to editorials and other partisan material which the editors inserted. The *Courant* did not yet cover the courts except to review briefly some of the cases already disposed of.[41] It was generally believed that the public discussion of trials might create prejudice in the mind of court and jury:

It is announced in the Mirror, that a robbery had been committed in the neighborhood of this city on Tuesday evening last. As this subject is, as we are informed, yet in a train of legal inquiry, we should not have noticed it if it had not been for the paragraph alluded to, and now do it only for the purpose of suggesting the propriety of a suspension of public opinion upon the subject.[42]

In addition to the shifting variety of weekly tidings from hither and yon, the Goodwins at one time or another embellished their paper with a number of small items which readers came to expect more or less regularly. Information pertaining to the seasons and the weather appeared in the "Weekly Almanac" and the "Meteorological Journal." [43] The former, placed beneath the ownership box on page one, recorded the phases of the moon for the month and the time of sunrise and sunset for seven days past. The "Journal" tabulated the readings of a Fahrenheit thermometer in downtown Hartford, indulging no predictions but reviewing the temperature along with the prevailing winds and weather of the previous week. From March to December the "Marine List" noted the names of sloops arriving and leaving the local river front. [44] Compiled from the New York papers, a "Banknote Table" revealed the exchange value of notes circulating in the East from various banks over the country. [45] Cattle market quotations were frequently given. [46] The editors printed the usual death notices but customarily excluded biographical sketches or eulogiums as uninteresting to the public. [47] Because of past imposition, they refused to insert marriage announcements unless submitted by responsible persons. [48] Beginning in 1822, short poems appeared under such titles as "The Sunday School," "The Infidel," "On the depressed state of Jewish Females," and "Lines Addressed to a Lovely Infant, expiring in its Father's Arms." [49] Besides reviving the New Year verses or "Carrier's Address," [50] an annual calendar, including government and population statistics, became a feature of the paper each January. [51]

All this affords no adequate description of the variety of reading matter. Local doings, still viewed by and large as not worth writing up, came to light through short editorial comments, printed addresses and resolutions, advertisements, and occasional articles copied from the *Mirror*. [52] The Hartford column sometimes contained lengthy editorials, sometimes brief paragraphs from other papers and magazines, and often a combination of both. The Goodwins were convinced that the great mass of readers wanted general information on the news, politics, and business of the day. [53] By 1825 they had come to believe that long moral essays and sermons were out of place in a newspaper and perhaps more fit for periodicals of a professed literary character. [54] Yet the diversity of tastes of the people who read the *Courant,* as well as their own long-established habits, made them strive to include a generous miscellany not easily catalogued. The tabulation of the contents of a paper selected at random shows the sort of material usually associated with fireside reading:

(July 26, 1825)

p. 1, cols. 1–2   Ownership box
                  "Weekly Almanac"
                  Advertisements
    cols. 3–6   Poems: "Lines On An Unfortunate Lady," "To the
                       Memory of William Power Watts (aged three
                       years)": (from English sources)
                  On earthquakes: "From Professor Silliman's American
                       Journal of Science"
                  "Decision of Character": from "Foster's Essays"
                  "The Maelstrom Whirlpool": "Letter from a gentleman
                       in Washington to the Hon. A. B. Woodward, Judge
                       of Middle Florida."
p. 2, cols. 1–6   "The Deserters": "Found among the papers of Mr.
                       Mason, Secretary to the Duke of Cumberland"
                  "Romantic Story" (a South Sea youth foiled his elders,
                       won his sweetheart): from the "Quarterly Review"
                  "Literary Anecdote" (a poor English clergyman had
                       dreams of wealth): source not specified
                  "Deaths by Drinking Cold Water," "Health in Town
                       and Country": "From the Boston Medical Intel-
                       ligencer"
                  Agricultural articles (surmounted by cut of semi-nude
                       female with farm implements draped about): on
                       sheep and the care of trees, from the Boston and
                       New York papers
                  "Foreign Intelligence" (news from Europe and Africa):
                       from the "Boston Gazette"
                  Domestic items (on canals, fires, accidental deaths, dis-
                       covery of human bones): from several newspapers
p. 3, cols. 1–3   "The Sabbath" (strictures on Lafayette for traveling
                       on Sunday): from "The Recorder and Telegraph"
                  "Extreme Warm weather": from several newspapers
                  Hartford column: reports from a number of sources on
                       canal building, banking, weather, heat prostration,
                       travel, marriages, and deaths
    cols. 4–6   "Marine List"
                  "Meteorological Journal"
                  Advertisements
p. 4, cols. 1–6   Advertisements.

Because it became increasingly difficult for the Goodwins to give
their readers a satisfactorily balanced offering, they began the publication of literary "supplements" in the fall of 1825 without any

increase in subscription price then or later.[55] These were printed on single sheets, about 17½ by 11½ inches, in such a way that the reader, after cutting and folding, might sit down to eight pages of improving entertainment. For some weeks before, advertisements had crowded the *Courant,* and the editors intended to issue the extra page during the busy periods only.[56] But the political and other news proved so compelling and the *Supplement* was evidently so well liked that it continued to be a regular fortnightly feature. This enabled the weekly *Courant* to offer a closer and more detailed account of public issues.

Between the regular and fortnightly issues, subscribers must have been struck with the scope of the writing that the Goodwins selected. The bulk of the latter consisted of prose—essays on education, travel, temperance, business, religion, biography, history, and romance, strange tales, handy hints, and moral maxims. It contained no book reviews, but the *Courant* itself gave editorial notice to several of the magazines of the period, among them Benjamin Silliman's *American Journal of Science & Arts,* Sarah J. Hale's *Lady's Magazine,* the *North American Review,* the *Knickerbocker,* and periodicals devoted to health, agriculture, education, geology, and railroads.[57] It printed complimentary announcements of new books, mostly texts which were probably sold in the store.[58] The verses printed in the *Courant* and *Supplement* came from the pens of the popular poets of the day. Readers got occasional glimpses of Wordsworth, Burns, Cowper, and Bryant,[59] but the favorites were Felicia Hemans, Reginald Heber, Bernard Barton, James Montgomery, W. B. Tappan, Jane Taylor, and the Americans: James G. Percival, Hannah Gould, and Lydia Sigourney. Though their thoughts might dwell upon anything from Lafayette to locomotives, the usual themes were faith, hope, charity, love, virtue, temperance, and death. Mrs. Hemans and her American counterpart, Mrs. Sigourney of Hartford, appeared oftener than the others. The sentiments of all were characterized by great delicacy and infused with the spirit of revived religion.

The production of finer paper, the progress of American type founding, and the invention of better presses made for improvement in the *Courant*'s size, print, texture, and general appearance during the 20 years of the Goodwin regime. The valedictory issue in 1836 was nearly 26 inches high and one and one-half feet wide.[60] Compared with the *Courant* of 1815, it had seven columns as against five, the reading was clearer, the paper thinner and whiter, the margins wider, and the content fuller, better organized, and more compactly arranged under brief, single-line captions. The greater variety of cuts, ranging from snuff bottles to chariots flying the clouds, and the growing use of space and heavier types, made advertisements more attractive and easier to look at. The *Courant*'s owners manufactured their own print paper, purchased types from the top-notch foundries of James Ronaldson, Elihu White, and D. & G. Bruce,[61] and equipped their office with the latest presses.

Since the Goodwins owned Ramage screw presses, it is likely that the *Courant* had been printed upon them for some years before February, 1816.[62] When they then acquired a newly invented "Columbian" from George Clymer of Philadelphia, visitors at the office saw the first all-iron press, resplendent with a Hermes on each pillar, alligators and other reptiles on the levers, and, surmounting the whole, an American spread eagle which acted as a counterweight to lift the platen. It was a decided departure from former presses since a pull on the handle bar operated through a series of compound levers to print one complete side of the *Courant* with uniform distinctness and at greatly reduced labor.[63] Some years later the paper was being turned out on a machine improved by John I. Wells of Hartford, which again increased the power of the pressman.[64] And in 1832 the Goodwins introduced into Hartford an Adams power press, which eliminated the inking of types by hand, made about 750 impressions an hour, and sounded the death knell for newspaper hand presses.[65] Since the old Ramage contrivance was so small that four impressions were necessary to print a single paper of the size of the first Goodwin issue, the distance from Ramage to Adams was indeed remarkable.[66]

The majority of the *Courant*'s readers, as always, lived outside the city of Hartford. Papers went by carrier and stage to people in the towns of Connecticut and neighboring states. As residents emigrated into upper New York and beyond the Alleghenies, the *Courant* followed them with tidings of "home."[67] Conscious of distant subscribers, the editors sometimes apologized for printing too much state news![68] In 1823 they claimed, as they had before, a much larger circulation than any other Connecticut paper,[69] but at no time were the figures disclosed. In 1830 and again when leaving the business, the Goodwins averred that their several competitors had not succeeded in diminishing their subscription list.[70] Throughout the period they sold advertising space for $.60 a square, and $1.00 for three weeks if the buyer consented to a place on the outside pages after the first insertion.[71] Between March and December, issues seldom listed less than 100 paid notices, and since the size and quantity of ads grew with the paper they almost always filled about half the printed surface. Subscription rates were likewise unchanged at $2.00 a year, or in quantities at $1.25.[72]

Whatever the income derived from the *Courant,* paper manufacturing was always deemed to be of equal or greater concern.[73] From the firm's correspondence it is clear that the mill business attracted more than an even share of the firm's promotional efforts. In 1821 young George moved to East Hartford to supervise the workers,[74] and when bookselling and publishing languished, Charles became a sort of traveling agent, canvassing the market in New York, Boston, and elsewhere.[75] For 20 years after the war the trade throve. Stock from the Goodwin mills went down the river by sloop for Boston, New York, and as far south as Mobile.[76] James Olmstead and Jonathan Seymour in New York, William Parker in Boston, and firms in Philadelphia served as distributing agents.[77] In the early years, all grades of paper were produced in quantity,[78] but as mills multiplied and rags appreciated in quality and price, stiffer competition induced them to specialize in fine writing paper.[79] After the early 1820's they continued to produce bank bill paper and some of coarser composition,[80] but they were compelled now and again to go elsewhere for their own wrapping and print paper.[81] Proud of the quality of their work, they boasted that they sorted their rags more closely than others, and that none could outdo them.[82] By inventing a rag-cleaning machine, William Debit, a foreman of one of their mills, enabled them to discharge a number of girl workers.[83] Acquiring the patent rights,[84] the firm profitably sold the cleaners to concerns in New England, New York, New Jersey, Pennsylvania, and Maryland.[85] Infringements occurred and protracted and expensive litigation ensued.[86] Their paper market seems to have expanded in the 1830's and the profits arising from this branch of the business doubtless led the Goodwins to think of reorganizing the family firm.[87] In the fall of 1836, when their father had attained the ripe age of 79, the brothers left the publishing business for paper making [88] and the *Courant* passed to other hands.

When Goodwin was appointed a member of the committee to plan the celebration of Hartford's 200th anniversary in 1835,[89] old-timers fell to recounting the town's recent progress. Many of the institutions and organizations, in which the *Courant* had shown pride, had also enlisted the personal support of the Goodwins. The father was a vice-president of the Retreat for the Insane and one of the founders of the American Asylum for the Deaf and Dumb.[90] Besides being directors of the latter, George, Charles, and Henry had helped establish or support the Savings Society, the Hartford Sunday School Society, the Tract Society, the Hartford Female Seminary, and the Bible Society.[91] Charles sat with the board of directors of the Hartford Bank and Edward was an officer of the Hartford Orphan Asylum.[92] The boys were good church workers, a fact especially consoling to the senior Goodwin who faithfully attended services in the First Church, sitting in a large, square pew with his children and grandchildren about him.[93]

Nobody knows with what reluctance the old printer and his *Courant* parted company. In 1836 he could hardly recall at what age he had first performed simple chores in the little office over Mookler's barber shop—he was either eight or nine at the time.[94] Family legend had it that Green hired him when he showed he could carry a pail of water upstairs.[95] He had peddled the *Courant* about the village of Hartford in the 1760's;[96] he had struggled with Watson in the early days of the Revolution and had managed the business for Watson's widow; with Hudson he had attained wealth and position, comfort for his family, and an education for his sons. Deprived of formal schooling, his years with the paper, his contacts with officers of state, members of the clergy, and prominent citizens who frequented the *Courant* office, had made him an educated, poised, and respected gentleman of the old school. In his sixties, as he walked the streets on his morning round, from his house to the market, John Spencer's barber shop, the post office, and the *Courant* office, he was described as the most notable personage in town:

. . . in full health and vigor, of a noble presence and carriage, six feet high, with a fine figure, and a handsome ruddy face. . . . an easy dignity and grace of manner, and a most becoming style of dress,—the Continental coat and waistcoat, small clothes, black silk stockings, low shoes with silver buckles, and a broad-brimmed hat.[97]

It may well have disappointed him that none of his sons chose to remain with the *Courant,* but he determined at any rate to find a successor worthy of maintaining the principles he had so long cherished. Alfred E. Burr, an excellent young workman to whom Henry had taught the printing trade, was urgently approached.

Burr, who later became editor of the *Hartford Times,* might become the *Courant's* proprietor if he were willing to fulfill two conditions: join the Whig party and become a member of the orthodox church.[98] To Goodwin's regret, Burr refused, and the paper was sold to John L. Boswell. On September 12, 1836, the *Courant* carried the old man's last message:

Since the paper has been under our control, we have endeavored to make it the advocate of correct principles, and the friend and supporter of good order and good morals. In politics, we have defended those doctrines and measures which we believed to be identified with the stability and success of our free institutions, and the true interests of the country. While we have sought to furnish a faithful record of passing events, and to keep our readers acquainted with the news and incidents of the day, we have also aimed to secure a higher object, by making our columns a vehicle of useful information, of correct moral sentiments, and rational entertainment. At the same time we have intended to exclude everything unfriendly to virtue, or offensive to delicacy, or in any way improper for a paper designed for a promiscuous family circle. How far we have succeeded, is for others and not for us to determine. That we have fallen far short of our wishes, is certain; though we would fain hope that we have not entirely failed of our object. The confidence and approbation manifested by the steady, uniform, and long continued support of a numerous list of patrons, have cheered us in our labors, and will hereafter be the subject of grateful recollection.

It is a gratifying circumstance that we leave the paper with an undiminished patronage—with a subscription list as large as at any period within the last fifteen years. And it is also a source of much satisfaction, that we leave it in the hands of a successor whose views on the most important questions of prevailing public interest correspond substantially with our own, and who, as we have good reason to believe, will sustain the same principles which have hitherto held a prominent place in our columns. Under the direction of Mr. Boswell, we trust the character of the Courant will not be essentially changed, except so far as it may be conducted with more ability and rendered more interesting and useful.

It could hardly be said that Goodwin's connection with the *Courant* ended in 1836. Such were his habits of industry and so fixed his associations that in the contract with Boswell he reserved the right to work in the office as formerly, a right which he exercised for several years afterward.[99] On his last New Year, the *Courant* looked back over his lifetime:

For more than three-quarters of a century has the *Courant,* in some form, made its uninterrupted appearance at the doors of a generous public. . . .

We have chronicled the death of nearly three generations of men. We have witnessed the greatest exploits upon the greatest stages of the world's modern history. States have risen, and fallen, kingdoms been over-turned, since we commenced our career. Men have set types for us, who have seen Washington. . . . The momentous events which made the close of the last century a memorable epoch in the world's annals, have found a place in our pages. . . . Of the brilliant though direful career of Napoleon, we were, in some sense, witnesses. We were here during the battles of Marengo, and Waterloo, and Lodi, and others on which the freedom of the world was staked.

. . . The resistance to the Stamp Act and to the Tax on Tea . . . the Signing of the Declaration of Independence, the Inauguration of the Father of his Country, the taking of the First Census of the United States, the adoption of the American Flag . . . the battles of Lexington, Bunker Hill and Yorktown, the framing of the American Constitution,—the tidings of all these great events, found us here at our work; for we have lived for a period *whereof the memory of few men runneth to the contrary.*

. . . We would fain hope that during our life-time, the world has grown better. Commerce has extended her snowy wings over vast seas. . . . Civilization and Christianity have . . . done immense and glorious work, in recovering the idolator and the heathen from stupidity and degradation.

. . . Facilities of intercommunication between the extremities of States and continents have increased almost beyond belief. Railroads and Canals, Steam-navigation upon the high seas, expresses which go from place to place with the ease and speed of *carrier pigeons,* and all the thou-sand improvements and influences which break down partition walls and make mankind brethren, have sprung into being, during our memory. . . . The manners and customs of society have changed vastly during our four score years. . . . The energy of our days we like. . . . But, the stability of the old time, the moral courage which dared to do right, whether the world smiled or frowned, the good old round-toed honesty of our Fathers, the purity of life and the easy simplicity of manners, the stern and rigid morality which led them to suspend worldly affairs from sundown on Saturday until Monday morning, the integrity which par-celed out exactly what justice demanded between man and man,—in these things, we are somewhat lacking. . . . The costly and tempting gaieties of the old world have crept in among us . . . and men are ashamed to live within their means, because the finery or equipage of their neighbors throws them into the shade.[100]

When Goodwin died on May 13, 1844, Boswell surmised that probably no man in the country had pursued his business for so long a time.[101] For 75 years he had worked with the *Courant.*

Lydia Sigourney wrote one of her sentimental poems to "Our Oldest Man":

Meek patriarch of our city,—art thou dead?
The just, the saintly and the full of days,
The crown of ripen'd wisdom on thy head,
The poor man's blessing, and the good man's praise?
Would that our sons, who saw thee onward move
With step so vigorous and serenely sage,
Of thee might learn to practise, and to love
The hardy virtues of an earlier age.[102]

PART FOUR
1836–1865

CHAPTER XI

CITY NEWSPAPER

JOHN L. BOSWELL, like Ebenezer Watson and George Goodwin, had served his apprenticeship with the *Courant.* Subsequently he had published two papers in Pennsylvania, the *Columbia Spy* and the *Lancaster Union.* When he became the owner and publisher of the *Courant,* he was 26 years of age, married, rather modest in his bearing, regular and methodical in his habits of work.[1] As a promising editor, a follower of Henry Clay, and a Congregationalist, he met squarely the specifications of his old master.[2] According to his salutatory, he approached his task with humility. The *Courant* would continue to uphold the great principles and measures which had long characterized it. Arrangements for editorial assistance had been made which he hoped would be acceptable. He entered a field where he knew that much was expected of him. He would do all in his power to sustain the high reputation of the newspaper. He asked the indulgence of the public.[3]

Boswell's 18 years with the *Courant* approximated the life span of the Whig party. In all the ways open to an enterprising, yet sedate and conservative journal, he promoted consistently the party's principles in Connecticut. The speeches and acts of the leaders of the day were appropriately praised or ridiculed. Good or evil motives were assigned hither and yon according to political predilections. In petty disputes with the opposition papers, especially the *Times,* the *Courant* for the most part refrained from personal abuse.[4] Campaign material, letters, reprints, and editorials formed an integrated partisan pattern. Boswell spoke to a statewide audience. His editorials were moderately well written, genial, and substantial. They were never flowery, seldom sprightly. On the need for tariff protection and the evils of an expanding slavery, they were reiterative and persistent. To paraphrase the words of a contemporary, the tone of his paper was always on the side of morality and good order.[5]

Boswell began publishing the *Daily Courant* in 1837,[6] claiming to have undertaken the venture more to gratify friends and advertisers than from the expectation of immediate profits.[7] The distressed state of federal finance and the impending special session of Congress made it desirable that local readers get the news more frequently.[8] He issued a prospectus on August 29, and planned to print the first regular number on September 6, but since the public response was weak, he waited until the 12th. If he were receiving adequate support by the first of the year, he said the subscription price would be $5.00 per annum, and $30.00 for advertisers who purchased a square a day.[9] On December 13, he confessed to have entertained strong doubts at the beginning. Thus far he had lost money. If he could get 400 subscribers and 30 yearly advertisers, the publication could go on. Terms for advertisers were reduced to $25.00 for the year, $20.00 without the paper but not including insertions in the weekly *Courant*.[10] Though by New Year's Day he had failed to achieve his goal, he decided to continue anyway. Mail from some quarter came to Hartford almost every hour in the day and night. Since the wealth, business, and population of the city could handsomely support such an enterprise, he declared he placed his trust in the future.[11] The size of the paper was about 12 by 16 inches, four pages with four columns to the page. Before long, advertisements filled three quarters or more of the printed surface. One page or less carried editorials, reprints, and an occasional letter. Most of the news was political.[12]

Daily journalism placed an emphasis upon speed in newsgathering. Since state elections were exciting and pre-eminently newsworthy, Boswell exploited Hartford's central location to scoop the annual returns in Connecticut. By the cooperation of postmasters and others, private expresses galloped by night to the *Courant* office from all corners of the state in time for the next morning's paper. In 1838, for example, vote tabulations were received from all but 10 towns by 7:00 A.M. Starting at five minutes after eight, special riders bore copies of the *Courant* to Boston, Norwich, Middletown, New Haven, and elsewhere.[13] To get the results of the New York state elections in the fall of that year, Boswell had expresses running from Albany and New York City.[14] To his annoyance, other editors sometimes appropriated the fruits of this system without acknowledgment. He complained of the expense and the trouble, took credit for originating the idea, and continued to furnish the earliest returns for a number of years.[15]

The *Courant* relayed the legislative news with as much dispatch as possible before telegraphic facilities were available. When the General Assembly met in Hartford, the day's proceedings were covered in the next morning's issue.[16] When the sessions were in New Haven, readers had to be satisfied at first with what took place until noon of the day preceding.[17] For more distant news, thanks to the local postmaster, papers and letters were collectible at the Hartford office at irregular hours of the day and night.[18] To report the Congress which convened in December, 1838, Boswell arranged for daily communications from an experienced correspondent in Washington.[19] Public documents were usually supplied by some of the Connecticut representatives.[20] On important occasions, extraordinary efforts were made to transmit information quickly. Van Buren's first message to Congress, delivered on September 5, 1837, arrived in Hartford sometime on the 6th to be printed in a *Courant Extra* the day following.[21] It traveled from Washington to Boston at an average speed of 18 miles per hour, hastened along the way by the 70 miles of railroad track between Baltimore and Philadelphia.[22] On December 6, 1838, Boswell stayed his press until noon, hoping to give readers a copy of another Van Buren message. He had planned to get it by express from New Haven but the boat from New York was detained. "It is very singular," he wrote, "that the great Southern mail, so important to all parts of New England, should be delayed 24 hours, in consequence of a little fog in the sound." [23] The *Courant* claimed to have established a record in 1841 by publishing one of John Tyler's speeches in less than 24 hours after its delivery in Washington.[24]

In the summer of 1846 Hartford was connected by telegraph with New York and Boston. Boswell arranged for daily market reports and for such other information from points along the line as might interest his readers. He could beat the mails from New York by a whole day.[25] About 2:00 P.M. on April 21, 1848, a ship arrived at New York with tidings of the revolutionary outbreaks in several European cities. By five o'clock that afternoon Hartford was reading Boswell's *Extra*.[26] He was proud of the celerity with which returns came in after the national election of 1848. Inside 12 hours he had heard from the votes of 16 states.[27] Synopses of the proceedings of Congress now appeared in the next day's *Courant*. Citing seven columns of a closely printed speech by Louis Kossuth in 1851, an editorial boasted that no paper in the state spent more money for such services.[28] Short reports by wire appeared usually under the heading, "By Magnetic Telegraph." Whatever arrived by evening telegraph or late train was included under "Postscript." [29] Boswell wrote in 1854:

... we believe a comparison of our files with those of a New York paper would show that the most important news of the day had been published by us at the same time it was issued in the larger cities. Our telegraphic intelligence is generally the same, our notices of foreign arrivals while they give all that is important, are often more readable than larger accounts, and as we receive by the evening mails from the east and south the morning papers from the principal cities between Portland and Philadelphia, and the New York and Boston evening papers, we are enabled early to publish whatever of interest they contain. Each morning we give reports of the New York markets, and stock sales, both first and second boards, of the day previous, and generally receive by telegraph notices of the market in Southern and Western cities.[30]

Boswell's personal reaction to the increased tempo of news reception was mixed. He spoke in 1850 of the annoyances and disappointments which afflicted the editor of a daily press with lines out of order, missing or obstinate operators, and general mismanagement by the telegraph companies.[31] With certain exceptions he thought the telegraph of questionable public value. Readers got their information earlier but paid for it by sacrificing accuracy, for the editor had no means of checking at the time whether the "news" was rumor, falsehood, or truth. People had been just as well off formerly when they got an accurate statement of Congressional debates three days afterward. The telegraph also aggravated the existing national trait of impatience. It began to make an impression on Hartford's merchants. Prompt, instantaneous decisions were characteristic of those now deemed to be top-notch business men. The calm, investigating judgment of yore was becoming passé. People, having little time for serious reflection, were constantly chasing novelties.[32] Boswell did not pursue the subject again.

An increasing amount of local news appeared. Readers wrote letters advocating or complaining about something. Private and public organizations issued resolutions or annual reports which were printed or commented upon. Lectures, recitals, and various entertainments were advertised and sometimes given editorial notice. Speeches were reported. College and school graduation or commencement programs were printed. The proceedings of the city government were recorded. Beginning in 1852, the city court was covered.[33] Little of what was written by Boswell and his associates would pass for reporting by modern standards. Accounts were seldom devoid of expressed or implied opinionativeness. They

were usually brief appraisals, deprecating, admonishing, or lauda-
tory in tone. For example, when bonds of the Hartford, Providence
& Fishkill Railroad were placed on sale, Boswell announced that
they were good investments.[34] When Horace Wells patented a
coal sifter, he recommended it to the public as a useful instrument.[35] When Barnum's circus came to town, the paper warned
people of pickpockets.[36] When reporting a fire, it suggested that
incendiaries were probably responsible.[37] Beginning in the late
1840's, as Hartford's business increased rapidly, the *Courant* indulged generously in city boosting, describing new and old industries, the growth of downtown streets, new buildings, population,
and the like, all in the spirit of exultation.[38] It had been possible for a
long time to find articles in the *Courant* which were essentially
editorials according to modern concepts. However, it was not yet
possible to observe commonly the straight reporting of city news.
Almost all of the writing betrayed a personal flavor.

What reading matter appeared in the *Daily* was utilized to compose the weekly *Connecticut Courant* which Boswell issued each
Friday or Saturday.[39] The two editions were virtually identical in
news and editorial content.[40] While politics predominated, both
daily and weekly carried nonpolitical foreign and domestic news
along with market reports, marriage and death announcements,
notices of books and magazines, an annual calendar, sloop arrivals,
occasional poetry and fiction. The "Carrier's Address" continued
for several years.[41] Fairs of the Hartford County Agricultural Society were reported at length.[42] The paper took an interest in the
mulberry craze of the late 1830's,[43] but agricultural news was featured much less frequently than formerly. Still less was printed,
including even the temperance material, that embodied the old
spirit of uplift so common in the 1820's.[44] These themes gave way,
especially after the mid-forties, to an interest in the local development of railroads, industries, insurance companies, mercantile establishments, civic projects, and population.[45] With the advent
of the telegraph, news reports were more succinct. The verbatim
publication of speeches became less usual.[46] Essays all but disappeared, though Isaac W. Stuart, under the pseudonym of "Scaeva,"
wrote excellently on the early history of Hartford in the papers of
1851 and 1852.[47] In this connection, the *Courant* published a full-
page, lithographed map showing the town in 1640.[48] During the
agitation against the Kansas-Nebraska Act in 1854, Boswell printed
the *Courant*'s first map of the United States depicting the states and

territories with reference to slavery.[49] With the outbreak of the Crimean War he distributed to subscribers a "Map of the Seat of War." [50] Subscribers to the weekly continued to receive the fortnightly *Supplement,* which contained tales of travel, history, biography, poetry, and a great variety of miscellaneous reading.[51]

Despite periodic enlargements of the daily and weekly *Courant,* advertisements continued to take the major portion of space. Besides soliciting the custom of patent medicine distributors, railroad companies, coal dealers, grocers, and others, Boswell kept an eye fixed on government advertising. In the early forties, with the Whigs in control of nation and state, the *Courant* printed the federal and state laws, fought with the local *Patriot & Eagle* for bankruptcy notices, and listed dead letters for the Hartford post office.[52] The last assignment was given to the *Times* in 1846 when, according to the law, it should have been awarded to the paper with the largest circulation. Boswell attacked the Democratic postmaster, appealed to the Postmaster General, and shortly recovered his plum.[53] In 1850 published commercial rates in the *Daily* were as follows, advertisements exclusively on the inside pages costing 50 per cent more: [54]

For 1 square with no change of advertisement—

1 day	$ 0.60
3 days	1.00
1 week	1.50
1 year	10.00

For 1 square with change of advertisement—

3 months	$ 7.00
6 months	12.00
1 year	20.00

Advertising became increasingly important. Partly to exploit this angle of the business, the publishers in Hartford agreed in 1837 to charge regular rates for public notices by fire departments, ecclesiastical and medical societies, literary institutions, and similar organizations.[55] Boswell also promised to make people pay for obituaries of more than five lines.[56] Aside from endorsing such measures, the Connecticut Newspaper Association in 1853 denounced the practice of selling space at less than the published rates.[57] It resolved to blacklist advertisers who broke their contracts and to take steps to boost rates by at least 25 per cent.[58] Boswell's predecessors had occasionally omitted advertisements for want of room. Boswell did likewise one time in 1838, but by the 1850's he chose to sacrifice reading matter rather than advertising.[59] In January, 1854, the pressure on his columns induced him to make the *Courant* the largest daily paper in the state.[60]

Although the *Daily* of 1854 was more than twice the size of the first issue of 1837, the annual price was about the same, $5.00 or $4.50 if paid in advance.[61] The weekly was advertised for $2.00 during the entire period.[62] Reduced rates were offered for quantity purchases and special rates for subscriptions during the sessions of Congress and the General Assembly.[63] Presumably most *Daily* readers resided in or about Hartford while the majority of weekly subscribers lived outside. Boswell chronically boasted of an increasing number of customers and laid claim traditionally to a larger distribution than any other Connecticut paper.[64] In 1846 the combined circulation of the two editions was over 5,500. Issues of the *Daily,* which had started at 200, had reached 720.[65] In Boswell's earlier years the mail stages and railroads carried newspapers without charge, but postal regulations ended this practice.[66] After July 1, 1851, the *Daily* was mailed to any point within a radius of 50 miles for $1.00 per year. The weekly was delivered free in Hartford County.[67]

The *Courant* prospered in Boswell's day. Local rivals appeared and disappeared, but none endured very long, some only for a few months.[68] In 1845 the *Courant* bought out the *Hartford Journal,* daily and weekly, and in 1849 took over the *Connecticut Whig.*[69] It had no Whig competitors worthy its mettle. Only the Democratic *Times* lasted through all these years. Alfred E. Burr, who published and edited it, was once Boswell's fellow apprentice. As press foreman he had printed the first issues of the *Daily Courant,* and on leaving Boswell's employment in 1839 the *Courant* had wished him success in all but his politics.[70] For brief times in the 1840's the *Courant* bore the names of associate editors, Chauncey Howard and Lucius E. Smith.[71] In 1850 Boswell formed a partnership with William Faxon, a native of West Hartford.[72] Since Faxon's subsequent business career was distinguished, his connection probably afforded Boswell more time and energy for editorial writing.[73] In this task he had the help of John P. Brace who remained with the *Courant* until 1861.[74] Assisting also were two future proprietors, Abel N. Clark and William H. Goodrich. Clark kept the books and acted as chief business manager. Goodrich was a journeyman printer.[75]

Boswell died unexpectedly of erysipelas on July 30, 1854, in the 47th year of his life.[76] To his associates the suddenness of his death was a great shock, but the *Courant* supposed that such dispensations were unquestionably wisely ordered. It spoke of his high standing in the community, his many relations with the city's business interests, his reputation for promptness, his unobtrusiveness, his private charities, and the large gathering of citizens who attended his funeral.[77] The paper went on without important change until January 1, 1855, when it became the property of Thomas M. Day of Hartford.[78]

The *Courant* entered a new era when it came under Day's management. In the first place, it severed connections with the expiring Whig party. Day wrote: "With regard to the party name by which we shall be known we are not tenacious—the word is not so important as the deed." [79] The *Courant* became a Know-Nothing journal and soon drifted into the Republican party, supporting Lincoln's administration during the Civil War.[80] Secondly, while wishing to sustain the *Courant*'s reputation as a "sound, safe and sober sheet," Day hoped to infuse more life and vigor into it. He promised changes in appearance and content. He wrote well and vowed to speak frankly. People might contribute their opinions, for he feared not to have readers see both sides of a question. Thirdly, the *Courant* would cover, sift, and condense news as it had never done before. It would employ reporters to collect all the floating items, attend public meetings, and keep in touch with everything newsworthy, especially in the city, county, and state. The out-of-state metropolitan papers supplied great quantities of foreign and national intelligence, but the local field particularly needed to be exploited.[81]

In another direction Day's control marked a new departure. For 90 years the *Courant*'s owners had been practical printers who were familiar with the mechanical as well as the editorial aspects of the business. To all this Day was a stranger. Graduated from Yale College in 1837, he had gained admission to the bar in 1840. After a brief practice, which deafness forced him to abandon, he engaged in mercantile pursuits. In 1850 and 1851 he traveled abroad. From the time he returned until he took over the *Courant,* he was not active in any business. He was financially comfortable.[82]

True to his promise, the *Courant* made changes during his decade of tenure. The editorials of the first year, when he exploited his Know-Nothing views, were pert, forthright, pungently written, and probably infuriating to the local Irish and Germans.[83] Partly because the Know-Nothing phase passed, and partly, one supposes, because experience taught him to be cautious where private opinion might be risky, his editorials were afterward less strongly personal in tone though they were always skillfully phrased.

The *Daily* increased its news content. Brief paragraphs appeared in columns neatly arranged under such headings as "City Items," "State Items," "Political Items," "Military Items," "Army Correspondence," "Religious Intelligence," "The Farm and the Garden." An occasional column entitled "Money and Business" very ably discussed corporate and financial affairs interesting to local investors.[84] Along with editorials, letters and book notices, these filled usually the seven columns of the *Courant*'s second page. Under "The Latest News by Telegraph," the brief foreign, Congressional, and Civil War news, along with market reports, took the middle column on page 3. The remainder of the paper was given over to advertisements set up in fine print and devoid of the assorted cuts of former years.[85] The typographical improvement was marked.[86] On the content, Day remarked in 1859 that the paper should be like a cheerful morning visitor, touching gracefully upon the topics of the hour and passing along. Readers wanted variety and they wanted it briefly:

The character of journalism in America is every day changing. Thirty years ago, only the public doings of public bodies, were chronicled in the driest way. Now-a-days, people . . . care more to know what is going on about their own homesteads. The local journal is becoming the chronicler of all the little local matters; the remembrancer, to call to mind the business of the day and jog the memory, in time for needful action. We think the *Courant* owes much of its success to the fact that it is eminently a family paper; is read at thousands of breakfast tables; contains something for both sexes; and is addressed to the young as well as the old.[87]

Since the *Daily* exemplified what the editor thought a local journal should be, the city news was covered closely. During the war Warren H. Burr and A. S. Hotchkiss were the city reporters.[88] They catered to the public interest in matters large and small—shows, concerts, sports, gardening, church activities, crime, and court trials.[89] Day warned citizens not to request that items be kept out of the paper, for he had an obligation to thousands of subscribers.[90] Hotchkiss counted it a duty to report the facts without bias. Sometimes he omitted the names of people where he believed injustice might follow, and he was abused sometimes for including names.[91] He wrote the *Courant*'s first Christmas shopping news.[92] Burr was responsible for the first spring style reporting:

Stepping aside from our usual custom we give this morning, for the benefit of our lady readers in and out of town, a slight description of the spring styles of millinery, as shown yesterday at the "opening" of several of our fashionable milliners. . . .

At Mrs. Daniels', we saw a lovely violet hat trimmed with moss roses and green grass, with barbes of lace running down the side; and another elegant one was a sort of brown crape with a large black lace leaf set upon one side of the lace curtain, and a brown mossy branch with frosted leaves . . . inside, scarlet pomegranite blossoms, with brown glistening wheat and black lace. A very pretty drab chip hat trimmed with a large bunch of roses peeping from a bed of moss, dotted with drops of dew, over which hovers a bright little humming bird. Barbes of black lace and a cape of the same with inside trimmings of mignonette and forget-me-nots finishes this beautiful hat.[93]

With the outbreak of war, the general contents of the paper took on a different flavor, not, however, at the sacrifice of local reporting. The quantity of foreign news, which had diminished over the years, reached a new low. Letters on political subjects, less common than formerly, virtually vanished.[94] A sprinkling of war poetry, casualty lists, excerpts from letters from the boys in camp, material on civilian war activities, appeals for volunteers, wartime politics, and the progress of federal arms accounted for a large part of the reading. In a few issues, editorials discussed "freedom of the press," finding nothing in the Constitution to keep the government from bearing down on "Copperhead" newspapers.[95] On the other hand, the War Department's censorship goaded the editor into an occasional outburst, mostly on grounds that important tidings came late and that false rumors injured public morale.[96] In the latter connection the *Courant* assumed editorially that Jefferson Davis was dead on September 7, 1861. Several weeks prematurely, a *Courant Extra* announced Vicksburg's surrender.[97] The capture of Richmond was falsely reported from Philadelphia in May, 1863.[98] In 1864 a forged proclamation, purporting to have originated in Washington, caused local excitement and dejection.[99] Bulletins displayed important news at the *Courant* office on holidays and the owners were not adverse to printing extras on Sundays.[100] Sometimes the speed of war reporting was relatively slow. The battle at Gettysburg, for example, reached a decisive phase on Friday, July 3,

1863; but because of the holiday week end, no *Courant* bore news of the results until the following Monday.

However, the *Courant* generally maintained its tradition for speed in getting the news. It purchased the services of the New York Associated Press, beginning sometime under Boswell. Day wrote on January 31, 1855: "It has not been sufficiently understood heretofore, that we have *all* the telegraphic information within reach of the Associated Press in New York. Of course, we pay for it, and pay handsomely." [101] The greatest sort of thrill came in August, 1858, with the completion of the transatlantic cable. Day eulogized Cyrus W. Field, and the citizens in Hartford, as elsewhere, held a civic celebration; but the cable broke on September 1, and news from Europe continued to be labeled "5 days later" until after the Civil War. [102] In November, 1860, the *Courant's* expresses and the telegraph brought the Connecticut election news from all but two towns by three o'clock in the morning. No state in the Union had its returns gathered as completely within 10 hours of the closing of the polls. Day got congratulations from a number of out-of-state newspapers. [103] The reception of Lincoln's speech to Congress on December 1, 1862, surpassed previous records:

The Message was sent North yesterday by telegraph. Its receipt in this city commenced at 3:30 P.M., and continued without a moment's intermission till 11 o'clock. Mr. G. K. Walcott, the head operator in the Hartford office, received it entire by sound without making a single break during the whole time—a feat unparalleled in the history of American telegraphing. [104]

Most important of all, the *Courant* kept a circulation lead against three local dailies and numbers of weeklies. [105] The *Times,* Democratic throughout the war period and still its closest competitor, was now published by the Burr brothers. [106] In 1858 J. M. Scofield founded the Democratic *Post,* daily and weekly. [107] Because the city had no forthright Republican paper in 1856, 100 citizens, Gideon Welles and John R. Niles among them, launched the *Press.* [108] Soon on its staff were Joseph R. Hawley, Charles Dudley Warner, and Stephen A. Hubbard, men prominent in the *Courant's* postwar history. [109] Through the whole period Day's subscriptions increased annually. [110] With the firing on Sumter, daily circulation spurted and in a month's time the weekly soared from 17,000 to 26,000. [111] The *Courant* installed steam power and bought a Hoe press because the old Adams machine could no longer handle the load.[112] It had the biggest city circulation and repeatedly claimed the largest in the state.[113] In December, 1864, Day wrote that subscribers had trebled since 1855.[114]

Advertising increased, space cost more, and customers paid more for their papers. By 1865 ads and paid notices, set in small type, accounted for about five eighths the surface of daily issues that measured 26 inches by 18 inches with the usual four pages.[115] Supplementing income from regular commercial sources was whatever came from official printing for state and federal governments.[116] Because of the cotton shortage, the wartime rise in the cost of paper was disproportionately rapid, forcing a chronic upward revision of advertisement and subscription rates.[117] By the end of 1864 one square in the daily cost $35.00 per year, $1.00 for a single insertion in the weekly.[118] Annual subscribers to either paper paid $8.00 and $2.00.[119] The *Courant* charged for birth, marriage, and death notices.[120] The *Daily* sold on the streets for four cents.[121]

Four months before the end of the war Day sold his share in the paper to A. N. Clark who had been his business partner since 1857.[122] He had decided in 1855 to retain his post for only a decade. For the last two years he had taken small part in the management, but he looked back with pride on the *Courant*'s progress.[123] Jacob A. Turner, who worked for Day as a compositor, recorded his memory of these years in 1914. As often happens in the reminiscences of old age, the chronology of events is a little confused, but the picture is interesting.[124] The office was that which the Goodwins had entered in 1815. The press was that which they had bought in the 1830's.[125]

Looking over the paper's outfit of today—its facilities for gathering news and its mechanical means of getting it before the public; its increased pages and the vast amount of reading matter spread upon them—it seems almost incredible to me, even though in daily touch with the various improvements. Turning back to the old place as it was it requires little brushing up of memory to see again the dark, time-worn little room devoted to the practical part of the establishment in which was done the typesetting, presswork, mailing, counting out carriers, and a hundred and one other incidentals that entered into the publication of the paper. Five or six compositors, a woman to "feed" the Adams press, a good strong man to furnish the "steam" for propelling it, completed the outfit. The business and editorial end of the establishment was massed in a little seven-by-nine room facing Main street. A. N. Clark handled the business end, tucked away in one corner of the room. A very plain studded railing fenced the "intellectual" people away from the ordinaries. It required little room for this force, which amounted to a mere trio. Thomas M. Day, editor-in-chief, "Al" Hotchkiss, city editor, were the principal occupants, J. P. Brace, the "heavy" editor, making his home in a dusty, spider-webbed sort of a library on the floor above, reached by a rickety stairway that might have been in use in Methuselah's day. W. H. Goodrich, then foreman of the practical department, tossed in a few city items occasionally, mostly in the nature of "puffs" for one thing and another that drifted into the office. Aside from these tid-bits Hotchkiss was the whole city department. Later Mr. Goodrich came to be clerk of the police court, which enabled him to turn out a real news item now and then. Aside from these, the city, editorial comment, and news comment devolved on the three worthies named—Day, Brace and Hotchkiss. Mr. Clark for a long time combined editing the telegraphic news with his not overformidable labors at the books. He hiked down to the telegraph office, too, to get the dispatches. All this was boy's play as compared with present-day newspaper work. Oftener than otherwise the telegraph office was closed before 9 o'clock in the evening and the outside local world for the most part was in bed and asleep! Compositors quit soon after 9 o'clock, a member of the day force coming around at about 1 o'clock in the morning to "make up" the paper and get it ready for the press, and he usually "fed" the morning's edition 'till the girl came in.

It was a four page paper then, the "outside" (first and fourth) pages being printed in the day time, without news or reading matter of any kind, or any changing of ads, the outside pages for three days being run off the same day, merely the date being changed. It will interest printers, and likely amuse them, to know that the night work—the setting type part of it—was done in shifts, usually only two men being required to put up the meager telegraphic news, these remaining till shortly after 9 o'clock, or until Mr. Clark had turned in his last bit of telegraphic news, with his always cheery "Good night." [126]

Two months before Day retired, the *Courant* celebrated its 100th anniversary by printing and distributing a facsimile of Thomas Green's first issue.[127] "The life of the COURANT," wrote the editor, "extends over the most eventful century in the history of man." According to Day, in no period had the march of progress been so rich and diversified in its manifestations. The old weekly newspaper had been enlarged from time to time until it exceeded five times the size of the original.[128] Even the fortnightly *Supplement* was more than twice its size. The *Courant* had always been self-supporting. Public calamities and financial panics had left it unscathed. Its circulation and advertising patronage were never before so large, its prospects never more promising for an indefinite career of influence and usefulness. Day offered his personal best wishes:

THE COURANT: *esto perpetua!* [129]

CHAPTER XII

WHIG POLITICS

WHEN the people elected Martin Van Buren to the presidency, the *Courant* disparaged their choice:

The truth is, he has the confidence of nobody but office-holders, and office-seekers. They are certainly a numerous, active, and efficient body, scattered throughout the Union, and working with all their might to secure their own places, and their own incomes. Still, he will be, in name at least, PRESIDENT OF THE UNITED STATES, and what he may fall short in public spirit and patriotism, will be made up in the gratification of his ambition and vanity. That he will come into office with a smooth, cajoling, flattering exterior—the contrast of everything in the character and conduct of his predecessor—there is very little reason to doubt. The consequences of his administration will be better known hereafter.[1]

The Whigs made effective capital of the depression which blighted the country during Van Buren's years in the White House. According to Boswell, hard times were the miserable consequences of Jackson's political chicanery. He had wrought the destruction of the United States Bank. He had fostered the multiplication of small, unsound "pet banks." He had issued his ill-advised Specie Circular. He had wrecked the credit of the entire country. Not only the government treasury, but all branches of the economy had suffered. Banks suspended specie payment, stocks fell, mills closed or curtailed output, commerce waned, agricultural prices were deflated, profits and wages diminished, unemployment set in, and land values were down. The Whigs had clearly foreseen the results.[2]

Since the *Courant* regarded Van Buren as Jackson's henchman, its editorial reproaches were almost ready-made. Jackson had wrecked the United States Bank because he was unable to convert it to his peculiar political uses; Van Buren's Independent Treasury was a scheme for grand and petty fraud.[3] Jackson had been the enemy of sound currency; Van Buren's treasury notes were akin to the "continentals" of years ago.[4] Jackson had introduced a system of administrative corruption; in 1840 Boswell called Van Buren's presidency "the most unfaithful, mischievous, unprincipled, and corrupt administration that has ever presided over the concerns of the nation."[5] In four years the *Courant* approved only the joint resolution of Congress which in effect repealed the Specie Circular.[6]

The most important measure of the Van Buren administration created the Independent Treasury, an arrangement whereby the government became the custodian of its own funds in its own vaults. Boswell remarked that a number of proposals had been made to help put the currency system in order, but he hoped that the Whigs would propose nothing new. The country had suffered too much from untried experiments, and all that was called for was to re-establish the United States Bank. The administration plan seemed to the *Courant* to place federal funds where politicians would misuse them.[7] In this connection were cited 100,000 office holders and Amos Kendall's army of political postmasters.[8] In the earlier years, the President's chief motives arose allegedly from a desire to employ the treasury in buying a personal popularity which his merits and talents denied him. Since his predecessor had filled most of the federal offices, he was accused of needing a substitute for "patronage." [9] Later, the *Courant* insisted that the Democrats were attempting to reproduce the panic of 1837 in order to push the plan through Congress.[10] When finally enacted in 1840, it was said to have been designed for Van Buren's re-election. Although he had run the government in debt and had now achieved private control of its funds, at least the country had avoided the imposition of a large standing army. To all intents and purposes, Jackson's successor was even then a monarch. All he lacked, to believe Boswell's propaganda, was an effective means to prevent the people from expressing their disapproval of him.[11]

Throughout his term the *Courant* accused Van Buren of standing for the wholesale plunder of the public domain. The question of the disposal of public lands had come to the fore at the end of Jackson's administration. Thomas H. Benton and others advocated two points of policy: (1) to throw the lands open to individual settlement on the most liberal terms possible; and (2) to cede to the states the unsold residue of national territory within their boundaries. In supporting Clay's arguments against Benton, the *Courant* disliked the first point and found the second even less tolerable.[12] The lands were yielded to the government by the original states with the understanding that they be held in trust for the common benefit. Benton's proposed reduction, pre-emption and graduation laws would allow aliens from the poorhouses of Europe to erect huts, chop a few trees, plant a few potatoes, and gain possession of the property.[13] As a matter of fact, the land had been pledged to secure the payment of the national debt. With the debt extinguished, title to the land was morally reinvested in the states. Congress had no authority to use the income from the sale of their property, much less to sell it cheaply to trespassers and speculators or to donate it to the rising states of the West. The proceeds should be divided among the states. Connecticut's stake could probably be estimated at more than $30,000,000, enough to support all her schools and colleges for ages to come.[14] Benton was a demagogue.[15] Van Buren was indulging in outright bribery for the sake of western votes.[16]

Month after month, as the tide of opinion moved against the administration, the *Courant* was filled with abuse. One theme predominated: "Gold for the Office-Holders—Rags for the People." [17] After 1837 the Whigs won the annual state elections.[18] Connecticut Democrats or "loco focos," Niles, Welles, Isaac Toucey and others, were made to look prosperous, dishonest, and ridiculous.[19] Opposition journals, especially the *Times* and the New Haven *Register,* lacked ordinary decency.[20] Van Buren was ill fitted to rally his followers. At first he was merely unheroic, tedious, inept, and corrupt. By 1839 he lived like a prince on the people's money.[21] French bedsteads, imported wine coolers, hemmed dishrags, rich carpets, costly mantle sets, gilt and satin covered settees, *fauteuils,* taborets, ottomans, and music stools ornamented the White House. He owned a French china set of 440 pieces. As long as he drew the presidential salary of $25,000, little did he care for small business men, humble workers, and honest farmers.[22] It was suggested repeatedly that he and his party would employ fraud to keep themselves in power. If necessary they would resort to force.[23]

To oust the administration, the Whigs rallied beneath the banner of "Harrison and Reform." Since little was known of the leader, the *Courant* explained him to the public. William Henry Harrison was not an "old granny," nor was he under the tutelage of "managers" or "keepers." He was no military weakling skulking from danger. Neither did he lack the talents necessary for high office. On the contrary, no man in the country had held more civil and military posts. He possessed learning, scholarship, and a favorable religious character. If his views were obscure, so much the worse for his enemies. The Whigs were satisfied with his principles.[24] Fun was poked at his humble living habits, the alleged log cabin and hard cider. But ". . . his strict integrity in the public service,

added to a high and delicate sense of personal honor, and his unbounded benevolence of heart, have kept him comparatively poor
and in debt." [25] He was "the poor man's friend." [26] Tippecanoe
clubs were formed.[27] The *Courant* printed poetry, songs, addresses,
resolutions, and the varied propaganda of an exciting campaign.[28]
For headquarters, Hartford Whigs erected a log cabin complete
with chairs, stools, coon skins, musket, powder flask, shot bag,
snowshoes, and George Washington's portrait.[29] Better a cabin
with independence, plenty, and suitable currency than a palace with
English coach, gold plate, and an empty treasury.[30]

Despite the fact that Van Buren's enemies conducted the colorful campaign of 1840 without benefit of political platform, the
Courant hailed Harrison's inauguration as the commencement of
the "New Era." [31] When John Tyler of Virginia became President one month later, it supposed his views to be sound and promised that the party program would go forward without interruption.[32] What the items of the program were, the editor made abun-
dantly clear. Before Congress convened, readers were told that the
question of the disposal of the income from public lands would
certainly be decided. Provision for distributing the funds should be
made before the admission of new states added senators and representatives who favored the schemes of Benton. The Independent
Treasury would be abolished. As an election device, it had no present value; as a financial institution, it was useless.[33] After Clay
revealed his program, Boswell announced that the proposed national bank should take the general form of the institutions of 1791
and 1816. The country could have no other large-scale regulator of
currency and credit.[34] Last but not least, Congress would have
to undertake a general upward revision of the tariff, which would
necessarily repeal the famous compromise of 1833. Of all the issues,
this one commanded the most editorial space.[35]

The protective tariff was justified on grounds of "general welfare." The *Courant* asseverated that the industry of the people had
an indisputable right to the support of the people's government.
Free trade was nonsensical.[36] The opposition in the South arose
from a willingness to depress northern manufacturing for the sake
of making the slave system work. Elsewhere it was based upon
the miserable delusion that one class of people in a modern community could prosper without bringing benefits to others.[37] For
the farmers the tariff created markets, for the laborers, jobs, and
for the consumers, lower-priced goods. It therefore was not class

legislation. In the first place, protection alone was desired, for anything higher would be of no advantage even to manufacturers.
Secondly, fact, not theory, had already demonstrated that protection reduced the prices of commodities, for it encouraged competition.[38] Moreover, given an adequate law, the country need have
no fear of panics and depressions in the ordinary times of peace—
no slumps, no shutdowns, no unemployment. Protection produced
general prosperity.[39]

According to Boswell, the tariff and distribution issues were
intertwined. John C. Calhoun was derided for supporting Benton's views. The South Carolinian derived his motivation from a
hatred of the tariff. If the lands funds were given to the states,
legislators might argue more tellingly that the government needed
a tariff for income.[40] When Whig ideas of distribution were enacted
into law in 1841, the *Courant* accepted the news with gloating. The
debt-ridden states could discharge their obligations, and Connecticut, in the future, would be relatively free from taxes.[41] The only
alternative now remaining to the tariff was a direct federal tax,
which the people would never countenance.[42] But when the tariff
came up for battle, the tune changed. Because of President Tyler
and a certain legal commitment, it was impossible to raise the tariff
rates without sacrificing the distribution law already passed. The
Courant felt then, if the income from the lands were to be taken
from the states and applied to the ordinary expenses of the federal
government, that ideas of protection would fare ill in the future.[43]
However painful this dilemma, Boswell never hesitated to support
the tariff. The *Courant* not only sermonized constantly upon its
prosperous implications but damned and harassed the Congressmen from New England who ventured to think otherwise.[44]
Within a month after the passage of the tariff of 1842, readers were
offered the news of reviving prosperity. At the end of a year, such
tidings were shouted.[45]

Because of John Tyler, what the Whigs looked forward to as a
"new era" eventuated into a nightmare. A *Courant Extra* bore the
news of the veto of the first bank bill. Boswell, feeling upset and
sarcastic toward the hair-splitting "metaphysician," argued the constitutionality of the measure.[46] In a fortnight, his composure returned. He would stand by Tyler, said he, as long as Tyler adhered
to Whig principles, differences on the bank question notwithstanding.[47] One week before Clay's followers quit the President's
Cabinet, the *Courant* laid the inefficacy of Congress to Democratic

intrigue, to the circulation of fabrications about differences among the Whigs.[48] Even after the second bank veto produced the breach with Tyler, Boswell counseled unity, claiming that intraparty warfare might endanger the measures already passed. He thought that the distribution law and the abolition of the Independent Treasury deserved the country's thanks.[49]

Only when Tyler struck down a Whig tariff bill in August, 1842, did the *Courant* begin to treat him like an enemy. Jackson had been criticized for his vetoes, it said, but when the people began to appreciate the implications of Tyler's use of the power, they would remonstrate in language not to be gainsaid or misunderstood. He was making himself a constituent part of the legislature. He was negating the will of the majority.[50] Well before his term was concluded, the *Courant* spoke of "apostasy" and "treachery." [51] Crude words expressed bitter contempt:

We doubt whether stronger delusion was ever sent upon a public man, than is at this moment visiting the *Accidental Mr. Tyler*. The poor lunatic considers himself popular. . . . Is the man smitten with sudden idiocy? . . . We have heard of men who imagined themselves teapots, or that they stood on glass feet; but the case like Mr. Tyler's is not yet recorded in any of the books.[52]

Before the election of Tyler's successor, the disturbing question of Texas came sharply into the political foreground:

Here are the vacant lands, and a pretty large lot of them too. Any citizens of Connecticut that wish to emigrate to the land of Bowie knives and Toothpicks, can have their choice of all varieties. Here are fine mountainous deserts, wild prairies ready stocked with full-blood Camanches and wild horses that will do excellent service—when you catch them, plenty of villages, Taos, Sante Fe, Albuburque [sic], Sibelletta, &c., already inhabited by some 18 or 20,000 Mexicans, copper-colored near to a black, and who will make capital slaves.

To be sure they have been given away by one King after another, Spanish and Mexican, and are now occupied by Mexican subjects as Mexican provinces; and one Jacob Barker alone claims some 130 million acres or so; but what of that? We are the strongest and have followed the advice of the old crone to the Artful Dodger,

Steal from the weak uns, so when
they go for to say you steal you
can go for to lick em.

Besides Texas gives them to us. Why look at the Treaty. There is our title deed all signed, though not sealed, to mines and lands, and buildings and arsenals, and stores, &c. &c., like the songs in the handbill, too tedious to mention. She gives them to us! Aye, so the old Farmer gave away his lands on his death bed. "I will," said he to the attorney, "to my son John 500 acres of land, to James 400 acres." "Stop," says the scribe, "where are they to get them?" "Get them? Why work for them as I did." She gives them, but we must lie and cheat and fight for them as she did.

The fact is that there are no vacant lands belonging to Texas in existence, and all that debt of 20 millions or more will come out of the Treasury of the United States: and the citizens of Connecticut are to bear their share of this and of the war that must succeed.[53]

The *Courant* advanced several reasons to explain the developing sentiment in favor of annexation. The slaveholders of the South desired to expand their empire. Their political agents in Washington were apprehensive of the threat of the Northwest. They would need the representation of additional slave states to preserve their Congressional power. Americans who had acquired Texan bonds were anxious to guarantee their investments. Speculators, who had validated their land claims by the rebellion against Mexico, were hoping to stimulate settlement.[54] Bad faith had been manifest through all the proceedings terminating in the Texan revolution. The complaints and grievances to Mexico were the sham work of a minority. This "struggle of an oppressed people for freedom" was a farce.[55] The incorporation of Texas and California would jeopardize our relations with Mexico. Worst of all, it would perpetuate the national disgrace and curse of slavery.[56]

Though the Texas and Oregon questions were politically linked, Boswell had little to say about the distant Northwest. The election excitement generated by the Democrats appeared to him foolish. Why talk of terminating the treaty of joint occupation with England? The nation had no more use for Oregon than for Tartary, but the westerners were in a better position than the British to settle it. Therefore it would eventually be American.[57] When Webster and Lord Ashburton composed the treaty to end the Maine boundary dispute, the *Courant* thought that no two governments on the globe had more substantial reasons to maintain lasting peace and friendship than did England and the United States.[58]

The presidential choice of 1844 was a great disappointment to the *Courant*. During Tyler's years it had engaged earnestly in state political campaigns. It had fought the "vile and levelling principles of Loco Focoism." [59] It had appealed to workers, farmers, merchants, shoemakers, hatters, tailors, young men, debtors, abolitionists, and honest men generally.[60] It had played the currency and tariff issues for all they were worth.[61] But Connecticut's Whigs had been trounced in 1842 and 1843.[62] In the spring of 1844 the Whigs carried the state in what the editor called a victory for the protection of American industry.[63] This brought hopes that Henry Clay, the great Whig leader, might at last be rewarded in the national election of November. The tariff and the Texas issues were paramount. Poems, clubs, parades, conventions, and all the elements of the election institution were recorded in the *Courant*.[64] James K. Polk and his party wanted to reinstall the odious Independent Treasury. They sought the repeal of the tariff of 1842. In effect, they stood for the destruction of the currency, of industry, and eventually of the Union. They favored the annexation of Texas, the perpetuation of slavery, and immediate war with Mexico.[65] A vote for James G. Birney, candidate of the Liberty party, was a vote for Polk. For "slavery and disunion," vote Democrat. For "liberty and the Union," vote Whig. For "a fair day's wages for a fair day's work," cast your ballot for Clay.[66] The *Courant* attributed Polk's election to four factors: (1) the votes of the New York abolitionists for Birney; (2) the seductiveness of British gold in spreading the gospel of free trade; (3) the weight of recent immigrants and the Catholic priesthood; and (4) the influence of the holders of Texan bonds.[67]

The policies of Polk's administration, as the *Courant* interpreted them, were unfavorable to the successful prosecution of business. Although the paper was distressed when Congress set out to reestablish the Independent Treasury, agitation of the old bank and currency issues never appeared thereafter.[68] Editorials on the distribution of the proceeds from the public lands were stopped for the nonce, to be resumed a few years later from a somewhat different point of view.[69] Polk was accused of betraying his election promises and of seeking to gain Oregon by accommodating the British with "free trade" legislation. He and his party were "panic makers." [70] All the old arguments for the beneficence of protection paraded through the paper, year in and year out, even after the rates of the recent Whig tariff were lowered by the Walker tariff of 1846. In the early days of Polk's tenure, as if the Independent Treasury and the impending revision of the tariff were not enough, his unstatesmanlike management of the Oregon question and the worsening relations with Mexico tended to shake the confidence of the business fraternity, if Boswell is to be believed. Enterprise saw no encouragement ahead, he said, and commerce felt the blight, chiefly from the lack of stability in public policy and from the fear of war. The recklessness with which numerous papers in the country spoke of the prospect of hostilities with Great Britain or Mexico, or with both, was ill advised and contemptible.[71]

Although what the paper regarded as the cooked-up dispute with Great Britain was peaceably settled, no such happy issue characterized the Texan affair. From beginning to end, editorials censured the measures leading to the Mexican War. Months before annexation, readers were rallied to protest.[72] When Texas entered the Union, the names of Connecticut's congressmen who voted for admission were held up to shame in prominent type.[73] To believe the *Courant,* the ease with which northern and western representatives yielded to demands for living space for surplus slaves was more than mere baseness: it was the saddest commentary ever written upon the professed principles of the American Republic.[74] As war approached, readers were told that American occupation of the east bank of the Rio Grande constituted military aggression.[75] All this was the work of a single political party, but the fighting which followed belonged to the nation:

The war is upon us, and the nation must make the best of it. It will cost less treasure and sacrifice, less number of human beings, to prosecute it vigorously, and to a speedy termination. It is too late perhaps, to retrieve the errors of a gigantic scheme of folly and ambition, and the nation must show its strength in putting an end to hostilities. But the mournful and humiliating history of the proceedings which involved us in the contest, cannot be forgotten or forgiven by a people who are peaceful in their pursuits, and abhor the carnage and devastation inflicted upon nations by warring armies.[76]

Since the *Courant* attributed to Polk the responsibility for instigating the war, it wanted to know his plans for its prosecution. Was the American Army merely to occupy what was claimed to be the Texas boundary or was it to march forward, multiplying its "conquests"? Were the troops to invade Mexico by different routes, finally to "revel in the Halls of the Montezumas"? Was the navy to besiege the ports of Mexico? Was the conflict to be terminated quickly, or was it to be protracted for the sake of glory, plunder, and revenge? Did he intend to conduct the war as it suited his tastes without informing the people? If the President's habitual bungling supplied the clue, wrote Boswell, the country might anticipate a long guerrilla struggle with steep taxes, crushing debts, federal bankruptcy, industrial paralysis, and a loss of national prestige.[77]

The *Courant's* editorials continued to harass the administration. The conduct of the war was said to be inefficient, costly, and waged for the promotion of slavery. It was a war of conquest.[78] Those who volunteered to fight were advised sarcastically to share whatever immortality the affair might bring to Polk and his Cabinet.[79] The alleged pompous behavior and bloated assumptions of Brigadier General Stephen Kearny and Commodore Robert Stockton were derided,[80] but Zachary Taylor and Winfield Scott, both Whigs, were defended against all criticism.[81] Repeatedly the *Courant* demanded to know the government's war aims.[82] Taking a stand against territorial acquisitions, it assumed nevertheless that such gains were in the cards.[83] When Polk visited Hartford in June, 1847, Boswell proclaimed his feeling of indifference.[84] He confessed little patience with the doctrine of Manifest Destiny:

We have no sympathy with that lust for territorial aggrandizement which a spurious patriotism attempts to pass off for the "destiny" and "mission" of this country. The area of true freedom can never be thus forcibly extended. We trust that such ideas of national growth may become obsolete as speedily as possible, and give place to the true and just notion of progress our elder statesmen in time past were wont to cherish—progress in knowledge, arts, science, religion, and in everything which is lovely and of good report. But if, by the action of the constitutional rulers of our land, territorial expansion must enter into our policy, a regard to the character and the best good of the present and all succeeding generations, requires that the one institution, which has retarded the growth of half the Union, shall not exert a malign influence over a single acre of newly acquired territory.[85]

By thus insisting upon the exclusion of slavery, the *Courant* fought steadfastly for the Wilmot Proviso. After a few months of war Boswell saw indications that people would not accept calmly the geographical extension of human bondage.[86] In his opinion the liberality which had suffered slavery to remain unmolested when the Constitution was formed did not sanction or contemplate its expansion. Northerners felt deeply upon this subject. They had no intention of violating the letter or spirit of the Constitution. They desired not to tamper with the Missouri Compromise. Nor did they in any sense wish to disturb slavery within the southern states. But as for its intrusion into new federal territories, they were staunchly against it. The great issues involved could not long be evaded or postponed. Their discussion might well test the ties that bound the Union together.[87] When the House of Representatives passed the proviso in 1847, Boswell knew that the Senate would not concur. Nevertheless he rejoiced that such action heralded an eventual extinguishment of the dominance of the slave power. It was "one of the greatest triumphs of freedom since the declaration, on the fourth of July 1776, that ALL MEN ARE CREATED EQUAL." [88] In heavy black frame the *Courant* displayed the names of "Betrayers of Freedom," a full list of senators and representatives from the free states who had voted against the bill.[89]

What the *Courant* objected to was the effect of the slave system upon the society of white men. Common schools and slavery, it held, were incompatible. As a result, the great majority of southern whites were uneducated and kept in ignorance. Moreover, because of values created by the slaveholding minority, free labor could attain no dignity. This oligarchy, which already controlled the legislative policy of the federal government, now asked Congress to extend such a state of affairs into new territories.[90] Neither then nor later was the *Courant* tinged with abolitionism. Yet Boswell's views on the Negro were not illiberal:

That in many points the European race is superior to the Asiatic and African no one denies. That among European races the British, or, to use a more fashionable name, the Anglo-Saxon race, is elevated above the others, in some respects, is generally asserted by all who belong to it, and we regard it as a very salutary and comfortable belief. But to speak of the African race as in any peculiar sense inferior, as if they lacked some of the essential characteristics of human nature, is doing great injustice.[91]

When the war ceased, the question of the status of the acquired territories dominated the campaign of 1848. The *Courant* wanted Henry Clay or Daniel Webster to be nominated; but when the Whigs chose Taylor and Fillmore, Boswell nailed their names to the editorial page.[92] Although Zachary Taylor was a slaveholding resident of Louisiana, the *Courant* professed to believe that he would approve a bill excluding slavery from the territories.[93] The Democratic nominee, Lewis Cass of Michigan, was presented as a two-faced northerner pledged to veto the Wilmot Proviso.[94] Would the supporters of the small Free Soil party play into the hands of Cass by opposing Taylor for being a southerner? Even George Washington owned slaves.[95] The country could get a protective tariff with Taylor, but not with Cass.[96] Taylor stood for peace and republicanism, Cass for war and "destiny." [97] "Rough and Ready" clubs appeared, enthusiasm was whipped up, and in November the *Courant* felt gratified to have the government once again delivered to the Whigs.[98]

Until the last weeks of the long contest which led to the Compromise of 1850, the *Courant* adhered rigidly to the doctrine of free territory. To the contentions of Calhoun and the southern radicals that Congress had no right to legislate the exclusion of slavery, Boswell cited the Ordinance of 1787 and the Missouri Compromise.[99] To advocates of "popular sovereignty," who hoped that settlers in the territories might determine the status of slavery, he replied that Congress alone could wield the authority.[100] Toward those who would extend the line of the Missouri Compromise, he turned a deaf ear.[101] When the people of California, adopting an appropriate constitution, sought admission to the Union as a free state, the *Courant* approved.[102] But when the President proposed that the inhabitants of other territories likewise be allowed to frame constitutions of their choice, the *Courant* demurred. Boswell insisted on the ideas of the proviso.[103] Texas had been admitted as a slave state because slavery existed there. The Missouri Compromise had permitted bondage in the Louisiana Territory where it had been established previously. Conversely, it had been barred north of the Ohio, and in Louisiana north of 36° 30′, where it had gained no hold. In line with these precedents, the federal government should prohibit slavery in the territories north of Texas. Arguments that they were now free and therefore required no legislation were aside from the point. The proviso would continue the policy of the forefathers.[104]

This great objective, wrote Boswell, ought never to be abandoned. With Calhoun he could agree on the one point that compromise was inadmissible. That free and slave states should come into the Union *pari passu,* he resolutely denied. The question of free California ought in no shape or form to be bracketed with New Mexico, Utah, fugitive slave laws, or other extraneous measures.[105] The *Courant* rejoiced to have Clay take his post in the momentous Congress which convened in December, 1849. Though a slaveholder from a slave state, he believed, supposed Boswell, that slavery ought not to be extended. He might propose a plan which would satisfy moderate men of all parties.[106] The broad compromise proposals of Clay and the support which Webster gave them left the

Courant unswayed. Boswell viewed the latter's 7th of March speech
with amazement and regret. Webster's grounds were not those of
the Whigs of Connecticut: while they would brook no interference
with slavery in the states, they favored the abolition of slave trade
in the District of Columbia, and insisted on the prohibition of
slavery in the territories.[107] Despite Clay, despite Webster, despite
even a majority of members of the Senate, the *Courant* was
adamant.[108] In May, 1850, Boswell conceded victory to the com-
promisers and scored the defection of northern Whigs.[109] At that
time he wrote as follows:

We desire the admission of California, and that immediately, before
her exasperated population shall be led to seek for independence, as a
necessary means of self government. We wish the establishment of territorial governments with such expressed prohibitions of slavery as shall
forever make them free. We ask for a decision of the question of Texan
boundary by the competent tribunal, and then the formation of new
states or the purchase of her territory will stand as questions to be hereafter determined by their own expediency or right. We shall then be
satisfied to see the requirement of the Constitution carried into effect
respecting the delivery of fugitive slaves, but not one single step taken
in advance of the requisitions of that instrument; and expect to see a
prohibition of the slave trade in the District of Columbia.[110]

The growth of disunion sentiment in the South induced the
Courant to surrender its stand. Months before, Boswell believed
that good sense would prevail over the disorganizing views of the
followers of Calhoun, that "prince of agitators and disruption-
ists." [111] As the conflict intensified, Connecticut readers were cau-
tioned not to underestimate the resolutions and pronouncements
of southern conventions, politicians, and newspapers.[112] Calhoun's
speech on March 4, 1850, might have seemed "weak" and "toneless"
to the northern press, but not to the *Courant*. Sincerity rang from
every phrase.[113] The rulers of the South were impelled more by a
fear of loss of power than by loss of rights.[114] Already ambitious
young men were dreaming of a southern federation free from
tariffs, committed to an expansionist policy, and made prosperous
by the needs of northern and British industry.[115] By July, Boswell
wrote that even a decision against the wishes and feelings of the
North would be less evil than the developments which threatened.
People in the deep South had been made to believe that northerners wished to free their slaves forcibly. The slightest cause might
kindle the flames of dissolution. Mutual forbearance was abso-

lutely essential.[116] In the end, therefore, the *Courant* approved all items of the compromise. Boswell was disappointed; the fugitive slave law was a bitter pill to swallow, but he rejoiced at the passing of the crisis.[117] A great public meeting in Hartford condemned all sectional strife.[118] As the *Courant* had written in August:

We trust that the Almighty does not yet intend to punish us for our presumption as a nation, and our pride in our own power and resources; and that he will still employ us as the instrument in his hand of disseminating the principles of liberty in the world, and of sheltering in our domains and protecting by our power the oppressed of all nations.[119]

During the national tranquillity which followed, the *Courant* turned to several subjects. Tariff editorials reaffirmed the need for protection, hoping for revision of the measure of 1846.[120] Solicitous paragraphs disclosed a reviving interest in the prospects of colonizing Liberia.[121] Louis Kossuth's resplendent reception, reminiscent of the Lafayette tour, filled the columns of the paper for over six months.[122] Though the *Courant* repudiated the doctrine of Manifest Destiny in general and invasions of Cuba in particular,[123] its pages glowed with pride in the expanded "empire." Boswell boasted of the merchant marine,[124] advocated a larger navy,[125] displayed a warm interest in water and rail projects to span the Isthmus of Panama,[126] and urged the annexation of the Sandwich or Hawaiian Islands to keep them from Britain or France. The latter would stimulate the China trade.[127] The California gold rush had appealed to him as the folly of human weakness but he welcomed the impetus it gave to the settlement of the western coast.[128] A transcontinental railroad, he thought, would form the crowning emblem of the spirit of Yankee enterprise.[129]

Editorials on the disposal of the western lands were of two kinds: those which opposed the donation of farmlands to individuals, and those which approved grants to railroad corporations. In the former, Boswell depicted proposed homestead laws as the work of agrarian socialists and levelers. Land obtained for nothing would soon be relinquished, said he, while those who paid money would have an interest in cultivating, improving, and preserving their holdings. If the government adopted the system of doling small parcels to actual settlers, the stripping of present owners of all but the allowed acreage would logically follow. At any rate the lands were pledged to the payment of the public debt.[130] The existence of the debt made the old Whig doctrine inadvisable. It had called for the distribution to the states of the proceeds from sales.[131] The next best move, to follow Boswell's reasoning, was to subsidize the building of railroads through the public domain, a policy which Congress initiated in 1850. This would encourage settlement, raise land values, and bring products rapidly to the seaboard states. It also seemed expedient from the point of view of "revenue." Moreover, indomitable pioneers who braved the wilderness deserved this fostering paternalism, for they should not be isolated from the civilized East.[132]

Presently the *Courant*'s political tone became listless. Taylor had died during the compromise crisis and the beloved leaders, Clay and Webster, passed on before the election of 1852. Millard Fillmore carried on as chief executive but the Whigs lacked control of Congress. For nomination, the *Courant* supported General Winfield Scott rather than Fillmore.[133] The party was supposedly contesting the presidency with sectionalists, with the disciples of nullification, with the enemies of the tariff and internal improvements;[134] but the excitement was less contagious than formerly. The Democrats had captured Connecticut,[135] and in November the people chose Franklin Pierce, the "unknown man," the third-rate New Hampshire lawyer, to guide the destinies of the Republic.[136] This was the last national canvass in which the Whigs presented a presidential candidate.

CHAPTER XIII

REPUBLICANISM AND SLAVERY

IN January, 1854, when Stephen A. Douglas introduced bills into the Senate to organize the territories of Kansas and Nebraska, the *Courant* renounced all faith in sectional compromises. According to its editorials, Douglas had acted against a solemn compact between the North and the South. Boswell's views were straightforward. Douglas wished to be President. He needed southern votes. Therefore he proposed legislation which provided that, whenever those territories should be admitted into the Union as states, they should come in with or without slavery, whichever their constitutions at the time of admission might prescribe. Since Kansas and Nebraska were a part of the old Louisiana Purchase, his bill repealed the Missouri Compromise of 1820. No question existed about the constitutionality of the measure, but were there simply no moral obligations attached to the keeping of these great historical agreements? It was bootless to argue that the Compromise of 1850 had superseded the Missouri Compromise. They had nothing to do with each other. Douglas's infamous violation of public faith had reopened the whole slavery question. Henceforth no truce would be possible.[1]

In line with these feelings, Boswell called upon the press and the people of the North to unite. Legislators should be compelled to vote "No." Mass meetings should be held in every city and town.[2] The fact that the Democratic papers were not solidly supporting Douglas was the brightest omen Boswell had seen. The defection of the local *Times* was particularly pleasing.[3] On February 24, Hartford citizens attended a large protest gathering, where, among other speakers, was John R. Niles, the *Courant*'s old political enemy.[4] In March, Boswell inserted the following notice in sorrowful black frame:

Isaac Toucey
A Senator from the State of Connecticut, voted on the 4th day of March, 1854, for the "Bill for the Government of Nebraska and Kansas," by which the prohibition of Slavery, in the territory ceded to the United States by France, North of Latitude 36° 30', commonly called the Missouri Compromise, is declared *inoperative and void.*[5]

In April the *Courant* had no disposition to claim the state election victory for the Whigs alone: it was a vote against the extension of the slave system.[6] In May, when the bill passed the House of Representatives, Boswell could not write temperately. It was the first telling stroke against the federal Union. No compromise could ever again be made. Mistrust replaced confidence. The feeling of brotherhood with the South, nourished by the American Revolution and by countless common sacrifices, would wither away in the hearts of northerners. It would die from memory. The North threatened nothing, but southerners might depend upon it: confidence in their honor had been woefully wrecked by the repeal of the Missouri Compromise.[7]

In the months following, the *Courant* supported three movements designed in different ways to harass, counteract, or check the dynamics of the slave system.[8] One aimed to obstruct the operation of the fugitive slave law. The second intended to prevent Kansas from joining the ranks of the enemy. The third was the search for a northern political alignment committed to the prohibition of slavery in the territories. All three made plain that sectional good will and the old spirit of compromise had flown.

To Boswell, the federal fugitive slave act was an odious measure. Of all parts of the Compromise of 1850, this one he accepted with the greatest reluctance; and then only, so he explained, because he believed that the South regarded its enforcement as the criterion of northern sincerity.[9] On the day when Pierce affixed his signature to the Kansas-Nebraska Act, the *Courant* renounced its uneasy acceptance and thereafter supported the passage of legislation to hamstring the effectiveness of its execution in Connecticut.[10] Boswell favored a policy of state non-cooperation and the passage of an antikidnaping bill making it hazardous for a slave hunter to attempt to recover any fugitive who had found lodgment within the state. The southerners had broken faith, said the *Courant,* and the people of Connecticut were no longer bound by the Compromise of 1850 or by any related agreements. They would set up every available obstacle to the recovery of runaway Negroes.[11]

Accepting Douglas's law at its face value, the *Courant* on June 1, 1854, ran an editorial endorsing the activities first advertised by the Massachusetts Emigrant Aid Society. Similar organizations, wrote the editor, should be formed in every free state. Connecticut's young men should be encouraged to go to Kansas and Nebraska so that free-soil settlers would fill the territories. Funds should be raised, routes marked out, and agents hired to assist them in gaining their titles.[12] Before the year's end, the paper told of emigrating parties, composed of uncommonly persevering men. Carrying with them the school and the Bible, the weapons of their ancestors, they would cultivate the soil and populate the land with thriving communities. Would they quail at the threats of the Arkansas and Missouri bullies with their bowie knives and revolvers? It would be easy to predict victory in any struggle for supremacy. On the character of these emigrants, the citizens of the North could base their hopes that Kansas and Nebraska would one day enter the Union as free states.[13]

The *Courant's* first call for political reorganization appeared on May 27, 1854, under the editorial heading, "A New Party":

To oppose the extent of the area of slavery is a principle that can bind and ought to bind American freemen together in one great party. . . . No matter by what name they may have been hitherto known—whether as Whigs, or Democrats, or Free Soilers. It is time that minor differences should be forgotten or laid aside, and that all who feel alike in this matter should collect around the same standard and join in the support of the same principle—NO MORE SLAVE TERRITORY.

Before the end of 1854 the *Courant* favored a policy which would allow the Whigs to keep their identity in local and state elections, but which would enable them to unite with others in supporting candidates for federal office. According to its editorials, the national Whig party was doomed. The northern and southern wings could not be expected to act together again, and many northern Democrats and Free Soilers, who were opposed to extending slavery, would never be willing to call themselves Whigs. Yet it was not advisable to throw away the heritage and influence that belonged to the party.[14] The *Courant* noted the appearance of the new Republican party.[15] Of the Know-Nothing or American movement, it was not surprising that men, tired of compromising politics, should rush into a fresh, rising organization with principles so flattering to American prejudices. The Know-Nothings took a stand against the election influence of foreigners, particularly of Irish Catholics. Therefore they leaned more toward the Whigs because the latter were the inveterate enemies of the Democrats who courted the foreign votes. But their party lacked the elements of breadth, stability, or permanency.[16] Whatever the arrangements for fusion, the *Courant* emphasized that there should be no treading upon abolitionist grounds. There should be no interference with the sovereignty and rights of southern states, only an insistence upon the nonextension of slavery.[17]

On New Year's Day, 1855, five months after Boswell's death, the *Courant* ceased to be an organ of the dying Whig party. Day declared that it mattered not what readers called the paper. It might be known as Whig or American or Republican. For Pierce's truckling administration it would show no sympathy. For the stimulation of American manufacturing it would advocate the protective tariff. It would encourage every judicious effort to stay the further encroachments of the slave power. Moreover, it would support measures to check the undue influence of foreigners at the polls.[18] In effect, for over a year and a half, the *Courant* was a spokesman for the local Native American or Know-Nothing movement.

In keeping with the *Courant*'s new role, Day took for his theme, "America for the Americans." Unreserved and spirited editorials bore down upon the newcomers from Ireland.[19] Not long would Connecticut remain the "Land of Steady Habits" if the Democratic demagogues could continue to recruit votes from the dregs of Europe each year.[20] If Germans drew less comment than Irish fellow citizens, they were nevertheless depicted as intemperate Sabbath violators, scoffers at religion, and radical adherents to notions of a "red-republican" government.[21] While Day admitted that the country owed much to immigrants in the past, and also that continued immigration was desirable for reasons not mentioned, good immigrants, said the *Courant,* were in the minority.[22]

Although the paper displayed such sentiments consistently until the presidential campaign of 1856, Day soon became less assured of the political promise of Native Americanism. His support of the victorious Know-Nothing or American party in the state election of 1855 was zestful.[23] But a Know-Nothing national convention at Philadelphia, in June of that year, side-stepped the Kansas-Nebraska issue, and Connecticut's members were among those from the North who withdrew in protest. Day regretted the split, but backed the stand of the state's delegates.[24] In February, 1856, when a national convention again split on the same issue, the Connecticut delegation withdrew again, and the party nominated Millard Fillmore for the presidency. Day approved neither the convention nor Fillmore.[25] Meantime the *Courant* had embraced the platform and candidates of the Connecticut Know-Nothings for the April election of 1856.[26] Day was now in the position of being identified with a party which he was convinced had no national merits. In March, despite the *Courant*'s appeal for fusion support of the American ticket,[27] Connecticut's recently formed Republican party nominated its own candidates whom Day approved and even defended without being able to endorse.[28] The American party made its distinctive appeal by a demand for native officeholders and stricter naturalization laws.[29] While Day believed these to be important, only the Republican party took an approved stand on what appeared to him to be the paramount national issue.[30] Since the *Courant*'s subsequent campaign was not very spirited, Day probably suffered from divided allegiance.[31]

The developments in Kansas brooked no indifference. For Day's first three months the *Courant*'s editorials generally neglected the Kansas issue.[32] But beginning in April, 1855, with news of the fraudulent election of a proslavery territorial legislature, the editor became excited.[33] In August he wrote:

Let us look at the matter calmly. A solemn compact of more than thirty years standing, by which slavery was prohibited north of latitude 36:30, has been repealed. This repeal has reopened the entire question. It has disturbed every settlement—every compromise; has revived, with added bitterness, every controversy between the North and the South; has brought out, in its full proportions, the determination of the slave States to extend the system of slavery over every territory of the Union, where, by possibility, it can exist; and has exhibited to the world the spectacle of an armed invasion of a peaceable community by an organized band of ruffians from the State of Missouri, who drove the rightful electors from the polls, and carried the election in favor of slavery, *at the point of the bayonet*. The Legislature chosen by such means is in session. It is recognized by the General Government. A governor who attempted, by mild measures, to prevent the successful accomplishment of this unparalleled outrage, has been dismissed for the attempt, and a tool of the Missouri ruffians has been appointed in his place. One of the first enactments of the infamous Legislature has been a law which makes it a state prison offence to declare, by word or writing, that slavery cannot by law exist in Kansas. . . . The indignation of the free people of the North, sufficiently aroused before, has been kindled to a fever heat by the scenes which they have witnessed.[34]

Henceforth, Day recorded his personal concern for the free settlers in Kansas in almost every issue of the *Courant* along with maledictions upon popular sovereignty, Pierce, Jefferson Davis, and the entire South. He bespoke support for Eli Thayer, who addressed large audiences in Hartford, urging money and emigrants for the New England Emigrant Aid Society.[35] In February, 1856, the *Courant* declared editorially that, if words, votes, and measures sufficed not to stay the curse of slavery, the settlers ought to be supplied plentifully with Sharp's rifles. Kansas should be free, cost what it might.[36]

With such feelings, Day eagerly endorsed John C. Frémont when the Republicans made him their standard bearer in the summer of 1856.[37] As the *Courant* had argued earlier, no real conflict existed between the Know-Nothing and Republican creeds. The whites were superior in all ways to the Negroes. Though some belittled the new party with taunts of "Black Republicanism," it was really an aristocratic, white man's party, for it intended to preserve as much of the land as it could from "the pestilential presence of the black race."[38] Averring now that nothing in Frémont's platform required the surrender of Know-Nothing or Whig principles, the *Courant* presented him as the presidential candidate of the "People's Party." It was necessary for all free men, regardless of peculiar views or past affiliations, to support the single principle of no more slavery in the territories.[39]

Frémont was described in the *Courant* as a masterful man of the Andrew Jackson type, native born, possessed of strong moral feelings and an iron will.[40] James Buchanan, his Democratic opponent, was an experienced administrator, more conservative than Pierce or Douglas, but withal a tricky politician as his complicity in the Ostend Manifesto made plain.[41] Frémont was the friend of free settlers in Kansas and the champion of free workingmen everywhere.[42] Buchanan, whose sectionalism was rank, was inimical to the tariff, no friend of free white labor, and a partisan apologist for popular sovereignty.[43] Did readers wish New England settlers to be arrested, imprisoned, and murdered in Kansas? Would they be indifferent to the extension of slavery into New Mexico, Utah, and Southern California? Did they hope for the annexation of Cuba and possibly war with England and Spain? Did they want the government to reopen the slave trade? If so, their votes had best be cast for Buchanan.[44] If popular sovereignty ever had possibilities, it was now useless in Kansas. Slavery had been legalized, thanks to the Missouri bullies, and the government supported their handiwork. The only hope for saving the territories lay in a complete change of the national administration.[45]

During the campaign, Day's paper devoted little space to his usual Know-Nothing diatribes.[46] Towns all over the state sprouted Frémont camps and liberty poles. Write-ups of political rallies and Kansas meetings vied with charges and countercharges assailing the integrity of opposition candidates and newspapers.[47] Fillmore was allegedly a Roman Catholic.[48] Frémont was cleared of similar charges, nor was he an abolitionist or slaveholder.[49] The *Courant* favored no rebellion in Kansas, but the Missouri partisans should be fought with weapons of their own choosing. The Topeka Constitution was neither insurrectionary nor unconstitutional and Congress ought to sanction it at once.[50] Buchanan's followers were "nigger-democrats." [51] Disunion threats from the South were nonsense.[52] On a drizzling Election Eve, Hartford's Frémonters staged a great torchlight parade. The city was brightly illuminated. Youthful Democrats fired rockets into the crowd, threw stones, frightened the horses with firecrackers, and generally enacted a local version of border ruffianism.[53] Not since 1840 had any campaign generated so much excitement.

After Buchanan's success the *Courant* renounced its alliance with the Know-Nothings. No opposition paper, wrote Day, could begin to represent the feelings of the Hartford community unless it gave vent, freely and often, to the indignant sense of wrong and injustice which haunted the North as a result of the repeal of the Missouri Compromise. Questions of naturalization, of birthplace, of religious connections, and of foreign allegiance were important but secondary. The commanding problem was the survival of the social system of the North or the social system of the South, for one or the other would predominate. Frémont had carried all New England. It was a glorious victory and the *Courant* hoped to fight shoulder to shoulder with the Republicans in future campaigns. Day called upon local clubs to hold meetings, disseminate propaganda, and preserve their organizations intact. They should begin work immediately to win the election four years hence.[54]

Two days after Buchanan's inauguration in March, 1857, Chief Justice Roger B. Taney delivered the Dred Scott decision, making it unconstitutional for Congress to exclude slavery from the territories. According to the *Courant,* this was a voice from Calhoun's sepulcher, contradicted by the sentiments of the age, men's consciences, and the teachings of political economy. It was the heaviest blow ever dealt the dignity of free labor. It had made slavery national, freedom sectional. Ere long the hated system of the South might invade even the free states. Day wrote of the Court daring to divulge its long premeditated judgment now that the elections were over. The justices of the majority were cunning tools of the Negro owners. Declaring a necessary respect for the United States

Supreme Court, however, the *Courant*'s editorials endorsed two avenues of escape. If free men gained local control, slavery could not exist in any of the territories, despite a dozen abstract decisions as to its legality. Secondly, northerners could redouble their efforts to achieve control of the national government. The federal circuit courts could be recast and men with backbone placed on the Supreme Court bench. The infamous decision could be reversed.[55]

During the first year of the new administration Kansas affairs continued to draw the *Courant*'s fire. When the votes of proslavery settlers endorsed the Lecompton constitution, Day wondered at what point the free inhabitants might be justified to wage civil war for the right of self-government. Administration leaders, he warned, might have the blood of such tragedy upon their heads.[56] Citizens held an anti-Lecompton mass meeting in Hartford and the *Courant* urged that the state election of 1858 be fought on the single issue of returning the constitution to the people of Kansas for a fair verdict.[57] The *Courant* had always contended that Congress was sovereign over the territories and not now did it complain of any violation of "popular sovereignty." When Douglas broke with the administration in assuming the ground, the paper believed him to be logical in view of his premises, but his premises were still those of a demagogue. Day's views differed. In denying Kansans the chance to approve or disapprove the proslavery constitution *in toto,* Buchanan's followers flouted "state sovereignty." The territorial stage was passing away in Kansas. Settlers had a right to mold their own state institutions. Those who talked of popular sovereignty, which had a democratic speciousness about it, were now engaged in denying the rights of statehood.[58]

When northern votes defeated the Lecompton forces in the House of Representatives, Hartford's people fired guns and celebrated.[59] Day felt assured of the future of Kansas. Freedom, too, had been aggressive. The North had discovered colonization to be more effective than acts of Congress and party compromises. Free settlers were moving into Missouri and Virginia. Others would take up land in Arizona and even in Texas. Whatever could be done peacefully and constitutionally to spread freedom and hedge in slavery would now be undertaken by energetic Yankees and liberty-loving Germans.[60]

Since the *Courant*'s leading *motif* was to emphasize the evils of slave-power politics, subordinate themes were given play accordingly. The depression of 1857 was construed to be the result of a deficiency of protection which the incumbent administration sanctioned. It pointed the need for public as well as private economies.[61] However, river and harbor dredging, a transcontinental railroad, and other improvements were deemed worthy of good Republican support.[62] Especially noticeable was the *Courant's* increasing concern for the welfare of northern workingmen. Though Day doubted the wisdom of child labor legislation and regarded demonstrations of the unemployed during the hard times of 1857–1858 as degrading and subversive,[63] in a partisan tiff with the *Times* in 1860 he defended the right to strike.[64] The call for homestead legislation became a basis for appealing to workers and foreigners to vote the Republican ticket. In aspersing slavery, much was said at election time about the dignity of free labor.[65]

The most exciting event of the late 1850's was John Brown's raid at Harper's Ferry. After Brown lectured at Hartford two years earlier, Day had told his readers: "Brown is just the man we need in Kansas; and if every man who loves Freedom and can spare a dollar or two, would put it in Brown's purse, we will warrant they get their money's worth out of Brown, hereafter." [66] The *Courant* proclaimed that his work in Kansas had been excellent, but that his fantastic and treasonable plans in Virginia revealed him to be a monomaniac.[67] The *Times* might display his pikes and scream that Republicans had given him encouragement and supplies, but his action was plainly the result of the policy of the Buchanan administration in Kansas.[68] Moreover, it disclosed the fear psychosis of the slaveholders and commented eloquently upon the security of their vaunted "system." It stimulated a revival of seditious talk and disloyalty in the South. It presaged a sectional split in the Democratic party, thus injuring Douglas's chances for the presidency in 1860. Above all, it dramatized for the public the Republican disapproval of northern radicalism or abolitionism.[69] Brown's death would glorify the supremacy of the laws of the United States.[70] If local Democrats held meetings assuring the South of their disapprobation of Brown's misdeeds, the Republicans had no need for such ceremonies.[71] Finally, it was impossible not to see traits of the grim old Puritan in Brown's character. His name would go down to posterity because he lived and died for his belief in freedom. He was a man of no compromise.[72]

In 1860 the *Courant* never doubted the election of Abraham Lincoln. At first thought it seemed to Day that no man had better qualifications for the Republican nomination than Edward Bates of Missouri. A conservative, in good repute, he could give the ticket a national rather than a sectional character. He alone might draw votes from south of the Mason and Dixon line.[73] But when Lincoln spoke in Hartford on March 5, the *Courant*'s editor was wonderfully impressed. Lincoln's speech was the clearest exposition of Republican views he had ever heard.[74] After the Chicago convention he was elated. Not since 1840 had any candidate presented the appeal to the common people which "Honest Abe" somehow embodied. The Illinois Rail Splitter was an intellectual giant, clear-headed, straightforward, sincere, and equipped with the simple habits of the backwoodsman. He eschewed abolitionism, but hated slavery and would keep it within bounds. He respected the sovereignty of the southern states, and politicians would never cajole him into transgressing the Constitution. The country had seen enough of tricky and compromising sophists.[75]

The outcome of recent Connecticut elections had been pleasing to the *Courant*. The state's Civil War governor, William A. Buckingham, took office in 1858.[76] Since the *Courant* entered the Republican camp with Whig and Know-Nothing antecedents, Day preached heartily for the unity of antiadministration forces. The main tenets of Republicanism were so important that he hoped no differences on minor points would sacrifice the united front of Republicans, Know-Nothings, old Whigs, and anti-Lecompton Democrats.[77] All campaigns were fought on national issues and the one in the spring of 1860 was extended to merge with the national campaign of that summer and fall.[78]

Editorials often discussed the talk of disunion and southern secession which threatened in case of Republican victory.[79] Day admitted that the economic dependence of the South was profitable to New England, but not for the sake of supplying clocks, clothespins, and coffee mills would Yankees be budged from their territorial principles.[80] He was tired of the eternal question of slavery. Only by Lincoln's election could it be politically domesticated in the southern states where it belonged.[81] For 60 of the 72 years past, those states had controlled the Union. Neither by their numbers, population, or the character of their productions were they entitled to dominate. The handwriting was on the wall.[82] The most encouraging development in national history was the growth of population in the upper Mississippi Valley. The great issues of the future would be decided there. The newer states, having no embittering recollections of old contests, no sectional hatreds, no rankling jealousies, could well afford to be just and generous. Lincoln was a splendid example of a northwest American.[83] Threats of secession were mostly bluff. The Republican party would not suffer the Constitution to be trampled upon or the Union to be dissolved.[84]

Day conceded that all the presidential candidates were men of ability.[85] John C. Breckinridge, who had been nominated by the southern wing of the Democracy, might be expected to carry the slave states.[86] Douglas, whose campaigning proved his perseverance, would draw the votes of northern Democrats who might otherwise vote for Lincoln; but his doctrine of popular sovereignty was now so equivocal and contradictory that good judges gave him the chance of carrying not more than three states, possibly only one.[87] The Constitutional Union party, presenting John Bell of Tennessee, might attract old Whigs and make a showing in the border states, but it straddled the issue of the status of slavery in the territories. It was several years behind the times.[88] In Connecticut most of the Democratic papers supported Breckinridge, but the Douglas faction was dominant.[89] Maine went Republican in September. Party schisms all over the North and state Republican victories in Pennsylvania, Ohio, and Indiana in October made predictions for Lincoln more assured.[90] With the possible exception of California and Oregon, Lincoln would carry every free state. There was an inherent power in the Republican cause, wrote Day, that made victory as fixed as fate.[91]

Among the more colorful features of the long and exciting campaign were the activities of the young Republican Wide-Awakes who appeared at rallies, escorted speakers, and marched in night processions, bearing aloft their lantern torches and wearing caps and capes of enameled cloth which oil and rain could not harm. The local club, which first accompanied Lincoln when he visited Hartford, was the parent of hundreds of Wide-Awake organizations which appeared in the North before November.[92] The *Courant* posted speakers' schedules, speeches, rallies, and parades.[93] Day adopted a satirical tone in reporting the doings of the opposition, rubbing salt into the wounds of the Democrats,[94] and accusing the editors of the local *Times* and *Post* of being obsequious to Douglas when the "little giant" spoke in Hartford.[95] It seemed as if the *Courant* campaigned endlessly for free homes, free men, and free territories.

Great joy greeted Lincoln's success on November 6. A large congregation of citizens awaited the returns at the Republican camp.

The South Windsor Glee Club and a brass band supplied music. The *Courant* furnished the telegraphic tidings. People shouted, drums rolled, bedlam broke loose, and crowds followed the parading Wide-Awakes, cheering the *Courant* office and rousing leading citizens for speeches in the early hours of the morning. A few days later Republicans staged a city-wide celebration.[96]

Exultation changed to anxiety. Within a fortnight Day wrote both that the southern states had no right to secede and that they ought to be allowed to do so.[97] His convictions were transient as well as contradictory. By the beginning of 1861 he had discovered his stand. He believed that Connecticut's men should be drilling, that arms factories ought to be producing, and that the government ought to equip itself for war.[98] The compromises offered by the Virginia convention and by Senator John J. Crittenden and others were unacceptable. Republicans could be magnanimous in many ways but they could never abandon two principles: no slavery in the territories and no secession from the Union.[99] In the month before the call to arms, Day hoped strongly that Lincoln's sterling character and conservative good sense might somehow heal the wounds of the broken Republic.[100]

CHAPTER XIV

RAILROADS, INDUSTRY, AND CULTURE

JOHN WARNER BARBER, Connecticut's chronicler of a century ago, recorded this description of Hartford in the middle 1830's:

The city is rather irregularly laid out, and is divided at the south part by Mill or Little river. Across this stream a fine bridge of free stone has been thrown, which connects the two parts of the city. . . . Another bridge, across the Connecticut river, 1,000 feet long, and which cost over $100,000, unites the city with East Hartford. Hartford is very advantageously situated for business, is surrounded by an extensive and wealthy district, and communicates with the towns and villages on the Connecticut above, by small steamboats, (now 8 in number) two of which, for passengers, ply daily between Hartford and Springfield. The remainder are employed in towing flat bottomed boats of 15 to 30 tons burthen, as far as Wells' river, 220 miles above the city. The coasting trade is very considerable, and there is some foreign trade, not extensive, carried on. Three steamboats form a daily line between here and New York. The manufactures of this city . . . exceed $900,000 per annum; among these are various manufactures of tin, copper, and sheet iron; block tin and pewter ware; printing presses and ink; a manufactory of iron machinery; iron founderies, saddlery, carriages, joiners' tools, paperhangings, looking-glasses, umbrellas, stone ware, a brewery, a web factory, cabinet furniture, boots and shoes, hats, clothing for exportation, soap and candles, 2 manufactories of machine and other wire cards, operated by dogs, &c. &c. More than twice as many books are published here, annually, as are manufactured in any other place of equal population in the United States. There are 15 periodicals; 12 weekly newspapers, (5 sectarian,) 2 semi-monthly and 1 monthly. The city is well built, and contains many elegant public and private edifices. The state house, in which are the public offices of the state, is surmounted by a cupola, and is a very handsome and spacious building. The city hall, built for city purposes, is also spacious and elegant; it has two fronts, with porticoes, supported each by six massy columns. In the city are 12 places of worship—5 for Congregationalists, 1 Episcopal, 2 Baptist, 1 Methodist, 1 Universalist, 1 Roman Catholic, and 1 African; several of them are very handsome, and the Episcopal, a Gothic edifice, is much admired for its elegance. There are 5 banks, a bank for savings; 3 fire and marine insurance offices, an arsenal, museum, 2 markets, &c. The American Asylum for the deaf and dumb, the Retreat for the insane, and Washington College, are all beautifully located, in the immediate vicinity of the city. The population within the city limits in September, 1835, was nine thousand and eight hundred.[1]

The advent of the steamboat and the railroad prompted the *Courant*'s writers to think of Hartford's future in terms of increased wealth; that is to say, in terms of population growth, enhanced land values, increasing trade, and expanding industry. These were the fundamentals of "progress." But Hartford's first great enthusiasm for railroads, which superseded an earlier one for canals, was suspended by the depression of 1837.[2] In the gloomy spring of that year, when the Hartford banks stopped specie payment, Boswell gave assurances of their solvency and pleaded with the public for patience.[3] For many a moon thereafter the *Courant* printed meager tidings of local business activity. Not until late in 1840 did it show signs of wishing to revive an interest in the promotion of railroad investment.

The road from New Haven to Hartford was completed in 1839.[4] The following year the *Courant* began to urge an interest in extending the line to Springfield. Boswell himself was on the committee to solicit funds for a survey of routes. The distance was about 24 miles and the cost was expected to be something less than $400,000. The project seemed pressing because it appeared that other routes were beginning to divert business from Hartford. Goods were being shipped from New York to Norwich or Stonington and overland to Boston. The advantages of building to Springfield and hence facilitating an inland route between New York and Boston sounded obvious. The distances from one port to the other by way of Norwich, Stonington, or Hartford were approximately equal, but the average speed of steamboats was about 13 miles per hour, that of railroad cars about 25.[5] But investors were slow. When the line opened in December, 1844, Boswell lamented that New York freight was being hauled over a Long Island road and transshipped to Boston. He hoped that the New Haven, Hartford, and Springfield route might quickly eclipse its rivals.[6]

With the Springfield line completed, the old zeal for railroad construction set in again. The *Courant* gave a great deal of publicity to the promotion of a road from Hartford to New York by way of Danbury. By cutting through the central and western parts of the state, it was supposed that Hartford would expand its hinterland, that manufacturing might be encouraged there, and that still more trade might be snatched from the shore-line routes north of New York. New Haven enterprisers were promoting a rival line designed to draw business from those areas into their own city.[7]

Old Connecticut Valley plans were refurbished. Hartford men sat on the board of directors of a line from Springfield to Northampton. Boswell and others urged the organization of a long road running north from southern Vermont.[8] According to one booster:

The greatly augmented earnings of the Hartford and New Haven road, since its opening to Springfield, and the additions it will receive, on the successive sections up the valley being opened to its business, which will greatly exceed any estimates which have or can be made, will place this among the most valuable stocks in the country, even should a part of the business be diverted hereafter from the south end of the road, by any other route.[9]

In 1846 the General Assembly authorized the building of a drawbridge over the Connecticut River at Middletown to accommodate what was to be known as the "Air Line Road" from New York to Boston. This piece of legislation, which Boswell termed "gross and outrageous," thoroughly alarmed Hartford's business men.[10] In the first place, the Air Line threatened to divert New York and Boston traffic, competing directly with existing and proposed lines through Hartford. In the second place, the bridge menaced Hartford's river traffic. Middletown was only 20 miles to the south.

The citizens of Hartford instructed their Common Council to appropriate the necessary funds to prevent the Middletown interests from erecting the bridge.[11] The fight lasted for several years in and out of the legislature.[12] In the *Courant,* at city meetings, and before the General Assembly, the spokesmen for Hartford advanced arguments alleging the damage which would befall the state from a drawbridge over the river below Hartford.[13] In 1845, according to the *Courant,* there were 2,700 arrivals and departures of vessels registered at the local wharves. All the vessels passed Middletown and few of their owners lived in Hartford. The bridge would delay traffic, create bars and shoals, divert the river channel, and, by arresting the ice, retard the opening of navigation and cause floods. The people had established themselves in businesses, invested in farms, storehouses, dwellings, and mills in full confidence of free navigation. Boswell wrote of trading rights granted by the Creator, guaranteed by the Constitution of the United States, and exercised by successive generations of Americans.[14]

During this struggle between competing railroad interests, Hartford countered with a bold stroke. The *Courant* announced, on February 14, 1848, that $627,000 had been raised locally toward the building of the first segment of a line through eastern Connecticut to Providence, Rhode Island. It would cut athwart the Air Line Road. The supporters of the latter fought Hartford's proposition in the legislature by threatening to go to Boston by way of Providence. The lawmakers denied them the right to be circuitous and the bridge was not erected.[15] Needless to say, the fight ended to the complete satisfaction of Boswell, the Common Council, and the business men of Hartford.

The arguments against the bridge were the more interesting because many of Hartford's citizens were coming to feel that the future depended little upon her river traffic. New England was being industrialized, Hartford lacked water power, and Boswell, among others, thought that the city had better become alert to changing circumstances. Most local men of business were constrained to admit, according to an editorial in November, 1843, that the trade of the city had for some years been gradually declining. Something else was needed:

To every body, it must be obvious, that for a city of our size and population, Hartford is very deficient in manufactures. We should be our own producers; and not merely a halfway house for the transhipment of goods and produce from and to flourishing points on each side of us. . . . We should not be subjected to the costs of freight now incident to getting goods into this market. So evident is this necessity, that manufacturers in other towns have seriously thought of locating their establishments here to be put in motion by steam, in the absence of water power—but on the whole, deeming that impracticable, have gone back again some twenty or thirty miles into the country to manufacture their goods, and send them here at the increased cost of transportation. Any thing which would obviate this difficulty would become at once, of vast importance to the interests of Hartford. It would bring many men of business energy among us, put new life into the affairs of the city, enlarge our population and enable us to produce for ourselves many of the staple articles of our trade, for which we are now dependent upon manufacturing establishments around us.[16]

For the next four years the *Courant* provided space for the water-versus-steam controversy. It was proposed to furnish the city with water power by digging a canal from Enfield Falls, several miles to the north. This had been discussed chronically for a number of years.[17] Boswell supported it in the fall of 1843 and suggested action. He proposed also to expend money for erecting a "steam cotton mill." In 1844 a lecture at Gilman's Saloon by C. L. James of Newburyport presented the brief for this case. James contended that steam was cheaper than water.[18] Since most disputants regarded the two proposals as alternatives, the proponents of each appealed for public support. Letters appeared in the *Courant* and mass meetings were held.

The steam-and-water controversy was an interesting manifestation of the anxiety which accompanies the breakup of traditional patterns of thought. Heretofore Hartford's future had been projected in men's minds within an old frame of reference. In years gone by, Hartford was said to have profited from certain dominant advantages of location. First, she was astride the main coach road, midway between Boston and New York. Secondly, she lay at the head of navigation on the Connecticut River. Newer arteries of inland transportation between the great seaports might circumvent Hartford. This was to be avoided. By canal and railroad construction, rival cities might tap and drain trade from the long Connecticut Valley north of Hartford. This was to be feared. But contrariwise, if Hartford's capitalists were foresighted, the Boston and New York trade and the riches of the entire Connecticut Valley might pour down upon a great commercial city abounding in population and teeming with enterprise. This was Hartford's dream.[19]

Because local business men had inherited an assumption with respect to Hartford's position between New York and Boston, they were the more strongly moved, for example, to fight the Air Line Road. Because they assumed also the promise of Hartford's station on the river, they were eager to support railroad construction along the valley to the north of them. All this, which accorded with old ways of thinking, served the purposes of the future. But the very multiplication of rail lines and the proliferation of water-power manufacturing introduced doubts. Men were beginning to see that Hartford was not destined to develop into a wealthy commercial mart. The old dream was becoming untenable. The future was unclear.

Most writers agreed with Boswell that Hartford's heavy mercantile business had fallen off. The number of boats engaged in up-river trade was alleged to have declined notably. Boston supplied the city's former customers with more of their groceries and dry goods, Albany furnished them with more flour and feed, New York with more cotton, rags, dye stuffs, and other raw materials for manufacturing.[20] Hartford was known now only for its position in the wool trade:

Railroad facilities were called for, and the works which have since been constructed, the Western Road on the north, the Norwich and Worcester on the east, the Housatonic Road on the west, and the Hartford and New Haven which passes through our city, have furnished to the manufacturer and consumer facilities which have given to him a selection of markets, at any of which he can supply himself as easily, as cheaply upon as advantageous terms, and with as good opportunity of making a selection as he could do at this city.[21]

Whether Hartford's decline in business was absolute, or only relative to that of neighboring cities, the feeling of unrest persisted. Providence, Worcester, Springfield, Troy, New Haven, and other communities were observed to be pulling ahead:[22]

Whether Hartford is really falling off in capital and industry, or not— a point about which there is some diversity of opinion—certain it is that there is no such increase in these elements of productiveness as proves our city to be prosperous, or as suits its history and natural advantages, or as satisfies the wants and desires of the citizens at large. The progress of our population, as compared with that of hundreds of other cities and towns, and many within our own State too, is slow. . . . Our trades and professions are far from expanding as we wish. Our real estate begins, some of it, to lose value. Commerce exhibits no striking improvement. Our instruments and facilities of transportation have been increased, but without in full proportion enlarging business in our midst. Agriculture and manufactured products do not flow in upon us and heap in increased abundance from the surrounding country. Our mechanics complain that they have not sufficient work, and quite a number of them, the past year, have left us. Supply exceeds demand in many occupations. If we are not as a city actually declining in prosperity, we begin in some points to look ready for a decline.—Certainly we are not advancing as we should be.[23]

Boswell accused Hartford's capitalists of lacking courage and energy, of sleeping on their money bags.[24] They were charged with investing their riches elsewhere to the detriment of their own community.[25] Others joined in attempting to prod them into sponsoring meetings to endorse water- or steam-power projects.[26] Boswell thought that, if enterprises of either sort were promoted with spirit, Hartford's population and real estate values might be doubled in a decade.[27]

In 1846 a so-called citizen's committee argued the feasibility of organizing a steam-driven cotton mill. According to the report, a factory of 10,000 spindles, capitalized at $125,000, would reap profits of not less than 10 per cent under proper management.[28]

In January, 1847, another committee announced that sufficient water could be brought from Enfield, a distance of over 12 miles, to drive 300,000 spindles. The estimated cost was $748,427.[29] The month following, the *Courant* covered a timely sermon by Horace Bushnell, Hartford's widely known preacher. Bushnell selected his text from II Chronicles, Chapters 32 and 33: "This same Hezekiah also stopped the water-course of Gihon, and brought it straight down on the west side of the city of David. And Hezekiah prospered in all his works." Proclaiming it the Christian duty of the city to prosper, he continued:

I cannot ascertain that we have suffered or begun to suffer any real diminution of numbers or of resources. But the opening of new avenues of trade and travel on every side of us has compelled the business of our city to change its form. Some kinds of trade have been partially destroyed, but others have been and are being created. And it is natural, while these changes are going on, that we should all suffer a degree of anxiety. . . . This, at least, is certain, that we have come now to a great and final crisis. The causes that are going to affect the interests of our city, as a place of business, in all future time, are now displayed and coming into action. Hereafter no great change is to be anticipated. It is not as when we lost our West India commerce. We have come to the last trial—the final crisis. And now it is to be decided, within the next five or ten years, whether we are to go on maintaining our growth and numbers, or to sink into decline. Up to this time, our city has maintained an even, healthy, and generally constant growth, from the very first day of the settlement.—The river has been its life. Now, at last, there are opening rivers of trade and motion above us and back of us on every side, and it is very soon to be seen whether we can turn the resources left us in such a way as to escape injury.[30]

In the years following these events Hartford prospered. No canal led water to the city, nor did mills with spindles flourish there. Yet, as early as 1849, a visitor had never seen so many signs of prosperity. Asylum Street, with its drays, wagons, boxes, bales, great and small packages directed to all parts of the country, resembled a slice from the busiest portion of New York's Pearl Street.[31] Railroads were built, industries grew, insurance companies flowered. The *Courant* was never tired of noting these pleasing symptoms of growth.

On Saturday, November 10, 1849, the editor of the *Courant* accompanied the directors of the Hartford and Providence Railroad on the opening of the line from Hartford to Willimantic. The engine chugged across the new bridge spanning the Connecticut and headed east. Spectators cheered and waved their hats.[32] About one month later, cars were running west from Hartford to Plainville and by June, 1850, to Bristol.[33] In the middle of July, citizens met to decide whether the municipality should loan $500,000 to what was now known as the Hartford, Providence & Fishkill Railroad. It seemed desirable to push to the west as rapidly as possible in order to compete with a line running up the Naugatuck Valley from the south.[34] Letters in the *Courant* prior to the city meeting attempted to show that the railroads were really "public utilities" and therefore deserving of public credit.[35] A correspondent suggested, perhaps ironically, that the city should float a million dollars' worth of bonds rather than the proposed $500,000. Half could be delivered to the railroad; the remainder could be used as a "safety fund" to secure payment of the fire insurance policies issued by Hartford companies.[36] Editorially, the *Courant* felt that serious objection might be raised to placing public credit behind a railroad corporation, that it might be wrong in theory, but that circumstances seemed to warrant it in the case before the people. The paper had already advised readers to invest in the bonds of the company, the loan would certainly be safe, and the building of the road would give a mighty impetus to Hartford's business.[37] The directors, for their part, resolved not to use the money from the city until subscriptions to stock assured the completion of the road to the Naugatuck Valley on the west, and to Providence or Boston in the other direction. On July 15, by a vote of 430 to 17, the citizens loaned the credit of the city to the railroad.[38]

By 1850, also, the Connecticut Valley had been lined and tapped with tracks. Readers were asked to recall how the exciting convention at Windsor, Vermont, 14 years earlier, had stimulated pamphlets, resolutions, and what appeared to some to be unattainable dreams. Most of the construction had been done within the last four years. Now a traveler might leave Burlington in midwinter at 8 A.M. and arrive in New York by way of Rutland and Hartford in time for a full night's rest.[39]

New industries came to Hartford and old ones throve. Industrialization placed a premium upon steam engines and railroad equipment. Woodruff & Beach made engines for most of the local concerns, exported them to Cuba, California, and elsewhere, manufactured cotton presses, and produced machinery for the growing textile industries.[40] Tracey & Fales, later Fales & Gray, made railroad cars for the Connecticut roads, built them for the Pennsylvania and Erie lines, and sent them into many states of the Union.[41] The expanding market for boots and shoes, for silver products, for books, and for a host of other articles, brought business. Late in 1848 the *Courant* estimated that 1,100 persons were employed in Hartford's boot and shoe trades, many of them doing "homework" in residences outside the city. Several workshops produced silverware, using fifty-cent pieces for raw material.[42] Among successful publishing firms, Case, Lockwood & Co., successors to Case & Tiffany, did a national printing business, printed thousands of school texts each year, and were the sole publishers of Webster's dictionary in the late 1850's.[43] The Mexican War, the opening of California, and the European wars of the decade following gave fame to Colt revolvers and Sharp's rifles, both Hartford products. Samuel Colt's industry grew rapidly and became the largest in Hartford before the Civil War.[44] In 1852 the *Courant* marveled at the city. Streets and dwellings had spread over areas that were fields a short time before. Industries mushroomed:

In the mechanical department, particularly, a striking change has taken place, and now, early and late, the hum of business from hundreds of busy workmen may be heard, where only a few years since every thing wore a quiet and village-like aspect.[45]

Nor did the *Courant* fail to note the substantial position of local financial institutions. By the end of 1850 Hartford had six commercial banks with an aggregate capital of over $4,000,000; a savings bank with deposits of over $1,600,000; four fire insurance companies with $950,000, not to mention one mutual concern; and four new life insurance companies with $500,000 capital and large accumulated profits. The Connecticut Mutual Life Insurance Company, the first of its kind in the state, was chartered in 1846. Then followed the Hartford Life and Health (later, Hartford Life Insurance Company), the Charter Oak, and the Aetna, to name only the beginners. The Connecticut Company, in operation less than four years, had issued about 12,000 policies. The Hartford Life had sold 2,300 in 13 months. The others were commencing under excellent auspices.[46] The *Courant* carried editorials on the merits of this new brand of insurance.[47] According to Boswell, Hartford would soon be as distinguished for its life insurance as it was for its fire insurance.[48]

The city acquired better facilities for the accommodation of business men and travelers in an era of railroads. The *Courant* complimented the efficiency of express companies formed to run long-distance business errands, to carry papers and packages.[49] Magic messages were flying by telegraph to Boston and New York in the summer of 1846.[50] Citizens indicated the need for more accurate timekeeping, complained that public clocks disagreed, and that travelers sometimes missed the trains.[51] Hartford's public carriages were said to have resembled the vehicles of the wealthy and hackmen vied with each other for patronage.[52] Improved and newly constructed hotels catered to the comforts of living. In 1849 the United States Hotel had 400 rooms, hot and cold baths, well-appointed tables, and attentive waiters. The *Courant* thought that no public house in the country surpassed the aristocratic old City Hotel in orderliness and gentility. Allyn House, the city's most modern, was completed in 1857.[53]

"Merchant" wished to know, one day in 1848, if the citizens realized what disadvantages they labored under for want of proper lighting in their stores and public buildings. Were they aware that their neighbors in New Haven, Springfield, and Norwich had gas from which they obtained "elegant light"?[54] The *Courant* hoped that the Hartford Gas Light Company might have a plant in operation by November, 1849, in time for the opening of the railroad to Willimantic, but not until New Year's Eve was the city aglow with modern illumination. Supplementing or replacing some of the old street oil lamps were 50 newer ones. About three miles of main pipe had been laid.[55]

Because the gas company charged fees which the *Courant*'s editors and others thought to be excessive, Hartford's waterworks became a municipal enterprise. At first the paper commented favorably upon the formation of a private corporation.[56] But in the spring of 1852 gas rates began to get the editorial criticism which lasted for a decade: rates in other cities were lower, rates went down but bills went up, competition was needed, an impartial meter inspector was wanted.[57] By the summer of that year the *Courant* wished to prevent the water supply from being monopolized by private interests. The authority to float the necessary bond issue could be obtained from the next legislature. The cost would not exceed $200,000. The advantages for health and fire protection were obvious. Engines would pump the water from the Connecticut River to a reservoir from which a network of pipes would carry it over the city.[58]

The *Courant* was jubilant when voters adopted the project after considerable controversy in 1853.[59] Editorials argued strongly against the use of lead pipes. Clashes ensued over the disposal of the bonds.[60] Finally, on July 4, 1856, the city celebrated the completion of its water system with fireworks, parade, regatta, torchlight procession, and bell ringing.[61] Five years later the *Courant* thought that no improvement in the decade had provided so much comfort, convenience, and protection. Yet even then the reservoir was proving inadequate for the needs of kitchens, laundries, and bathrooms. At the Asylum for the Deaf and Dumb, it was many times impossible to draw water in the rooms on the ground floor, to say nothing of those above.[62]

The *Courant* hoped also for public ownership of the bridge across the Connecticut River. When cattle fell through the bridge floor in 1850, it was alleged that the timbers had not been heavy enough to bear the traffic even some 30 years before. Hartford's trade from the east had long been handicapped. True, the bridge had paid large dividends to stockholders and had done yeoman's service for the city; but now it was beyond ordinary repair. Since Hartford was building a splendid stone bridge across the Little River for the convenience of residents who lived in the southern part of the city, why should not the public arrange to buy out the stockholders of the bridge to East Hartford? Such sentiments flared up but came to naught. Even then the bridge company was successfully defending its rights in litigation which eventually reached the Supreme Court in Washington.[63]

As the downtown section of the city spread over old residential areas and as new and old families erected houses away from the center, new streets were laid out. Older streets were widened, straightened, and graded.[64] Until the late 1850's complaints were not frequent in the *Courant* about the construction of streets, sewerage, sidewalks, or crosswalks.[65] Main Street was macadamized, near-by streets were apparently kept generally passable, and walks were well paved with Bolton stone.[66] In the business district, boxes, bags, bales, and casks frequently cluttered the walks, while dry goods, coats, pantaloons, and the like sometimes fluttered in the faces of pedestrians.[67] In summertime, ball playing in the streets was a problem,[68] and on wintry days, young people raced their sleighs up and down Main Street. To counter this, citizens adopted a speed law in 1852 imposing a five-dollar fine upon any who drove over six miles per hour or who drove sleighs without bells.[69] The *Courant*'s editors advocated more cleanliness for both walks and streets. People trundled swill carts along the walks and, in the season for watermelons, littered the streets with rinds. Shopkeepers were urged specifically to wash the sidewalks, at least on Saturday nights, so that ladies might attend church without soiling their expensive skirts.[70]

In 1855 the *Courant* became eloquent on the subject of Main Street:

So broad—so gracefully curved, so well sewered, so well lighted, supplied with good cross-walks, so cheerfully sprinkled with vehicles, not lonesome and not overcrowded, not so noisy as the cobblestone pavements would make it, and not so muddy as the absence of McAdam would leave it—an occasional tree to relieve the monotony of straight lines, and not trees enough to conceal the graceful spires and tasteful buildings which fringe its outlines.[71]

When the trees and awning posts were removed about five years later, the thoroughfare looked nude to old-timers. To believe the *Courant,* the consensus of feeling was that the trees obstructed the view and injured real estate values by hiding the buildings.[72]

Much of the beauty of Hartford, according to the *Courant,* came from the excellent taste of the citizens in flowers, shrubs, and trees. The paper gave space to the frequent exhibits of the Horticultural Society. A "Society for Public Improvement" was organized. The *Courant* spoke of the abundance of flowers from the violets and heartsease of early spring to the gorgeous dahlias and chrysanthemums of autumn.[73] A stranger was impressed by their fashionable cultivation, especially about the suburban dwellings. Of the several kinds of maple trees, he noted none more pleasing than the sugar variety with its rich, dark green foliage. In no city had he ever seen so many tulip trees.[74]

The paper remarked also the changing appearance of public buildings and dwellings:

The taste of Hartford has wonderfully improved within the last twenty years in both public and private architecture. The people of Boston say that Hartford is distinguished for its well built churches. In our private erections, there have been lately many new models followed, so that the eye is not wearied by any tiresome uniformity of buildings. The spots where these new dwellings are erected have been well chosen. . . . A few artists of skill and taste, settling among us, have done wonders, within twenty years, for the ornamental character of the town.[75]

In 1853, partly to beautify the city, Horace Bushnell urged the municipal council to convert a number of acres of land along the

Little River into a park.[76] The *Courant* had argued the need previously.[77] According to Bushnell, the new Statehouse might be erected there; it would be accessible to the poor as well as the rich, and it would impress travelers entering Hartford by railroad. Also, it would raise the value of property and might induce the rich, in search of picturesque residence, to move into Hartford.[78] The *Courant*'s writers strongly supported Bushnell.[79] The project was adopted and eventually, after some irritation at delay, completed.[80] Though Frederick Law Olmsted, designer of New York's Central Park, remarked in 1861 that Hartford's efforts had been expended upon an ill-digested plan badly fitted to difficult terrain,[81] the park nevertheless delighted the citizens.[82]

Between 1847 and 1860 the municipal limits were twice extended, the city was divided into wards, city meetings were abolished, and the government reorganized.[83] A municipal court was established[84] and policemen were equipped with uniforms and badges, but not with guns. In 1860 there were 19 regulars and eight supernumeraries.[85] In 1849 the reorganized Hartford fire department consisted of sack and bucket, hook and ladder, hose, and engine companies. Since none of the companies used horses, the 481 firemen pulled trucks and engines as well as fought flames. All were volunteers.[86]

In recounting the progress of a decade, the *Courant* noted in 1861 that the city's jail capacity had doubled.[87] From time to time the editors offered generalizations to account for crime growth not only in Hartford but over the country. According to them, it was an urban phenomenon with tangled roots: poverty, disease, intemperance, cultural maladjustment on the part of foreigners, the waning of religious and moral instruction, weak parental discipline, uncertainty of punishment, opportunities for concealment.[88] In Hartford the *Courant* deplored gambling but conducted no vice crusade.[89] It carried this comment when advocating the founding of a city court in 1851:

When gambling saloons, with their attendent evils are permitted to be kept on every corner of our streets; when houses of prostitution are allowed to be opened in the very heart of our city, and within the toss of a biscuit of the residence of our most respected and influential citizens, it is time that we should awake from the lethargy in which the former quiet and good order of our city has placed us.

With an increase of population as rapid as that which we have experienced for a few years past, will necessarily come an increase of vices, and our citizens will be wise if they make provision in the outset to keep them in check.[90]

To judge from the paper, the city was freer from fires than from crime. A number of conflagrations in the earlier years were attributed to incendiaries;[91] but after 1849 the absence of losses was noteworthy.[92] The burning of the Grove Works on Potter Street in 1861 was the largest in the generation before the war. The property was evaluated at $10,000.[93]

In one way or another the *Courant* pursued its old interest in the preservation of health and life. Patent medicines were hawked more than ever. In one period, tomato pills were being pushed as substitutes for calomel, efficacious for impurities of the blood, for ailments of the stomach, liver, and so forth.[94] Dentists continued to advertise. Chief among them was Horace Wells whose claims to the discovery of anesthesia were duly publicized.[95] Only in 1849 was the city threatened with disease of epidemic proportions. In July the paper gave almost daily attention to the cholera in other cities, and in August its presence was reported in Hartford; but fortunately the visitation was brief.[96] By 1852 the *Courant* saw the need for a local hospital. When an explosion at the Fales & Gray factory killed 18 people, the deficiency was more apparent.[97] In 1856 the paper reprinted the first annual report of the Hartford Hospital, which was located near the South Green. Conceding that the "general public" feared that the institution might create epidemics, the editor explained that no contagious cases were admitted and that each patient was provided with a fresh bed of oat straw.[98] New buildings were opened for the reception of patients in 1860.[99]

In 1847 the city established a high school.[100] This was welcome news to a paper which had shown an enduring interest in education. Not only did the *Courant* follow the progress of all the older local educational institutions; until the 1850's it continued to abet the movement for better common schools.[101] Emphasis was put upon the need for qualified teachers. In the late 1830's, the *Courant* publicized the work and objectives of the recently appointed state Board of Commissioners of Common Schools.[102] In 1839 it related in detail the early efforts to train teachers at the Hartford Grammar School for the common schools of the state.[103] A decade later, when the legislature provided for the first state normal school, Boswell not only appreciated its promise but hoped in vain that Hartford might have the educational advantages of its presence.[104]

According to correspondents, the public high school had the great merits of the common schools. It placed education within the reach of all the children of all the people.[105] In 1856 the *Courant* first printed an account of the graduation exercises in which it carefully included the names of the several clergymen who took part but omitted the names of the graduates.[106]

The *Courant* claimed in 1861 that all of Hartford's finest churches had been built in the decade preceding.[107] Congregations were not only better housed but good Christians attempted to meet the challenge of an industrializing city. Unattached young men came to town to seek a living, including Irish and German immigrants. The Young Men's Moral and Social Union provided them with sociability and reading matter.[108] Hartford had a Young Men's Christian Association in 1857.[109] City missions were established with evening classes for the untutored and aid for the indigent.[110] With the short-lived depression of 1857 came daily prayer meetings to solace the manufacturers and business men.[111]

By erecting the Wadsworth Atheneum in the early 1840's, provision was made for a sort of local enshrinement of the arts and sciences. Daniel Wadsworth gave the land for a building to contain a gallery of fine arts and to provide accommodations for the several literary and scientific associations then existing in Hartford. Gideon Welles, John M. Niles, Henry Barnard, and others were influential in raising the necessary funds by public subscription. The Connecticut Historical Society, the Natural History Society, and the Young Men's Institute were given rooms for reading, lecturing, and debating.[112]

Hartford had no tax-supported library, but the Atheneum rooms of the Young Men's Institute partially fulfilled the needs for one. Barnard was the Institute's president when it was founded in 1838. The Hartford Library Association transferred its books to the organization and others made bequests. The rooms were opened to the public, magazines were made available, and by 1861 the library contained 12,000 volumes. The *Courant* highly approved this service.[113] It approved also the reading rooms maintained by other organizations, chief among them the Hartford Arts Union, formed in 1849 for men interested in technical and scientific subjects.[114] This is not to say that the paper looked with favor upon current reading tastes. On the contrary, Boswell described contemporary novels as feeble, shallow, and even "vicious." He regretted to the end of his days that people read them and that the old veneration for the English classics had well-nigh gone. It distressed him equally that so much of the periodical literature of the period was infested with transcendentalism and "other dim dreams and fantasies."[115]

Throughout these years the lecture held first rank among the activities designed for intellectual enlightenment. As the local lyceums became inactive, the Institute brought a dozen or more speakers to the Atheneum each winter.[116] Ralph Waldo Emerson, Mark Hopkins, Horace Greeley, Oliver Wendell Holmes, Henry Ward Beecher, Elihu Burritt, John Quincy Adams, Caleb Cushing and Thomas Hart Benton were a few of the better known names.[117] After 1849, when the Arts Union inaugurated a similar service, ambitious citizens could attend approximately 30 lectures a season.[118] Until about this time, the *Courant* reported the remarks of speakers in considerable detail and with the courtesy usually accorded to local doings.[119] Since the Mexican War was disliked, an exception was made in the case of Sam Houston:

Hon. Isaac Toucey presided, and in introducing the orator to the meeting passed a warm eulogy upon him and bespoke for him a warm reception, but the cheering was rather cool. Once or twice they managed to get up rather more of a racket, but there did not seem to be very much enthusiasm.[120]

The popular and fine arts were given sparse notice in the *Courant*. Traveling daguerreotypists supplanted the itinerants who once painted miniatures and cut silhouettes.[121] Citizens might visit the gallery of fine arts where Rosa Bonheur's "The Horse Fair" attracted comment in 1860.[122] Panoramas and dioramas still commanded public patronage.[123] Stereoscopes became popular.[124] Lessons in water coloring and oil painting were available.[125] After the death of Hartford's native son, Edward S. Bartholomew, the sculptor, the *Courant* supported a movement to raise $5,000 to place his works in the Atheneum. The editor adjudged his *Repentant Eve* to be one of the finest productions of modern times.[126]

The *Courant* thought that Hartford needed a large public hall, especially for the numbers who attended an increasing variety of concerts and music recitals.[127] Church choirs, the German *Liederkranz,* the Beethoven Society, several brass bands, and groups of pupils were repeatedly in the news.[128] In 1854 at the Center Church some of the old people sang the "quaint music" of their youth, and such revivals were popular for several years.[129] Among the great artists visiting the city were Ole Bull, peerless violinist, Louis M. Gottschalk, American pianist, Adelina Patti, then a child prodigy, and Henriette Sontag whose rich, mature voice captivated her listeners.[130] Most exciting of all was Jenny Lind. The *Courant* saluted her American tour in 1850. Citizens were advised to travel to New York to hear her. Editorials compared the simplicity of her singing with the affectations of the Italian school and hoped that she might revolutionize American taste: [131]

All this love of the artificial in music, this fondness for the mere display of the perfectibility of its mechanical part may be done away with by the genuine, unaffected, simplicity of Jenny Lind's singing, and her advent here be marked as an era in the history of American music.[132]

Miss Lind sang in Hartford at the new Fourth Church in 1851. Tickets were sold privately before being placed on public sale. Twelve hundred persons sat in the audience but many more were turned away. Since the windows were open, crowds perched on fences and the roofs of near-by houses. Halfway through the recital, the disgruntled citizenry rioted. Window panes were shattered, women fainted, the singer was frightened. Neither the mayor nor the chief of police could stop the commotion. An hour after the singing ceased, Miss Lind fled the church, was hustled to the railroad station, and quit Hartford. The *Courant* was deeply humiliated by the reception the people had given her.[133]

The theater emerged slowly from ill repute. In 1837 letters appeared in the paper pointing out the inevitable accompaniment of thieves, pickpockets, and loose females. Actors, it was said, customarily frequented grogshops and brothels. Boswell himself thought the theater to be the most pernicious of all places of amusement.[134] By the 1850's, however, citizens were petitioning the city council, under a local option law, to remove the restrictions in Hartford. The question had entered the city elections for several years and the law had been violated.[135] Boswell approved Shakespearean readings but clung to his old position on the theater.[136] After Day became editor, the *Courant* gave attention to the roving companies which infrequently visited the city.[137] On October 16, 1855, appeared this comment:

The play of Uncle Tom, was performed last night to a crowded house at Wyatt's Lyceum. The Eva of little Cordelia Howard is a beautiful creation. . . . Our citizens ought not to miss this chance, to see an excellent moral drama, admirably performed. We were pleased to see last night, some of the best people of the city present, with their wives and children.[138]

Certain games and sports, hitherto without respectable status, were at least winning a degree of public tolerance. The *Courant* associated bowling and billiards with gambling and drinking, but no amount of complaining did away with them.[139] It disapproved boxing as brutish,[140] but in 1859 gave two columns to the famous Heenan-Sayres fight in England. "We give the account," wrote the editor, "not because we approve of such things, but because the public is intensely interested to know the details."[141] In 1860 Heenan gave an exhibition bout in Hartford.[142] In Boswell's mind horse racing was disreputable too. He spoke of its deleterious effects upon community morals.[143] Remarking that raising and training horses for the track was the work of aristocracy, Day hoped that Hartford might never be cursed with a course.[144] Yet Hartford had a trotting park in 1855 and the *Courant* admitted that many of the city's most respectable people patronized the races, which were popular almost immediately.[145]

Readers spotted the appearance of newer and less objectionable activities. At South Green, in 1858, 20 Trinity College students had a game of "foot ball" with a like number of town boys.[146] Baseball teams were playing in 1860 as were cricket teams.[147] A number of local boat clubs composed the Hartford Navy, which sponsored races and reviews. In 1860 it accepted the challenge of the Springfield Navy to a three-mile race between two boats, each of which was to be a "6 oar lapstreak."[148] Because the *Courant* thought that city life was debilitating, it bespoke the need for gymnasiums.[149] The local Germans had their own gymnastic society, the Turnverein.[150] Day favored more physical activity for young people even at the expense of intellectual education. The urbanized sons of hardy farmers were soft. New inventions and facilities deteriorated the physical powers of Yankee women. Girls as well as boys, he thought, should play ball, hike, skate, and swim.[151]

Girls did participate in some of the sports. The editors called for public bathing accommodations, perhaps chiefly for those who had no bathrooms at home.[152] Day proposed that someone set up bath houses on the banks of the Connecticut where ladies and gentlemen might bathe together in "Cape May fashion."[153] In the winter of 1858–1859 a "skating fever" broke out and the paper noted that both sexes of all ages and pursuits carried skates with none of the feeling of shame which would have afflicted them, especially the ladies, even the winter before.[154] In 1861 the people of Hartford were alleged to be spending more than $500 per week on dances, which averaged better than one each night.[155]

Other occasions provided fun for young and old. River and rail excursions, picnics, sleighing parties, fairs, and outdoor band concerts were common.[156] In 1860 the *Courant* professed to find nothing but noise, confusion, and intemperance in the modern way of celebrating July 4.[157] Glass blowers, magicians, organ grinders, rope walkers, freaks, and menageries offered commercial entertainment.[158] Representations ranging from Napoleon's funeral to the beauties of the Alps could be seen by panorama.[159] Traveling minstrel groups played in Hartford.[160] P. T. Barnum's circus came to town in 1851. On the opening day, from twelve to fourteen thousand persons flocked to see General Tom Thumb, the Ceylon elephants, and the other wonders of the world's greatest show.[161] The *Courant* preferred the "hippodrome" to the "circus" since the clowns attached to the latter sometimes indulged in obscene jokes.[162]

In 1856 the paper recorded an exciting event, singular and sorrowful, that attracted great numbers of people. Poems were afterward written in its memory: [163]

The Charter Oak is Prostrate!

Our whole community, old and young, rich and poor, were grieved to learn that the famous old Charter Oak, in which Wadsworth hid King Charles' Charter of the old colony of Connecticut, in 1687, . . . had been prostrated by the wind. It fell about ten minutes before one o'clock, in the stormy morning of August 21, 1856. This tree has been for centuries one of the "Hartford institutions." No tree in the country has such legendary associations. Our citizens thronged in crowds to the spot. Chief Justices and Reverend Doctors intermixed with sturdy laborers to view the fallen Monarch. A dirge was played at noon, by Colt's Armory Band, over the fallen tree; it was a touching thing for these mechanics, some of them sons of Connecticut, and some of them born the other side of the Atlantic, thus to volunteer their sympathy; and many a manly eye was nourished as the Dead March in Saul was played, followed by "Home Sweet Home" and rounded off with "Hail Columbia." The bells all over the city, were tolled at sundown, as a token of the universal feeling, that one of the most sacred links that bind these modern days to the irrevocable past, had been suddenly parted.[164]

Through all the years of Hartford's change, Boswell, Day, and their associates took space to record their passing delights and pet aversions respecting a miscellaneous assortment of matters. The *Courant* noted red petticoats and hoop skirts.[165] It recorded the advent of "Bloomerism" in 1851 when some local women appeared in short kilts and Turkish trousers, but it had little use for the women's rights movement.[166] It was annoyed at women who forsook the home to mingle in election crowds or who wore silk attire on the streets when it belonged in the parlor.[167] Stamping the feet at concerts and lectures, pommeling the chairs with canes, and even handclapping were denounced as crudities.[168] The tobacco habit was nasty.[169] Other things were frowned upon: Sunday bathing, taking babies to evening entertainments, racing horses in hot weather, racing sleighs, racing steamboats, shooting sparrows and robins, tolling the bells at funerals, men loafing on corners, and women parading the streets.[170] Spiritualism or "Rochester rappings," transcendentalism, clairvoyance, mesmerism, Millerism, and Mormonism were deceptive and vicious.[171] Boswell thought the country had swung from an era of skepticism into one of credulity.[172] Of the several *isms* which disfigured the age, according to Day, spiritualism was the most dangerous since it led to other illusions, vices, insanity, and suicide.[173] When Day endorsed the politics of the Know-Nothings, the *Courant* had little respect for "German Infidels," "German Pantheists," [174] and it spoke of the Irish section of Hartford as "Pigville." [175] Strangers whose remarks complimented the city always pleased the editors. Charles Dickens visited Hartford in 1842 and was handsomely feted; [176] but when his *Notes on America* were published, Boswell declared that the author had made himself supremely ridiculous: "Never, if we may judge from his works, since his return to his own land, did any foreign traveller with any pretensions to intelligence, gain so poor and meagre an idea of any people among whom he travelled." [177]

Humanitarian reforms, redolent of the 1820's and 1830's, were now and again in the wind. The editors wrote strongly for the establishment of a state school for delinquent boys.[178] They demanded provisions for the institutional separation of paupers, criminals, and the mentally diseased.[179] They spoke with scorn of proposals to abolish capital punishment for murder.[180] But no reform movement, not even the struggle for better public schools, received as much newspaper space or as many high hopes as did the fight against old John Barleycorn.

In 1841 a "Washington Temperance Society" was organized in Hartford by 11 reformed drinkers. In three weeks, 100 members were meeting almost every night. At the end of one year, about

1,800 persons, including the city mayor and council, took part in religious exercises, dinners, and speeches, celebrating the remarkable growth of the total-abstinence movement.[181] By 1843, besides the Washington Society, Hartford had a Martha Washington Society, a Young Men's Temperance Society, a Catholic Society, a Hope Total Abstinence Society, and a Cold Water Army.[182] John Hawkins and John B. Gough, nationally known temperance missionaries, came to town to speak.[183] Men, women, and children made abstinence pledges.[184] The *Courant* rejoiced and did what it could, in the years ahead, to preserve enthusiasm for the Washington movement. Boswell believed that nine tenths of the crime and a large share of human poverty and degradation were plainly traceable to the drinking of liquor.[185]

In 1854 Connecticut adopted the "Maine law" prohibiting the manufacture and sale of alcoholic beverages except for sacramental, medicinal, and manufacturing purposes. This was an experiment of great worth, according to the *Courant,* even if only partially successful. It would destroy the roots of wretchedness and misery.[186] The law became effective on August 1. On August 10, the *Courant* was delighted that local grogshops were closed and that nights were free from brawling and loud profanity. By August 15, it conceded that excitement over the liquor question was pushing aside interest even in the famous Nebraska bill. It was regrettable, thought the editor, that the issue was assuming a partisan, political character.[187]

The law was unpopular in the city from the beginning. Citizens were asked to authorize the selectmen to appoint town agents to handle the legal sales. They refused.[188] The selectmen appointed an agent anyway. The citizens appropriated no money. The *Courant* said that none was needed. Attempts were made to enjoin the agent from acting.[189] The *Times* took up the battle for "personal liberty." The *Courant* accused the *Times* of demagogic appeals to foreigners, of confusing the restrictions of the Republic with old-world tyrannies, and of wishing to brutalize the masses by alcohol.[190] At the end of a year Day believed that prohibition had been vindicated and that its "principle" had been established forever, even though there were secret violations all the time.[191] The editor stood by his guns in 1856 and 1857 while admitting the breakdown of enforcement in Connecticut cities. The friends of temperance were doing good work, he said, despite large numbers of shops operating openly in Hartford.[192] As time passed, the *Courant* observed a local revival of the old Washington movement. Once again total abstainers were holding regular meetings. Once again John B. Gough came to Hartford to speak.[193]

Within a month of the firing on Fort Sumter, despite disappointments, the *Courant* looked back upon Hartford with immense pride.[194] The city had grown in territory, population, and wealth. The old dwellings of the first settlers had given way to splendid stores. Solitary lanes and uninhabited byways had become thickly populated streets. Building lots, which begged for purchase at $50 a foot a dozen years before, could not now be bought for four times that amount. Colt's great industry, other factories, railroads, public institutions, and modern facilities for living were the measure of Hartford's progress. In a few months, promised the *Courant,* citizens were to enjoy the conveniences of a modern horse railway system.

CHAPTER XV

THE COURANT *IN THE CIVIL WAR*

IN the springtime of 1861, when news of the bombardment of Sumter reached the cities and towns of the North, excitement was unbounded. Resentments, long pent up, found release in the fervid emotions of patriotism. The *Courant* bore its sensational tidings under a display head, one column wide. Editorially, it vented its wrath:

The awful fact that CIVIL WAR has begun in bloody earnest seems to be only too well authenticated. Our telegraphic columns tell the sad story, so far as it has come to hand. The South Carolinians took the initiative. Let it be forever remembered, that the greatest crime committed since the crucifixion of our Saviour, was wantonly and wilfully committed in behalf of American Slavery. . . . Slavery has sown the wind; it will soon reap the whirlwind. . . . Let the South remember that they who live by the sword are sure to die by the sword; and that any temporary advantage that the fortune of war may give them, though pleasant to their palate for the moment, will prove bitterer than wormwood and gall in their bellies. Let not him who putteth on his armor boast himself like one who putteth it off; but may we all, sobered by the grim reality of internal war, gird up our energies and [ac]quit ourselves like men. It is sweet to die for one's country; and never had mortal a better cause than that which now summons all who feel themselves to be men, to rally around the flag of our fathers. Men of Connecticut! TO ARMS!! [1]

Two days later, on Monday morning, April 15, Lincoln's proclamation calling for 75,000 volunteers was published in the papers of the North. Along the line of the Great Lakes, the *Courant* heard the tramp of gathering hosts; along the seaboard from Cape May to Passamaquoddy Bay, the roll of drums drowned out the roar of the Atlantic. Men fighting for the right, the Constitution, and the country were invincible: "Thrice armed is he that has his quarrel just . . ." [2] Inflamed patriots, including Thomas Day, were anxious, eager, and impatient for a major trial of arms. Within a fortnight Hartford's citizens had raised over $60,000 to equip volunteers and the *Courant* thundered for action. [3] Ever since November 6, the government had been faltering and palliative in policy. It seemed that a defensive psychology inhibited even the Republicans in Washington. Treason asked for nothing but force. Volunteers had enlisted for a fight. Something ought to be done somewhere and done immediately. Even initial reverses would be preferable to inaction. As for Lincoln's dallying with Maryland, Baltimore should be entered and placed under military rule. If her people resisted, they should be shot down like dogs. If Maryland rebelled, Maryland should be conquered. If the South sprang to her aid, the South must be whipped. On April 26, in such a spirit, the editor hoped to chronicle a battle within the next few days. If Winfield Scott were too old to lead troops, he hoped that a younger man might be placed at his post.[4]

Throughout the long strife with its grievous disappointments, the first of which was the battle of Bull Run in July, 1861, the *Courant* displayed an unwavering faith in the favorable issue of the conflict. In many ways it attempted to support the cause of federal arms. It sought to stimulate volunteering. It encouraged participation in civilian war activities. It demanded heavier taxes. Crying out for national unity and scorning ideas of appeasement, it sprayed venom upon speculators and "copperheads." It relayed tales of southern atrocities. It berated Great Britain for her attitude toward the conflict. It criticized the conduct of the war. It criticized the generals. It criticized the politicians. It criticized the government. For four years Day's policy was impatient, aggressive, and demanding, calling for competence, calling for action, and summoning whatever measures he supposed might place a decisive and early end to the great civil combat. This was the first time since the Revolution that the *Courant* could engage heartily in prosecuting an American war.

When new regiments were called for after the failure of George B. McClellan's Virginia campaign in 1862, state authorities all over the North conducted enlistment drives. The *Courant* roused patriotism and publicized mass meetings to stir up sentiment for local volunteering.[5] According to Day, it was not enough for citizens to contribute money. Neither rich nor poor, educated nor ignorant, could claim moral exemption from personal services. Educated people in particular owed it to society to offer their sons so that the humbler might be encouraged to make similar sacrifices. This was a war of the whole people.[6] One year earlier Day thought enlistment bounties were extravagant and inappropriate,[7] but now he promoted them strongly from private and public sources. The Citizen's War Committee was formed to give cash to volunteers and to the dependents they left behind them.[8] The *Courant* praised the example of one wealthy resident who would supplement bounties by giving to each of the families of 10 good men the sum of $10.00 per month for one year.[9] For prospective three-year recruits, the following was placed at the head of the editorial page: [10]

Volunteers who enlist in this town within the next few days will receive in bounties and wages for three years' service, the following sums:

Town of Hartford bounty,	$ 175.00
State bounty ($50, and $30 yearly),	140.00
U. S. bounty, in advance,	27.00
" " " at close of service,	75.00
Wages for three years,	468.00
	$ 885.00

If the volunteer has a wife, and two children under 14 years of age, he will draw the following additional pay:

State bounty to wife and two children	$ 360.00
Town bounty to wife and two children	216.00
	Total, $1461.00

Part of the fervor exhibited in procuring enlistments in 1862 was stimulated by a desire to avoid the stigma of conscription. The War Department had warned that a draft would be ordered in states failing to meet their quotas. The *Courant* hoped drafting would be unnecessary, but raised no important objections to the principle.[11] As local recruiting lagged, Day believed that hundreds of young men were simply standing by, hoping to get large sums of money as substitutes for wealthy men whose names might be drawn but who would be unwilling to fight.[12] Some of the latter were said to be anticipating this plight by bidding for substitutes on condition they were called. Citing one man who provisionally offered $2,000, the *Courant* deplored the practice on grounds that it would inflate the exemption market to a point beyond the reach of men of moderate means.[13] When the draft was applied in Hartford's district in September, it was apparently not very successful. According to Governor Buckingham, from over 1,200 men drafted in the Connecticut towns, only 76 principals and 142 substitutes were mustered into the service. A number deserted after reporting to camp, still more were unaccounted for, and the majority were exempted by local doctors and selectmen.[14] In retrospect, the effects of this draft looked bad to the *Courant*. Day wrote that previous requisitions had been fairly met, but when conscription was threatened, whole communities had become panic-stricken. In an effort to fill quotas, officials had dragged in the halt and the maimed, enormous bounties were voted, the recipients were debauched, and many of them were discharged afterward as physically unfit.[15]

A more comprehensive conscription law in 1863, which permitted draftees to procure substitutes or to buy one year's exemption for $300, also placed a premium upon local recruitment. The *Courant* at first objected to the new measure, citing the previous year's experience, and discerning a despotic centralization of power in Washington; but it was accepted as inevitable and later defended.[16] Editorials urged bounties for conscripts as well as for volunteers; finally they supported arrangements by which the public treasuries doled out to individuals part of the cost of getting substitutes.[17] Private brokers sold the latter at so many hundred dollars apiece, apparently procured them from as far away as conquered slave state territory.[18] The *Courant* preached on the superior fitness of volunteers, endorsed any expedient measure to place men in the field, and withal was disgusted with the whole spectacle of recruitment. On July 13, 1863, the editor remarked that large numbers of men had left town to avoid the draft of that day. Additional cars had been placed on the railroad, so great was the exodus during the 10 days preceding. In August, 1864, Day charged that the community had come to regard the avoidance of military service as the paramount obligation of the crisis. According to him, the facts afforded a painful commentary on the decline of popular patriotism.[19]

Civilian war work took the form of sewing, knitting, making bandages, preparing jellies, wines, dried foods, collecting books, and giving money to one or another of the organizations supplying aid and comfort at the front. Early in the war the *Courant* questioned the wisdom of some of the work of the United States Sanitary Commission. Why should it appeal to charity for essential army supplies when the government ought to finance the costs of blankets, hospital materials, and the like, by equitable taxation?[20] The Hartford Soldiers' Aid Society collected and distributed these items, some of them through the Sanitary Commission, some directly to Connecticut regiments in the South, some to hospitals within the state.[21] The *Courant* urged "soldiers' gardens," collected books, praised the devotion of Hartford's ladies, asked donations for the Commission and the Aid Society.[22] In 1864 it editorialized on the need for supporting the United States Christian Commission, another service organization.[23] Throughout the war it gave space for appeals and acknowledgments.

From beginning to end, also, the *Courant* worried about the nation's public credit, conceiving it to be threatened by the unprecedented wartime expenditures. To follow the pattern of editorials, as large a proportion as possible of federal and state income should be derived from taxation. The more the government taxed, the less it would need to borrow; the less it borrowed, the greater the security of its credit.[24] The several legal tender acts, perhaps necessary expedients, impaired contracts.[25] Although soldiers were paid in legal tender currency, United States bondholders should be paid in gold, for this was the very symbol of government solvency.[26] Greenbacks made it imperative to increase taxation. Otherwise the government's paper would depreciate rapidly, taking a customary toll of the savings of insurance companies, retired clergymen, widows, and so forth.[27] With this point of view, the *Courant* made no great issue of the different taxes imposed during the war. While favoring a uniform national currency, it feared the working of Salmon P. Chase's proposed national banking system, principally, according to the editor, because the national banks might achieve a stake in the preservation of legal tender.[28] In conclusion, heavy taxes made both public and private retrenchment imperative. Different localities were pressing for internal improvements on grounds of their value for national defense, but Day favored the general suspension of such projects until after the war.[29] For individuals and families, he recommended the moral worth of a return to the simpler, less expensive habits of living.[30]

The *Courant* had no tolerance for those who were supposed to be disrupting the war effort. Day wrote of the bounty racket, of graft in the army, of the "harpies" and "vultures" who fattened on government contracts, of "vampires" who speculated in cotton and foodstuffs.[31] Not much better, if at all, were the government's political enemies. Local Democratic leaders were attacked savagely as malignant and seditious. Their followers were allegedly traitors, hypocrites, disguised rebels, Copperheads.[32] The meeting at Middletown in 1862 was "Jeff. Davis' Convention." [33] The local *Times* was a Vallandigham sheet, the Jeff Davis organ, "The Traitor's Advocate." According to Day, no stronger proslavery paper could be found in the entire country, and yet it howled about the wartime suppression of civil liberties.[34] Nor was the *Times* alone in Connecticut:

The copperheads, always noted for venom, are daily becoming more open and deadly in efforts to break down the government, and if the sting fails to prove mortal, it will be from no lack of poison and malignanty. The press represents the party. Painful as the fact is, it must nevertheless be confessed that the opposition organs of Connecticut echo the sentiments of a large minority at least, of the people of the State. If these papers were printed in South Carolina instead of New England, they could hardly exhibit more virulence in denouncing the government of the United States and the cause which it is struggling so heroically to maintain. Bare rumors of disaster to the federal arms are heralded by alarming announcements displayed in conspicuous type. Defeats, such as must unavoidably occur amid the vicissitudes of war, are served up in all styles with plentiful exaggerations for the delectation of sympathizing readers. Reverses are hashed and re-hashed till even the nostrils of the loco-foco loathe the foul mess concocted by his own ingenuity. The blunder of a General is a perfect wind-fall to the copperheads. It affords a fresh excuse for hissing at the President. . . . and long columns of figures are paraded to show the credulous the enormous expenditures of men and money incurred by the president in furtherance of personal ends. When the facts are brought out before judicial boards so as to stamp the lie upon such fabrications, the inventors of the falsehoods not only abstain from disseminating the truth, but with unblushing effrontery continue to reiterate their lies. A loyal man can see the difference between the tone of the Jeff. Davis organs at the North and at the South. In both sections they are equally bold, reckless and malignant. Editorials that appear in the one would not be at all out of place in the columns of the other. If the confederacy was distracted by a Union element at all approximating in strength and hardihood to the rebel element at the North, it could not survive a month. And yet one of the favorite dodges of the faction that plots and speaks with utter impunity, is to harp on the dangers to our liberties! Loyal people resort to no violence to close their venomous mouths. Davis would deal more summarily with malcontents to his bastard government, treating them at short notice to the prison or the rope.[35]

The British Government's friendly attitude toward the South likewise drew uncomplimentary appraisal. The *Courant* told readers that John Bull had always been adept at seeing the sins of others, shutting his eyes to the opium, calicoes, and cheap hardware which had long underlain British naval policy; exalting such executioners as Clive and Hastings; forgetting India, China, Ireland, the coolie trade, the demoralization of colonial peoples with a deceptive mixture of trinkets, ardent spirits, and pious missionaries. The British were a nation of shopkeepers, enforcing trade by the bayonet. With them, might and right were commensurate. For years they had preached against slavery and flooded the country with abolitionist tracts. Who would have thought their philanthropy so shallow that they now supported the rebels? Despite past wars, Americans had traditionally felt close to the English people. Not soon would they forget this hostility to the Republic in its days of supreme trial.[36]

In granting belligerent status to the Confederacy at the beginning of the war, Day argued that Britain and France had not recognized southern "nationality." They were asking only that the government's blockade of southern ports be more than a mere paper affair, a point that everybody conceded. This was a hollow victory for the South.[37] When Captain Charles Wilkes took Mason and Slidell, Confederate envoys to England and France, from the British steamer *Trent,* the *Courant* joined in the popular approval. Arguments ran as follows: (1) that the "right of search" of a belligerent nation was incontestable; and (2) that the transportation of messengers and dispatches of a belligerent was equivalent to carrying contraband. Editorials were certain that the prisoners would not be handed over to Britain, let the consequences be what they might. Secretary Seward's decision was therefore unpalatable, but the paper supported him, opining that Jefferson Davis would gnash his teeth now that the prospects of an Anglo-American war had appreciably diminished.[38] The case of the Confederate *Alabama,* built in the dockyard at Liverpool, was less conclusive but sharply resented. Day conceded that the United States could do nothing at the time but averred that the hour of reckoning would surely come.[39] Also disliked were the plans of England, France, and Spain to enforce their claims upon Mexico. If these were passing infractions of the Monroe Doctrine, exercised while the Union was distraught, Louis Napoleon's attempt to establish an empire there was a challenge of a bolder sort. The *Courant* believed that a clash of arms between the United States and France could not long be averted.[40]

In the first half of the war, editorials discussed the possibility of an intervention of European powers to break the blockade of the South. In 1862 Day wondered if Europe, especially England, could stand the loss of three successive cotton crops. The loss of two appeared to be certain. British mills were shut down, unemployment was rife, shipping was distressed.[41] Although intervention constituted the hope of the South, circumstances were observed to be making it unlikely. In the first place, Napoleon and the British Government could not agree on an appropriate time.[42] Secondly, the Russian Government sympathized with the North and therefore opposed interference.[43] Most important of all, continental wheat crops in 1861 and 1862 were insufficient to meet European wants. The latter seemed to the *Courant* to be one of the tokens of divine care. As long as the rulers of England and France depended upon the North for bread-stuffs for their people, they could be held in check. The favorable trade balance, by allowing the North to accumulate specie, also promoted the soundness of northern finances. The cereals of the West took the place of cotton in supporting the banks. Day believed that all this not only discouraged foreign interventionists, but it furnished a magnificent spectacle of a mighty nation placing hundreds of thousands of men on the battlefield and simultaneously feeding Europe's millions.[44]

The purposes for which the war was fought, as the *Courant* presented them, underwent change after the first months of conflict. In the beginning Day was opposed to emancipation. The sudden freeing of millions of Negroes would bring suffering to whites and blacks for generations. It would react disastrously upon the border states that were loyally supporting the cause. It would convert the war into an antislavery crusade and thus render it unpopular. People in the North were fighting the southern aristocracy for equal rights and for the preservation of the Union, but for nothing more.[45] In October, 1861, the *Courant* ran a lead editorial by "R." which announced a change in outlook. The rebels were stubborn, federal leniency brought nothing but harm, and the time had come for strong measures. What sounded radical six months before seemed appropriate now from a military point of view. The slaves of the rebels must be declared free.[46]

Henceforth the *Courant* called repeatedly for emancipation. It rejoiced when slavery was abolished in the District of Columbia, called for a bill prohibiting it forever in the territories, urged freedom for contraband Negroes, and their employment at federal arms.[47] Lincoln's proclamation on January 1, 1863, was hailed as the most fruitful document of the century. With it, the nation stood committed to the fundamental principles of the forefathers. To justify the American Revolution, they had declared a belief in certain inalienable rights which had been given the lie by the growth of the institution of slavery. This anomaly had now passed. The cause for which the North fought was as clear as crystal. The war would make America free in reality as well as in name.[48] But what to do with the Negroes was puzzling. The editor believed that the Republican party could never stand the charge of having set the blacks into direct competition with free white labor. The *Courant's* suggestions, which accorded with old Whig convictions, contemplated a wholesale removal of ex-slaves to the tropics, preferably Haiti and Liberia. Their leaders, ennobled by experience in the war, might take the seeds of civilization to those benighted regions. The United States Navy could provide transportation.[49]

For three years the *Courant* pleaded persistently for a more energetic prosecution of the war. At the outset, Lincoln's policy was said to have been unwisely magnanimous. Southern spies and sympathizers were allegedly swarming the offices in Washington, doing what they could to sabotage the government and the war. After a year the administration had not shot a single spy, hung a traitor, or condemned a pirate. The *Courant* cried for a Cromwellian policy of vigorous and unrelenting severity.[50] In the paper's opinion, the administrative leniency seemed to give tone to the psychology that dominated the movements of the army of the Potomac. McClellan's inaction was galling, Lincoln's reticence exasperating.[51] Editorials ascribed the failure of 1862 to the meddling of politicians, to the incompetence and conceit of Edwin M. Stanton in the War Department, finally to a lack of appropriate talent on the part of McClellan himself.[52] In days of defeat the editor was infuriated by the censorship of news, charging that the administration lacked faith in the people.[53] As the stars of successive generals rose and fell around Richmond, none of the paper's impatience abated. Editorials demanded dash, audacity, and a hailstorm of assaults upon enemy positions.[54] Confederate officers were admitted to be more competent and better trained.[55] If we should believe what was printed, the remoteness from Washington of the armies of the West preserved them from political interference, hence accounted for their greater successes.[56] But Gideon Welles in the Navy Department was defended against all strictures. Since naval commanders were not traditionally presidential candidates, Welles was said to have been free from political annoyances. Naval victories were attributed in part to this fortunate circumstance.[57]

The paper cried down all talk of peace and compromise, mostly around election time. The Republicans returned William A. Buckingham to the governorship each spring.[58] The Democrats, early in the war, were stigmatized as unpatriotic appeasers.[59] As the editor remarked, all parties hoped for an end of hostilities, even the Confederates, but the Republicans alone would assure victory with the complete restoration of the Union and the thorough destruction of slavery.[60] Such sentiments, repeated without interesting variation, culminated in the national election of 1864. The *Courant* favored Lincoln, assuming that the party would renominate him and the people would elect him.[61] General McClellan, his Democratic opponent, was complimented for virtually repudiating the peace plank in his party's platform, but editorials damned him as a pliable character who could be expected to succumb to the wiles of the Copperheads.[62] The editor appealed for a campaign without claptrap and indeed the contest was a rather mild one.[63]

Pleased at Lincoln's re-election and the strong, favorable tide of the war, the *Courant* took time for retrospection.[64] Since 1861 the country had passed through days of discouragement and gloom as if God had forsaken it. In the beginning the people had been inexperienced, self-confident, and impetuous, disposed to chafe irrationally under the sore trials through which they passed. The early generals had disappeared, the Cabinet had been remodeled, civil officers had been displaced to make room for rising talent. Through all the months Lincoln had been the central, immovable pivot of the government. He had shown as much shrewdness in the choice of measures as in the selection of men. Since it had been impossible at first to understand the full implications of the crisis, the formulation of a policy adapted to evolving circumstances had become the test of executive intelligence. The administration had moved steadfastly until the military, naval, and civil affairs were managed with consummate skill and statesmanship. Lincoln had shown remarkable forbearance, wisdom, and determination. The nation had achieved a new consciousness:

We have carried on a war of greater magnitude than ever before witnessed in any country; but, knowing our cause to be just, and learning at fearful cost our strength as a nation, we have held, and are determined to hold on, until the authority of the government is acknowledged in every State in the Union, and the laws obeyed in every one of the States which ever have been a part of the Union. We have not only learned the value of the Union, but we have been taught our strength, financially and morally; we have learned that we are a powerful people—one to be feared and respected by all nations. We have been led through terrible war to look upon slavery as the cause of the rebellion, and as a curse to the nation which must, and shall be removed. While four years ago the people were ready to conciliate the South by guaranteeing slavery by amending the Constitution, to-day the people . . . will have no more buying and selling of human beings, but all shall be free as the air of heaven, firmly resolved that this shall be the home of the *free* and the *brave*.[65]

If the editor had thumbed back through his volumes of the *Courant,* he could have found a recording of the eager hopes, the pride, the discouragements, the joys and bitter sorrows which were intimate ingredients of these years of national crisis. Public confidence surrendered to dismay and consternation with the initial encounter at Bull Run.[66] Gloom characterized the first winter, gave way to assurance and expectancy in the spring. "On to Richmond" became the cry; enthusiasm soared.[67] Naval successes and the progress of arms in the West scarcely assuaged the grief that followed McClellan's failure.[68] After another winter of melancholy came mixed fortunes: Lee's invasion of Pennsylvania, Meade's glorious victory at Gettysburg, Grant's triumph at Vicksburg, and the turning tide of the war.[69] Here and there in the papers, in periods of adversity, were editorials counseling courage, determination, and optimism.[70] Short consoling items recorded the distress, the loss of morale, and the food shortages in the South.[71] Other paragraphs evinced hatred, telling of torture, starvation, and death in the prison camps of the Confederacy.[72] Scattered throughout the issues were neat lists of names of the boys in blue who would never return to Connecticut's towns and farms.[73] Not least of all were the unmistakable signs of prosperity, thriving enterprises, rising prices, good profits, lagging wages, and the quickening tempo of city life.[74]

The *Courant* marveled at Hartford's wartime prosperity. Munition factories, chiefly Colt's and Sharp's, ran day and night, employing hundreds of workers, producing thousands of arms each month for the government. Leather concerns made straps, knapsacks, and ammunition boxes. Clothing and shoe factories throve.[75] The imposing Charter Oak Bank building was erected.[76] Allyn Hall was built with a seating capacity of over 2,000, equipped for rally, lecture, or theater.[77] A "Bryant, Stratton & Co.'s Commercial College" was dedicated.[78] For the Travelers Insurance Company, offering the novelty of accident insurance, the *Courant* prophecied a national future.[79] Horse cars appeared on Main and Asylum streets.[80] The editor demanded an enlarged city police force armed with revolvers.[81] A disastrous fire at Colt's, causing a property loss of over

$1,000,000, resulted in a paid city fire company with horse-drawn steam engines.[82] Social life intensified. Masquerade balls and tableaus became popular.[83] An Italian opera troupe played the *Bohemian Girl, Barber of Seville, Il Trovatore.*[84] Clara Louise Kellogg made her Hartford debut.[85] People saw John Wilkes Booth in *Richard III,* Laura Keene in *Our American Cousin,* and others in such favorites as *East Lynne* and *Ten Nights in a Bar-Room.*[86] Bailey's circus, George Christy's minstrels, and Dan Rice's popular show attracted large patronage.[87] Hundreds attended stereopticon displays. This "culmination of the dagguerrian art" was counted a wonderful scientific discovery.[88] Trotting races, national horse shows,[89] state billiard tournaments,[90] exhibitions of laughing gas,[91] boat races, glass blowing, skating, dancing, baseball, boxing,[92] lectures, concerts, and no end of entertainment catered to all shades of preference. "No one would imagine," wrote a visitor, "that any of the evils of war could have been felt here."[93]

In April, 1865, the *Courant* described how joyously the city greeted the tidings from Appomattox:

The news of the surrender of Lee's army was received by the COURANT through a special dispatch fifteen minutes before the official announcement came and our flag was at once given to the breeze. Messengers were immediately dispatched to notify the police, and have the bells of the city rung. This was about 9:45. Shortly after the church bells sent forth their merry peals, the fire department responded at first supposing there was a fire, and subsequently thousands of people leaving their houses appeared upon the streets, and such a scene of rejoicing has never been witnessed in Hartford before.

Around the telegraph office an immense crowd collected, and cheered and re-cheered amid the wildest enthusiasm. Bonfires were lighted, and Main street was a blaze of light. Christy's Minstrel band was speedily engaged and came out, doing splendid service, when a procession was formed, and with flags flying, chinese lanterns displayed, etc., marched down Main street, headed by the fire steamers and hose carriages, to the South Green and then countermarched. In the meantime an extra COURANT on a small slip had been issued and was rapidly distributed. Many buildings were illuminated, gas jets being turned on in full force, and ladies appeared at windows waving flags and handkerchiefs. Trinity College was well lighted, and a number of students came down town in a body, and marched in the procession, singing and blowing horns. In addition to the band and horns, bells, gongs, drums, etc., were brought into use, and the noise made was immense. The enthusiasm can hardly be imagined; it was beyond anything this people have witnessed before.[94]

These events, which followed so closely the *Courant*'s centennial anniversary, concluded a century in the development of the nation. When the *Courant* first saw the light of day, the American Revolution had not been fought, the federal Union had not been born. The people of that generation crystallized institutions of lasting and profound import in American history. Those who followed them spanned a continent and contributed in various ways to the building of a great Republic. Washington, Hamilton, Jefferson, Jackson, Clay, Calhoun, Webster, and countless forgotten people had played their roles and passed on. Not easily, across the bridge of decades, could the readers of 1865 appreciate with what misgivings, joy, bitterness, and hope Hartford's *Courant* had itself been a part of the life stream of the nation.

What mattered now to the editor was that the nation survived. It seemed to him that people had fought not so much from enmity toward the South as from a devotion to the Union. The victory had been for those who believed in the future of the Republic, who had faith in man's capacity for self-government.[95] Lincoln's tragic death received this comment:

His death at this time is a national affliction—not, strictly speaking, a national calamity. Above all the sorrow; rising out of the heavy weight of anguish which bears upon the popular heart; independent of everything which the assassin has accomplished, there is this cheering consolation—*The Nation lives!* The mission of our late President to save that which was threatened with destruction, to build anew on ground which had before been wet with bondsmen's tears, and to give the world assurance that our system of government could and should stand, was accomplished fully. So we say our weeds of mourning are for the loss of so good a man—respect for his great personal and public worth—for what he has done for us and for our children, rather than on account for any great calamity to the nation.[96]

NOTES

CHAPTER I

COLONIAL NEWSPAPER

1. John Warner Barber, *Connecticut Historical Collections, Containing a General Collection of Interesting Facts, Traditions, Bibliographical Sketches, Anecdotes, &c. Relating to the History and Antiquities of Every Town in Connecticut, with Geographical Descriptions* (New Haven, 1836), p. 49; Albert C. Bates, "Thomas Green," *Papers of the New Haven Colony Historical Society* VIII (1914), 293. The shop was located on the west side of Queen St. (Main St.) on the north corner of the cemetery, about where the south corner of the Waverly building now stands. Barber talked to George Goodwin who worked in the original office.

2. The Heart & Crown sign was for many years before and afterward the emblem of the Fleets, a Boston publishing firm, and was used by them at their shop and on some of their printed works. Bates, *loc. cit.,* p. 294. The almanac was advertised in the prospectus: "Just Published, and to be sold by the Printer hereof, ELLSWORTH's ALMANACK for the year 1765. Calculated for the Meridian of Hartford . . ." Green is credited with having published it in Albert Carlos Bates, *The Work of Hartford's First Printer* (Cambridge, 1925), p. 346.

3. The first issue of the *Connecticut Gazette* appeared on Apr. 12, 1755, under the name of James Parker and, beginning with the issue of Dec. 13, 1755, was published by James Parker & Company. Holt, junior partner of the firm, was the printer of the paper and Parker's deputy at the post office. Parker never lived in Connecticut and was concerned with the printing business in New York and New Jersey. Holt moved to New York in June, 1760, and Green took over his work until the suspension of the *Gazette* on Apr. 14, 1764. Isaiah Thomas, *The History of Printing in America, with a Biography of Printers, and an Account of Newspapers* (Albany, 1874), I, 188–189; Clarence S. Brigham, comp., *Bibliography of American Newspapers, 1690–1820*, Proceedings of the American Antiquarian Society, XXVII (1917), 291; *Conn. Gaz.*, Apr. 12, Dec. 13, 1755, June 21, 1760; Bates, "Green," p. 290; Jarvis Means Morse, *Connecticut Newspapers in the Eighteenth Century* (New Haven, 1935), pp. 1–2; articles on John Holt, *Dictionary of American Biography*, IX, 180–181; Benjamin Mecom, *ibid.*, XII, 488–489; James Parker, *ibid.*, XIV, 226–227; Thomas Green, *ibid.*, VII, 558–559; Beverly McAnear, *James Parker versus John Holt*, Proceedings of the New Jersey Historical Society, LIX (1941), 77–95, 198–212.

4. The facts are taken from Bates, *Hartford's First Printer*, p. 345; Bates, "Green," pp. 289–290; *The Public Records of the Colony of Connecticut*, V, 477; Thomas, *Hist. of Printing*, I, 185–191; articles on Samuel, Bartholomew, and Thomas Green, *DAB*, VII, 555–556, 537–538, 558–559.

5. Bates, *Hartford's First Printer*, p. 346; Morse, *op. cit.*, p. 4; Bates, "Green," p. 291. The *Conn. Gaz.* was revived by Mecom on July 5, 1765, with a sample issue. The first regular issue appeared on July 12, 1765. Brigham, *loc. cit.,* p. 291. The printery at New Haven had been originally established by Franklin who intended it for Mecom; but when the latter had other plans James Parker took it over. Articles on Holt, Mecom, Parker, *DAB,* IX, 180–181; XII, 488–489; XIV, 226–227.

6. Green was born in New London, Aug. 25, 1735, and married on Sept. 30, 1761. His first two children were born in New Haven in 1762 and 1764. Bates, "Green," pp. 290, 308–309.

7. Connecticut censuses of 1756 and 1774 are in *Col. Records*, X, 617–618 and XIV, 483–492.

8. Timothy Green issued a prospectus of the *New London Gazette* on Oct. 12, 1763. The first regular issue appeared on Nov. 18, 1763.

9. New York papers published at the time were: John Holt's *The New-York Gazette; or, The Weekly Post-Boy;* Hugh Gaine's *The New-York Mercury;* and William Weyman's *The New-York Gazette*. Brigham, *loc. cit.,* pp. 417, 421, 456.

10. Hartford's recorded population in 1761 was 3,938. *Col. Records,* XI, 574–575 n.

11. Cf. *post,* pp. 18–19.

12. *Connecticut Courant,* Oct. 29, 1764.

13. *Ibid.,* May 13, 1765, contains notice that the printing shop had been moved to the store of James Church opposite the Court House and next to Bull's Tavern. Advertisements of Caleb Bull (*ibid.,* June 8, 1767) and James Church (*ibid.,* Oct. 24, 1768) show that the shop occupied the upper floor of the building.

14. Advertised in issues of Oct. 29, Dec. 3, 1764; July 1, Sept. 2, 1765; Jan. 13, Feb. 24, Mar. 10, Apr. 28, Sept. 8, Sept. 15, 1766.

15. A list of Green's Hartford imprints is in Bates, *Hartford's First Printer,* pp. 348–361.

16. The prospectus, numbered "00," appeared Oct. 29, 1764; the issue numbered "2" is dated Dec. 3, 1764; issue "1," of which no known copy exists, was presumably dated Nov. 26, 1764.

17. The emblem was missing from issues of Oct. 7, 1765 to Nov. 3, 1766. He began to use 10-point type for news columns. With the issue of Sept. 9, 1765, he began to use 12-point type.

18. Such papers were issued on Mar. 17, Apr. 21, May 5, Sept. 22, Sept. 29, Oct. 6, 1766.

19. Half-sheet papers were issued on Aug. 12, 19, Oct. 14, Mar. 17, Apr. 21, Sept. 29, 1766; Jan. 5, 19, Apr. 13, 1767. The first supplements appeared with the issues of Step. 15 and 22, 1766.

20. *Cour.,* Oct. 29, 1764–Dec. 28, 1767, *passim.*

21. *Ibid.,* Dec. 24, 31, 1764; Mar. 4, 1765; Jan. 6, Feb. 3, 1766; Mar. 16, Dec. 28, 1767.

22. *Ibid.,* Dec. 17, 1764.

23. *Ibid.,* Nov. 30, 1767.

24. *Ibid.,* Apr. 18, May 30, 1768; Mar. 26, 1771.

25. The partnership was announced in the issue of Apr. 18, 1768, and the Green & Watson imprint appeared with the issue of Apr. 25, 1768. Despite this, in Dec. 12, 1768, Watson wrote of the year of partnership as ending in December, 1768; three years later, although the partnership was clearly dissolved Dec. 18, 1770 (*ibid.,* Mar. 26, 1771), Watson's name did not appear alone in the *Courant* until Mar. 26, 1771.

26. Green's house in Hartford was advertised for rent or sale in the issue of Feb. 8, 1768; Mecom published the last issue of the *Conn. Gaz.* in Feb. 1768, appealing to his subscribers to pay him enough money to get out of town.

27. Watson announced that he had complete charge of the *Courant* in the issue of Apr. 18, 1768.

28. Thomas Watson, *John Watson of Hartford, Conn., and his Descendants* (New York, 1865), p. 17.

29. *Cour.,* Dec. 12, 1768.

30. Advertisements. *Ibid.,* June 13, Dec. 26, 1768; Oct. 2, 1769; Feb. 26, 1771; Apr. 26, Nov. 21, Dec. 12, 1774; May 22, 1775; Apr. 29, 1776; May 5, 1777.

31. *Ibid.,* July 28, Aug. 18, 1772; June 29, 1773.

32. *Ibid.,* July 18, 1768.

33. Advertised in issues of Nov. 14, 21, 1774; May 22, 1775; Apr. 29, 1776. Watson's identified publications are listed in James Hammond Trumbull, *List of Books Printed in Connecticut 1709–1800* (Hartford, 1904) and Albert Carlos Bates,

Supplementary List of Books Printed in Connecticut 1709–1800 (Hartford, 1938).

34. *Cour.,* Jan. 4, July 18, 1768; Sept. 3, 1770; Mar. 5, 1771; Feb. 16, 1773.

35. *Ibid.,* Sept. 26, 1768; Apr. 3, July 17, Oct. 16, 1769; Apr. 9, May 7, July 9, Nov. 20, 1770; Nov. 19, 1771.

36. *Ibid.,* Apr. 18, 1768; July 9, Nov. 20, 1770; Dec. 19, 1774.

37. *Ibid.,* Jan. 2, Feb. 20, Sept. 18, 1769; Sept. 10, 1771. People sometimes wished to sell Negroes. *Ibid.,* Feb. 20, Sept. 18, 1769; Sept. 10, 1771; Feb. 23, May 25, Dec. 14, 1773; Jan. 2, 23, Nov. 20, 1775; Jan. 22, 1776.

38. *Ibid.,* Apr. 27, 1773; Sept. 6, 1774.

39. *Ibid.,* Dec. 28, 1767; Mar. 6, 1769; Jan. 1, 15, 1770; Feb. 19, 1771; Jan. 14, Mar. 3, 31, Apr. 7, 1772.

40. Published on Tuesday from Sept. 25, 1770, to Sept. 12, 1774.

41. *Ibid.,* May 1, 8, 1775.

42. *Ibid.,* May 1, Nov. 6, 1775.

43. *Ibid.,* Apr. 3, 1775.

44. *Ibid.,* Nov. 25, 1776.

45. The King's Arms regularly appeared from Dec. 28, 1767 to Jan. 22, 1776, except for the issues between Aug. 13, and Dec. 18, 1770. The Connecticut seal appeared with the issue of Jan. 29, 1776.

46. Appeared from June 7, 1774 to Apr. 24, 1775. Green had entitled the paper *The Connecticut Courant and the Weekly Advertiser* for a few weeks starting with the issue of Sept. 29, 1766.

47. Appeared from Dec. 3, 1764 to Oct. 14, 1765; Watson placed it in the heading off and on until it permanently disappeared with the issue of Sept. 18, 1775.

48. The steed first appeared on Jan. 29, 1770. Watson also used the cut of a house. *Ibid.,* May 3, 1774.

49. The "Poet's Corner" appeared regularly at the top of column 1 on the back page from Dec. 25, 1770 to May 22, 1774; scattered from Mar. 22, 1774 to May 24, 1774; and regularly from June 7, 1774 to Dec. 26, 1774. It dwindled away after the war started.

50. Marriage notices were fairly common from Nov. 23, 1773 to May 10, 1774, and death notices from Nov. 27, 1770 to June 7, 1774.

51. For apologies for paper and types, see subsequent paragraphs. Apologies for typographical and spelling errors appeared in issues of Sept. 11, 25, Oct. 30, 1764; Apr. 11, 1768; Feb. 12, 1770; June 2, 1772.

52. *Ibid.,* June 5, 1769; Mar. 12, 1770; Mar. 25, June 3, 1776.

53. *Ibid.,* Nov. 9, 16, 1773.

54. *Cf. post,* pp. 28–31.

55. *Cour.,* Dec. 12, 1768.

56. *Ibid.,* May 2, 1768; Dec. 4, 1769; Jan. 1, Aug. 6, 1770.

57. *Ibid.,* Nov. 6, 1769. This presumably excluded income from advertisements for which rates were 3s. for 10 lines for three weeks and 6d. for each week thereafter. *Ibid.,* May 2, 9, 1768; Dec. 25, 1770.

58. *Ibid.,* Nov. 6, 1769.

59. *Ibid.,* Dec. 4, 1769.

60. *Ibid.,* Dec. 25, 1770.

61. *Ibid.,* Mar. 26, Dec. 17, 1771; Dec. 15, 1772; Feb. 2, July 20, Dec. 14, 1773; Feb. 1, June 7, 1774; Jan. 22, 1776.

62. *Ibid.,* Nov. 21, 1774.

63. *Ibid.,* Apr. 28, 1777.

64. Green never advertised for rags before he started getting paper at the Norwich mill. First advertisements appeared on June 30 and July 14, 1766.

65. *Ibid.,* Mar. 5, 1771; Aug. 21, Oct. 16, Dec. 11, 1775.

66. *Public Records of the State of Connecticut,* I, 549–550. Austin Ledyard was born in Hartford in 1751, died in 1776. Undated manuscript genealogy by John

Austin Stevens, *The Family of Ledyard, Descendants of John Ledyard, in Two Generations,* Connecticut Historical Society. First announcement that the mill was being built appeared in *Cour.,* Aug. 21, 1775. Its location is placed on the Hockanum River at "Five Miles," now Manchester, in Joseph O. Goodwin, *East Hartford: Its History and Traditions* (Hartford, 1879), pp. 154–158.

67. *Cour.,* Oct. 16, 1775.

68. *Ibid.,* Dec. 11, 1775.

69. Issue No. 572 was dated Dec. 11, 1775, and the next extant issue was No. 574, dated Jan. 22, 1776.

70. The issues from Jan. 22, 1776 until after Watson's death were 10 inches wide and 16½ inches high.

71. One rider called for payment from customers in East Hartford, Bolton, Andover, Coventry, East Windsor, Tolland, Stafford, Somers, Enfield, Suffield, and West Windsor—Connecticut towns to the east, northeast, and north of Hartford (*Cour.,* Jan. 15, 1770, Apr. 16, 1771); another rode through Middletown to Durham, south of Hartford (*ibid.,* Dec. 17, 1771); one rode fortnightly to towns west of Hartford—Litchfield, Torrington, Goshen, Canaan, Sharon, New Milford, New Fairfield, Simsbury, and into New York as far as Poughkeepsie (*ibid.,* Mar. 10, 1772); one rode up the Connecticut Valley weekly in summer and fortnightly in winter as far as Northfield near the northern Massachusetts border (*ibid.,* Aug. 6, 1770); still another traveled each fortnight to Berkshire County, Massachusetts, as far north as Pittsfield (*ibid.,* Sept. 17, 1771). Newsriders frequently dunned their customers in the *Courant. Ibid.,* Mar. 12, June 25, Sept. 25, Nov. 27, 1770; Oct. 15, 1771; Mar. 15, 1772; Mar. 30, Nov. 23, 1773; Apr. 3, 1775; Feb. 12, Sept. 16, 1776; Mar. 3, Apr. 28, June 23, 1777.

72. *Ibid.,* Dec. 11, 1775.

73. *Ibid.,* Nov. 18, 1776; Apr. 28, 1777.

74. *Ibid.,* Nov. 11, 1776.

75. Thomas, *Hist. of Printing,* II, 90.

76. *Cour.,* Mar. 11, Oct. 14, 1776.

77. *Ibid.,* Aug. 21, Sept. 4, 1775; Oct. 14, 1776.

78. *Ibid.,* Aug. 21, 1775.

79. *Ibid.,* Dec. 15, 1772.

80. *Ibid.,* July 20, Dec. 14, 1773; June 7, 1774.

81. *Ibid.,* Mar. 3, 1777.

82. *Ibid.,* May 19, 1777.

83. The new type appeared with the issue of Jan. 13, 1778.

84. Probate files of the estate of Ebenezer Watson of Hartford, 1777, deposited in the Connecticut State Library, Hartford Probate District, No. 5716.

85. Watson married Elizabeth Seymour of Hartford in 1767 and she died on Apr. 11, 1770, leaving him two children. On Aug. 1, 1771, he married Hannah Bunce Watson. Watson, *John Watson of Hartford,* p. 17.

86. Goodwin was born in Hartford on Jan. 7, 1757, according to James Junius Goodwin, *The Goodwins of Hartford, Connecticut* (Hartford, 1891), p. 640. Thomas, *Hist. of Printing,* I, 191, deemed Goodwin to be a "correct printer" but said of Watson: "It does not appear that Watson was a thoroughly taught printer, though he practised the art ten years."

87. *Cour.,* Feb. 3, 1778.

88. Watson taught and led singing in the Second Church Society. One year's rent on the house and lot he occupied was abated by the Church at the time of his death. See Edwin Pond Parker, *History of the Second Church of Christ in Hartford* (Hartford, 1892), pp. 143, 152. His interest in military affairs preceded the war by several years, and in Aug., 1777, he was made an ensign of the Governor's Guard. *Col. Records,* XIII, 544–545; *State Records,* I, 379, 427, 427 n.

89. The widows petitioned the General Assembly for a loan without interest

and the Assembly granted the lottery. According to the widows, their loss was more than £5,000. *Connecticut Archives, Industry* (1st Series), II, 59, 60; *State Records,* I, 503; *Cour.,* Feb. 24, 1778.

90. *Cour.,* May 12, 1778.

91. *Ibid.,* Dec. 30, 1777.

92. In the issue of Sept. 8, 1778, appeared the following:

"The Protest against the proceedings of the state of Vermont, can be published, if desired, in a pamphlet but not in the Courant.

The method proposed by J. W. to raise and establish the credit of our currency, is too plain to need publication.

The answer to the Countryman contains nothing of consequence enough to claim a place in this paper.

The author of the Dream exhibits the marks of real honesty and original genius; but his Dream is fitter for an appendix to the Pilgrim's Progress, than for the Connecticut Courant."

See also issue of Aug. 4, 1778.

93. The issue of Mar. 10, 1778 carried no seal, and none afterward appeared.

94. *Ibid.,* Dec. 30, 1777; Oct. 6, 1778; June 22, 1779; Dec. 5, 1780.

95. *Ibid.,* Feb. 3, 1838. The Ledyard and Watson petition to the General Assembly, early in 1778, claimed that more than 8,000 papers per week were printed in Hartford. *Conn. Archives, Industry* (1st Series), II, 59.

96. *Cour.,* Mar. 2, 1779.

97. *Ibid.,* Apr. 14, 1778. Hudson and Mrs. Watson were married on Feb. 11, 1779. Watson, *John Watson of Hartford,* p. 17.

98. Hudson's first wife and Watson's first wife were cousins, and the families lived in adjoining houses. William DeLoss Love, *The Colonial History of Hartford Gathered From the Original Records* (Hartford, 1914), p. 306. Hudson collected bills for Watson in 1771 (*Cour.,* Dec. 17, 1771), and upon the latter's death was appointed administrator of his estate by the Court. Probate files of the estate of Watson, 1777.

99. Appointed Jan. 17, 1777 and resigned in 1779. *State Records,* I, 157; II, 246.

100. Hudson was born at Bridgewater, Massachusetts, in 1741 and was not a printer. Nahun Mitchell, *History of the Early Settlement of Bridgewater, in Plymouth County, Massachusetts, including an Extensive Family Register* (Boston, 1840), p. 201; Thomas, *Hist. of Printing,* I, 191.

101. *Cour.,* May 18, Aug. 24, 1779; Mar. 28, 1780. Two rooms were beneath the printing shop. The printers' store occupied one of them and the other was used at this time by Samuel Buell, goldsmith and jeweler. *Ibid.,* Dec. 21, 1779; Mar. 14, 1780.

102. Advertisements. *Ibid.,* Aug. 21, Oct. 30, 1781; Jan. 1, 1782; Jan. 21, 1783.

103. *M'Fingal* was first advertised in the issue of July 30, 1782, and Webster's spelling book (then comprising the first part of his *A Grammatical Institute of the English Language*) on Sept. 16, 1783.

CHAPTER II

POLITICS AND REVOLUTION

1. *Connecticut Courant,* Oct. 29, 1764. Other items of protest were in the same issue.

2. Material for this and the following paragraph was taken from *Cour.,* Dec. 3, 1764 ("Extract of a Letter from New England"); May 20, 1765 (letter from New London); Aug. 17, 1767 (letter by "A Well-Wisher to His Country"); Mar. 21, 1768 (letter by "Memorialist"); July 20, 1773 (advertisement by William Gris-

wold); and some excellent historical letters in Dec. 9, 1783 (by "P. C."); Mar. 2, 9, 1784 ("Policy of Connecticut"); Aug. 31–Oct. 5, 1789 ("The Freeholder"); and Jan. 2–Feb. 27, 1792 ("The Patriot").

3. In 1761, the recorded population of Hartford was 3,938. *The Public Records of the Colony of Connecticut,* XI, 574–575 n. For the Connecticut censuses of 1756 and 1774, see *Col. Records,* X, 617–618 and XIV, 483–492.

4. The story of an informer being whipped out of town in New Haven appeared in *Cour.,* Feb. 10, 1766.

5. Item from New York with particulars from several sources. *Ibid.,* May 6, 1765.

6. *Ibid.,* July 8, 1765–Mar. 3, 1766, *passim.*

7. *Ibid.,* Sept. 2, 30, Oct. 14, Dec. 30, 1765; Mar. 3, 1766.

8. *Ibid.,* May 6, Aug. 19, Sept. 9, 1765.

9. *Ibid.,* June 10, July 22, 1765.

10. *Ibid.,* July 22, Dec. 30, 1765; Feb. 17, Apr. 28, 1766.

11. *Ibid.,* Dec. 30, 1765; Jan. 6, 1766.

12. Report from Boston. *Ibid.,* Oct. 14, 1765.

13. Report from New York. *Ibid.,* Jan. 13, 1766.

14. Report from Newport. *Ibid.,* Jan. 13, 1766.

15. *Ibid.,* June 10, 1765.

16. *Ibid.,* Sept. 2, 9, 16, 1765.

17. *Ibid.,* Sept. 2, 1765.

18. In New London, Lebanon, and Windham. *Ibid.,* Sept. 2, 1765.

19. *Ibid.,* Sept. 23, 1765. It was dated Sept. 1.

20. *Ibid.,* Sept. 23, 1765.

21. *Ibid.,* Sept. 9, 1765.

22. The Oct. 28, issue (in the possession of the Yale Library) is No. 49. The three following issues have not been located, but No. 53 (in the library of the Connecticut Historical Society) is dated Dec. 30, 1765. The presumption is made that no papers were issued for five weeks beginning Nov. 4. Issue No. 50 would then have appeared on Dec. 9.

23. *A List of Newspapers In the Yale University Library* (New Haven, 1916), pp. 10, 14, 30, 32, 47, 82.

24. *Ibid.,* pp. 10, 14; George Bancroft, *History of the United States of America, From the Discovery of the Continent* (New York, 1883), III, 159–160

25. Some years later, President Ezra Stiles of Yale branded Green with Toryism. Franklin Bowditch Dexter, ed., *The Literary Diary of Ezra Stiles, D.D., LL.D., President of Yale College* (New York, 1901), II, 549.

26. *Cour.,* Sept. 23, Dec. 30, 1765; Jan. 27, Feb. 3, 24, 1766.

27. *Ibid.,* Feb. 3, 1766.

28. *Ibid.,* Feb. 24, 1766.

29. *Ibid.,* Feb. 3, 10, Mar. 24, 31, 1766.

30. *Ibid.,* Mar. 31, 1766; article on Thomas Fitch, *Dictionary of American Biography,* VI, 427–428.

31. *Cour.,* Apr. 7, 21, 1766.

32. *Ibid.,* May 26, 1766.

33. *Ibid.,* June 2, 1766.

34. *Ibid.,* Jan. 26, 1767.

35. *Ibid.,* May 18, 1767.

36. *Ibid.,* May 25, 1767.

37. *Ibid.,* June 1, 15, Aug. 3, 17, 1767; July 25, 1768.

38. *Ibid.,* Dec. 22, 1766; Aug. 17, 1767; Mar. 21, May 9, 1768; Feb. 18, 1771.

39. Unsigned letter. *Ibid.,* Mar. 11, 1765.

40. Letter by "A. B." *Ibid.,* Mar. 11, 1765. See also issue of Dec. 14, 1767.

41. Letter from New York. *Ibid.,* Dec. 1, 1766. See also issues: Feb. 22, 29, 1768.

42. *Ibid.,* Sept. 30, 1765.

43. *Ibid.,* Oct. 29, 1764. This funeral economy originated in Boston and spread to other colonies. *Ibid.,* Dec. 3, 17, 1764; Jan. 21, Aug. 26, 1765; Nov. 16, 1767; Nov. 21, 28, Dec. 26, 1774; Aug. 21, 1775.

44. *Ibid.,* Dec. 3, 17, 1764; June 10, 1765.

45. *Ibid.,* July 29, 1765.

46. *Ibid.,* Mar. 25, Apr. 1, 1765; Mar. 31, Apr. 7, June 16, July 28, 1766.

47. *Ibid.,* Jan. 21, 1765.

48. *Ibid.,* Oct. 10, 1768.

49. *Ibid.,* Jan. 11, July 25, Nov. 28, 1768; Jan. 16, Sept. 11, 1769; July 23, Aug. 6, 1770; Sept. 17, 1771.

50. *Ibid.,* June 16, 1766; Nov. 30, Dec. 14, 1767.

51. *Ibid.,* Apr. 7, 1766; Feb. 20, Apr. 17, July 17, 1769.

52. *Ibid.,* Oct. 29, Dec. 3, 31, 1764; Jan. 14, 1765; Nov. 16, 1767; Jan. 25, Feb. 15, 1768; Mar. 5, June 4, 1770.

53. *Ibid.,* Jan. 11, Mar. 7, 14, 21, May 9, 1768; Jan. 29, 1769; Feb. 5, 12, 19, May 7, 1770.

54. Twelve letters by John Dickinson. *Ibid.,* Dec. 21, 1767–Apr. 18, 1768.

55. *Ibid.,* July 4, 1768.

56. *Ibid.,* July 11, 1768 ff.

57. *Ibid.,* June 12, 1769. Other resolves to the same end are in the issues of May 9, Aug. 1, Sept. 26, 1768.

58. *Ibid.,* May 22, July 10, 24, Nov. 13, 1769.

59. *Ibid.,* May 8, Sept. 4, Oct. 16, 30, 1769; Jan. 1, 22, Mar. 12, 1770.

60. Excerpt from a letter from London, Philadelphia dispatch. *Ibid.,* July 3, 1769. Other consoling reports are in the issues of Apr. 24, May 1, June 5, Dec. 11, 1769.

61. *Ibid.,* Sept. 25, Nov. 13, 1769.

62. *Ibid.,* Jan. 1, 1770.

63. *Ibid.,* Nov. 6, 1769.

64. *Ibid.,* Jan. 15, 1770.

65. *Ibid.,* Feb. 26, 1770.

66. *Ibid.,* Dec. 26, 1768; May 22, June 19, July 17, Sept. 25, Oct. 30, Nov. 6, 1769; Mar. 12, 19, May 21, 1770.

67. Reprinted from the *London Evening Post. Ibid.,* Feb. 19, 26, 1770. Another letter of this type from a London paper is in the issue of May 14, 1770.

68. Resolves of Connecticut merchants. *Ibid.,* June 11, July 23, 30, Aug. 6, 13, Sept. 17, 1770. Statement by the *Courant's* printer. *Ibid.,* Aug. 27, 1770.

69. Letter by "Issachar." *Ibid.,* Jan. 15, 1771.

70. *Ibid.,* Mar. 10, May 5, 12, June 2, Aug. 25, Sept. 15, 1772.

71. *Ibid.,* June 5, 1769.

72. *Ibid.,* June 9, July 7, 1772; June 8, 15, 1773.

73. *Ibid.,* Mar. 10, 17, May 12, 26, June 9, Dec. 29, 1772; Aug. 17, 1773.

74. *Ibid.,* Mar. 23, 1773. Other material on Writs of Assistance appeared in *Cour.,* Feb. 16, 23, Apr. 6, 1773.

75. *Ibid.,* Dec. 29, 1772; Jan. 12, Apr. 27, June 1, 8, 1773.

76. *Ibid.,* Apr. 27, 1773.

77. New York dispatch. *Ibid.,* Oct. 12, 1773.

78. *Idem.*

79. *Ibid.,* Oct. 12–Dec. 14, 1773, *passim.*

80. *Ibid.,* Dec. 14, 1773.

81. *Ibid.,* Nov. 30, Dec. 14, 1773.

82. *Ibid.,* Dec. 21, 1773.

83. Excerpt from a Baltimore letter under Boston date line. *Ibid.,* Apr. 12, 1774.

84. *Ibid.,* May 17, 1774.

85. A letter from London (*ibid.,* Nov. 14, 1774) said: "I have been [on] a Tour

upwards of 1500 miles——I do assure you in my whole Travels I have found two out of three in favour of Boston, and the People in general seem to be much pleas'd that you make such a steady Stand." Other examples may be found in the issues of May 24, Aug. 2, Oct. 3, 17, 1774; Feb. 13, May 1, 1775.

86. *Ibid.,* May 24, 1774.

87. *Idem.*

88. *Ibid.,* June 7, 14, 1774.

89. *Ibid.,* June 7, 1774 ff. Watson printed supplements to the issues of June 21 and 28, 1774, to carry briefs of the many resolutions.

90. Unsigned letter. *Ibid.,* June 14, 1774.

91. *Ibid.,* June 14, 1774.

92. *Idem.*

93. *Ibid.,* June 7, 1774 ff.

94. *Ibid.,* June 19, Aug. 9, 1774.

95. *Ibid.,* Aug. 16, 1774.

96. *Ibid.,* Sept. 12, 1774.

97. *Ibid.,* Aug. 23, Sept. 19, 1774.

98. As one writer expressed it (*ibid.,* Oct. 31, 1774): "The society for propagating the gospel may now resign their charter, for they are in a great measure superseeded by the establishment of Popery in Canada."

99. *Ibid.,* Sept. 19, 1774.

100. *Idem.*

101. *Ibid.,* Sept. 12, Oct. 17, 1774.

102. *Ibid.,* Oct. 17, 1774. Other letters appear in the issues of June 5, 1775 and Nov. 18, 1776.

103. *Ibid.,* Jan. 2, 1775.

104. *Ibid.,* Feb. 20, 1775.

105. *Ibid.,* Jan. 23, 1775.

106. *Ibid.,* Jan. 23, 1775.

107. *Ibid.,* Jan. 23, Feb. 20, Mar. 6, 13, 1775.

108. *Ibid.,* Jan. 30, 1775.

109. *Idem.*

110. *Ibid.,* Nov. 14, 1774; Jan. 9, 16, 30, 1775.

111. *Ibid.,* Apr. 3, 24, 1775.

112. *Ibid.,* Feb. 13, 1775.

113. Letter by "Juridicus." *Ibid.,* May 8, 1775.

114. *Ibid.,* May 8, 1775.

115. Virtually every issue from the spring of 1775 into the late summer of 1776 carried information on the hounding of the Tories. The following is typical of the "confessions" which the paper printed (*ibid.,* May 15, 1775):

"I the subscriber do hereby freely and openly declare to the world, that I have advanced sentiments contrary to the general opinion of the colonies in America, respecting proper methods of obtaining relief of our grievances; for which I am heartily sorry, and desire forgiveness of all and every one for anything I have said, that in the least appeared to be inimical to the cause and general good of the American colonies; and hereby promise, that for the future, I will both in word and deed, conduct [myself] as a true and hearty friend to the rights and liberties of America."

Of notices exposing Tories, this one from Milford is typical (*ibid.,* Aug. 21, 1775):

"The Committee of Observation for this town having had due process against *Arthur Knowles* and *Henry Straight,* both of this town, according to the association of the Continental Congress, and finding them obstinately fixed in full opposition to the spirit of said association——hereby give notice thereof to the public, that they may be treated with all that neglect and contempt which is so justly their due, for this incorrigible enmity to the rights of British America."

The resolution of the governor and Committee of Safety that all transients in Connecticut should carry credentials from selectmen or committees of inspection is printed in the issue of July 22, 1776.

116. *Ibid.,* Nov. 27, 1775; May 20, July 8, 1776.

117. *Ibid.,* Apr. 8, 1776. Whether Watson actually collected the dollars is not known.

118. *Ibid.,* Sept. 23, 1776.

119. *Ibid.,* May 8, 1775.

120. *Ibid.,* Apr. 22, 1776.

121. *Ibid.,* July 8, Aug. 12, 1776.

122. *Ibid.,* Sept. 9, 1776.

123. Earliest reports are in the issues of July 24, Aug. 7, Nov. 27, 1775; Apr. 29, 1776.

124. *Ibid.,* Oct. 23, 1775.

125. *Ibid.,* Apr. 1, 1776.

126. In approving the Declaration of Independence in Oct., 1776, the General Assembly declared that the king had abdicated the government of Connecticut by unjustly waging war against her and the other colonies, thereby absolving the people of Connecticut from their allegiance and subjection to the Crown. *The Public Records of the State of Connecticut,* I, 3.

127. Extract from a Philadelphia letter under New York date line (*Cour.,* Aug. 7, 1775) said: "Last night a vessel in 14 days from Barbados, brings papers to the 7th of June——All in confusion——mobs in every street——the parliament was called together——Lord North is gone to France, and it is thought the troops will be recalled from Boston——stocks fallen 10 per Cent." Also, *ibid.,* Oct. 23, Nov. 13, 1775.

128. *Ibid.,* Nov. 27, 1775.

129. *Ibid.,* Feb. 19–Mar. 11, 1776.

130. *Ibid.,* Feb. 19, 1776.

131. *Ibid.,* May 27, 1776.

132. *Ibid.,* Apr. 8, 22, May 20, June 10, July 1, 1776.

133. *Ibid.,* Aug. 7, Oct. 23, Nov. 13, 1775; Dec. 2, 1776; May 5, 1778; May 18, 1779.

134. *Ibid.,* Jan. 27, 1777; May 5, 1778.

135. Philadelphia dispatch, letter from Shrewsbury. *Ibid.,* Nov. 23, 1779.

136. *Ibid.,* Sept. 9, Nov. 25, Dec. 30, 1776; Jan. 20, May 12, June 2, 16, 23, 1777.

137. *Ibid.,* Sept. 9–Oct. 28, 1776, *passim.*

138. *Ibid.,* Dec. 9, 1776.

139. *Ibid.,* Oct. 14, 1777.

140. *Ibid.,* June 20, 27, July 4, 1779.

141. *Ibid.,* Nov. 27, 1775.

142. *Ibid.,* Aug. 25, Sept. 29, Nov. 4, 1777; Oct. 30, 1781 ff.

143. *Ibid.,* June 12, 19, Aug. 7, 14, 1775; Jan. 6, 1776; Feb. 3, May 19, 26, June 2, Sept. 22, 1777; Nov. 17, Dec. 8, 1778; June 27, 1779; Jan. 9, 16, 1781.

144. *Ibid.,* Mar. 18, 1776; May 5, July 14, Sept. 29, Nov. 10, 1778.

145. *Ibid.,* June 22, 29, July 20, 1779.

146. *Ibid.,* July 17, 1775.

147. *Ibid.,* Oct. 16, 1775; Jan. 29, Mar. 11, 25, Apr. 8, May 27, 1776.

148. *Ibid.,* Apr. 8, 1776.

149. *Ibid.,* Apr. 15, 1776.

150. *Ibid.,* June 24, July 8, Aug. 12, 1776.

151. *Ibid.,* Nov. 18, 1776.

152. *Ibid.,* Feb. 17, 1777.

153. *Idem.*

154. *Ibid.,* Feb. 17, 24, Apr. 14, May 19, 26, 1777.

155. *Ibid.,* Feb. 17, Oct. 21, 1777.
156. *Ibid.,* Sept. 8, 1777.
157. *Ibid.,* Apr. 14, May 26, 1777; Oct. 20, Nov. 3, 1778.
158. *Ibid.,* Feb. 17, Sept. 29, 1777; Mar. 24, June 16, 1778; July 27, Aug. 3, Sept. 14, Oct. 12, Nov. 16, 1779.
159. For example, in issues of Feb. 29, July 25, Aug. 22, Oct. 24, 1780; June 19, 1781.
160. There was a high number of such letters. Some of them may be found in the issues of Oct. 16, 1775; Jan. 29, Mar. 11, 25, Apr. 8, May 27, Aug. 12, Nov. 18, Dec. 23, 1776; Jan. 13, Feb. 24, Mar. 17, Apr. 14, May 12, 26, Dec. 2–30, 1777; Aug. 4, 25, Oct. 20, 27, 1778; Sept. 17, 1782.
161. *Ibid.,* Feb. 22, 1779.
162. *Ibid.,* Feb. 29, 1779; Nov. 29, 1781.
163. Scores of references are in the papers of 1779–1782.
164. *Ibid.,* May 16, 1779; May 26, Apr. 2, 1782.
165. *Ibid.,* June 25, 1782.
166. *Ibid.,* July 23, Aug. 20, 1782.
167. *Ibid.,* July 30, 1782.
168. *Ibid.,* June 25, 1782.
169. *Ibid.,* Nov. 20, 1781.
170. *Ibid.,* Dec. 24, 1782.
171. *Ibid.,* Aug. 20, 1782.
172. *Ibid.,* Sept. 3, 1782; Mar. 4, 1783.
173. *Ibid.,* Apr. 1, 1783.
174. *Ibid.,* May 6, 1783.

CHAPTER III

CULTURAL REFLECTIONS

1. *Connecticut Courant,* Nov. 27, 1769.
2. *Ibid.,* Nov. 16, 1784.
3. *Ibid.,* Feb. 26, 1771.
4. *Ibid.,* Feb. 3, 1784.
5. *Ibid.,* Feb. 2, 1767; also, Feb. 16, 1767.
6. *Ibid.,* Mar. 13, 1775; also, May 27, 1765 and June 10, 1765.
7. *Ibid.,* Apr. 27, 1773.
8. *Ibid.,* Jan. 12, 1767; Jan. 9, 1786.
9. *Ibid.,* May 13, 1765; essay on matrimonial happiness in issue of Feb. 16, 1773.
10. *Ibid.,* Aug. 13, 1771. Other notices are in the issues of June 4, 1770; July 6, 1773; Oct. 31, 1774; Aug. 21, 1775; Oct. 13, 1778; Oct. 10, 1780; Mar. 26, 1782.
11. *Ibid.,* Sept. 25, 1770; Feb. 19, 1771; Apr. 9, Oct. 15, 1782.
12. From Kingston, Jamaica. *Ibid.,* Apr. 29, 1765.
13. Advertisements. *Ibid.,* Dec. 3, 24, 1764; Jan. 8, June 24, 1765; Aug. 25, 1772; May 1, 1775; Feb. 27, 1781.
14. Letters. *Ibid.,* May 27, 1765; May 8, 1769; Sept. 25, 1770.
15. Letters. *Ibid.,* July 22, 1765; Feb. 4, 1783.
16. *Ibid.,* Sept. 15, 1766.
17. *Ibid.,* May 13, 1765.
18. *Ibid.,* Aug. 18, 1788.
19. *Ibid.,* Oct. 30, 1770; May 14, 1771.
20. *Ibid.,* Apr. 5, 1774.
21. *Ibid.,* Sept. 30, 1783.
22. *Ibid.,* Nov. 12, 1771.

23. *Ibid.*, Aug. 14, 1769.
24. *Ibid.*, Sept. 29, 1766.
25. *Ibid.*, June 16, 1766.
26. *Ibid.*, May 5, 1766.
27. *Ibid.*, May 11, June 1, 1767.
28. *Ibid.*, Feb. 26, 1770.
29. *Ibid.*, Nov. 3, 1778.
30. *Ibid.*, Aug. 13, 1771.
31. *Ibid.*, Aug. 13, 1771.
32. *Ibid.*, Dec. 16, 1776.
33. *Ibid.*, Dec. 28, 1784.
34. *Ibid.*, Feb. 10, June 16, 1777.
35. Advertisements. *Ibid.*, Sept. 21, 1767; Apr. 3, Oct. 30, 1769; Aug. 13, 1770; Mar. 26, 1771; Jan. 7, 1772; Oct. 26, Nov. 23, 1773; Jan. 2, May 22, 1775; June 24, July 15, Oct. 21, 1776; Apr. 21, 1777.
36. Discussed in letter. *Ibid.*, June 30, 1777.
37. *Ibid.*, July 8, 1765.
38. *Ibid.*, June 10, 1765.
39. *Ibid.*, May 12, 1766.
40. *Ibid.*, Aug. 24, 1767; Feb. 13, 1769.
41. *Ibid.*, Sept. 25, 1775. "Cures" for consumption, cholic, jaundice, whooping cough are in the issues of Oct. 20, 1766; Feb. 13, Apr. 3, 1769; July 25, 1771; June 2, 1777.
42. *Ibid.*, July 13, 1767; July 11, 1768.
43. *Ibid.*, Jan. 25, 1774; Oct. 31, 1785.
44. *Ibid.*, May 11, 1767.
45. *Ibid.*, Sept. 18, 1769.
46. *Ibid.*, Sept. 25, 1769.
47. *Ibid.*, Feb. 4, 11, 1772; Oct. 10, 1785.
48. *Ibid.*, Apr. 23, 1770. This poem, which did not originate locally, was widely circulated in the colonial newspaper press.
49. Most advertised book lists contained them. For example, in the issue of Sept. 8, 1778, Watson & Goodwin advertised *Domestic Medicine; or, the Family Physician* by an Edinburgh doctor.
50. Recently discovered and said to have been patronized by "thousands." *Ibid.*, Sept. 30, 1765. Dispatch from Boston. *Ibid.*, Aug. 18, 1766.
51. *Ibid.*, June 15, 1767.
52. *Ibid.*, Aug. 18, 1766.
53. *Ibid.*, Aug. 18, 1766.
54. *Ibid.*, Aug. 11, 1766.
55. *Ibid.*, Nov. 2, 1767; Apr. 23, 1770; Apr. 21, 1772; Mar. 8, 1774; Nov. 7, 1785. Letters commending or criticizing the medical societies are in the issues of June 19, July 31, Aug. 7, Oct. 30, Dec. 25, 1769.
56. *Ibid.*, Apr. 16, 1771.
57. *Ibid.*, Nov. 27, 1769.
58. *Ibid.*, Feb. 23, 1767. Orations delivered at subsequent meetings of the society are in the issues of Sept. 7, 14, 1767.
59. *Ibid.*, Apr. 12, 1774.
60. *Ibid.*, Feb. 1, 1780.
61. *Ibid.*, Feb. 1, 1780.
62. *Ibid.*, Mar. 30, 1784.
63. *Ibid.*, Apr. 29, Aug. 5, 1765; June 30, Sept. 8, 22, Dec. 1, 1766; Feb. 2, Apr. 20, Aug. 24, 1767; Feb. 15, 1768; and in scattered issues thereafter. See especially advertisement in the issue of July 20, 1784, which speaks of Boston as the asylum of runaways.

64. *Ibid.,* Apr. 9, 1770. Advertisements for runaway apprentices are also scattered throughout the issues of this period.

65. *Ibid.,* Oct. 13, 1772.

66. Counterfeiters at New Haven were branded on foreheads with the letter C (*ibid.,* Mar. 14, 1768); they were cropped, branded, and ears were cut off at Kingston, Rhode Island (*ibid.,* Oct. 30, 1770); they were pilloried, cropped, and branded on both cheeks at Newport (*ibid.,* Apr. 30, 1771); at Litchfield they were whipped, fined £50, and confined for four years (*ibid.,* Aug. 24, 1784).

67. *Ibid.,* Aug. 10, 1767; Feb. 1, 29, Apr. 11, 25, May 2, 1768; May 29, 1769; Oct. 30, 1770; June 23, 1772; Nov. 16, 1779; June 13, 1780; Oct. 28, 1783; Sept. 14, 21, 1784; Jan. 25, Feb. 22, Sept. 12, 1785.

68. *Ibid.,* Mar. 19, 1770; May 5, 1777; Nov. 10, 1778; Mar. 14, 1780; Jan. 30, 1781; Nov. 26, 1782; Jan. 21, 1783; July 13, Sept. 14, 28, 1784; Apr. 26, Nov. 28, 1785.

69. *Ibid.,* Nov. 23, 1779.

70. *Ibid.,* Dec. 19, 1768; Aug. 21, 1769. A letter decrying imprisonment for debt is in the issue of Feb. 1, 1784.

71. Cases are noticed in the issues of Sept. 7, 1767; Aug. 1, 22, Sept. 5, 1768; Dec. 17, 1771; Feb. 9, 1779; Mar. 15, 1785.

72. *Ibid.,* Apr. 23, 1771. Other references are in the issues of Dec. 4, 1770; Jan. 8, Feb. 5, Mar. 5, Apr. 2, 30, Aug. 27, 1771; Sept. 19, Nov. 28, Dec. 5, 1774; July 14, 1778.

73. *Ibid.,* Aug. 5, 1765; Aug. 10, Sept. 7, 1767; Feb. 8, 1768; Feb. 20, Nov. 27, 1769; Feb. 12, 1770; Dec. 8, 1772.

74. *Ibid.,* Jan. 9, 1786.

75. *Ibid.,* Dec. 18, 1770; Mar. 24, 1777.

76. *Ibid.,* Mar. 17, 1777.

77. *Ibid.,* Nov. 17, 1766; Aug. 22, 1768; Oct. 16, 1770; Aug. 11, 1772; Feb. 1, 1785.

78. In the issues between Dec. 4, 1770, and June 5, 1775, advertisements of 22 breaks were noticed, not counting breaks from the common jails in either county or from the colonial prison at Simsbury in Litchfield County.

79. *Ibid.,* Jan. 11, Apr. 12, 26, Nov. 28, 1774; June 19, Aug. 28, 1775; Nov. 18, 1776; Feb. 24, 1777; May 22, Aug. 28, 1781; Nov. 12, 1782.

80. *Ibid.,* Nov. 28, 1774.

81. *Ibid.,* May 22, 1781.

82. *Ibid.,* Feb. 24, 1777; Nov. 12, 1782.

83. *Ibid.,* Apr. 22, 1776.

84. *Ibid.,* Apr. 10, 1775.

85. *Ibid.,* June 5, 1781.

86. Material for these assertions was taken from advertisements in the issues of June 25, 1770; Nov. 17, 1772; Sept. 14, 1773; Sept. 25, 1775; Feb. 3, 1777; Nov. 30, 1779; Nov. 28, 1780; May 21, Nov. 12, 1782; Apr. 1, 8, 29, Dec. 30, 1783; Jan. 11, 1785.

87. *Ibid.,* Nov. 30, 1779.

88. *Ibid.,* May 21, 1782.

89. *Ibid.,* Nov. 12, 1782; Apr. 1, 29, 1783; Jan. 11, 1785.

90. *Ibid.,* May 21, 1782.

91. *Ibid.,* June 25, 1770.

92. *Ibid.,* Feb. 3, 1776.

93. *Ibid.,* Oct. 14, Dec. 30, 1783. This school was never established. Emily Ellsworth Fowler Ford (Emily Ellsworth Ford Skeel, ed.), *Notes on the Life of Noah Webster* (New York, 1912), I, 64, 65.

94. *Cour.,* Sept. 25, 1775; Nov. 28, 1780.

95. A series of letters by "Philometis" advocating more education for girls appeared in the issues of Nov. 17, Dec. 15, 22, 1772; Jan. 12, 26, 1773.

96. *Ibid.,* Sept. 14, 1773.

97. *Ibid.,* June 25, 1770.

98. *Ibid.,* Nov. 30, 1779; June 5, 1781.

99. *Ibid.,* Jan. 11, 1785.

100. *Ibid.,* Apr. 8, 1783.

101. Besides Dartmouth and Yale, activities of the colleges at Cambridge, Providence, New York, Princeton, and Philadelphia were noted, sometimes in detail. *Ibid.,* July 29, 1765; Apr. 14, July 28, Aug. 4, 1766; Feb. 2, July 20, Sept. 14, 1767; May 9, 16, July 25, 1768; May 29, June 5, July 24, 1769; Apr. 9, July 23, Aug. 6, 1770; July 23, Oct. 29, 1771; June 9, Sept. 15, 1772; July 27, Sept. 14, 1773; Feb. 15, June 14, Oct. 24, 1774; Apr. 15, 1776. The genesis of Dartmouth from the Indian Charity School at Lebanon, Connecticut, may be traced in the issues of July 14, 1766; Nov. 2, 1767; Sept. 10, 1770; Oct. 29, 1771; Oct. 20, 1772. The commencements at Yale were noticed annually. *Ibid.,* Aug. 5, 1765 and yearly thereafter.

102. *Ibid.,* Sept. 15, 1772.

103. Letters. *Ibid.,* July 28, 1778; Feb. 11, 1783.

104. Letters by "Parnasus." *Ibid.,* Feb. 4–May 27, 1783, *passim.* Letters pro and con by other writers were in issues of Mar. 18, 25, Apr. 15, 22, 29, June 3, 10, 1783; Apr. 20, 27, May 11, 1784.

105. *Ibid.,* Feb. 10, 1784.

106. *Ibid.,* May 27, 1783.

107. Almost every issue of the early *Courant* bore some news of this sort.

108. *Ibid.,* May 13, 1765; Apr. 7, July 28, 1766; Jan. 15, Feb. 9, June 1, 1767; Dec. 2, 1783.

109. *Ibid.,* Dec. 2, 1783.

110. *Ibid.,* June 17, 1765; Mar. 14, 1768.

111. *Ibid.,* Aug. 31, 1784.

112. *Ibid.,* Apr. 18, 1768.

113. *Ibid.,* July 8, 1765; June 29, 1767.

114. *Ibid.,* June 17, 1765; Feb. 3, Mar. 3, 1766; Jan. 12, 1767; July 18, 1768.

115. *Ibid.,* June 17, 1765.

116. *Ibid.,* June 17, 1765; March 3, 1766.

117. *Ibid.,* June 17, 1765.

118. *Ibid.,* June 17, 1765.

119. *Ibid.,* Oct. 16, 23, 30, 1769.

120. Strong wrote the essays. *Ibid.,* Oct. 16, 23, 30, 1769. The diagram is in the issue of July 16, 1770. Reports on comets by others are in the issues of Apr. 14, May 5, 1766; Sept. 4, 11, 18, Nov. 6, 13, 27, 1769; July 9, 1770; Jan. 27, Feb. 3, 1784.

121. *Ibid.,* June 4, Sept. 10, 1770; Mar. 26, 1771.

122. *Ibid.,* Mar. 25, 1765.

123. *Ibid.,* May 23, 1768.

124. *Ibid.,* May 23, 1780.

125. *Ibid.,* Aug. 27, 1771.

126. *Ibid.,* Nov. 18, 1783.

127. *Ibid.,* Jan. 18, 1785.

128. *Ibid.,* July 13, 1784.

129. *Ibid.,* Feb. 8, 1785.

130. *Ibid.,* Sept. 5, 1785.

131. *Ibid.,* June 8, 1784.

132. *Ibid.,* July 6, 1784.

133. *Ibid.,* July 28, Dec. 1, 1778; Mar. 3, July 13, 1779; June 26, 1781.

134. *Ibid.,* Dec. 9, 1776; Feb. 17, Mar. 17, 1777; June 29, 1779; Sept. 18–Oct. 2, 1781.
135. *Ibid.,* Apr. 28–May 26, 1777.
136. *Ibid.,* Mar. 24, June 23, July 14, 1777; July 13, 1779; June 26, July 10, Aug. 7, Sept. 11, 1781.
137. *Ibid.,* Jan. 29, June 24, Aug. 5, Oct. 7, 1776; Mar. 10, 1777; Apr. 14, 1778; Sept. 14, 1779.
138. *Ibid.,* July 28, Dec. 1, 1778; Aug. 17, 1779; Mar. 14, Apr. 11, Sept. 26, 1780; June 26, 1781.
139. *Ibid.,* Apr. 7, 1777.
140. *Ibid.,* Sept. 23, Nov. 4, 1776; Nov. 11, Dec. 16, 30, 1777; Feb. 15, Nov. 20, 1780.
141. *Ibid.,* July 17, 31, Sept. 4, Nov. 27, 1775; Jan. 22, July 15, 1776.
142. *Ibid.,* Nov. 27, 1775; May 20, 27, June 24, July 8, Aug. 5, 12, 26, Nov. 25, Dec. 30, 1776; Jan. 20, 1777; June 9, Sept. 1, 1778.
143. *Ibid.,* July 1, 8, 1776.
144. *Ibid.,* Apr. 8, May 20, June 10, 24, July 8, Nov. 18, Dec. 2, 1776; Feb. 17, May 19, Aug. 11, Sept. 8, 1777; Feb. 22, 1780.
145. *Ibid.,* Dec. 26, 1780.
146. *Ibid.,* Sept. 3, 1782.
147. Cf. *ante,* pp. 35–36.
148. *Cour.,* Sept. 3, 1782.
149. *Ibid.,* Apr. 7, 1766; also, Oct. 22, 1771.
150. *Ibid.,* Sept. 12, Oct. 24, Dec. 5, 1768.
151. *Ibid.,* June 12, 1769.
152. *Ibid.,* June 12, 1769.
153. *Ibid.,* Oct. 17, 1768; Sept. 24, Oct. 1, 29, Nov. 19, 1771; Feb. 4, 1772.
154. *Ibid.,* May 26, 1772.
155. *Ibid.,* Dec. 12, 1785.
156. *Ibid.,* Sept. 24, 1771.
157. *Ibid.,* July 24, 1769.
158. Most of the eulogies printed in the *Courant* before the Revolution had this flavor.

CHAPTER IV
FEDERALIST PRESS

1. *Connecticut Courant,* May 13, July 29, Aug. 12, 26, Sept. 2, 9, 23, 30, Oct. 14, 1783; Mar. 30, 1784.
2. *Ibid.,* July 29, Aug. 12, Sept. 2, 9, 23, 30, Oct. 14, 1783.
3. *Ibid.,* Sept. 9, Nov. 4, 1783; Apr. 6, 1784.
4. *Ibid.,* Oct. 28, 1783. Noah Webster claimed the authorship of the editorial. This and subsequent articles attributed to Webster were identified by him in his personal volumes of the *Courant,* now in the New York Public Library and the Yale University Library.
5. *Ibid.,* Dec. 23, 1783; Mar. 30, Apr. 6, 1784.
6. *Ibid.,* Sept. 23, 30, 1783; Mar. 9, 1784.
7. *Ibid.,* Sept. 23–Oct. 21, 1783; Dec. 30, 1783–Jan. 27, 1784; Feb. 10, 1784; Mar. 16–Apr. 13, 1784.
8. By Noah Webster. *Ibid.,* Jan. 6, 1784.
9. *Ibid.,* May 13, 1783; Feb. 3, 10, Mar. 30, 1784. For other issues with resolutions, letters, and addresses favoring the cause of the Convention, cf., *ante,* n. 1.
10. *Ibid.,* Mar. 16–Apr. 20, May 4, 1784.
11. *Ibid.,* Mar. 30–Apr. 20, 1784.

12. *Ibid.,* Jan. 13, 20, 27, Apr. 6, May 4, 1784.

13. *Ibid.,* Apr. 6, 13, 1784.

14. *Ibid.,* June 3, July 8, Nov. 4, 1783; Mar. 30, 1784.

15. *Ibid.,* Dec. 10, 1782.

16. *Ibid.,* Oct. 22, 1782.

17. "Honorius" letters. *Ibid.,* Aug. 26, Sept. 2, 9, 16, 30, Oct. 14, 21, 1783; Jan. 13, 27, 1784. Cf. *post,* pp. 118–119.

18. *Cour.,* May 25, 1784.

19. *Ibid.,* Feb. 24, 1784.

20. *Ibid.,* May 25, 1784.

21. *Ibid.,* May 22, July 10, 31, Aug. 14, 28, Sept. 25, 1786; Mar. 5, 19, Apr. 9, 1787.

22. *Ibid.,* May 21, June 25, 1782; June 3, Sept. 2, 1783; Aug. 28, 1786–Apr. 9, 1787, *passim;* May 28, 1787.

23. *Ibid.,* Sept. 18, 1786.

24. Reprinted from the *Norwich Packet* with approval. *Ibid.,* Mar. 27, 1786.

25. Seven articles published concurrently in the *Courant* and the *American Mercury,* beginning on Jan. 3, 1785.

26. *Cour.,* Feb. 15, 1785.

27. The "Anarchiad" appeared in *The New-Haven Gazette and the Connecticut Magazine* in 12 installments (Oct. 26, 1786–Sept. 13, 1787, *passim*) and was reprinted in the *Courant.*

28. *Cour.,* Nov. 27, 1786.

29. *Ibid.,* Feb. 5, 1787.

30. *Ibid.,* Feb. 5, 12, 26, Mar. 5, Oct. 29, Nov. 12, 1787; Mar. 17, 1788.

31. *Ibid.,* Nov. 12, 1787.

32. *Ibid.,* May 28, 1787.

33. *Ibid.,* Oct. 1, 1787.

34. *Ibid.,* Nov. 5–Dec. 24, 1787.

35. *Ibid.,* Dec. 24, 1787.

36. *Ibid.,* Oct. 8, 1787.

37. *Ibid.,* Nov. 26, 1787.

38. *Ibid.,* Jan. 14, Feb. 4, 1788.

39. *Ibid.,* Apr. 30, 1787.

40. *Ibid.,* Oct. 1, 1787–Jan. 14, 1788.

41. *Ibid.,* Dec. 10, 24, 1787.

42. *Ibid.,* Dec. 10, 1787.

43. *Ibid.,* Jan. 14–June 30, 1788, *passim.*

44. *Ibid.,* June 30, 1788.

45. *Ibid.,* June 23, 1788.

46. *Ibid.,* Feb. 11–May 3, 1790, *passim;* Dec. 13, 1790; July 4, 1791; Mar. 5, 1792.

47. *Ibid.,* Aug. 29, 1791.

48. *Ibid.,* Sept. 5, 1791.

49. *Ibid.,* Dec. 6, 1790.

50. *Ibid.,* July 23, 1792. Previously Burke had been derided for his dislike of the Revolution. *Ibid.,* Aug. 22, 1791.

51. *Ibid.,* Oct. 8, 1792.

52. *Ibid.,* July 29, Aug. 12, 19, 1793.

53. *Ibid.,* Aug. 12, 1793.

54. *Ibid.,* Feb. 3, 1794.

55. *Ibid.,* Aug. 12, 1793 ff.

56. *Ibid.,* Nov. 25, 1793.

57. *Ibid.,* Feb. 11, 1790; Apr. 11, 1791; Dec. 3, 10, 1792.

58. *Ibid.,* Jan. 14, 1793.

59. *Ibid.,* Feb. 4, 1793.

60. *Ibid.,* July 22, 1793; Jan. 6, Feb. 3, Mar. 17, 24, Apr. 7, May 5, Sept. 29, 1794.

61. *Ibid.,* Jan. 6, 1794.

62. *Ibid.,* Nov. 4, 1793.

63. *Ibid.,* Jan. 27, 1794.

64. *Ibid.,* Aug. 18, 1794; Jan. 5, Apr. 20, 1795.

65. *Ibid.,* Jan. 6, 1794 ff.

66. *Ibid.,* Mar. 24, 31, 1794.

67. *Ibid.,* Mar. 24, Apr. 21, 1794.

68. *Ibid.,* May 19, 1794.

69. *Ibid.,* Aug. 4, 1794.

70. *Ibid.,* July 13, 1795 ff.

71. *Ibid.,* Oct. 6, 1794; Jan. 5, July 20, 1795.

72. *Ibid.,* July 20, 27, Aug. 3, 1795.

73. *Ibid.,* July 13, 1795 ff.

74. *Ibid.,* Aug. 3, 1795.

75. *Ibid.,* July 27, 1795.

76. *Ibid.,* June 27, 1796.

77. *Ibid.,* Aug. 3, 31, Sept. 14, Nov. 9–23, 1795; Dec. 28, 1795–Jan. 18, 1796; Feb. 8, Apr. 18, 1796; May 22, 1797; June 18, July 9, 23, 1798.

78. *Ibid.,* Dec. 28, 1795–Jan. 18, 1796; Nov. 14–Dec. 5, 1796; Mar. 6, Apr. 17, May 15, 1797.

79. *Ibid.,* July 17, 1797; Jan. 1, 8, Jan. 22–Feb. 12, Sept. 3, 1798; Jan. 28, Feb. 11, 1799.

80. *Ibid.,* Aug. 14, 1797 ff.

81. *Ibid.,* Sept. 25, 1797.

82. *Ibid.,* June 20, 1796; Mar. 6, 1797; June 16, 1800.

83. *Ibid.,* Mar. 6, 1797.

84. *Ibid.,* Jan. 29, 1798.

85. *Ibid.,* June 18, 1798.

86. *Idem.* The "Gustavus" letters which ran in the *Courant* from Apr. 24 to Sept. 11, 1797, summarized this whole interpretation.

87. *Ibid.,* July 30, 1798.

88. *Ibid.,* Nov. 19, 1798.

89. *Ibid.,* Oct. 22, 1798.

90. *Ibid.,* Mar. 19, 1798.

91. *Ibid.,* Dec. 17, 1798–Jan. 14, 1799, *passim;* Apr. 1, May 13, June 3, 1799.

92. *Ibid.,* Mar. 19, 1798.

93. *Ibid.,* Feb. 19, 1798.

94. *Ibid.,* Mar. 5, 1798.

95. *Ibid.,* May 27, June 10, 17, 1799.

96. *Ibid.,* June 18, Sept. 10, 1798; July 29, 1799.

97. *Ibid.,* Apr. 9, 1798.

98. *Ibid.,* Sept. 30, Oct. 7, 1799.

99. *American Mercury,* Oct. 3, 1799.

100. Hudson & Goodwin reprinted an article from the *Mercury* in the *Courant* of Feb. 9, 1801, and wrote: "As this is the first open and direct attack upon the government of the State of Connecticut, we felt it a duty to give the piece a place in our paper, that all may read and judge for themselves. No comment can be necessary—the thing speaks clearly its own meaning; at once unveiling a design, which has been long in operation—often predicted—and at last realized; having for its object, nothing less than the subversion of that ancient and steady order of things, so long cherished and preserved, by the wisdom and vigilance of the good people of this State."

101. *Cour.,* Nov. 11, 1799; June 2, 1800.

102. Granger defended himself against charges appearing in the *Courant. Ibid.,* Apr. 23–May 21, 1798. References to Baldwin are in issues of May 7, 21, 1798; Sept. 15, 22, Nov. 17, Dec. 1, 1800.

103. *Ibid.,* Sept. 1, 8, 1800.

104. *Ibid.,* May 19, Oct. 27, 1800.

105. *Ibid.,* Feb. 2, 1801.

106. *Ibid.,* Apr. 2, Sept. 3, 1798; May 13, 1799; Mar. 24, 1800.

107. Letters by "Burleigh." *Ibid.,* July 7, 14, 21, 28, Aug. 11, Sept. 1, 1800.

108. From the "Burleigh" series, *passim.* The prospectus appeared in the issue of June 23, 1800, and the 15 letters between June 30, and Oct. 6, 1800.

109. *Cour.,* June 23, 1800.

110. By "Burleigh." *Ibid.,* July 21, Aug. 11, 18, 1800.

111. By "Burleigh." *Ibid.,* Sept. 15, Oct. 6, 1800.

112. *Ibid.,* Sept. 8, 1800.

113. "Burleigh" letter. *Ibid.,* Sept. 15, 1800.

114. *Ibid.,* Nov. 21, 1796. Another "Pelham" letter was in the issue of Dec. 12, 1796.

115. *Ibid.,* Aug. 14–Sept. 11, 1797.

116. *Ibid.,* Mar. 19, 26, 1798. The issue of Apr. 9, 1798 carried an additional letter over the same pseudonym.

117. *Ibid.,* June 23, Sept. 22, 1800.

118. *Ibid.,* Sept. 22, 1800.

119. *Ibid.,* Sept. 29, 1800.

120. *Ibid.,* Dec. 29, 1800; Jan. 5, 12, 1801.

121. *Ibid.,* Jan. 12, 26, Feb. 2, 9, 1801.

122. *Ibid.,* Feb. 2, 1801.

123. From the *Courant*'s New Year's poem by Theodore Dwight. *Ibid.,* Jan. 5, 1801. Cf. *post,* pp. 122–123.

CHAPTER V

FIGHTING THE NEW ORDER

1. Since few of Jefferson's Connecticut partisans were foreigners and none were southerners, they became fools and profligates in the Federalist demonology. According to one writer, they were of three kinds: "Their principal leaders are men, desperate in fortune, and still more desperate in morals. . . . The next class consists of a few, who have been lucky in the accumulation of wealth; but who are so deplorably deficient in knowledge, judgment and capacity, that their vanity itself despaired of rising by fair means into office. . . . The residue are composed of the dregs of mankind." *Connecticut Courant,* Mar. 30, 1803.

2. *Ibid.,* July 20, 1801–Mar. 1, 1802, *passim;* Jan. 12, June 8, Aug. 31, Dec. 21, 1803; Jan. 11, 18, 1804.

3. *Ibid.,* June 8, 1801–Jan. 18, 1802, *passim;* Sept. 7, 1803.

4. *Ibid.,* Nov. 16, 1801. It was announced in a single exclamatory sentence.

5. *Ibid.,* Mar. 23, Aug. 10, 1801.

6. *Ibid.,* Aug. 16, 1802.

7. *Ibid.,* Mar. 1, 22, 29, Nov. 22, 1802; Jan. 5, 12, Apr. 27, May 25, 1803; *American Mercury,* Dec. 23, 1802.

8. *Cour.,* Feb. 3, Mar. 2, Aug. 18, 1803.

9. *Ibid.,* May 24, Aug. 16, Sept. 20, 1802; Mar. 23, July 20, Aug. 18, Sept. 14, 1803; Mar. 28, Aug. 22, Oct. 17, 24, 1804; Mar. 20, Apr. 3, 10, Sept. 11, 1805.

10. *Ibid.,* Jan. 4, 1802.

11. *Ibid.,* July 27, Aug. 10, 17, 1801.

12. *Ibid.,* Feb. 8–Apr. 5, Aug. 30, 1802.

13. *Ibid.,* Feb. 8–22, 1802.
14. *Ibid.,* July 5, Sept. 6, 1802.
15. *Ibid.,* Nov. 16, 1801; Apr. 5, May 24, Sept. 20, 1802; Mar. 23, Apr. 6, 1803; Mar. 28, 1804.
16. *Ibid.,* Jan. 18, 1802.
17. *Ibid.,* Jan. 18–July 19, 1802, *passim.*
18. *Ibid.,* Mar. 29, 1802.
19. *Ibid.,* Feb. 8, 1802.
20. *Ibid.,* Feb. 15, 22, Mar. 22, 1802.
21. *Ibid.,* Oct. 12, 1801; Feb. 8, 15, Apr. 5, 1802.
22. *Ibid.,* Feb. 8, 1802.
23. *Ibid.,* Apr. 18, 25, Dec. 12, 1804; Feb. 20–Apr. 10, 1805.
24. *Ibid.,* Feb. 22, 1804.
25. *Ibid.,* Aug. 11, 1803.
26. *Ibid.,* Aug. 11, 25, Sept. 7, 1803.
27. *Ibid.,* Aug. 25, 1803; June 27, Oct. 10, 1804.
28. *Ibid.,* Aug. 11–31, Nov. 23, 1803.
29. *Mercury,* May 17, 1804.
30. *Cour.,* June 27, 1804.
31. *Ibid.,* Mar. 9, 1801.
32. *Ibid.,* Apr. 6, 1801.
33. *Ibid.,* Sept. 14, 1801.
34. *Ibid.,* Mar. 23, 1801.
35. *Ibid.,* Mar. 16, 1803.
36. *Ibid.,* Apr. 6, 20, 27, May 18, Sept. 7, 1801; Mar. 1, 22, 1802; July 20, 1803.
37. *Ibid.,* Mar. 26, 1806.
38. *Ibid.,* Dec. 1–15, 1802.
39. *Ibid.,* Jan. 5, 1803.
40. *Ibid.,* Aug. 10, 1801; Mar. 30, 1803.
41. *Ibid.,* Mar. 23, Apr. 6, Aug. 10, Sept. 28, 1801; Jan. 4, 1802; Mar. 30, Apr. 6, 20, May 11, June 15, 1803; Dec. 12, 1804; Jan. 2, 23, 1805. With the upswing of antifederalist agitation in Connecticut during Jefferson's first term, the Baptists presented petitions to the General Assembly requesting the abolishment of tax-supported churches. *Ibid.,* June 14, 1802; June 1, 1803; July 3–Aug. 22, 1805. The editors wrote: "The object . . . is, the repeal of all the laws of this state for the support of the institutions of religion. It is not doubted that many of the denominations of Christians called Baptists are entirely sincere in their endeavors to obtain this object. . . . At the same time it is believed that many have countenanced these Petitions as mere political engines. . . . A great majority of the citizens of Connecticut, believe that their welfare is intimately connected with the preservation of our religious institutions, and that the Legislature, charged with the great interests of the community, would betray both weakness and wickedness, in abandoning these strong bulwarks of society." *Ibid.,* June 1, 1803.
42. *Mercury,* May 21, 1801.
43. *Cour.,* May 18, 1801; Sept. 27, 1802; May 11, 1803.
44. *Ibid.,* Nov. 9, 16, 23, 1801.
45. *Ibid.,* June 1, 1803.
46. *Ibid.,* May 11, Sept. 21, 1801; Feb. 8, May 17, 1802; Mar. 9–30, May 4, 1803.
47. *Ibid.,* June 28, 1802; July 20, Aug. 25, 1803.
48. *Ibid.,* Sept. 20, 1802.
49. Reprint from *Gazette of the United States. Ibid.,* Mar. 16, 1801.
50. *Ibid.,* Aug. 16, 1804.
51. *Mercury,* Jan. 6, 1803.
52. *Cour.,* Apr. 3, 1805.
53. *Ibid.,* Feb. 13, 1805.

54. *Ibid.,* Aug. 22, 1804.
55. *Ibid.,* Nov. 15, 1802; Sept. 12, 1804; Aug. 28, 1805.
56. *Ibid.,* Mar. 9, 16, 1803; Nov. 28, 1804.
57. *Ibid.,* Aug. 28, 1805.
58. *Ibid.,* Nov. 15, 1802; Aug. 28, 1805.
59. *Ibid.,* Aug. 1–Oct. 24, 1804, *passim;* Mar. 6, 1805.
60. *Ibid.,* Aug. 22, Oct. 24, 1804.
61. *Ibid.,* Aug. 29, Nov. 14, Dec. 26, 1804.
62. *Ibid.,* Oct. 24, Nov. 7, 14, Dec. 26, 1804; June 12, 1805.
63. *Ibid.,* Sept. 12, 1804; July 17, 1805.
64. *Ibid.,* Aug. 31, Sept. 14, 21, Oct. 19, 1801; Mar. 22, 29, Sept. 6, 1802; June 1, 8, Sept. 7, 1803; Mar. 28, Apr. 4, 1804.
65. *Ibid.,* Sept. 7, 1803.
66. *Ibid.,* July 31, 1805.
67. *Ibid.,* Oct. 2, Dec. 11, 1805.
68. *Ibid.,* July 3, Aug. 22, 1805.
69. *Ibid.,* Oct. 10, 1804.
70. *Ibid.,* Oct. 9, 1805 ff.; Dec. 30, 1807.
71. *Ibid.,* July 8–Sept. 23, 1807.
72. *Ibid.,* Apr. 6, 1808.
73. *Ibid.,* Mar. 23, Apr. 6, 1808.
74. *Ibid.,* Apr. 6, Aug. 10, 31, Sept. 14, 1808; Feb. 1, Mar. 8, 1809.
75. *Ibid.,* Apr. 6, 1808.
76. *Ibid.,* May 11, Aug. 10, 31, 1808.
77. *Ibid.,* Mar. 30, 1808.
78. *Ibid.,* June 1, 8, July 6, Aug. 17, Sept. 28, 1808.
79. *Ibid.,* Aug. 31, Sept. 7, 14, 1808.
80. *Ibid.,* Apr. 6, 1808.
81. *Ibid.,* Sept. 7, 1808.
82. *Ibid.,* Jan. 20, Feb. 24, Mar. 16, 23, May 4, 25, June 8, 15, Aug. 17, Nov. 9, Dec. 7, 28, 1808; Jan. 11, Mar. 29, 1809.
83. *Ibid.,* Nov. 30, 1808–Mar. 15, 1809.
84. *Ibid.,* Mar. 1, 1809.
85. *Ibid.,* Feb. 8, 1809.
86. *Ibid.,* Oct. 4, 1809.
87. *Ibid.,* June 7, 1809.
88. *Ibid.,* Sept. 13, 1809.
89. *Ibid.,* Jan. 3, 1810.
90. *Ibid.,* Feb. 27, Mar. 27, July 31–Sept. 18, 1811, *passim.*
91. *Ibid.,* Nov. 8, 15, 22, 1809; Apr. 4, 1810.
92. *Ibid.,* Sept. 27, 1809; Feb. 28, 1810; Feb. 27, Mar. 6, 1811.
93. *Ibid.,* Feb. 28, Aug. 29, 1810.
94. *Ibid.,* Feb. 28, 1810.
95. *Ibid.,* Oct. 31, 1810; Feb. 20, Apr. 24, July 17, Sept. 25, 1811.
96. *Ibid.,* Sept. 25, 1811.
97. *Ibid.,* Sept. 5, 1810.
98. *Ibid.,* Feb. 20, 1811.
99. *Ibid.,* Sept. 27, 1809.
100. *Ibid.,* May 29, 1811.
101. *Ibid.,* Oct. 4, 1809; Aug. 29, 1810.
102. *Ibid.,* June 19, Sept. 4, 1811.
103. *Ibid.,* Sept. 4, 1811.
104. *Ibid.,* Mar. 6, May 29, Oct. 9, 1811.
105. *Ibid.,* Dec. 4, 1811.
106. *Ibid.,* Aug. 29, 1810.

107. *Ibid.,* Sept. 11, Nov. 13, 1811.
108. *Ibid.,* Sept. 11, 1811.
109. *Ibid.,* May 30, Aug. 15, 22, 1810; Feb. 20, 1811.
110. *Ibid.,* Aug. 15, 1810.
111. *Ibid.,* Apr. 11, 25, Dec. 5, 1810; July 3, Dec. 4, 1811.
112. *Ibid.,* Aug. 22, 1810.
113. *Ibid.,* Jan. 31, 1810.
114. *Ibid.,* July 3, 1811.
115. *Ibid.,* Oct. 25, 1809; Apr. 3, July 17, Sept. 18, 1811; Feb. 5, Mar. 11, 1812.
116. *Ibid.,* Apr. 8, 1812.
117. *Ibid.,* Apr. 3, 1811.
118. *Ibid.,* Jan. 15, 1812.
119. *Ibid.,* May 5, 1812.
120. *Ibid.,* Sept. 18, 1811.
121. *Ibid.,* Dec. 5, 12, 1810; Apr. 17, Oct. 30, 1811.
122. *Ibid.,* Oct. 30, 1811.
123. *Ibid.,* Jan. 22, Apr. 8, 1812.
124. *Ibid.,* May 19, 26, June 16, 1812.
125. *Ibid.,* June 23, 1812.
126. *Idem.*
127. *Ibid.,* July 7, 28, 1812; Mar. 2, 1813.
128. *Ibid.,* July 21, 1812.
129. *Ibid.,* Aug. 24, 1813; Feb. 22, Mar. 15, 1814.
130. *Ibid.,* Mar. 7, 1815.
131. *Ibid.,* June 30, 1812.
132. *Ibid.,* June 30, 1812; Mar. 2, Oct. 26, 1813.
133. *Ibid.,* Oct. 20, 27, 1812; Feb. 2, Sept. 21, 1813.
134. Summarized in the issue of Apr. 26, 1814.
135. *Ibid.,* Sept. 15, Oct. 6, 1812; Mar. 30, Apr. 6, 1813.
136. *Ibid.,* Oct. 6, 1812.
137. *Ibid.,* July 21, Oct. 6, 20, Nov. 3, 1812; Mar. 2, Apr. 13, July 6, Sept. 21, 1813.
138. *Ibid.,* May 4, 1813; June 14, 21, July 12, 1814; Aug. 2, Oct. 4, 31, 1815.
139. *Ibid.,* June 14, 1814.
140. *Ibid.,* July 12, 1814.
141. *Ibid.,* Aug. 18, 1812; Mar. 2, Apr. 6, Aug. 3, 1813; Feb. 1, 1814.
142. *Ibid.,* Aug. 3, 1813.
143. *Ibid.,* Jan. 11, 1814.
144. *Ibid.,* May 18, 1813; Aug. 30, 1814.
145. *Ibid.,* Feb. 9, Mar. 2, 16, Apr. 6, 1813.
146. *Ibid.,* Mar. 16, 1813.
147. *Ibid.,* Mar. 16, 1813; Aug. 30, 1814.
148. *Ibid.,* July 28, Aug. 18, Nov. 17, 1812; Jan. 12, 1813.
149. *Ibid.,* Sept. 15, 1812; Jan. 19, Mar. 2, Aug. 24, Dec. 21, 1813; Mar. 15, Apr. 26, 1814; Jan. 17, 1815.
150. *Ibid.,* Mar. 23, 1813; Mar. 15, 1814; Nov. 8, 1815.
151. *Ibid.,* Dec. 22, 1812.
152. *Ibid.,* Sept. 8, 15, Oct. 6, 1812; July 20, Aug. 10, Nov. 16, 1813; Jan. 4, 1814.
153. *Ibid.,* July 20, 1813.
154. *Ibid.,* Oct. 6, 13, 1812.
155. *Ibid.,* July 20, 1813.
156. *Ibid.,* Dec. 29, 1812.
157. *Ibid.,* July 13, 1813.
158. *Ibid.,* Nov. 30, 1813.

159. *Ibid.,* July 13, Nov. 30, 1813.
160. *Ibid.,* Oct. 27, 1812; Aug. 3, 17, 24, 1813.
161. *Ibid.,* Dec. 21, 1813; Aug. 2, 1814.
162. *Ibid.,* Sept. 6, 1814.
163. *Ibid.,* Aug. 23, 1814.
164. *Ibid.,* Oct. 25, Nov. 8, Dec. 20, 27, 1814; Jan. 10, 31, Feb. 7, 1815; Jan 6, 1815 (extra).
165. *Ibid.,* Nov. 22–Dec. 27, 1814, *passim.*
166. *Ibid.,* Nov. 15, 1814; Jan. 3, 10, 1815.
167. *Ibid.,* Feb. 14, 1815.
168. Reprinted from the *Connecticut Mirror. Ibid.,* Feb. 21, 1815.
169. *Ibid.,* Mar. 7, 22, Apr. 5, 1815.
170. *Ibid.,* Mar. 29, 1815.

CHAPTER VI

NEWSPAPER GLIMPSES OF EARLY HARTFORD

1. *Connecticut Courant,* Sept. 22, 29, 1766.
2. Early issues, *passim.*
3. Cf. *ante,* pp. 6–7, 18.
4. Cf. *post,* chaps. IX, XIII.
5. *Cour.,* May 20, Nov. 18, Dec. 9, 16, 30, 1783.
6. *Ibid.,* July 8, 22, Dec. 30, 1783; May 3, July 25, Oct. 17, 1785.
7. *Ibid.,* June 1, 1784.
8. *Ibid.,* July 6, 1784.
9. *Ibid.,* July 27, 1784; Apr. 5, 1785.
10. *Ibid.,* May 18, 25, June 1, 1784.
11. *Ibid.,* Dec. 9, 1783; Mar. 2, 9, May 25, 1784.
12. *Ibid.,* Mar. 2, 9, 16, 1784; Jan. 2, 1792.
13. *Ibid.,* May 25, 1784.
14. *Ibid.,* Jan. 2, 9, 1792.
15. *Ibid.,* Mar. 28, 1791; Jan. 16, 1792.
16. *Ibid.,* Jan. 9, 1792.
17. *Ibid.,* May 25, 1784; Jan. 30, 1792.
18. *Ibid.,* Feb. 24, 1784; Mar. 28, Nov. 7, 1791; Jan. 23, 1792.
19. *Ibid.,* Jan. 23, 1792.
20. *Ibid.,* Apr. 30, June 4, 11, 18, Aug. 6, 1792.
21. *Ibid.,* June 4, 1792.
22. *Ibid.,* Aug. 6, 1792.
23. *Ibid.,* July 27, Aug. 31, Sept. 7, 1789.
24. *Ibid.,* Aug. 31, Sept. 7, 14, 1789.
25. *Idem.*
26. *Ibid.,* Oct. 8, 1787; Dec. 31, 1789; Mar. 22, July 5, 1790; Oct. 3, 1791.
27. Barzillai Hudson was one of the owners. Advertisements. *Ibid.,* Sept. 15, Nov. 10, 1788; Sept. 14, 1789; Apr. 12, Nov. 1, 1790; Apr. 11, 1791; Oct. 22, 1792; July 7, 1794.
28. *Ibid.,* Oct. 26, 1789; Jan. 14, May 17, 1790.
29. *Ibid.,* May 17, 1790.
30. *Ibid.,* Jan. 7, 1790.
31. *Ibid.,* Sept. 26, 1791.
32. *Ibid.,* Sept. 12, 26, 1796.
33. *Ibid.,* Oct. 3, 1796; May 22, 1805.
34. *Ibid.,* Feb. 20, 1792.
35. *Ibid.,* May 1, 8, 22, 29, June 26, 1797; Feb. 19, 26, Nov. 26, 1798; Jan. 14, Oct. 7, 14, 1799.

36. *Ibid.,* Aug. 2, 9, 1809.
37. *Idem.*
38. Advertisements. *Ibid.,* Apr. 13, 1779; June 30, 1794; Aug. 3, 1795; June 17, 1799.
39. *Ibid.,* Mar. 10, 1794.
40. *Ibid.,* Aug. 1, Sept. 5, Oct. 3, 1810.
41. *Ibid.,* Jan. 16, 1811.
42. *Ibid.,* Feb. 7, 1815.
43. *Ibid.,* Nov. 16, 1789.
44. *Ibid.,* July 21, 1794; Apr. 20, 1801; Aug. 9, 1815.
45. *Ibid.,* Dec. 8, 1788; Feb. 14, 1791; July 21, 1794; Jan. 26, 1803.
46. *Ibid.,* Oct. 8, 1798; Nov. 23, 1801; Nov. 5, 1806.
47. *Ibid.,* Nov. 7, 1810.
48. *Ibid.,* June 30, 1794; Feb. 27, 1797; Apr. 20, 1801; Jan. 26, 1803.
49. *Ibid.,* Nov. 16, 1789.
50. *Ibid.,* July 21, 1794; Aug. 9, 1815.
51. *Ibid.,* Aug. 2, 1790; Jan. 6, 1794; Mar. 2, 1795; Oct. 26, 1813; Apr. 5, 1815.
52. *Ibid.,* June 30, 1794; Oct. 26, 1813.
53. *Ibid.,* Aug. 12, 1799.
54. *Ibid.,* Sept. 2–Nov. 11, 1793; Sept. 1–Oct. 20, 1794; Sept. 7–Nov. 2, 1795; Aug. 28–Oct. 30, 1797; Sept. 3–Oct. 29, 1798; Sept. 8–22, 1800; Nov. 2, 1801; Aug. 2, 1802; Aug. 25, 1803; Sept. 18, 1805.
55. *Ibid.,* Sept. 28, 1795.
56. *Ibid.,* Aug. 19–Sept. 16, 1799.
57. *Ibid.,* Sept. 30, Oct. 7, 1793; Sept. 10, 1798.
58. *Ibid.,* June 6, 1804; July 31, 1805.
59. *Ibid.,* Jan. 17, 1795.
60. *Ibid.,* Oct. 10, 1796.
61. *Ibid.,* Dec. 8, 1788; Apr. 22, 1793; July 21, 1794; Mar. 6, 1797; Sept. 2, 1799.
62. *Ibid.,* Oct. 5, 1784; Apr. 16, 1792; Mar. 13, 27, Dec. 11, 1797; Oct. 20, 1812.
63. *Ibid.,* Nov. 9, 1801.
64. *Ibid.,* Apr. 22, 1793.
65. Letters. *Ibid.,* July 6, Aug. 3, 10, Oct. 19, 1801; Jan. 25, Mar. 8, 1802; Aug. 3, 1803; May 8, 1805.
66. *Ibid.,* Jan. 9, Feb. 13, 1811.
67. *Ibid.,* May 21, Aug. 20, 1787; May 1, 1797; Mar. 25, 1799; Nov. 14, 1810.
68. Exceptions may be found in issues of Mar. 19, 1787; May 18, 1795; May 30, 1804; Apr. 26, 1814.
69. *Ibid.,* Mar. 31, 1788; July 27, 1795; Oct. 8, 1798; Sept. 30, 1799; Sept. 22, 1800; Oct. 5, 1801; Oct. 26, 1803; June 6, 1804; Dec. 25, 1805; Nov. 19, 1806; Sept. 21, 1808; Nov. 23, 1813; Sept. 20, 1814; June 14, 1815.
70. *Ibid.,* Sept. 23, 1793; Dec. 25, 1805.
71. *Ibid.,* Mar. 3, 1794; June 21, 1795; Sept. 18, Oct. 9, 1797; Mar. 5, 1798; June 2, 1800; July 19, 26, 1802; Aug. 18, 1803; July 16, 1806; Aug. 15, 1810.
72. *Ibid.,* Sept. 17, Dec. 10, 1798; Sept. 16, 1799.
73. *Ibid.,* Jan. 12, June 22, 1801.
74. *Ibid.,* Oct. 6, 1772; Mar. 30, Aug. 10, 1773; Sept. 30, 1783; Apr. 26, 1785.
75. For example, *ibid.,* Mar. 5, 1798.
76. These are scattered throughout the issues of the 1780's and 1790's.
77. *Ibid.,* June 12, 1797.
78. *Ibid.,* Mar. 13, 1797; May 4, 1801.
79. *Ibid.,* Mar. 27, 1786; Jan. 19, 1789.
80. *Ibid.,* Nov. 3, 1788; July 20, 1789; Apr. 12, 1790; Apr. 29, Sept. 30, 1793; Sept. 4, Oct. 2, 1797; Aug. 6, Oct. 29, 1798; Apr. 17, 1805; July 16, 1806; Oct. 25, 1809; May 23, 1810; May 29, 1811; Nov. 10, 1813.

81. *Ibid.*, July 20, 1789; Apr. 12, 1790; Sept. 22, 1794; Aug. 3, 1795; Sept. 4, 1797; June 4, Oct. 29, 1798; Jan. 7, 1799; Jan. 25, Sept. 19, 1804; Mar. 19, Sept. 17, 1806; Feb. 1, 1809; Feb. 28, 1810; May 29, 1811; Nov. 29, 1814.

82. *Ibid.*, Sept. 30, 1793; Sept. 12, 1796; Nov. 19, 1798; Sept. 14, 1803; Mar. 7, 1810; Apr. 17, May 29, July 10, 1811; Mar. 18, 1812; June 29, Nov. 10, 1813.

83. *Ibid.*, Aug. 24, 1813.

84. *Ibid.*, Feb. 22, Apr. 26, 1774.

85. *Ibid.*, Mar. 27, 1775.

86. *Ibid.*, Mar. 29, 1790; May 2, 1791; Dec. 3, 1792.

87. *Ibid.*, Feb. 10, 1794; Dec. 25, 1805; May 6, 1807; Nov. 23, 1813.

88. *Ibid.*, Sept. 25, Nov. 20, 1769; May 14, Aug. 27, 1771; Sept. 14, 1773; Mar. 8, 1774; June 30, 1778; Dec. 23, 1783; June 13, 1785.

89. *Ibid.*, Aug. 8, 1796.

90. *Ibid.*, Nov. 19, 1798; Aug. 26, 1799 (supplement); Jan. 4, Dec. 29, 1802; Sept. 19, 1804; Feb. 28, 1810; Mar. 18, Dec. 8, 1812.

91. *Ibid.*, Nov. 25, 1793; Dec. 14, 1795; May 8, Dec. 4, 1797; Feb. 25, May 27, Dec. 30, 1799; Oct. 10, 1804; Oct. 26, 1808; Dec. 26, 1810; Jan. 29, Feb. 26, Dec. 29, 1812; Feb. 15, 1814.

92. *Ibid.*, Aug. 9, 1790; Oct. 20, 1794; Sept. 19, 1804; July 24, 1805; May 4, 1808.

93. *Ibid.*, Sept. 19, 1804; July 24, 1805; May 4, 1808.

94. *Ibid.*, July 21, 1788; Feb. 15, 1796; May 19, 1800; Sept. 20, 1802; May 13, 1807; Oct. 5, 1813; May 17, 1815.

95. The museum was moved later from the State House to a building nearby. *Ibid.*, Jan. 30, June 12, 1797; Nov. 16, Dec. 21, 1808.

96. *Ibid.*, Apr. 13, 1803; May 16, 1804; May 15, Oct. 2, 1805; May 4, 1808; May 2, 1810.

97. *Ibid.*, Sept. 13, 1815.

98. *Ibid.*, July 28–Sept. 8, 1794; July 27–Oct. 19, 1795; July 11–Aug. 15, 1796; June 26–Oct. 2, 1797; Nov. 13, 1797; Aug. 5–Sept. 2, 1799.

99. *Ibid.*, July 27, 1795.

100. *Ibid.*, Aug. 3, 1795.

101. *Ibid.*, Mar. 9, 1795.

102. *Ibid.*, Aug. 10, 1795.

103. *Ibid.*, Aug. 31, Oct. 12, 1795; July 18, Aug. 15, 29, 1796; June 26, July 3, Aug. 28, Sept. 25, 1797; Sept. 9, 1799.

104. *Ibid.*, July 18, 1796.

105. *Ibid.*, June 2, 1800.

106. The last performances in Hartford were in 1799. *Ibid.*, Aug. 5–Sept. 2, 1799.

107. *Ibid.*, June 11, 1787; Dec. 22, 1788; Mar. 28, 1791; Aug. 17, 1795; May 16, 1796; Apr. 15, 1799; June 16, 1800.

108. *Ibid.*, May 28, 1806; Mar. 18, 25, 1807.

109. *Ibid.*, Mar. 21, May 16, 1796; May 7, Oct. 15, 1798; May 18, 1801; Feb. 22, 1809.

110. *Ibid.*, May 18, 1789; May 24, 1790.

111. For example, *ibid.*, May 16, 1791; May 14, 1792; May 18, 1795; July 4, 1796; July 3, 10, 1797.

112. *Ibid.*, Oct. 19, 1784; Apr. 20, Oct. 26, 1789; Aug. 6, 1798.

113. The local merchants were meeting monthly in 1790 (*ibid.*, Mar. 29, 1790), and came to call their meeting place the "Chamber" (*ibid.*, Feb. 3, 1800).

114. *Ibid.*, Aug. 6, 1792.

115. *Ibid.*, Dec. 12, 1791; Oct. 1, Nov. 19, 1792; Jan. 21, 1793; Oct. 25, 1815.

116. *Ibid.*, May 3, June 7, Sept. 27, 1809; July 31, 1811.

117. *Ibid.*, Dec. 17, 1787; June 15, 1789; June 14, 1790.

118. *Ibid.*, July 7, 1788; June 14, 1790; Sept. 17, 1792; July 4, 1796; July 11, 1804.

119. *Ibid.*, Apr. 13, 1767; June 3, Dec. 19, 1768; Mar. 24, 1772; Jan. 26, Apr. 6, 13,

May 11, 1773; Sept. 12, Oct. 3, 1774; Jan. 2, 1775; May 19, 1777; Sept. 20, 1790; May 16, 23, 1791.

120. *Ibid.*, Dec. 18, 1786.

121. *Ibid.*, July 7–Oct. 27, 1788; Nov. 30, 1789; Feb. 2, Aug. 1, 1791; Sept. 27–Nov. 8, 1809.

122. *Ibid.*, Sept. 5, 1791; Nov. 7, 1796; Apr. 24, 1797; June 7, 1802; May 27, 1807.

123. *Ibid.*, Mar. 5, 1792.

124. *Ibid.*, Nov. 14, 1791.

125. *Ibid.*, Sept. 5, 12, 19, 1791.

126. *Ibid.*, Sept. 5, 1791.

127. *Ibid.*, Feb. 2, 1795.

128. *Ibid.*, Aug. 11, 1788; May 20, Aug. 26, 1793; Aug. 25, 1794.

129. *Ibid.*, Aug. 25, 1794.

130. *Ibid.*, June 17, 1793; Jan. 17, Feb. 2, 1795.

131. *Ibid.*, Oct. 13, 1800.

132. *Ibid.*, Dec. 31, 1789.

133. *Ibid.*, Jan. 12, 1767; Oct. 23, 1775; Mar. 23, 30, 1801; Feb. 4–25, 1807; Aug. 29, 1810.

134. For example, *ibid.*, June 9, 1772; May 13, 1783; Oct. 26, 1784; Jan. 19, 1789; Nov. 1, 1790; May 28, 1792; Nov. 25, 1793; Nov. 14, 1796; Oct. 11, 1809; Sept. 13, 1815.

135. *Ibid.*, Feb. 27, 1792.

136. For references, cf. *ante*, n. 134.

137. *Ibid.*, May 17, 1815. A small steamboat ran between Hartford and Middletown. *Ibid.*, Aug. 31, 1813.

138. *Ibid.*, Aug. 13, Oct. 15, 1771; Feb. 18, Apr. 28, June 16, 1772.

139. *Ibid.*, Oct. 14, 1783; Jan. 13, May 4, 1784; Jan. 23, 1786.

140. *Ibid.*, Dec. 20, 1790; Aug. 24, Nov. 2, 1795; Mar. 21, 1796; June 24, 1807; June 15, Nov. 22, 1808; Oct. 11, 1814.

141. *Ibid.*, May 2, 1810; Aug. 16, 1814.

142. *Ibid.*, Dec. 7, 14, 1795; Feb. 19, 1806; Dec. 9, 1807; Mar. 2, 1808; Feb. 9, 1813,

143. *Ibid.*, Dec. 9, 1807.

144. *Ibid.*, June 14, 21, July 26, Aug. 23–Sept. 13, 1814.

145. S. G. Goodrich, *Recollections of A Lifetime or Men and Things I Have Seen: in a Series of Familiar Letters to A Friend, Historical, Biographical, Anecdotical, and Descriptive* (New York, 1856), I, 410–413.

CHAPTER VII

HUDSON & GOODWIN, PUBLISHERS

1. Bavil Webster's *The Freeman's Chronicle; or the American Advertiser* ran from September 1, 1783, into the summer of 1784. The last known issue was July 8, 1784. Webster left Hartford in the spring or summer of that year and the issues starting on June 3, 1784, were printed by Zephaniah Webster. James Hammond Trumbull, *List of Books Printed in Connecticut 1709–1800* (Hartford, 1904), p. 142.

2. Joel Barlow was co-editor with Elisha Babcock from the first issue, dated July 12, 1784, to November 14, 1785. Cf. *post*, n. 105.

3. The *Mercury* had not yet appeared.

4. *Connecticut Courant*, Dec. 30, 1783.

5. Titles of acts were printed (*ibid.*, Nov. 30, 1773 ff., *passim*); acts were printed (*ibid.*, Nov. 18, 1776 ff., *passim*); synopses were printed (*ibid.*, Oct. 28, 1783 ff., *passim*).

6. *Ibid.*, July 17, 1786. Spectators were allowed to attend sessions of the lower house. *Ibid.*, Oct. 26, 1784.

7. *Ibid.,* Oct. 23, 1786.

8. *Ibid.,* Dec. 14, 21, 28, 1784; July 27–Dec. 2, 1784, *passim.*

9. *Ibid.,* Dec. 19, 1785–Sept. 17, 1787, *passim.*

10. Advertisement of New London tavern keeper. *Ibid.,* Feb. 8, 1785; *ibid.,* April 5, 1785 ff.

11. Webster's contributions, including many not cited in the text, were identified by himself in his private copies of the *Courant,* now in possession of the New York Public Library and the Sterling Memorial Library at Yale University.

12. *Cour.,* Mar. 14, 21, 28, 1791.

13. *Ibid.,* Apr. 26, 1785; Sept. 5, 26, 1791.

14. "Policy of Connecticut" letters. *Ibid.,* Feb. 24, Mar. 2, 9, 16, Apr. 6, May 18, 25, 1784. Eight "Patriot" letters. *Ibid.,* Jan. 2–Feb. 27, 1792.

15. Under Hartford date line. *Ibid.,* May 25, 1784.

16. *Ibid.,* Apr. 26, 1785.

17. *Ibid.,* July 9, Aug. 6, 1792.

18. "Candor" letters. *Ibid.,* July 8, Aug. 5, 1793.

19. Cf. *ante,* pp. 62–63.

20. *Cour.,* Apr. 30, 1792.

21. Under Hartford date line. *Ibid.,* Apr. 11, 1792.

22. Cf. *ante,* p. 61.

23. From a manuscript by Webster inserted in the 1784 volume of the *Courant* in the New York Public Library; written in 1787, 1824, and 1832.

24. Twenty essays by "The Prompter." *Cour.,* Dec. 6, 1790–June 13, 1791, *passim;* Harry R. Warfel, *Noah Webster Schoolmaster to America* (New York, 1936), pp. 204–205; cf. *post,* p. 134.

25. *Cour.,* Feb. 14, 1791.

26. Identified by Webster. *Ibid.,* Apr. 13, Sept. 9, 1784.

27. Identified by Webster. *Ibid.,* Mar. 23, 1784. The choice was presented as one between "Goosecap" (William Pitkin, member of the Council and aspirant to the governor's office, who was unsympathetic with the Cincinnati) or a man of sound principles and sense. Governor Jonathan Trumbull had resigned office in the fall of 1783 after 14 years of service. Another letter by Trumbull, arguing the cause of the Cincinnati, is in the issue of Jan. 20, 1784.

28. Authorship identified by Webster. *Ibid.,* Aug. 5, 1783. Wolcott wrote "Political Creed" in the issue of Jan. 6, 1783.

29. *Ibid.,* Dec. 30, 1783; cf. *ante,* pp. 59–60.

30. Cf. Louie M. Miner, *Our Rude Forefathers, American Political Verse 1783–1788* (Cedar Rapids, 1937), p. 169 n.

31. Miner, *op. cit.,* p. 162; Luther G. Riggs, ed., *The Anarchiad: A New England Poem, Written in Concert by David Humphreys, Joel Barlow, John Trumbull, and Dr. Lemuel Hopkins* (New Haven, 1861), pp. 105–106; *Hartford Daily Courant,* Aug. 1, 5, 1861.

32. Rhythmic version attributed to Noah Webster in Miner, *op. cit.,* p. 169 n., but not identified by Webster.

33. *Conn. Cour.,* Oct. 23, 1786. Hopkins was a coppersmith. *Hart. Daily Cour.,* Aug. 5, 1861.

34. For a full account, cf. Miner, *op. cit.,* pp. 159–184.

35. *Conn. Cour.,* Nov. 20, 1786. Webster wrote: "People in general are too ignorant to manage affairs which require great reading and an extensive knowledge of foreign nations. This is the misfortune of republican governments. For my own part, I confess, I was once as strong a republican as any man in America. Now, a republican is among the last kinds of government I should chose. I should infinitely prefer a limited monarchy, for I should sooner be subject to the caprice of one man, than to the ignorance and passions of a multitude."

36. The "Anarchiad" appeared in *The New Haven Gazette, and the Connecticut*

Magazine in 12 installments (Oct. 26, 1786–Sept. 13, 1787, *passim*) and was widely republished throughout the northern colonies. It was reprinted in the *Courant,* omitting the 10th installment, between Nov. 13, 1786, and Sept. 23, 1787. The 11th installment was published in the *Courant* before it appeared in the *Gazette. Cour.,* Aug. 6, 1787; *Gaz.,* Sept. 13, 1787.

37. *Cour.,* Jan. 1, 1787.

38. *Ibid.,* Nov. 13, 1786.

39. Reprinted from the *New London Gazette. Ibid.,* Jan. 1, 1787.

40. *Ibid.,* Feb. 26, 1787. Other answers to W. W., in letter form, are in the issues of Jan. 22, 29, and Apr. 2, 1787.

41. *Ibid.,* March 26, 1787. The celebration of his death was premature for Williams was re-elected to the Council in May, 1787 (*ibid.,* May 14, 1787), and for many terms thereafter.

42. John Warner Barber, *Connecticut Historical Collections, Containing a General Collection of Interesting Facts, Traditions, Biographical Sketches, Anecdotes, &c. Relating to the History and Antiquities of Every Town in Connecticut, with Geographical Descriptions* (New Haven, 1836), p. 49.

43. Printed on a separate half sheet and inserted in the *Courant* volume for 1786, Connecticut Historical Society.

44. *Cour.,* Jan. 4, 1796.

45. *Ibid.,* Jan. 8, 1798.

46. *Ibid.,* Jan. 5, 1801. Authorship identified in Trumbull, *List of Books,* p. 68; cf. *ante,* pp. 78–79.

47. Joel Barlow wrote the verses in *Cour.,* Jan. 1, 1787. Theodore Albert Zunder, *The Early Days of Joel Barlow A Connecticut Wit* (New Haven, 1934), pp. 200–201. Verses for Jan. 1, 1788, printed on a half sheet, were written by "some of the authors of 'The Anarchiad' " (Trumbull, *List of Books,* p. 80); Webster versified in *Cour.,* Jan. 7, 1790 (identified by himself, *Cour.* files in NYPL); Webster identified Mason Fitch Cogswell as the author in *Cour.,* Jan. 3, 1791; Lemuel Hopkins wrote the poem for 1794 in *Cour.,* Jan. 5, 1795 (Trumbull, *List of Books,* p. 99); Hopkins was the author also in *Cour.,* Jan. 9, 1797, according to Albert Carlos Bates, *Supplementary List of Books Printed in Connecticut 1709–1800* (Hartford, 1938), p. 35; Richard Alsop, Hopkins, and Theodore Dwight composed "The Political Green-House for 1798," one of the best-known works of the Wits (*Cour.,* Jan. 7, 1799; Trumbull, *List of Books,* p. 155); a eulogy of George Washington, rather than the usual rhythmic satire, appeared in *Cour.,* Jan. 6, 1800.

48. *The echo, with other poems, printed at the Porcupine Press by Pasquin Petronius* was published in New York. Some of the pieces had been published in the *Mercury.* Annie Russel Marble, *The Hartford Wits* (New Haven, 1936), pp. 5–6; *Cour.,* June 3, 1807.

49. *Cour.,* Apr. 20, 1789 ff., *passim.*

50. "The Secretary of State for the United States, having directed that the laws of the United States for the district of *Connecticut,* be published in the *Connecticut Courant,* we have this day commenced with the laws of the last session of Congress, and shall pursue the publication until they are all printed." *Ibid.,* May 6, 1799.

51. Cf. *ante,* pp. 14, 29, 36–37, 60, 64–65.

52. *Cour.,* July 18, 1804; *Mercury,* Aug. 9, 1804. Sampson was a Yale graduate of 1773, preached at Plympton, Massachusetts for 20 years until his voice failed, and then moved to Hudson, New York. In company with Harry Croswell and George Chittenden, he established *The Balance, and Columbian Repository* in 1801. He continued to write off and on for the *Courant* until 1817. Clarence S. Brigham, comp., *Bibliography of American Newspapers, 1690–1820,* Proceedings of the American Antiquarian Society, XXVII (1917), 249–250; *Appleton's Cyclopedia of Amer-*

ican Biography (1888), V, 382; J. Munsell, *The Typographical Miscellany* (Albany, 1850), p. 146.

53. For example, *Cour.*, Jan. 2, July 31, Aug. 15, Sept. 11, 1805. Abraham Bishop and Oliver Wolcott, Jr., were alleged to be writing the *Mercury*'s editorials. *Ibid.*, Sept. 11, 1805.

54. *Ibid.*, Aug. 15, 1805; *Mercury*, Sept. 5, 1805.

55. The column appeared regularly from Aug. 1, 1804 to Apr. 3, 1805; irregularly to Apr. 30, 1806.

56. *Cour.*, July 18, Sept. 12, 1804.

57. Ellsworth wrote regularly from Aug. 1, 1804 to Apr. 3, 1805. *Mercury*, Aug. 30, 1804; William Garrott Brown, *The Life of Oliver Ellsworth* (New York, 1905), pp. 336–337. Noah Webster contributed twice. *Cour.*, Oct. 24, 31, 1804.

58. *Cour.*, Sept. 5, 1804.

59. *Ibid.*, Sept. 19, Oct. 17, Nov. 7, 14, 1804; Brown, *Ellsworth*, p. 336.

60. *Cour.*, Aug. 1, 1804–Apr. 3, 1805, *passim*. Articles on gypsum are in the issues of Aug. 15, Sept. 26, Oct. 10, Nov. 28, Dec. 12, 1804.

61. *Ibid.*, Dec. 5, 19, 26, 1804; Jan. 16, 1805.

62. *Ibid.*, Sept. 12, Oct. 17, 1804.

63. *Ibid.*, Oct. 10, 1804. He was accused in the *Mercury* of attempting to peddle political propaganda. *Mercury*, Aug. 30, Sept. 6, 1804; Jan. 3, Apr. 11, 1805.

64. *Cour.*, Dec. 12, 1785; Sept. 1, 1788; Aug. 29, Oct. 17, 1791; Feb. 9, 1795; June 10, 1799.

65. *Ibid.*, Jan. 5, Apr. 6, 1795; Mar. 19, 1798.

66. *Idem;* also, *ibid.*, Mar. 19, 1798.

67. *Ibid.*, July 18, 1804.

68. *Ibid.*, Apr. 2, May 28, June 11, July 2, Sept. 10, 17, Oct. 8, 1806.

69. *Ibid.*, May 7, 1806.

70. *Ibid.*, Sept. 31, 1806.

71. The United States *v.* Hudson and Goodwin, 7 *Cranch*, 32; Noah Webster (Hampden, *pseud.*), *A Letter to the President of the United States, Touching the Prosecutions, Under his Patronage, Before the Circuit Court in the District of Connecticut: Containing a Faithful Narrative of the Extraordinary Measures Pursued, and of the Incidents Both Serious and Laughable, That Occured, During the Pendency of These Abortive Prosecutions* (New Haven, 1808), pp. 5–23; Richard Hildreth, *A History of the United States of America* (New York, 1863), V, 592; *Cour.*, May 13, Sept. 30, 1807.

72. In the eighteenth century, paper was often taken from the mill wet and unsized. The demand greatly exceeded the supply largely because of the scarcity of rags. "Everything like rags was ground up together to make paper, which accounts for the peculiar colors often observed in the paper of this time." J. Munsell, *A Chronology of Paper and Paper-Making* (Albany, 1857), p. 29.

73. The shorter title appeared with the issue of Mar. 21, 1791. In 1783 the *Courant* was issued on Tuesday; on Monday beginning May 16, 1785; on Thursday beginning Dec. 12, 1789; back to Monday on Mar. 8, 1790; on Wednesday with the issue of Dec. 1, 1802; on Tuesday beginning Apr. 21, 1812; on Wednesday from Mar. 22, 1815; and on Tuesday with issue of Oct. 31, 1815.

74. At the end of the Revolution the *Courant* measured 14 x 10 inches; it was soon enlarged to approximately 10½ x 16½ inches (*Cour.*, Sept. 9, 1783 ff.) with 3 columns to the page; with the issue of Oct. 27, 1794, the size was increased to 11½ x 18 inches, four columns per page; beginning with Jan. 7, 1799 there were 5 columns; and the size increased to 13 x 19½ inches on Oct. 11, 1809, making the columns slightly wider than before.

75. Issues of Apr. 17, 1798 (XYZ Affair); Oct. 17, 1798 (Lyon); Nov. 26, Dec. 5,

1798 (Battle of Nile); June 23, 1812 (declaration of war); Jan. 6, 1815 (Hartford Convention).

76. It is impossible to know how many supplements were issued each year. Fifteen issued in 1799 and 17 in 1800 are preserved in the *Courant* files of the Connecticut Historical Society. Fewer are preserved or were issued earlier. Notices that advertisements were omitted for lack of space were common.

77. *Cour.,* Feb. 28, 1815.

78. The price was boosted to 9s. with the issue of Nov. 9, 1795; with issue of Feb. 23, 1803, it was quoted as $1.50 per annum, apparently the dollar equivalent of 9s.; $1.75 with issue of Dec. 11, 1805; and $2.00 with issue of Nov. 30, 1813.

79. Carriers' advertisements for payment are in *Cour.,* May 27, Sept. 16, Dec. 23, 1783; Mar. 23, 1784; Oct. 10, Dec. 19, 1785; Sept. 4, 1786; Dec. 8, 1788; June 21, 1790; Apr. 9, 1792; Oct. 1, Nov. 26, 1798; Dec. 2, 1799; Jan. 23, 1805; Aug. 3, 1808; Oct. 20, 1812.

80. *Ibid.,* Jan. 12, 1795.

81. *Ibid.,* Jan. 7, 1799; July 18, 1804.

82. *Ibid.,* Oct. 12, 1808.

83. S. N. D. North, *History and Present Condition of the Newspapers and Periodical Press of the United States, with a Catalogue of the Publications of the Census Year* (Washington, 1884), pp. 6–7.

84. The paper mill in East Hartford belonging to Daniel Butler and Hudson & Goodwin was razed by fire on Dec. 2, 1788, at an estimated loss of over £700; the papers for about three months afterward were reduced in size. In 1807 spring freshets ruined a mill and dam. *Cour.,* Dec. 9, 1788, Mar. 4, 1807; William DeLoss Love, *The Colonial History of Hartford Gathered From the Original Records* (Hartford, 1914), p. 312 n.; Joseph O. Goodwin, *East Hartford, Its History and Traditions* (Hartford, 1879), p. 160.

85. *Cour.,* Sept. 26, 1785; Jan. 9, 23, 1786; Dec. 31, 1792; Nov. 18, 1793.

86. Advertisements. *Ibid.,* Jan. 23, 1786; Dec. 20, 1790; June 1, 1801; Nov. 30, 1813.

87. *Ibid.,* Mar. 30, May 11, July 20, 1789; July 11, 1791; Mar. 25, July 29, 1793; Feb. 10, Sept. 29, 1794; May 18, 1795; Feb. 5, 1798; Jan. 19, 1801; June 26, 1805; Mar. 13, Dec. 18, 1811; June 16, Dec. 29, 1812; June 22, Sept. 14, 1813; June 14, 1815.

88. Love, *Colonial History,* p. 312; *Cour.,* Apr. 18, 1796.

89. Book advertisements in *Cour.,* July 20, 1784; Mar. 29, 1785; June 19, 1786; May 11, 1789; May 9, 1791; Feb. 13, 1792; June 24, 1793; May 5, 1794; Nov. 23, 1795; Sept. 12, 1796; Dec. 9, 1799; Nov. 15, 1802; Sept. 9, Oct. 28, 1807.

90. The small dictionary was first advertised in the issue of Feb. 19, 1806.

91. *Cour.,* Oct. 28, 1783; Jan. 21, 1788; Aug. 3, 1789; Dec. 27, 1809; Dec. 26, 1810.

92. *Ibid.,* July 25, 1791; Aug. 26 (supplement), Dec. 9, 1799; Apr. 28, 1800; June 22, Nov. 9, 1801; July 3, Aug. 7, 1805; Feb. 18, 1807.

93. *Ibid.,* June 24, 1793.

94. *Ibid.,* Feb. 24, 1784; Mar. 29, Nov. 7, 1785; June 19, 1786; May 5, 1788; May 25, 1789; May 31, 1790; Aug. 8, 1791; Mar. 25, 1793; Oct. 20, 1794; Dec. 14, 1795; Feb. 20, 1797; July 7, 1800; May 25, Aug. 3, Nov. 16, 1801; Mar. 16, 1803; Sept. 19, 1804; Jan. 30, May 15, 1805; July 29, Oct. 21, 1807; Nov. 15, 1809; Aug. 8, 1810; Aug. 21, 1811; July 27, 1813; Mar. 8, 1814.

95. *Ibid.,* Nov. 7, 1791.

96. *M'Fingal: a modern Epic Poem, in Four Cantos.* Advertised as in press (*Cour.,* July 30–Aug. 20, 1782), publication was announced in the issue of Sept. 10, 1782. This was the first edition of the complete work although it had been published in part at Philadelphia in 1776. Henry A. Beers, *The Connecticut Wits and other Essays* (New Haven, 1920), p. 14.

97. John Trumbull, *The Poetical Works of John Trumbull, LL.D. Containing M'Fingal, A Modern Epic Poem, Revised and Corrected, with Copious Explanatory Notes* (Hartford, 1820), I, 18–19.

98. Patten's first advertisement in the *Courant* appeared on Dec. 30, 1776. Webster set up his business about 1778. Thompson R. Harlow, *Early Hartford Printers* (Hartford, 1940), p. 8.

99. *Cour.*, Dec. 24, 1782.

100. Trumbull, *Lists of Books,* pp. 192–193.

101. *Cour.*, Jan. 7, 1783. For authorship, cf., Alexander Cowie, *John Trumbull Connecticut Wit* (Chapel Hill, 1936), pp. 187–188. Noah Webster thought Trumbull to be the author.

102. *Cour.*, Feb. 25, 1783.

103. Published for 1779 as *The Connecticut Almanack* (Watson & Goodwin); for 1780 and 1781 under the same title by Hudson & Goodwin; for 1782–1789, as *An Astronomical Ephemeris, Calendar, or Almanack.* Trumbull, *List of Books,* p. 9.

104. Babcock appeared in Hartford in 1777 and apparently ran the paper mill in which Hannah Watson had an interest. Early in 1782, he and Anthony Haswell, who had been employed for about a year by Hudson & Goodwin, started the first paper in Springfield, Massachusetts. The first issue of *The Massachusetts Gazette and general Advertiser* appeared on May 14, 1782, and the partnership continued to May 13, 1783, when Haswell moved to Bennington, Vermont. Babcock ran the paper for another year and returned to Hartford to go into partnership with Barlow. Royal R. Hinman, *A Catalogue of the Names of the Early Puritan Settlers of the Colony of Connecticut* (Hartford, 1852), pp. 93–94; *Cour.*, Oct. 21, 1777; Harlow, *Early Hartford Printers,* p. 9.

105. The rejoinder was probably written by Barlow. *Cour.*, Nov. 16, 1784; Zunder, *Early Days of Joel Barlow,* pp. 174–175.

106. *Cour.*, Dec. 28, 1784. Adv. by Barlow & Babcock. *Ibid.*, Nov. 9, 1784.

107. *Ibid.*, Nov. 9, 1784.

108. *A Grammatical Institute of the English Language, Comprising, An easy, concise, and systematic Method of Education, Designed for the Use of English Schools in America, In Three Parts. Part I, Containing a new and accurate Standard of Pronunciation.* The first advertisement was in *Cour.*, Sept. 16, 1783.

109. Emily Ellsworth Fowler Ford (Emily Ellsworth Ford Skeel, ed.), *Notes on the Life of Noah Webster* (New York, 1912), I, 59–60.

110. Warfel, *op. cit.*, pp. 60–61.

111. Ford, *Notes,* II, 447.

112. Webster's letters to Hudson & Goodwin, *Ford Collection,* New York Public Library, *passim;* Ford, *Notes,* I, 53–57, 90–122; Warfel, *op. cit.*, pp. 51–88.

113. *Cour.*, Nov. 9, 1784; letter from N.W. to H. & G., Sept. 10, 1786, *Ford Coll.* NYPL.

114. Letter from N.W. to H. & G., June 22, 1788, *Ford Coll.*

115. Deposition by N.W., Feb. 28, 1789, *Ford Coll. Cour.*, Jan. 26, 1788.

116. Letter from N.W. to H. & G., June 22, 1788, *Ford. Coll.*

117. Letters from N.W. to H. & G., June 22, Aug. 16, 1788; Feb. 27, 1789, *Ford Coll.*

118. Letter from N.W. to H. & G., June 22, 1788, *Ford Coll.;* copy of letter from George Goodwin & Sons to Solomon Warriner, Jan. 30, 1822 in George Goodwin & Sons, *Letter Books,* III, Connecticut Historical Society.

119. Deposition of N.W., Feb. 28, 1789, *Ford Coll.; Cour.*, Jan. 19, 26, 1789; letters from Samuel and Robert Campbell to H. & G., Jan. 6, May 3, 1788, in possession of CHS; copy of letter from H. & G. to Samuel Campbell, Dec. 30, 1787, CHS; manuscript records of the Connecticut Superior Court in session at Hartford, Dec., 1788 and Sept., 1789, Connecticut State Library.

120. *Cour.*, Jan. 19, 26, 1789; May 24, 1790; *American Mercury,* May 31, 1790; Patten's petition to the Superior Court at Hartford, Feb. 22, 1790, CSL.

121. *Cour.*, May 24, 1790.

122. Letters from N.W. to H. & G., July 24, 1786; Feb. 27, 1789, *Ford Coll.;* *Cour.,* Jan. 19, 1789; May 24, 1790.

123. *Cour.,* Jan. 19, 26, 1789; May 24, 1790.

124. Letters from N.W. to H. & G., Jan. 18, Feb. 20, 1789, *Ford Coll.;* deposition of N.W., Feb. 28, 1789, *Ford Coll. Cour.,* May 24, 1790. Webster advertised Campbell's 14th edition as an inferior one in *Cour.,* Sept. 17, Nov. 12, 1792.

125. Warfel, *op. cit.,* pp. 72–73. Patten had printed "Dilworth" before. *Cour.,* Dec. 18, 1781.

126. Bates, *Supplementary List of Books,* pp. 69–70.

127. The last-named was published in 1791 as *The Prompter, or a Commentary on Common Sayings & Subjects.* Legal notice of the copyright is in *Cour.,* Nov. 7, 1791; cf. *ante,* n. 24. A checklist of Webster's writings is in Ford, *Notes,* II, 523–540; Trumbull, *List of Books* and Bates, *Supplementary List of Books,* record the H. & G. publications before 1801.

128. *Cour.,* Jan. 1, May 14, 1787; Zunder, *Early Days of Joel Barlow,* p. 207; H. & G. issued a second edition in 1788. *Cour.,* Oct. 29, 1787; May 26, 1788.

129. *Cour.,* Jan. 1, 1787.

130. Trumbull, *List of Books,* pp. 5–6.

131. John Pell, *Ethan Allen* (Boston, 1929), p. 228. Allen's "Bible," entitled *Reason, the Only Oracle of Man, or a Compendious System of Natural Religion . . . ,* was published at Bennington, Vermont, in 1784.

132. Trumbull, *List of Books,* and Bates, *Supplementary List of Books, passim.*

133. William Beer, *Checklist of American Periodicals 1741–1800* (Worcester, 1923), p. 8; Rosalie V. Halsey, *Forgotten Books of the American Nursery A History of the Development of the American Story-Book* (Boston, 1911), pp. 101–102. Four numbers (Jan.–Apr., 1789) were advertised. *Cour.,* Feb. 2, Mar. 2, 16, Apr. 20, May 11, 1789.

134. *Cour.,* Feb. 2, 1789.

135. *Ibid.,* Dec. 19, 1785; May 5, Sept. 1, 1788; Mar. 2, 1789.

136. The CHS has a complete file. H. & G. distributed them. Letters to H. & G. dated 1800–1802, *passim,* CHS. Circulation figures appear in George Leon Walker, "The Historical Address," *Commemorative Exercises of the First Church of Christ in Hartford, at its Two Hundred and Fiftieth Anniversary, October 11 and 12, 1883* (Hartford, 1883), pp. 87–88.

137. In 1784 The General Association of the Congregational Churches of Connecticut voted to revise *Watt's Book of Psalmody* then in use. The Barlow revision was well received by the New England churches until Barlow was chiefly remembered for his fall from orthodoxy in France. Timothy Dwight's edition succeeded Barlow's. H. & G. had printed Barlow's third edition in 1791. Trumbull, *List of Books,* p. 199; Charles Burr Todd, *Life and Letters of Joel Barlow, LL.D. Poet, Statesman, Philosopher With Extracts From His Works and Hitherto Unpublished Poems* (New York, 1886), p. 48.

138. *Cour.,* Nov. 15, 1802; Oct. 10, 1804.

139. *Ibid.,* Oct. 18, 1809; James Junius Goodwin, *The Goodwins of Hartford, Connecticut* (Hartford, 1891), p. 641.

140. John Wright, *Early Bibles of America* (New York, 1892), p. 135.

141. Henry Baldwin, "Social Life After the Revolution," *The Memorial History of Hartford County Connecticut 1633–1884,* J. Hammond Trumbull, ed. (Boston, 1886), I, 581 n. George Goodwin and Hudson & Goodwin were among the incorporators of the Hartford Library Company. *Resolves and Private Laws of the State of Connecticut,* I, 718–719. Goodwin signed the petition for incorporating the insurance company and H. & G. bought 100 shares of the original stock. Charles Hopkins Clark, "Insurance," *Mem. Hist.,* I, 500; *Connecticut Archives, Corporations,* I, 10–12.

142. *Cour.,* July 7, 1784; Apr. 3, 1786; W. A. Ayres, "Manufactures and Inventions," *Mem. Hist.,* I, 564–565.

143. *Cour.,* Apr. 5, 1790; Apr. 4, 1791; Apr. 2, 1798; Apr. 1, 1799; Apr. 7, 1800; Mar. 30, 1808; Mar. 29, 1809; Mar. 28, 1810.

144. George Leon Walker, *History of the First Church in Hartford, 1633–1883* (Hartford, 1884), pp. 378 n., 460. He was a bank director from 1794 to 1817. P. H. Woodward, *One Hundred Years of the Hartford Bank Now the Hartford National Bank Of Hartford, Conn.* (Hartford, 1892), p. 168. He was advertised as among the directors of the turnpike company in *Cour.,* May 27, 1807.

145. Henry was already a member of the firm when Richard joined in 1808. *Cour.,* Nov. 2, 1808. The firm's financial interest in the mercantile establishments is revealed in *Cour.,* Oct. 11, 1814, Oct. 25, 1815.

146. *Cour.,* June 8, 1813.

147. *Ibid.,* June 7, 1809; July 4, 1810; May 18, 1813; May 17, 1814; June 7, 1815. At one time he was local collector for the "American Board of Commissioners for Foreign Missions." *Ibid.,* Nov. 24, 1812.

148. Advertisements for Oliver Goodwin, Goodwin & Whiting, George Goodwin, Jr. & Charles Goodwin. *Ibid.,* Nov. 26, 1806; Oct. 11, 1809; Sept. 18, Oct. 9, 1811; Mar. 22, 1814. Of the six Goodwin boys who lived to maturity (Richard, Oliver, George, Jr., Charles, Henry, and Edward) all but Oliver were at one time or another members of the *Courant's* firm. Cf. *post,* p. 177. Oliver, who probably learned his trade with the firm, moved to Litchfield early in life and entered the bookselling and stationery business. Goodwin, *Goodwins of Hartford,* p. 648.

149. *Cour.,* Oct. 25, 1815; Goodwin, *Goodwins of Hartford,* pp. 642–643.

150. S. G. Goodrich, *Recollections of A Lifetime or Men and Things I Have Seen; in a Series of Familiar Letters to A Friend, Historical, Biographical, Anecdotical, and Descriptive* (New York, 1856), I, 410–413.

CHAPTER VIII

FROM FEDERALIST TO WHIG

1. *Connecticut Courant,* Jan. 23, 1816.
2. *Ibid.,* Mar. 19–Apr. 16, 1816.
3. *Ibid.,* Mar. 4–Apr. 15, Sept. 23, 1817.
4. *Ibid.,* Mar. 31–Apr. 21, 1818.
5. *Ibid.,* Sept. 23, 1817.
6. *Ibid.,* Mar. 19–Apr. 16, 1816; Mar. 4–Apr. 15, 1817.
7. *Ibid.,* June 16, Aug. 11, Sept. 15, 22, 1818.
8. *Ibid.,* Aug. 5, 1817.
9. *Ibid.,* Aug. 4, 1818.
10. *Ibid.,* July 28, Aug. 4, 18, 25, Sept. 15, 22, 29, 1818.
11. *Ibid.,* July 28, 1818.
12. *Ibid.,* Sept. 15, 1818; Apr. 27, May 4, 1819; June 4, 1822.
13. *Ibid.,* Sept. 29, Oct. 6, 18, 1818.
14. *Ibid.,* June 30, July 28, Sept. 15, Oct. 13, 27, 1818.
15. *Ibid.,* Jan. 14, Nov. 11, 1817; July 21–Aug. 4, 18, Sept. 22, Oct. 13, 1818.
16. *Ibid.,* Oct. 13, 1818.
17. Fourteen letters written by H. G. Otis and reprinted from the *Boston Centinal* justified the Hartford Convention. *Ibid.,* Feb. 24–May 4, June 15–July 6, 1824.
18. *Ibid.,* June 11, 1822.
19. *Ibid.,* June 11, 1822; Mar. 11, 1823; Mar. 23, 1824; Feb. 28, 1826.
20. *Ibid.,* Jan. 11, 1825.

21. *Ibid.*, June 11, 1822; June 24, Sept. 30, Nov. 11, 18, 1823; Feb. 3, Oct. 19–Nov. 2, 1824.

22. *Ibid.*, Mar. 11, 1823. The editors favored districting the state for the election of state senators and United States congressmen as a substitute for the caucus. *Ibid.*, Sept. 19, Oct. 17, 1820; Apr. 1–15, Oct. 7–28, Nov. 11, 1828.

23. Enthusiasm dwindled from 1818 to 1823, in which year the Federalists took no organized part in the elections. The *Courant*'s political interest was at low ebb from the spring of 1823 (cf. *ibid.*, Apr. 8, 1823) until the fall of 1827.

24. *Ibid.*, July 1, Aug. 26, 1817.

25. *Ibid.*, July 20, 1819; Dec. 16, 1823.

26. *Ibid.*, Dec. 22, 1818; Dec. 7, 1819; Jan. 25, Mar. 14, 28, 1820.

27. *Ibid.*, July 1, 1817; Aug. 4, 1818; July 13, 1819; July 11, 1820.

28. *Ibid.*, July 20, 1819.

29. *Ibid.*, Mar. 9, 1819; Mar. 21, Sept. 12, 1820; Mar. 13, 1821.

30. *Ibid.*, Nov. 2, 1824. The same sentiment was expressed earlier in issues of Jan. 29, 1822; Apr. 29, May 27, July 1, Aug. 19, Nov. 4, 25, 1823; July 6, Aug. 17, 1824.

31. *Ibid.*, Feb. 24, Oct. 5, 1824.

32. *Ibid.*, July 1, 1823.

33. *Ibid.*, Oct. 19–Nov. 2, 1824.

34. *Ibid.*, Oct. 26, 1824.

35. *Ibid.*, Nov. 9, 1824.

36. *Ibid.*, Feb. 17, 24, Apr. 21, 1829; Oct. 12, 1835.

37. *Ibid.*, Feb. 22, 1825; Dec. 4, 1826.

38. *Ibid.*, July 16, 1827.

39. *Ibid.*, July 16, 23, Aug. 6–20, 1827.

40. *Ibid.*, July 16, Aug. 13, 1827 ff.

41. *Ibid.*, Jan. 28, 1828 ff.

42. *Ibid.*, Jan. 7, Feb. 25, 1817.

43. *Ibid.*, Oct. 28, 1823.

44. *Ibid.*, Oct. 7, 1823.

45. *Idem.*

46. *Ibid.*, Dec. 2, 1823; Jan. 6, 20, 1824.

47. *Ibid.*, Feb. 17, 1824.

48. *Ibid.*, June 25, July 2, July 23–Aug. 13, Nov. 19, 1827; Jan. 21, Apr. 22–May 20, 1828. Also, in earlier issues, Aug. 17, 1824; Jan. 3, Nov. 13–27, 1826.

49. *Ibid.*, Mar. 18, 1828.

50. *Ibid.*, May 27, Oct. 14, 1828.

51. *Ibid.*, Mar. 18, May 27, Nov. 11, 1828.

52. *Ibid.*, Nov. 19, 1827; Mar. 18, July 22, Aug. 5, 19, 1828.

53. *Ibid.*, Nov. 19, 1827.

54. *Ibid.*, Nov. 19, 1827; Mar. 18, 1828.

55. *Ibid.*, Mar. 11–Apr. 15, 1828.

56. *Ibid.*, Mar. 18, 25, 1828.

57. *Ibid.*, Mar. 11, 18, 1828.

58. *Ibid.*, Mar. 25, Aug. 12, 1828.

59. *Ibid.*, Aug. 26, 1828.

60. *Ibid.*, Nov. 18, 1828.

61. *Ibid.*, Mar. 10, 1829.

62. *Ibid.*, Mar. 17, Apr. 21, 28, 1829.

63. *Ibid.*, Apr. 28, 1829.

64. *Ibid.*, May 5, 1829.

65. *Ibid.*, Apr. 28, June 23, 1829.

66. *Ibid.*, Nov. 30, 1830; Oct. 11, 1831.

67. *Ibid.*, Mar. 17, Dec. 1, 1829.

68. *Ibid.,* Feb. 17, 1829.
69. *Ibid.,* Jan. 18, Feb. 15, Oct. 11, Nov. 1, 8, 29, 1831; June 19, 1832.
70. *Ibid.,* Oct. 11, 1831.
71. *Ibid.,* Jan. 18, 1831.
72. *Ibid.,* Aug. 17, 1824.
73. *Ibid.,* Oct. 11, 18, 1831; June 19, Oct. 30, 1832.
74. *Ibid.,* Feb. 2–Mar. 9, 1830; Apr. 30, 1833.
75. *Ibid.,* Oct. 26, 1830.
76. *Ibid.,* Dec. 15, 1829.
77. *Ibid.,* June 8, 1830.
78. *Ibid.,* Jan. 31, May 29, 1832.
79. *Ibid.,* July 17, Sept. 25, Oct. 2, 1832.
80. *Ibid.,* Oct. 30, 1832.
81. *Idem.*
82. *Ibid.,* Oct. 2, 9, 1832.
83. *Ibid.,* Oct. 7, 1817.
84. *Ibid.,* Aug. 11, 1829–Jan. 26, 1830.
85. *Ibid.,* Jan. 12, 19, 1830.
86. *Ibid.,* June 16, 1829; June 22, 1830.
87. *Ibid.,* June 22, 1830.
88. *Ibid.,* Jan. 11, 1831.
89. *Ibid.,* Feb. 17–Mar. 3, 1829.
90. *Ibid.,* Apr. 14, 1829.
91. *Ibid.,* Dec. 29, 1829; Feb. 16, Mar. 16, 1830.
92. *Ibid.,* Feb. 16, 1830.
93. *Ibid.,* Mar. 2–Apr. 13, 1830; Mar. 1–Apr. 12, 1831; Feb. 28–Apr. 10, 1832.
94. *Ibid.,* Feb. 17, 1829; Jan. 19, Dec. 28, 1830; Mar. 20, 27, Sept. 11, 25, 1832.
95. *Ibid.,* June 21, 1831.
96. *Ibid.,* July 16–Aug. 27, 1827, *passim.*
97. *Ibid.,* Oct. 11, 1831–Oct. 30, 1832, *passim.*
98. *Ibid.,* Feb. 22, Mar. 1, Apr. 26, May 3, June 28–Aug. 9, 1831.
99. *Ibid.,* Apr. 6, 20, 1830.
100. *Ibid.,* Oct. 30, 1832.
101. *Ibid.,* Sept. 11–Oct. 30, 1832.
102. *Ibid.,* Oct. 9, 1832.
103. *Ibid.,* Nov. 20, 1832.
104. *Ibid.,* Dec. 18, 1832.
105. *Ibid.,* Jan. 29–Apr. 30, 1833, *passim.*
106. *Ibid.,* Jan. 8, 15, 22, 1833.
107. *Ibid.,* Dec. 18, 1832; Jan. 1, 8, 1833.
108. *Ibid.,* Feb. 19, 1833.
109. *Ibid.,* Mar. 12, 1833.
110. *Ibid.,* Sept. 23, 1833.
111. *Ibid.,* Sept. 30, Oct. 7, 1833.
112. *Ibid.,* Dec. 9, 16, 1833.
113. *Ibid.,* Dec. 23, 1833; Jan. 13–Feb. 10, 1834.
114. *Ibid.,* Dec. 23, 1833.
115. *Ibid.,* Jan. 20, 1834.
116. *Ibid.,* Jan. 20–May 19, 1834, *passim.*
117. *Ibid.,* Mar. 17, 1834.
118. *Ibid.,* Mar. 24, 1834.
119. *Ibid.,* Apr. 2, 9, 1833.
120. *Ibid.,* Apr. 7, 14, Sept. 15–Oct. 13, Dec. 1, 1834.
121. *Ibid.,* Feb. 2, 1835.
122. *Ibid.,* Mar. 28, May 9, 1836.

123. Cf. *post*, pp. 172–174.
124. *Cour.*, Feb. 16–Apr. 13, 1835.
125. *Ibid.*, Apr. 13, May 11, 1835.
126. *Ibid.*, Apr. 13, 1835.
127. *Ibid.*, Feb. 29–Apr. 11, 1836.
128. *Ibid.*, Nov. 2, 1835.
129. *Ibid.*, May 23, 1836.
130. *Ibid.*, May 23–Sept. 19, 1836, *passim*.
131. Cf. *post*, pp. 187–188.
132. *Cour.*, Nov. 12, 1836. Boswell placed the names of Harrison and Granger on the editorial page when he took over the *Courant. Ibid.*, Sept. 19, 1836.

CHAPTER IX

BENEVOLENCE AND BUSINESS

1. *Connecticut Courant,* May 15, 1811, and annually thereafter.
2. *Ibid.*, May 28, 1816.
3. *Ibid.*, July 2, 1816.
4. *Ibid.*, Apr. 27, 1819; Apr. 17, 1821.
5. *Ibid.*, Jan. 30, Dec. 31, 1816; Jan. 4, 1820; Jan. 8, 1822; Sept. 21, 1824.
6. *Ibid.*, Sept. 3, 1816; Aug. 8, 1820; July 3, 1821.
7. *Ibid.*, Oct. 24, 1820.
8. *Ibid.*, Nov. 5, 1822.
9. *Ibid.*, Jan. 28, 1823; Dec. 14, 1824.
10. *Ibid.*, Aug. 7, 1826; Apr. 15, 1828.
11. *Ibid.*, June 9, 1818; June 15, 1819; June 12, 1821.
12. For example, *ibid.*, Feb. 24, Mar. 17, Apr. 7, May 5, 26, June 16, 23, July 14, Aug. 4, 18, Sept. 1, Dec. 3, 1818.
13. *Ibid.*, June 2, 1829.
14. *Ibid.*, Apr. 23, 1822; June 24, 1823.
15. Cf. *post*, p. 180.
16. *Cour.*, Oct. 18, 25, 1831.
17. *Ibid.*, Feb. 21, 1832.
18. *Ibid.*, Aug. 20, 1822; Apr. 6, 1824.
19. *Ibid.*, Dec. 30, 1823–Jan. 20, Feb. 10, 1824; Mar. 5, 1827; Mar. 11, Nov. 11, 1828; Jan. 17, June 19–July 3, 1832.
20. *Ibid.*, Oct. 19, 1819; July 30, 1822; June 26, 1826; Feb. 25, 1828; June 2, 30, Aug. 11, 1829; May 25, June 15, 1830; June 14, 1831; July 31–Aug. 28, 1832; Mar. 12, May 10, 14, Oct. 21, 1833; July 4, 1836.
21. *Ibid.*, May 5, 12, 1818.
22. *Ibid.*, Oct. 15, 1816; Sept. 30, 1817; Feb. 26, Aug. 13, 20, 1822; Oct. 26, 1824; Apr. 1, Oct. 7, 1828; Apr. 13, 1830.
23. *Ibid.*, Nov. 22, 29, 1831; Dec. 4, 1832; Jan. 15, Dec. 2, 1833; Dec. 29, 1834; Oct. 19, 1835; Jan. 4, 1836.
24. *Ibid.*, Feb. 26, 1833; May 26, Aug. 11, 1834.
25. *Ibid.*, Aug. 5, 1823.
26. *Ibid.*, Jan. 5, 1835.
27. *Ibid.*, Dec. 31, 1816. Cf. *post*, pp. 186–187.
28. *Cour.*, Mar. 25, 1817.
29. James Monroe and Andrew Jackson visited it. *Ibid.*, July 1, 1817; June 24, 1833. Public exhibitions are recorded in issues of Sept. 2, 1817; June 2, 1818; Apr. 17, 1821.
30. *Ibid.*, Sept. 2, 1817
31. *Ibid.*, June 12, 1821.

32. *Ibid.,* June 12, Oct. 9, 1821.

33. *Ibid.,* Nov. 5, Dec. 10, 31, 1822; Aug. 19, 1823; Mar. 9, 1824.

34. *Ibid.,* Mar. 9, 1824.

35. For example, *ibid.,* Aug. 31, 1824; May 24, 1825. Reports were published annually.

36. *Ibid.,* July 6, 1819.

37. *Ibid.,* July 13, 20, 27, Aug. 17, 31, 1819; July 19, 1825; Nov. 30, 1835. Cf. *post,* pp. 186–187.

38. *Cour.,* Sept. 7, 1819.

39. Now Trinity College. *Ibid.,* Feb. 24, Mar. 2, 16, Apr. 13, 20, 27, May 11, June 15, 1824; Aug. 6, 1827.

40. *Ibid.,* Mar. 5, 1827; Oct. 27, 1829; Apr. 27, Nov. 2, 1830; Nov. 2, 1835. Cf. *post,* pp. 186–187.

41. *Cour.,* Apr. 16, July 29, Aug. 5, 1833.

42. *Ibid.,* Sept. 9, 16, 1828; May 26, 1829; Sept. 28, 1830.

43. *Ibid.,* May 27, 1833.

44. *Ibid.,* Feb. 14, 1826.

45. *Ibid.,* Apr. 2, 1827.

46. *Ibid.,* July 13, 1830.

47. *Ibid.,* July 13, Oct. 26, 1830.

48. *Ibid.,* Aug. 24, 31, Oct. 12, Nov. 9, 23, Dec. 28, 1830; Jan. 25, 1831.

49. *Ibid.,* May 31, Dec. 6, 1825; May 23, 1836.

50. *Ibid.,* Aug. 25, 1818; June 25, 1822; Mar. 25, 1828.

51. *Ibid.,* Aug. 13, 1822; Nov. 11, 1823; May 21, Nov. 12, 1827; Apr. 21, 1834; Feb. 16, 1835.

52. *Ibid.,* Dec. 3, 31, 1816; May 13, 1817; Jan. 29, 1822; June 3, 1823; Aug. 7, 1826; Apr. 30, 1827; Mar. 11, Apr. 15, 1828.

53. *Ibid.,* Sept. 14, 1830.

54. *Ibid.,* Mar. 30, 1835.

55. *Ibid.,* Jan. 26, Dec. 21, 1835.

56. *Ibid.,* Apr. 1, Oct. 7, 1828; Sept. 22, 1829.

57. *Ibid.,* Aug. 7, 1826; May 28, 1827; Apr. 15, 1828; Feb. 3, May 12, June 30, Aug. 11, 1829; Feb. 9, Aug. 3, 1830.

58. *Ibid.,* Sept. 29, 1829.

59. *Ibid.,* July 1, 1817; June 23, 1818; June 27, 1820; June 22, 1830; June 29, 1835.

60. *Ibid.,* Sept. 4, 1821; Jan. 15, 1822; July 17, 1826.

61. *Ibid.,* Oct. 14, 1817; Mar. 3, Nov. 3, 1829.

62. *Ibid.,* Mar. 3, 1829.

63. *Ibid.,* July 13, 1819; Jan. 14, Dec. 30, 1823; Nov. 23, 1824; Mar. 1, May 31, 1825; May 15, 1826; May 14, 1827; Apr. 15, Sept. 16, Oct. 7, Nov. 4, Dec. 16, 1828; Jan. 20, Mar. 3, May 19, 1829; Sept. 21, 1830; Dec. 13, 20, 1831; Mar. 19, Dec. 9, 1833; Apr. 21, June 2, Sept. 1, Nov. 3, 1834; Mar. 16, Aug. 24, Sept. 14, 1835; Sept. 5, Dec. 24, 1836.

64. *Ibid.,* Feb. 7, 21, 1832.

65. *Ibid.,* Sept. 22, 1829.

66. *Ibid.,* Mar. 24, Sept. 22, 1829; Jan. 26, 1830; Jan. 15, 1833.

67. *Ibid.,* Mar. 24, 1829.

68. *Ibid.,* Jan. 26, 1830; Jan. 4, 1831.

69. *Ibid.,* Jan. 26, 1830.

70. *Ibid.,* June 25, 1822; Aug. 17, 1835.

71. *Ibid.,* June 28, 1831; Jan. 13, 1834; Oct. 12, 1835.

72. *Ibid.,* June 19, 1811; Jan. 19, 1819; Jan. 11, 1820; Mar. 27, 1821; Sept. 7, 1824; Nov. 8, 1825; Jan. 11, 1836.

73. *Ibid.,* Oct. 23, 1821; May 6, 1828.

74. *Ibid.,* Nov. 9, 1819.

75. *Ibid.,* Nov. 19, 1816; Oct. 7, 1817; Apr. 28, Dec. 22, 1818; Apr. 20, 1819; Nov. 11, 1823.

76. *Ibid.,* Aug. 19, 1823.

77. *Ibid.,* Dec. 16, 1823; Dec. 23, 1828.

78. *Ibid.,* July 15, 1823; July 13, 1824; June 5, 26, 1826; July 1, 1828; July 7, 1829.

79. *Ibid.,* July 17, 1821; May 7, 1827; May 20, 1828.

80. *Ibid.,* May 20, 1828. The General Assembly restricted the sale of tickets in 1828. *Ibid.,* June 10, 1828.

81. *Ibid.,* Dec. 14, 1824; May 24, Aug. 9, 1825; Apr. 10, 1826.

82. *Ibid.,* Dec. 14, 1824; May 24, 1825; Apr. 10, 1826.

83. *Ibid.,* Feb. 28, 1826. Reprinted essays on the city theaters as saloons of vice appeared in issues of Jan. 24, 1826 and July 16, 1827.

84. *Ibid.,* Feb. 28, 1826.

85. *Ibid.,* May 1, 1826.

86. *Ibid.,* July 1, 1828.

87. *Ibid.,* Aug. 5, 12, Sept. 2, 1823.

88. *Ibid.,* Aug. 12, 1823.

89. *Ibid.,* Oct. 22, 1827; Sept. 23, 1828.

90. *Ibid.,* July 29, 1828.

91. *Ibid.,* Mar. 18, 25, 1828; Oct. 20, Nov. 24, 1829; Oct. 25, 1831; Aug. 24, 1835.

92. *Ibid.,* May 4, 1830.

93. *Ibid.,* Nov. 15, 1831.

94. *Resolves and Private Laws of the State of Connecticut,* II, 810–812; *Cour.,* Jan. 24, Nov. 20, 1826.

95. *Cour.,* July 31, 1832.

96. *Ibid.,* June 26, 1826; June 30, 1829; June 15, 1830; June 14, 1831.

97. *Ibid.,* June 15, 1830.

98. *Ibid.,* June 10, 1833.

99. *Ibid.,* July 8, 22, Aug. 26, Oct. 16, 1833.

100. *Ibid.,* June 10, 24, July 8, 1833.

101. *Ibid.,* Oct. 20, 1834; June 15, Aug. 17, 1835.

102. *Ibid.,* Oct. 9, 1833; July 21, Aug. 18, 1834.

103. *Ibid.,* Aug. 24, 1835.

104. *Ibid.,* July 21, 1834.

105. *Ibid.,* July 29, Aug. 12, 1833; Aug. 31, Sept. 28, 1835.

106. *Ibid.,* Aug. 31, Sept. 21, 28, 1835.

107. *Ibid.,* Sept. 28, 1835.

108. *Ibid.,* July 4, 1836.

109. *Ibid.,* Feb. 15, 1825; June 26, Aug. 14, 21, 1826.

110. *Ibid.,* July 19, 1825.

111. *Ibid.,* Feb. 15, 1825.

112. *Ibid.,* Sept. 9, 1828.

113. *Ibid.,* Aug. 14, 1826.

114. *Ibid.,* Aug. 21, 1826.

115. *Ibid.,* Aug. 28, 1826.

116. *Ibid.,* Apr. 15, 1828.

117. *Ibid.,* Jan. 27–Feb. 10, Nov. 3, 1829; Mar. 16, 1830; Dec. 24, 1836; Jan. 21, 1837.

118. *Ibid.,* July 29, 1828.

119. *Ibid.,* Feb. 15, Nov. 29, 1825; Apr. 15, 1828; Mar. 16, June 22, 1830.

120. *Ibid.,* July 19, 1825; Mar. 16, 1830.

121. The *Courant* editorially advertised and urged the use of coal (*ibid.,* Jan. 18, Nov. 1, 1825; Sept. 24, 1827; Jan. 6, 1829; Nov. 8, 1831); items on McAdam roads are in issues of Apr. 19, 1825; Dec. 31, 1827; June 28, Aug. 30, 1831; Aug.

28, 1832; fire insurance was urged (*ibid.,* Jan. 14, 1823; cf. *ante,* p. 104; and editorial notice of the formation of the Aetna Insurance Co. appeared in issue of June 22, 1819. Noticed also were the establishment of a local branch of the Second United States Bank (*Cour.,* Apr. 13, 1824) and the growth of local banking (*ibid.,* July 5, 1825). New manufactures were mentioned (*ibid.,* Jan. 18, 1820; July 31, Sept. 18, Oct. 2, 1826; Aug. 2, 1831); privately owned bathing establishments were in Hartford (*ibid.,* July 4, 1820; July 7, 1834; May 11, 1835); the oyster house was first advertised in issue of Nov. 11, 1817; and the soda water fountain in issue of June 30, 1818 (therapeutic claims were made for it); an advertisement for "elegant and fashionable corsets," the first noticed, was in the issue of Nov. 2, 1824. For material on steamboats and railroads, see subsequent paragraphs.

122. For example, *ibid.,* May 27, 1817.
123. *Ibid.,* Nov. 10, 1818.
124. *Ibid.,* Jan. 13, 1824.
125. *Ibid.,* Sept. 9, 1823.
126. *Ibid.,* May 4, 11, 1824.
127. *Ibid.,* Oct. 4, 1825; June 25, 1827; May 4, 1830.
128. *Ibid.,* May 25, 1824; June 25, 1827; May 4, 1830.
129. *Ibid.,* May 4, 1830.
130. *Ibid.,* Jan. 6, 13, Mar. 2, 1824; Jan. 18, Feb. 8, 22, 1825; May 8, 1826.
131. *Ibid.,* Jan. 6, 1824; Aug. 7, Sept. 11–Oct. 23, 1826.
132. *Ibid.,* Jan. 29, June 4, 1827.
133. *Ibid.,* Apr. 12, June 28, 1825.
134. *Ibid.,* Jan. 6, 13, 27, Mar. 2, Apr. 30, 1824.
135. *Ibid.,* July 17, 1826.
136. *Ibid.,* Dec. 4, 1826.
137. *Ibid.,* Dec. 11, 1826.
138. *Ibid.,* Dec. 4–25, 1826.
139. *Ibid.,* Dec. 11, 1826.
140. *Ibid.,* Feb. 7, 1826; Jan. 27, 1829.
141. *Ibid.,* Jan. 27, 1829.
142. *Ibid.,* Nov. 17, 1829.
143. *Ibid.,* July 27, Nov. 23, Dec. 7, 1830; Feb. 1, 8, 1831.
144. *Ibid.,* Feb. 1, 1831.
145. *Ibid.,* Aug. 10, 1835.
146. *Ibid.,* Mar. 1, Apr. 5, 1825.
147. *Ibid.,* Aug. 21, 1832.
148. *Ibid.,* July 21, 1834.
149. *Ibid.,* Jan. 5, 1835.
150. *Idem.*
151. On Jan. 9, 1835. *Ibid.,* Jan. 12, 1835.
152. *Ibid.,* Jan. 12, 1835–Aug. 22, 1836, *passim.*
153. *Ibid.,* July 13, 1835.
154. *Ibid.,* Mar. 30, 1835.
155. *Ibid.,* Aug. 3, 10, 1835.
156. *Ibid.,* Aug. 17, 1835.
157. *Ibid.,* Mar. 23, 30, May 18, June 15, 22, July 20, Aug. 10, Oct. 5, Dec. 14, 1835; Jan. 18, Feb. 8, July 4, 18, Aug. 15, 22, 1836.
158. *Ibid.,* Mar. 3, Nov. 10, 1818; Sept. 28, 1819; Feb. 15, 1820; Feb. 6, 1821; Jan. 7, 1823; Mar. 27, Dec. 11, 18, 1826; Mar. 26, May 14, Sept. 24, Oct. 29, Nov. 5, Dec. 3, 1827; Oct. 23, 1832.
159. *Ibid.,* Nov. 10, 1818; Mar. 27, 1826; Oct. 23, 1832.
160. *Ibid.,* Mar. 3, 1818; Feb. 6, 1821; May 14, 1827; Nov. 15, 1831; Nov. 4, 1833.
161. *Ibid.,* Nov. 10, 1818; Sept. 28, 1819; Feb. 8, 1820.

162. *Ibid.,* Dec. 18, 1826; Sept. 7, 1830.
163. *Ibid.,* Jan. 19, 1819; Sept. 6, 13, 1825; Aug. 29, 1836.
164. *Ibid.,* Jan. 19, Feb. 2, Oct. 5, Nov. 23, Dec. 28, 1819; Oct. 1, 1822.
165. *Ibid.,* Sept. 21, 28, 1819; June 27, 1820; Aug. 27, Sept. 10, 1822.
166. *Ibid.,* June 26–Nov. 27, 1832, *passim.*
167. *Ibid.,* June 26, July 3, 24, 1832.
168. *Ibid.,* Sept. 28, 1819; June 27, 1820; Aug. 27, 1822; Aug. 28, 1832; June 17, 1833; June 22, 1835.
169. *Ibid.,* Apr. 29, June 24, 1823; Sept. 28, 1824; Aug. 9, 1825; June 19, July 3, 1826; Feb. 24, May 5, Nov. 10, 1829; June 1, 1830.
170. *Ibid.,* Apr. 28, 1818; May 22, June 26, 1821; June 28, 1825; Nov. 4, 1828.
171. *Ibid.,* Nov. 4, 1828; Jan. 10, 1832; Jan. 20, 1834.
172. *Ibid.,* Jan. 11, 1820; July 3, 1826.
173. *Ibid.,* Oct. 12, 1830.
174. *Ibid.,* Aug. 21, 1826.
175. *Ibid.,* May 3, Aug. 30, 1831; May 27, June 3, 1833; Apr. 14, May 12, June 2, 1834.
176. *Ibid.,* Apr. 15, 1828; May 26, 1829.
177. *Ibid.,* Apr. 19, 1825; Dec. 31, 1827; June 28, Aug. 30, 1831; Aug. 28, 1832.
178. *Ibid.,* Feb. 15, 1836.
179. *Ibid.,* Aug. 24, 1835.
180. *Ibid.,* Nov. 9, 1835. Andrew Jackson visited Hartford in 1833 (*ibid.,* June 24, 1833), and Henry Clay was feted later the same year (*ibid.,* Nov. 11, 1833).
181. *Ibid.,* Sept. 7, 1824.

CHAPTER X

THE GOODWINS AND THE COURANT

1. The Goodwins conducted business under the name "George Goodwin & Sons" until November, 1822 (*Connecticut Courant,* Nov. 12, 19, 1822); as "George Goodwin" from November, 1822, to November, 1823 (*ibid.,* Nov. 18, 25, 1823); and as "Goodwin & Co." from November, 1823 until they sold the *Courant.*
2. George, Jr., was born in 1786 and graduated in 1806. Richard was born in 1782, graduated in 1807. Henry was born in 1793. James Junius Goodwin, *The Goodwins of Hartford, Connecticut* (Hartford, 1891), pp. 646, 652, 659.
3. Cf. *ante,* pp. 87–100, *passim.* Richard joined the firm in 1808. *Cour.,* Nov. 2, 1808.
4. "George Goodwin, Jr." (*Cour.,* July 11, 1810; Sept. 18, 1811); "George Goodwin, Jr. & Charles Goodwin" (*ibid.,* Oct. 9, 1811; Mar. 22, 1814); "Whiting & Goodwin" (*ibid.,* Nov. 26, 1806).
5. Goodwin, *Goodwins of Hartford,* p. 659; S. G. Goodrich, *Recollections of A Lifetime or Men and Things I Have Seen; in a Series of Familiar Letters to A Friend, Historical, Biographical, Anecdotical, and Descriptive* (New York, 1856), I, 410–411.
6. On the corner of Pratt and Main Streets. *Cour.,* Nov. 21, 1815; copy of letter from George Goodwin & Sons to Merchant Fire Insurance Co., Dec. 20, 1821 in George Goodwin & Sons, *Letter Books,* Vol. III, Connecticut Historical Society.
7. On arrangements for binding, cf. *post,* p. 179.
8. Copy of letter to James Olmstead, May 11, 1820. *Letter Books,* Vol. III.
9. Cf. *post,* p. 187.
10. Richard held the degree of M.A. from Yale College. *Catalogue of the*

Officers and Graduates of Yale University in New Haven, Connecticut (New Haven, 1924), p. 144.

11. *The Hartford Times,* Aug. 4, 1884.

12. Cf. *post,* p. 186.

13. Goodwin, *Goodwins of Hartford,* p. 656. Charles was still in other business late in 1817 (*Cour.,* July 2, 1816; Dec. 9, 1817) and apparently did not become a firm member for several years. Letters to John Mills, May 15, 1817 and Jonathan Seymour, Oct. 7, 1824 in *Letter Books,* Vols. II, IV. Edward, the youngest son, was graduated from Yale in 1823 and began the study of law at Litchfield when his father persuaded him to leave his studies, join the firm, and edit the paper. Goodwin, *Goodwins of Hartford,* p. 661. Both boys probably joined the firm in November, 1823, when the name "Goodwin & Co." appeared in the *Courant. Cour.,* Nov. 25, 1823.

14. William DeLoss Love, *The Colonial History of Hartford Gathered from the Original Records* (Hartford, 1914), p. 312 n.

15. In 1836 J. W. Barber thought that more books were published annually in Hartford than in any city of comparable size in the country. John Warner Barber, *Connecticut Historical Collections, Containing a General Collection of Interesting Facts, Traditions, Biographical Sketches, Anecdotes &c. Relating to the History and Antiquities of Every Town in Connecticut, with Geographical Descriptions* (New Haven, 1836), p. 33; cf. Thompson R. Harlow, *Early Hartford Printers* (Hartford, 1940), pp. 11–12. For newspapers and magazines, cf. *post,* pp. 179–180. In 1829 the Goodwins questioned whether any American city had more paper mills within a fifty-mile radius. Letter to Abijah L. Dunnell, Mar. 6, 1829. *Letter Books,* Vol. V.

16. *Cour.,* May 5, Sept. 15, 1818; Aug. 17, Dec. 7, 1819; Jan. 1, 1822.

17. Letters to Will E. Norman, Feb. 26, 1820; to Uriah C. Hatch, Dec. 9, 1821; and to Denis & Phelps, Feb. 27, 1822. *Letter Books,* Vol. III.

18. Letters to Messrs. Wells & Lilly, Mar. 2, 1816; to Durrie & Peck, Mar. 21, 1821; and to Rev. D. Catlin, Feb. 17, 1824. *Ibid.,* Vol. II, III, IV.

19. Letters to Uriah C. Hatch, Dec. 19, 1821; to Rev. J. S. Blake, Jan. 6, 1823; to Charles W. Whipple, July 8, 1824; and to Rev. Simeon Colton, July 28, 1824. *Ibid.,* Vols. III, IV; *Cour.,* Sept. 7, 1819, Sept. 16, 1823.

20. Letters to Sterling Woodford, July 4, 1828; to J. L. Cross, Feb. 26, 1830; and to E. M. Worthington, Aug. 21, 1834. *Letter Books,* Vols. V, VI.

21. Letter to Rev. R. R. Gurley, May 2, 1825. *Ibid.,* Vol. V. They had taken subscriptions earlier. *Cour.,* May 5, 1818.

22. *Cour.,* Sept. 28, 1830, Jan. 18, 1831; letter to E. M. Worthington, Aug. 21, 1834. *Letter Books,* Vol. VI.

23. The Goodwins obtained much of their book stock from printers and booksellers in other cities in exchange for their own publications. Hence, if the local market were poor, there would be less incentive to publish. Letters to Messrs. Wells & Lilly, Nov. 15 1815; to Jesse Bliss, Nov. 22, 24, 1815; to Samuel Greene, Dec. 21, 1815; to Caleb Bingham, Dec. 28, 1815; and to Thomas Dickman, Jan. 3, 1816. *Letter Books,* Vol. II. Letter to T. Grant, June 13, 1823. *Ibid.,* Vol. IV.

24. Letters to Messrs. Dodge & Sayer, Jan. 3, 1816; to Hezekiah Howe, Aug. 10, 1818; to Timothy Dwight, Dec. 10, 1818 and Dec. 25, 1821; to F. & R. Lockwood, July 1, 1823; and to Rev. John S. Blake, Jan. 8, July 10, 1824. *Ibid.,* Vols. II, III, IV; *Cour.,* June 9, 1818; Emily Ellsworth Fowler Ford (Emily Ellsworth Ford Skeel, ed.), *Notes on the Life of Noah Webster* (New York, 1912), II, 537; Albert Carlos Bates, *Check List of Connecticut Almanacs 1709–1850* (Worcester, 1914), pp. 88–96, *passim.*

25. Letter to Messrs. Wells & Lilly, Mar. 2, 1816. *Letter Books,* Vol. II. The firm of Durrie & Peck did the binding. Letters to Durrie & Peck. *Ibid.,* Vols. II, III, IV, V, *passim.*

26. Letter to T. Grant, June 13, 1823. *Ibid.,* Vol. IV. The best-known Hartford printers of the 1820's were Samuel G. Goodrich, Silas Andrus, David F. Robinson, O. D. Cooke, and H. & F. J. Huntington.

27. Letter to Benjamin Silliman, Sept. 4, 1823; to Robert Desilver, Sept. 16, 1823; to W. Hamlin, Sept. 30, 1823; to Cummings, Hilliard & Co., Jan. 2, 1824; to Russell Bronson, Jan. 3, 1824; to Rev. D. Catlin, Feb. 17, 1824; to Rev. Simeon Colton, June 3, 1824; to A. H. Maltby & Co., June 3, 1824. All in *ibid.,* Vol. IV. Letters to Wm. T. Turner, Sept. 9, 1826 (*ibid.,* Vol. V); and to A. Phelps, Sept. 30, 1833 (*ibid.,* Vol. VI). Exceptions are revealed in letters to Rev. D. Chapin, June 1, 1826, and to Durrie & Peck, Aug. 7, 1829. *Ibid.,* Vol. V. They printed *Beer's Almanac for 1825,* but none thereafter. Bates, *Check List,* pp. 96 ff.

28. Charles Hopkins Clark, "The Press, Newspapers, Publishing Houses, Etc.," *The Memorial History of Hartford County, Connecticut 1633–1884,* J. Hammond Trumbull, ed. (Boston, 1886), I, 612–613.

29. *Cour.,* Oct. 1, 1816. Letter to Samuel Greene, Jan. 3, 1817. *Letter Books,* Vol. II.

30. *Cour.,* Mar. 18, 1828; July 28, 1829; May 1, Sept. 18, 1832; Mar. 2, 1835; Clark, *loc. cit.,* I, 621; Winifred Gregory, ed., *American Newspapers 1821–1936 A Union List of Files Available in the United States and Canada* (New York, 1936), pp. 75–77. The *Independent Press* began on July 1, 1833 and absorbed the *Mercury.*

31. Clark, *loc. cit.,* I, 613–620, *passim.*

32. *Cour.,* Nov. 17, 1818. This was the longest and last series of didactic essays which the *Courant* printed. *Ibid.,* Apr. 5, 1815–Apr. 28, 1818.

33. *Ibid.,* Aug. 25, Nov. 17, 1818; Sept. 26, 1820.

34. *Ibid.,* Dec. 5, 1815.

35. The weekly column appeared from the beginning of 1817 (*ibid.,* Jan. 7, 1817) to the issue of Mar. 19, 1822, and in scattered issues thereafter until about 1825.

36. *Ibid.,* Nov. 30, 1824.

37. *Ibid.,* Jan. 7, 1817–Dec. 29, 1821, *passim.*

38. *Ibid.,* Nov. 23, 1824; Oct. 18, 1825; Dec. 25, 1832; Jan. 1, 22, Dec. 16, 1833; Feb. 10, 1834.

39. *Ibid.,* Apr. 2, 1816; Nov. 2, 1824.

40. *Ibid.,* Mar. 10, 1818; Oct. 20, 27, Nov. 3, 10, 1818; May 25, June 1, 8, 1830; May 10, 1831; May 29, June 5, Dec. 25, 1832. Also, letter to J. Barber, May 5, 1828. *Letter Books,* Vol. V.

41. *Cour.,* Mar. 16, 1819; Oct. 1, 8, 1827; Oct. 18, 1831; Feb. 28, Mar. 6, 1832; Mar. 5, May 14, Oct. 16, 1833; Mar. 2, 1835.

42. *Ibid.,* Nov. 13, 1821.

43. The "Almanac" appeared in *Cour.,* Jan. 4, 1814, and ran throughout the Goodwin period; the "Journal" started on Jan. 5, 1819, ran regularly for about three years, irregularly for three more, and then petered out.

44. *Cour.,* 1818–1836, *passim.*

45. Beginning on Aug. 8, 1828, it appeared frequently through the issues of 1832.

46. *Cour.,* 1818–1836, *passim.*

47. *Ibid.,* Feb. 4, 1823.

48. *Ibid.,* Sept. 16, 1828.

49. *Ibid.,* Aug. 20, Sept. 3, Nov. 5, 1822; Oct. 7, 1823.

50. *Ibid.,* Jan. 4, 1820; Jan. 9, 1821; Jan. 8, 1822; Jan. 6, 1824; Jan. 4, 1825; Jan. 18, 1836. The verses for Jan. 1, 1827 were printed on a separate sheet (in the *Cour.* files of the Connecticut Historical Society) as those for the missing years may possibly have been.

51. *Ibid.,* Jan. 12, 1819; Jan. 13, 1829; Jan. 11, 1831; Jan. 3, 1832; Jan. 8, 1833; Jan. 6, 1834; Jan. 5, 1835; Jan. 4, 1836.

52. Cf. *ante,* p. 6.

53. *Cour.,* Mar. 22, 1825.

54. *Idem.*

55. *Supplement to the Connecticut Courant.* The first number is dated Oct. 25, 1825. Volumes with very few numbers missing are in the library of the Connecticut Historical Society.

56. *Cour.,* Oct. 18, 1825. Letter to Elisha Swift, Dec. 8, 1825. *Letter Books,* Vol. V.

57. *Cour.,* Nov. 13, 1826; Sept. 24, 1827; Jan. 28, 1828; Oct. 27, Nov. 10, 1829; Jan. 4, July 12, 26, 1831; Jan. 3, 1832; Jan. 15, 1833.

58. *Ibid.,* Aug. 26, Dec. 30, 1828; May 5, Aug. 25, Oct. 20, Dec. 8, 1829; Aug. 17, Sept. 21, Dec. 28, 1830; Feb. 1, Nov. 29, 1831; Jan. 10, 24, Feb. 28, July 10, Aug. 21, 28, Sept. 4, 1832; Jan. 8, 1833–Sept. 12, 1836, *passim.*

59. *Supplement,* Sept. 17, 1827; Sept. 18, Oct. 8, 1832; Mar. 18, 1833; Apr. 27, June 15, 1835.

60. *Cour.,* Sept. 12, 1836. The *Courant,* 1814–1817, was about 14 x 18¾ inches (cf. *ante,* p. 128.) with 5 columns per page until Jan. 2, 1816, when the number of columns became 6. By 1826, the dimensions were 20 x 15 inches; by 1830, 21½ x 15 inches; 1831–1832, 22½ x 16¾ inches, still with 6 columns to the page; 1832–1836, the size and number of columns equaled that mentioned in the text.

61. Letters to D. & G. Bruce, Aug. 6, 1816 (*Letter Books,* Vol. II); to George Bruce, Oct. 10, 1822 (*ibid.,* Vol. IV); to Geo. Bruce, May 23, 1829 (*ibid.,* Vol. V); to James Ronaldson, Oct. 7, 23, Nov. 1, 1816 and Mar. 13, 1817 (*ibid.,* Vol. II); to E. White, Dec. 18, 1827 (*ibid.,* Vol. V); to Elihu White, Dec. 28, 1827 and Jan. 2, 1828 (*ibid.,* Vol. V) and Feb. 17, Mar. 7, 1831 (*ibid.,* Vol. VI); to White, Hagan & Co., July 28, 1834 (*ibid.,* Vol. VI). Frederick W. Hamilton, *Type and Presses in America A Brief Historical Sketch of the Development of Type Casting and Press Building in the United States* (Chicago, 1918), pp. 14–22.

62. Letters to Adam Ramage, Nov. 7, 1817; Mar. 12 and Apr. 27, 1818. *Letter Books,* Vol. II.

63. Letter to George Clymer, Nov. 1, 1815. *Ibid.,* Vol. II; *Cour.,* Feb. 13, 1816; Daniel Baker, *Platen Printing Presses A Primer of Information Regarding the History & Mechanical Construction of Platen Printing Presses, From the Original Hand Press to the Modern Job Press to Which is Added a Chapter on Automatic Presses of Small Size* (Chicago, 1918), pp. 3–4; *Dictionary of American Biography,* IV, 235–236.

64. *Cour.,* Mar. 11, Apr. 8, 1828.

65. Letter to Crocker & Brewster, May 30, 1832 (*Letter Books,* Vol. VI); to Greele & Willis, June 26, July 12, 1832 (*ibid.,* Vol. VI); *Dictionary of American Biography,* I, 71; Baker, *Platen Printing Presses,* p. 8–9.

66. Baker, *Platen Printing Presses,* p. 3; S. N. D. North, *History and Present Condition of the Newspapers and Periodical Press of the United States, with a Catalogue of the Publications of the Census Year* (Washington, 1884), p. 6.

67. Goodwin & Sons, *Account Books,* Vols. XIX–XXII, *passim,* CHS.

68. *Cour.,* June 16, 1818; May 17, 1825.

69. Letter to G. & R. Waite, Dec. 19, 1823. *Letter Books,* Vol. IV.

70. *Cour.,* Mar. 2, 1830; Sept. 12, 1836.

71. Letter to G. & R. Waite, Dec. 19, 1823 (*Letter Books,* Vol. IV); to Chas. Barrell, Oct. 17, 1828 (*ibid.,* Vol. V).

72. Letter to John Tallmadge, June 13, 1816 (*ibid.,* Vol. II); to S. & L. Hurlburt & Co., Jan. 23, 1832 (*ibid.,* Vol. VI).

73. Letters to Josiah C. Shaw, Nov. 28, 1817 and James Olmstead, June 29, 1818. *Ibid.,* Vol. II.

74. Letter to James Olmstead, Apr. 12, 1821. *Ibid.,* Vol. III; Goodwin, *Goodwins of Hartford,* p. 652.

75. Letter to Richardson & Lord, June 15, 1829. *Letter Books,* Vol. V. Letters to Erastus Ellsworth, Apr. 12, 1830; to Charles Goodwin, June 10, 1834; to Bennett & Walton, Feb. 11, 1833; to Francis Hamner, Sept. 20, 1833; to John Campbell & Co., July 7, 1835. All in *ibid.,* Vol. VI.

76. Letters to J. S. Kellogg & Co., Oct. 24, 1835; Nov. 22, Dec. 24, 1836; Jan. 24, 1837; to C. & W. H. Magarge, Nov. 6, 1835. *Ibid.,* Vol. VII; Letter to Abijah L. Dunnell, Mar. 6, 1829. *Ibid.,* Vol. V.

77. Letters to James Olmstead, Oct. 16, 1816; Apr. 12, 1821 (*ibid.,* Vols. II, III); to Jonathan Seymour, Mar. 20, 1820; June 20, 1823 (*ibid.,* Vols. III, IV); to J. Seymour & Son, Dec. 2, 1835 (*ibid.,* Vol. VII); to William Parker, Nov. 15, 1823 (*ibid.,* Vol. IV); to C. & W. H. Magarge, June 2, 1835 (*ibid.,* Vol. VI); to Campbell & Burns, June 24, 1835 (*ibid.,* Vol. VI).

78. *Cour.,* Dec. 26, 1815; Jan. 5, 1819.

79. Letters to Solomon Simpson, Oct. 10, 1822 and F. & R. Lockwood, Feb. 14, 1824 (*Letter Books,* Vol. IV); to Rev. Asabel Nettleton, Oct. 1, 1825 and M. M. Noah, May 26, 1828 (*ibid.,* Vol. V); to C. & W. H. Magarge, June 2, 1835 (*ibid.,* Vol. VI).

80. Letters to A. S. Beckwith, Aug. 5, 1828 and Geo. W. Callender, Feb. 3, 1829. *Ibid.,* Vol. V; *Cour.,* Sept. 28, 1830.

81. Letters to Gideon Hollister, Apr. 16, 1823 and Saml. Green, July 12, 1823 (*Letter Books,* Vol. IV); to Wm. Parker & Co., Sept. 9, 1826 (*ibid.,* Vol. V).

82. Letter to Jonathan Seymour, July 12, 1819 (*ibid.,* Vol. II); to James Olmstead, July 12, 1819; May 11, 1820; Apr. 12, 1821 (*ibid.,* Vols. II, III).

83. It saved the labor of about 12 girls and was patented in the name of the inventor on Jan. 13, 1829. Letter to Peter W. Gallandett, May 30, 1829 (*ibid.,* Vol. V); to Bennett & Walton, Mar. 4, 1833 (*ibid.,* Vol. VI).

84. Letter to Peter W. Gallandett, Aug. 7, 1829. *Ibid.,* Vol. V.

85. The machines were sold for $300. Letter to Asa Butler, June 20, 1829. *Ibid.,* Vol. V. Letters to S. & W. Meeteer, Feb. 17, 1832; to A. C. & W. Curtis, Nov. 25, 1831; to Bennett & Walton, Jan. 3, 1832; Mar. 4, 1833; to T. Crane, Apr. 23, May 16, 1833; to Mr. Donaghee, Nov. 11, 1834; to Messrs. Saflins, Dec. 22, 1834. All in *ibid.,* Vol. VI.

86. Letters to John H. Walsh, June 17, 1833; Feb. 4, 1835; Aug. 23, 1836; Feb. 17, 1837 (*ibid.,* Vols. VI, VII); to Allen Curtis, Feb. 4, 1835 (*ibid.,* Vol. VI); to John Carrington, Apr. 15, May 2, 1835; June 28, 1836 (*ibid.,* Vols. VI, VII); to A. E. Jessup, July 27, 1836; to H. V. Butler, Oct. 25, 1836; to Wm. L. Stone, Oct. 27, 1836; to Ely W. Blake, Nov. 9, 1837 (*ibid.,* Vol. VII).

87. Cf. *ante,* n. 77, n. 78.

88. They operated as two firms, Goodwin & Co. and H. & E. Goodwin. The latter was partly owned by Goodwin & Co. Letter to Abbot & Ely, May 29, 1838. *Letter Books,* Vol. VIII.

89. *Cour.,* Aug. 10, 1835.

90. *Resolves and Private Laws of the State of Connecticut,* I, 320; *Cour.,* June 11, 1816; May 27, 1833.

91. George served as trustee of the Society for Savings (*Cour.,* July 6, 1819; June 13, 1820) and was one of the incorporators (*Private Laws,* II, 1049-1051). Charles was a director of the Hartford Auxiliary Bible Society (*Cour.,* Sept. 3, 1816); he solicited funds for the Sunday School Society, was elected director and secretary, became superintendent of one of the four schools, helped establish a school for the Negro citizens (*ibid.,* Apr. 24, 1821; Z. Preston, *Statistics of the Hartford Sunday School Society, Organized May 5th, 1818* [Hartford, 1858],

pp. 6, 16–18); he is said to have started the Hartford branch of the Tract Society (Goodwin, *Goodwins of Hartford*, p. 656). Henry was on the list of incorporators of the Seminary (*Private Laws*, II, 1056–1058). All of them were among the incorporators of the school for the deaf and dumb. *Ibid.*, I, 320; *Cour.*, June 11, 1816.

92. Charles was a director from 1829 to 1835. Edward was one of the "Advisers" to the women officers of the Asylum. P. H. Woodward, *One Hundred Years of the Hartford Bank Now the Hartford National Bank of Hartford, Conn.* (Hartford, 1892), p. 168; *Hartford Orphan Asylum, 100th Anniversary 1833–1933* (Hartford, 1933), p. 25.

93. Goodwin, *Goodwins of Hartford*, pp. 644, 651, 656, 662; George Leon Walker, *History of the First Church in Hartford, 1633–1883* (Hartford, 1884), p. 415.

94. In 1835 or 1836 he helped J. W. Barber construct a dwelling map of Main Street at the time of the Revolution and Barber recorded that he began his apprenticeship with Green at the age of eight or nine years. Barber, *Historical Collections*, p. 49. He was born on Jan. 7, 1857 and began work in the office over the barber shop from which Green moved in May, 1765. Goodwin, *Goodwins of Hartford*, p. 640; cf. *ante*, p. 5. The *Courant* later stated that he was nine years of age. *Hartford Daily Courant*, May 14, 1844.

95. Goodwin, *Goodwins of Hartford*, p. 640.

96. Barber, *Historical Collections*, p. 49.

97. Goodwin, *Goodwins of Hartford*, pp. 643–644.

98. Clark, *loc. cit.*, I, 617. The passage cited was written for Clark by Frank L. Burr, brother of Alfred E. Burr. Also *Hartford Times*, Aug. 4, 1884.

99. *Hartford Daily Courant*, May 14, 1844. According to Joel Munsell, Albany printer: "Mr. Goodwin was yet hale and active when I knew him in Hartford in 1829, and for more than twelve years afterwards, was still in the habit . . . of walking to the printing office daily, and setting up paragraphs in type, to gratify long established habit." Isaiah Thomas, *The History of Printing in America, with a Biography of Printers and an Account of Newspapers* (Albany, 1874), II, 91 n.

100. *Conn. Cour.*, Jan. 6, 1844.

101. *Hart. Daily*, May 14, 1844.

102. *Ibid.*, May 20, 1844.

CHAPTER XI

CITY NEWSPAPER

1. *Hartford Daily Courant*, Aug. 1, 1854; *The Hartford Courant*, Oct. 25, 1914. He was born at Norwich, Connecticut, went to Hartford about 1822, and moved to Columbia, Pennsylvania in 1830. *The Columbia Spy and Literary Record* became the *Columbia Spy and Lancaster and York County Record* in 1831. He established the *Union* in 1834.

2. Cf. *ante*, pp. 187–188.

3. *Connecticut Courant*, Sept. 19, 1836.

4. Personal abuse was given to Henry A. Mitchell of the *Times* in *Conn. Cour.*, Jan. 6, Sept. 8, Dec. 22, 1838 and Feb. 23, 1839, but Boswell refrained thereafter. Alfred E. Burr left Boswell's employment in Jan. 1839 to become Mitchell's partner. Burr acquired full ownership of the *Times* in 1841 and wrote the editorials for many years. Boswell liked Burr. *Daily Courant*, Jan. 15, 1839; Charles Hopkins Clark, "The Press, Newspapers, Publishing Houses, Etc.," *The Memorial History of Hartford County Connecticut 1633–1884*, J. Hammond Trumbull, ed. (Boston, 1886), I, 617; cf. *post*, p. 199.

5. *Hart. Daily,* Aug. 1, 1854.
6. Changed from *Daily Courant* to *The Daily Courant* for a short time in 1838 and back to *Daily Courant* on Dec. 11 or 12, 1838. On Jan. 1, 1840, title became *Hartford Daily Courant.*
7. *Daily Courant,* Sept. 12, 1837. Hartford's first daily paper was the short-lived *New England Daily Review,* started in 1833 by Hanmer & Comstock. The daily edition of the *Times* appeared in 1841. Clark, *loc. cit.,* I, 615, 617; Winifred Gregory, *American Newspapers 1821–1936 A Union List of Files Available In the United States and Canada* (New York, 1936), p. 76.
8. *Daily Cour.,* Aug. 29, 1837. Congress was summoned to convene on Sept. 4.
9. *Idem; Conn. Cour.,* Sept. 9, 1837.
10. *Daily Cour.,* Dec. 13, 1837.
11. *Ibid.,* Jan. 3, 1838.
12. *Ibid.,* Sept. 12, 1837–Apr. 30, 1838.
13. *Ibid.,* Apr. 5, 1838.
14. *Conn. Cour.,* Nov. 10, 1838.
15. *Ibid.,* Apr. 18, 1840; *Daily Cour.,* Apr. 5, 1838; *Hart. Daily,* Nov. 8, 1848.
16. *Conn. Cour.,* Apr. 13, 1839.
17. *Daily Cour.,* Apr. 18, 1838.
18. *Ibid.,* Jan. 3, 1839.
19. *The Daily Courant,* Dec. 5, 1838.
20. *Conn. Cour.,* Aug. 20, 1842.
21. *Ibid.,* Sept. 9, 1837.
22. *Ibid.,* Sept. 16, 1837.
23. *The Daily Courant,* Dec. 6, 1838.
24. *Conn. Cour.,* June 5, 1841.
25. *Ibid.,* July 4, 1846. A person in New York had been hired to send him the news.
26. *Courant Extra,* Apr. 21, 1848.
27. *Hart. Daily,* Nov. 9, 1848.
28. *Ibid.,* Dec. 25, 1851.
29. *Ibid.,* Aug. 21, 1849 ff.
30. *Ibid.,* Jan. 2, 1854.
31. *Ibid.,* June 19, 1850.
32. *Ibid.,* July 26, 1850.
33. *Ibid.,* Jan. 3, 1852 ff.
34. *Ibid.,* Sept. 15, 1849.
35. *Conn. Cour.,* Nov. 9, 1839.
36. *Hart. Daily,* June 23, 24, 1851.
37. *Daily Cour.,* Nov. 10, 1837. *Conn. Cour.,* Dec. 1, 1838; Aug. 17, 1839; Aug. 2, 1845.
38. Cf. *post,* pp. 240 ff.
39. Published on Saturday (*Conn. Cour.,* Nov. 8, 1836); on Friday (*Hart. Daily,* Dec. 25, 1851); on Saturday (*Conn. Cour.,* 1861–1862).
40. Boswell removed the names of daily subscribers from the weekly list. *Daily Cour.,* Sept. 12, 1837. Similarity of content was generally true toward the end of the period. *Conn. Cour.,* 1861–1862. At that time the *Daily* contained virtually all that was published in the weekly plus the smaller local items which were not timely or of general interest to subscribers outside Hartford.
41. *Conn. Cour.,* Jan. 6, 1838; Jan. 5, 1839; Jan. 4, 1840; Jan. 9, 1841; Jan. 8, 1842; Jan. 6, 1844.
42. *Ibid.,* Oct. 8, 1842; Sept. 20–Oct. 11, 1845; Oct. 10–Nov. 21, 1846. *Hart. Daily,* Oct. 13–19, 1848; Oct. 15, 1849; Oct. 10, Nov. 7, 1850; Oct. 25, 1852; Oct. 12–14, 1853; Oct. 5, 23, 24, 1854.

43. *Conn. Cour.,* Nov. 10, Dec. 8, 1838; Mar. 30, Apr. 6, 20, May 11, July 27, Sept. 7, 14, 28, 1839; Apr. 16, 1842.

44. Cf. *post,* pp. 253–254.

45. Cf. *post,* chap. XIV.

46. Cf. *post,* p. 249.

47. *Hart. Daily,* Feb. 10, 1851–Feb. 18, 1852, *passim; Supplement to the Connecticut Courant,* Feb. 1, 1851–Mar. 6, 1852, *passim.* The essays were later published in book form. *Hart. Daily,* May 24, 1853.

48. *Hart. Daily,* Mar. 22, 1851.

49. *Ibid.,* Mar. 24, 1854.

50. Not printed in the *Courant. Ibid.,* Mar. 24, 1854.

51. Lydia Sigourney's poems are in scattered issues. Beginning in 1847 original literary essays appeared infrequently.

52. *Conn. Cour.,* June 5, Nov. 13, 1841; Feb. 12, 26, May 7, 1842.

53. *Ibid.,* Sept. 19, Oct. 17, 24, Nov. 28, 1846; *Hart. Daily,* Jan. 16, 18, 1847.

54. *Hart. Daily,* Jan. 1, 1850. Rates were approximately the same in 1839. *Daily Cour.,* Jan. 1, 1839. In 1845 the rate per square per year was reduced from $20.00 to $15.00. *Hart. Daily,* Dec. 4, 1844. In 1840 insertions in the weekly were 3 for $1.00 and $.20 thereafter. *Conn. Cour.,* Dec. 26, 1840; cf. *ante,* pp. 185–186.

55. *Conn. Cour.,* Aug. 26, 1837.

56. *Ibid.,* Apr. 25, 1840.

57. *Hart. Daily,* June 4, Nov. 10, 1853.

58. *Ibid.,* June 4, 10, 1853.

59. *Daily Cour.,* Mar. 30, 1838; *Hart. Daily,* Jan. 2, 1854.

60. *Hart. Daily,* Jan. 2, 1854.

61. In 1854 the *Daily* had 7 columns per page and measured 19 x 23½ inches. Dimensions in 1839 were approximately 14½ x 18 inches; in 1840, 15 x 20 inches; in 1847, 17½ x 22 inches. The price was reduced to $4.00 in 1845 (*Hart. Daily,* Dec. 4, 1844), and raised to $5.00 in 1850 (*ibid.,* Jan. 1, 1850).

62. *Conn. Cour.,* Dec. 4, 1841; *Hart. Daily,* Dec. 25, 1851. Boswell published a tri-weekly *Courant* on Tuesday, Thursday, and Saturday from the beginning of 1840 until sometime in July, 1841 which sold for $3.00. *Conn. Cour.,* Dec. 14, 1839; Jan. 4, 1840 ff.

63. *Conn. Cour.,* Nov. 24, 1838; Nov. 28, Dec. 19, 1840; June 21, 1845.

64. *Ibid.,* Feb. 3, 1838; June 20, 1840; Apr. 3, May 1, 1841; Jan. 8, Feb. 12, 1842; Jan. 17, Sept. 19, Oct. 17, 1846. *Hart. Daily,* Aug. 21, 1849; Dec. 25, 1851; Jan. 2, 1854.

65. Boswell's notarized statement is in *Conn. Cour.,* Oct. 17, 1846. For the three months before Sept. 22, the average figures were given as follows: *Daily* 720, and weekly 4,824. Boswell believed that the *Times,* his closest local competitor, printed about 500 daily and 3,600 weekly copies.

66. *Conn. Cour.,* Jan. 5, 12, 1839; Sept. 23, Oct. 7, 1843; June 21, 1845.

67. *Hart. Daily,* June 20, 1851.

68. Gregory, *Union List,* pp. 75–77; Clark, *loc. cit.,* I, 609–621.

69. The *Hartford Weekly Journal* and the *Hartford Evening Journal* were Whig papers established by Elihu Geer in 1843. The *Connecticut Whig* appeared in 1847; the *Daily Evening Whig* in 1848. *Conn. Cour.,* Nov. 4, 1843; Feb. 1, 1845. Gregory, *Union List,* pp. 76, 77; Clark, *loc. cit.,* I, 615.

70. *Daily Cour.,* Jan. 15, 1839; Clark, *loc. cit.,* I, 617.

71. Howard's name appeared from June, 1843 to August, 1844 (*Conn. Cour.,* June 24, 1843; *Hart. Daily,* Aug. 5, 1844); Smith's from April, 1847 to June, 1848 (*Hart. Daily,* Apr. 23, 1847; June 19, 1848).

72. The firm of "Boswell & Faxon." *Hart. Daily,* Jan. 1, 1850.

73. Faxon was a member of the firm which established the Republican daily

and weekly *Press* in 1856. Later he was chief clerk in the Department of the Navy under Gideon Welles, state bank commissioner in Connecticut for several years, and president of the Hartford Trust Company when he died in 1883. He was born on Apr. 17, 1822, and learned the printer's trade in the *Courant* office. *The Hartford Courant,* Oct. 25, 1914; Clark, *loc. cit.,* I, 609; George L. Faxon, *The History of the Faxon Family, Containing a Genealogy of the Descendants of Thomas Faxon of Braintree, Mass.* (Springfield, 1880), p. 261.

74. The *Daily* of Mar. 7, 1861, announced his resignation after almost 12 years with the *Courant.*

75. *Hart. Daily,* Dec. 29, 1864; Mar. 26, 1867. *Hart. Cour.,* Oct. 25, 1914; Julius Gay, *A Record of the Descendants of John Clark, of Farmington, Conn.* (Hartford, 1882), pp. 55, 71; Lafayette Case, *The Goodrich Family in America* (Chicago, 1889), p. 206.

76. *Hart. Daily,* July 31, 1854. He had worked in the office on the 25th.

77. *Ibid.,* Aug. 1, 1854.

78. *Ibid.,* Dec. 30, 1854; Jan. 1, 1855.

79. *Ibid.,* Jan. 1, 1855.

80. Cf. *post,* pp. 224 ff.

81. *Hart. Daily,* Jan. 1, 1855.

82. *Hart. Cour.,* Oct. 25, 1914; George E. Day, *A Genealogical Register of the Descendants in the Male Line of Robert Day of Hartford, Conn., Who Died in the Year 1648.* (New Haven, 1840), pp. 28–29. A nephew of Jeremiah Day who was President of Yale College from 1817 to 1846, he was born on Nov. 21, 1817 and died in 1905.

83. Cf. *post,* p. 225.

84. Appeared each Friday from Jan. 1 to July 1, 1855, and in the following issues: Feb. 26, Apr. 4, May 8, June 5, July 3, Aug. 20, Dec. 31, 1857; Feb. 12, Mar. 26, May 13, Aug. 20, Sept. 22, Nov. 18, 1858; Feb. 3, Mar. 31, June 2, Aug. 18, Oct. 27, Dec. 29, 1859; Feb. 23, Mar. 23, July 19, Oct. 12, 1860; Feb. 7, Aug. 29, Nov. 21, 1861; Feb. 27, 1862.

85. Large advertising cuts were discarded by Boswell in 1854. *Hart. Daily,* Jan. 2, 1854. Day continued to print the annual calendar or "Counting House Almanac" on or about the first of January.

86. The *Daily* appeared in new brevier and nonpareil on Apr. 2, 1855. New fonts of copper-faced type were put into use on Apr. 25, 1859. Other papers commented on the *Courant's* typographical excellence. *Hart. Daily,* Dec. 17, 1859.

87. *Hart. Daily,* Apr. 25, 1859.

88. Hotchkiss succeeded Burr in 1863. *Ibid.,* May 19, 1863; *Hart. Cour.,* Oct. 25, 1914.

89. Cf. *post,* p. 267. Murders, bank robbery, court trials are reported in issues of Mar. 14, 15, 1859; Nov. 7–21, 1861; May 6–9, Sept. 20, 1862.

90. *Hart. Daily,* Sept. 24, 1860.

91. *Ibid.,* Aug. 8, 1863.

92. *Ibid.,* Dec. 22, 1863; Dec. 21, 1864.

93. *Ibid.,* Apr. 15, 1863.

94. *Ibid.,* Apr. 23, 1861.

95. *Ibid.,* Aug. 26, 1861; Mar. 21, 1863; Mar. 26, 1864.

96. *Ibid.,* July 7, Aug. 22, 1862; May 14, June 24, 1863.

97. *Courant Extra,* May 23, 1863.

98. *Hart. Daily,* May 11, 1863.

99. *Ibid.,* May 19, 1864. The proclamation declared Grant's Virginia campaign a failure, called for 100,000 additional troops. The *Times* published an extra.

100. *Hart. Daily,* May 12, 1862; Dec. 26, 1864; Apr. 10, 1865.

101. *Ibid.,* Jan. 31, 1855.

102. *Ibid.,* Aug. 6–20, 1858; July 30, Aug. 1, 1866.

103. *Ibid.,* Oct. 31, Nov. 6, 7, 12, 1860. Similar arrangements were made for the national elections of 1856 and 1864. *Ibid.,* Dec. 12, 1856; Nov. 7, 1864.

104. *Ibid.,* Dec. 2, 1862.

105. The dailies are mentioned below. Counting a German language paper and three religious journals, Kenny recorded 11 weeklies published in Hartford in 1861. Daniel J. Kenny, *The American Newspaper Directory and Record of the Press* (New York, 1861), p. 11.

106. Frank L. Burr joined the firm in 1854. Clark, *loc. cit.,* I, 618. In 1862 the *Courant* claimed a city circulation of 600 more than the *Times.*

107. *Hartford Daily Post* and *Hartford Weekly Post. Hart. Daily,* Apr. 12, 1858; Clark, *loc. cit.,* I, 611; Gregory, *Union List,* p. 76.

108. *Connecticut Press* and *Hartford Evening Press,* published by Faxon and Pierce. Each of the citizens subscribed $100. Clark, *loc. cit.,* I, 609.

109. Hawley wrote editorials and became one of the publishers in 1857. Warner joined the staff as assistant editor in 1860; Hubbard, as editor, in 1861. Clark, *loc. cit.,* I, 609–611; *Hart. Cour.,* Oct. 25, 1914.

110. *Hart. Daily,* Jan. 31, 1855; Jan. 4, Dec. 12, 1856; Jan. 14, 1858; Apr. 25, 1859; Oct. 20, 1860; May 11, 1861; Jan. 8, Dec. 29, 1862; Jan. 1, Oct. 29, 1864.

111. *Ibid.,* May 11, 1861.

112. *Ibid.,* May 11, June 14, 1861.

113. *Ibid.,* May 11, 1861; Jan. 8, Dec. 29, 1862; Nov. 30, 1863.

114. *Ibid.,* Dec. 29, 1864.

115. Enlargements were made in Jan. 1861 and Jan. 1864. *Ibid.,* Jan. 1, 1861; Nov. 30, 1863. After Day retired, Clark enlarged the paper to 21 x 26½ inches, allegedly the largest daily in New England with a single exception in Boston. The number of columns to the page was increased from 7 to 8. *Ibid.,* Apr. 3, 1865.

116. *Ibid.,* July 8, 1857; Apr. 9, May 7, 1859; Jan. 7, 8, 10, 18, Mar. 10, 22, Apr. 2, June 4, 20, July 17, Oct. 20, 1862.

117. References to rising cost of paper are in issues of Dec. 2, 5, 17, 29, 1862; Jan. 21, 1863; July 1, 1864. Advertisement rates are in Dec. 12, 1862; Jan. 1, Apr. 4, Dec. 31, 1864. Changed subscription rates are in Dec. 5, 1862 and July 1, Dec. 19, 31, 1864.

118. *Ibid.,* Dec. 31, 1864.

119. *Ibid.,* Dec. 19, 31, 1864.

120. *Ibid.,* Nov. 25, 1856; Dec. 15, 1862; Apr. 4, Dec. 31, 1864.

121. *Ibid.,* Dec. 19, 1864.

122. The *Courant* was published by "Day & Clark" beginning on Jan. 1, 1857. Day's valedictory and Clark's salutatory were in the daily of Dec. 29, 1864. With the issue of Dec. 31, 1864, the firm name was "A. N. Clark & Co."

123. *Ibid.,* Dec. 29, 1864.

124. The excerpt below places Brace and Hotchkiss together as editorial writer and city editor, but Brace left the *Courant* in March, 1861, and Hotchkiss became city reporter in 1863. The Adams press was superseded by the Hoe in June, 1861. *Ibid.,* Mar. 7, June 14, 1861; May 19, 1863; account by P. Henry Woodward in *Hart. Cour.,* Oct. 25, 1914.

125. For the office and press, cf. *ante,* pp. 136, 185.

126. *Hart. Cour.,* Oct. 25, 1914.

127. The facsimile was printed on paper designed to resemble the original. Whether intentionally or by accident, it could be distinguished by the appearance of the modern rather than the old style *s* in the word "Thanksgiving" near the end of the paper.

128. Size was 22 x 28 inches. Cf. *ante,* p. 5.

129. *Hart. Daily,* Oct. 29, 1864.

CHAPTER XII

WHIG POLITICS

1. *Connecticut Courant,* Nov. 26, 1836.
2. *Ibid.,* Apr. 8–July 29, 1837, *passim.*
3. *Ibid.,* Aug. 12, Sept. 16, 1837. Cf. *ante,* p. 148.
4. Cf. *ante,* p. 154; *Conn. Cour.,* Sept. 23, 1837.
5. *Ibid.,* Nov. 21, 1840; cf. *ante,* p. 157.
6. *Conn. Cour.,* June 9, 1838.
7. *Ibid.,* Aug. 5, Sept. 9, 16, 1837; Feb. 3, 17, Sept. 8, Nov. 24, Dec. 22, 29, 1838; Jan. 5, 26, July 20, 1839; June 27, July 11, Aug. 8, 1840.
8. *Ibid.,* Sept. 16, 1837; June 27, 1840.
9. *Ibid.,* Aug. 5, Sept. 9, 1837; Feb. 3, 1838.
10. *Ibid.,* Aug. 3, 10, Oct. 9, 1839.
11. *Ibid.,* Aug. 8, 15, 1840.
12. *Ibid.,* Jan. 7, 14, Feb. 11, Mar. 4, 25, 1837; Feb. 3, 1838; Jan. 12, 19, 26, Apr. 20, Aug. 31, 1839; Jan. 4, Feb. 22, Aug. 8, 1840; Jan. 2, 9, 1841.
13. *Ibid.,* Jan. 16, 1841.
14. *Ibid.,* Aug. 31, 1839.
15. *Ibid.,* Jan. 7, 1837; Jan. 30, 1841.
16. *Ibid.,* Aug. 8, 1840.
17. The slogan in the state campaign of 1838. *Ibid.,* Mar. 3, 1838.
18. *Ibid.,* Apr. 7, 1838; Apr. 6, 1839; Apr. 11, 1840.
19. *Ibid.,* Jan. 6, 13, Aug. 25, Sept. 1, 8–29, Nov. 10, 17, 1838; Feb. 23–Apr. 6, 1839; July 4, 11, 1840.
20. *Ibid.,* Jan. 6, Dec. 22, 1838; Feb. 16, 23, 1839. Cf. *ante,* p. 193.
21. *Conn. Cour.,* Mar. 11, Oct. 21, 28, 1837; Jan. 20, 1838.
22. *Ibid.,* Oct. 19, 1839; July 11, 18, Aug. 1, 1840.
23. *Ibid.,* Aug. 1, 8, 1840.
24. *Ibid.,* Dec. 14, 1839; May 30, June 6, 13, 20, July 4, 11, Oct. 10, 1840.
25. *Ibid.,* June 20, 1840.
26. *Ibid.,* July 11, 1840.
27. *Ibid.,* Apr. 25, July 18, 25, 1840.
28. *Ibid.,* Dec. 14, 1839–Oct. 31, 1840, *passim.*
29. *Ibid.,* July 11, 1840.
30. *Ibid.,* June 20, 1840.
31. *Ibid.,* Mar. 6, 1841.
32. *Ibid.,* Apr. 10, 1841.
33. *Ibid.,* May 15, 1841.
34. *Ibid.,* June 19, 1841.
35. *Ibid.,* Oct. 30, Nov. 13, 1841. Tariff editorials began a steady run in October.
36. *Ibid.,* Nov. 13, Dec. 25, 1841; Jan. 1, Sept. 17, 1842.
37. *Ibid.,* Dec. 25, 1841; Sept. 23, 1842.
38. *Ibid.,* Jan. 1, Dec. 10, 1842.
39. *Ibid.,* Sept. 17, 1842.
40. *Ibid.,* Jan. 30, 1841; Mar. 5, 1842.
41. *Ibid.,* Sept. 11, 1841.
42. *Ibid.,* Nov. 13, 1841.
43. *Ibid.,* Jan. 5, 1842.
44. *Ibid.,* Jan. 29, Feb. 26, 1842.
45. *Ibid.,* Sept. 17, 24, 1842; Aug. 5–Nov. 4, 1843, *passim.*
46. News of the *Extra* was published in weekly issue of Aug. 21, 1841.
47. *Conn. Cour.,* Sept. 4, 1841.
48. *Idem.*

49. *Ibid.*, Sept. 11, Oct. 23, Nov. 6, 1841. Daniel Webster was commended for staying on as Secretary of State. *Ibid.*, Sept. 18, 1841.

50. *Ibid.*, Aug. 13, 20, 1842.

51. *Ibid.*, May 27, 1843.

52. *Ibid.*, Nov. 18, 1843.

53. *Ibid.*, Sept. 27, 1844.

54. *Ibid.*, Aug. 19, 1837; Aug. 5, 1843. *Hartford Daily Courant*, Oct. 1, Nov. 11, 1844.

55. *Hart. Daily*, Oct. 1, 1844.

56. *Conn. Cour.*, Oct. 22, 1842; *Hart. Daily*, Aug. 29, 1844.

57. *Hart. Daily*, Oct. 2, 1844.

58. *Conn. Cour.*, July 30, 1842.

59. *Ibid.*, Mar. 19, 1842.

60. *Ibid.*, Dec. 10, 24, 31, 1842; Jan. 7, 28, Apr. 1, 1843.

61. In the annual state elections from 1841 to 1844.

62. *Conn. Cour.*, Apr. 9, 1842; Apr. 8, 1843.

63. *Hart. Daily*, Apr. 2, 3, 1844.

64. The *Courant's* election campaign lasted one year. *Conn. Cour.*, Nov. 18, 1843 ff. and daily issues to Nov. 5, 1844.

65. *Hart. Daily*, Oct. 15, 24, 1844.

66. *Ibid.*, Oct. 7–30, 1844, *passim.*

67. *Ibid.*, Nov. 11–13, 1844.

68. Bank and currency editorials virtually disappeared after the election of 1844. On the Independent Treasury bill in 1846, an editorial said: "The freemen of this country will brook no such outrage, repeated after they have thundered their verdict against it. Down with the odious project." *Conn. Cour.*, Apr. 11, 1846.

69. Cf. *post*, pp. 220–221.

70. *Conn. Cour.*, Feb. 28, Aug. 8, 15, 1846.

71. *Ibid.*, Jan. 3, 1846.

72. *Hart. Daily*, Apr. 26, 29, 1844.

73. *Conn. Cour.*, Feb. 1, 1845.

74. *Ibid.*, June 28, 1845.

75. *Ibid.*, Sept. 6, 1845.

76. *Ibid.*, June 6, 1846.

77. *Ibid.*, Aug. 22, 1846.

78. *Ibid.*, Aug. 8, Sept. 12, Oct. 3, 1846; *Hart. Daily*, Jan. 5, 11, 21, 27, 1847.

79. *Conn. Cour.*, Nov. 28, 1846.

80. *Ibid.*, Dec. 26, 1846; *Hart. Daily*, Jan. 2, 1847.

81. *Hart. Daily*, Jan. 13, 20, 30, Feb. 3, 18, Mar. 2, 1847.

82. *Ibid.*, Jan. 21, Mar. 24, 1847.

83. *Ibid.*, July 24, Aug. 7, 25, 1847; Jan. 12, 1848.

84. *Ibid.*, June 26, 1847.

85. *Ibid.*, Aug. 25, 1847.

86. *Ibid.*, Jan. 11, 13, 14, 18, 21, 27, Feb. 12, 15–18, 22, Mar. 10, 17, Apr. 22, July 24, Oct. 26, Nov. 11, 1847; Feb. 24, 1848.

87. *Ibid.*, Jan. 21, Feb. 16, Oct. 26, 1847.

88. *Ibid.*, Feb. 17, 1847.

89. *Ibid.*, Mar. 10, 1847.

90. *Ibid.*, Apr. 22, Nov. 11, 1847.

91. *Ibid.*, Sept. 14, 1847. The *Courant* fought for Negro suffrage in Connecticut. *Ibid.*, Sept. 14, 29, Oct. 6, 7, 29, 1847.

92. *Ibid.*, Jan. 14, 15, 20, June 10, July 15, 1848.

93. *Ibid.*, July 15, Aug. 5, 1848.

94. *Ibid.*, July 20, 27, Aug. 5, Sept. 19, Nov. 6, 1848.

95. *Ibid.*, Aug. 16, 1848.

96. *Ibid.,* Aug. 5, 10, Oct. 17, 1848.
97. *Ibid.,* Oct. 4, 1848.
98. *Ibid.,* July 19–Nov. 8, 1848.
99. *Ibid.,* Feb. 16, July 24, Aug. 25, 1847; July 1, 1848; Jan. 24, 1850.
100. *Ibid.,* Oct. 26, 1847; Feb. 24, 1848.
101. *Ibid.,* Apr. 15, Sept. 4, 1847.
102. *Ibid.,* Jan. 30, Feb. 20, 26, Mar. 2, 1850.
103. *Ibid.,* Jan. 30, 1850.
104. *Ibid.,* July 24, Sept. 4, Oct. 26, 1847; Apr. 20, 1848; Jan. 24, 1850.
105. *Ibid.,* Apr. 15, 1847; July 1, 1848; Nov. 22, Dec. 8, 1849; Feb. 19, Apr. 3, 18, 1850.
106. *Ibid.,* Jan. 15, 1850.
107. *Ibid.,* Mar. 12, 1850.
108. *Ibid.,* Mar. 12, 18, 19, Apr. 5, 18, 20, 1850.
109. *Ibid.,* May 7, 1850.
110. *Ibid.,* May 15, 1850.
111. *Ibid.,* Dec. 27, 30, 1848.
112. *Ibid.,* Nov. 28, 1849; Jan. 24, Feb. 9, 19, Mar. 9, June 6, 1850.
113. *Ibid.,* Mar. 9, 1850.
114. *Ibid.,* Jan. 26, June 18, 1850.
115. *Ibid.,* Feb. 9, 19, 1850.
116. *Ibid.,* July 3, 30, Aug. 5, 1850.
117. *Ibid.,* Aug. 12, 14, 15, 20, Sept. 9, 12, 13, Oct. 4, Dec. 28, 1850.
118. *Ibid.,* Oct. 14, 15, 1850.
119. *Ibid.,* Aug. 5, 1850.
120. Tariff editorials had not disappeared during the crisis (for example, *ibid.,* Sept. 6, 1849; Feb. 28, May 1, 14, June 10, 20, July 8, 1850), but their frequency increased afterward. When the discussion of the Nebraska Bill filled the papers in 1854, they dwindled away.
121. *Ibid.,* Nov. 22, 1850; Apr. 30, Aug. 27, 1851; Jan. 10, 17, 1852; Jan. 24, 1853.
122. *Ibid.,* Dec. 9, 1851–July 16, 1852.
123. *Ibid.,* Sept. 27, 1849; Apr. 21, May 7, 14, Sept. 6–20, 1851; Nov. 24, 1852; Jan. 21, 1853.
124. *Ibid.,* May 3, 19, 1852.
125. *Ibid.,* Mar. 19, Apr. 18, 1853.
126. *Ibid.,* Aug. 19, 1850; Jan. 20, Aug. 5, Nov. 10, Dec. 4, 1850; also, Dec. 22, 1848; May 11, 29, 1850.
127. *Ibid.,* May 20, Aug. 20, Nov. 13, 1851; Nov. 12, 17, 1853. Later comments are in issues of Sept. 26, Nov. 17, 23, 1854.
128. *Ibid.,* Dec. 6, 12, 1848.
129. *Ibid.,* Apr. 16, Oct. 22, 1850; Jan. 16, 1851; May 24, 1852; Jan. 3, Feb. 3, Mar. 1, 7, May 23, Aug. 6, Sept. 8, 1853.
130. *Ibid.,* Feb. 2, May 1, Sept. 5, Oct. 7, 1850; May 20, Nov. 16, 1852.
131. *Ibid.,* Mar. 15, 1852.
132. *Ibid.,* May 1, Sept. 25, 1850; Mar. 15, 1852.
133. *Ibid.,* June 7, 1852.
134. *Ibid.,* Oct. 11, 13, 1852.
135. *Ibid.,* Apr. 6, 1852.
136. *Ibid.,* June 7, Oct. 13, Nov. 3, 1852; Mar. 14, 1853.

CHAPTER XIII

REPUBLICANISM AND SLAVERY

1. *Hartford Daily Courant,* Jan. 7, 9, 12, 17, 27, Feb. 1, 6, 8, 11, 16, 20, 23, 28, Mar. 2, 8, 18, 20, 21, 24, May 16, 20, 1854.

2. *Ibid.*, Feb. 8, 1854.
3. *Ibid.*, Feb. 8, 11, 1854. Most of Connecticut's leading Democratic papers supported the administration. *Ibid.*, Mar. 20, 1854.
4. *Ibid.*, Feb. 22–25, 1854.
5. *Ibid.*, Mar. 7–9, 1854.
6. *Ibid.*, Apr. 5, 1854.
7. *Ibid.*, May 24, 1854.
8. Boswell died on July 31, 1854, but the *Courant* underwent no significant change of view until Jan. 1, 1855.
9. *Hart. Daily,* Aug. 30, Oct. 4, Dec. 28, 1850; Mar. 6, 1851.
10. *Ibid.*, May 30, 1854.
11. *Ibid.*, June 26, July 3, 25, 1854.
12. *Ibid.*, June 1, July 18, 1854.
13. *Ibid.*, Aug. 31, 1854.
14. *Ibid.*, June 21, July 4, 28, Aug. 22, 1854.
15. *Ibid.*, July 22, 1854.
16. *Ibid.*, June 23, Nov. 16, 1854.
17. *Ibid.*, July 4, 1854.
18. *Ibid.*, Jan. 1, 1855.
19. *Ibid.*, Jan. 6, 1855 ff.
20. *Ibid.*, Jan. 10, 31, Feb. 6, 7, 9, Mar. 20, Apr. 5, 7, July 25, Sept. 5, 26, Nov. 5, Dec. 14, 1855; Jan. 8, 10, 15, Apr. 18, 1856.
21. *Ibid.*, Feb. 9, Apr. 5, Aug. 1, Nov. 7, Dec. 18, 1855.
22. *Ibid.*, Apr. 16, 1855.
23. *Ibid.*, Mar. 14–Apr. 5, 1855.
24. *Ibid.*, June 18–25, 1855.
25. *Ibid.*, Feb. 29, 1856.
26. *Ibid.*, Nov. 15, 23, 1855.
27. *Ibid.*, Nov. 23, 1855; Jan. 12, 1856.
28. *Ibid.*, Mar. 13, 1856.
29. Platforms of the Connecticut American party supported the protective tariff and demanded the nonextension of slavery. *Ibid.*, June 29, Nov. 15, 1855.
30. He praised the address issued by the first Republican national convention at Pittsburgh in February, 1856. *Ibid.*, Mar. 3, 1856.
31. The *Courant*'s campaign was conducted primarily against the re-election of Democratic Senator Isaac Toucey who had voted for the Kansas-Nebraska Bill. *Ibid.*, Aug. 30, 1855; Mar. 12, 15, 1856.
32. Day devoted his time to writing editorials against Catholicism and defending the state liquor prohibition law in preparation for the April election. For the *Courant*'s prohibition views, cf. *post,* pp. 253–255.
33. *Hart. Daily,* Apr. 9, 21, 28, 1855.
34. *Ibid.*, Aug. 30, 1855.
35. *Ibid.*, July 18, Oct. 23, Nov. 14, 1855; Feb. 1, 14, 15, 22, 1856.
36. *Ibid.*, Feb. 26, 1856.
37. *Ibid.*, June 19, 1856. Day's feelings were running high. On June 6, he signed the summons for a public meeting to denounce the assault on Charles Sumner.
38. *Ibid.*, Mar. 6, 1856.
39. *Ibid.*, June 19, 1856.
40. *Ibid.*, June 23, 1856.
41. *Ibid.*, June 7, July 2, 1856.
42. *Ibid.*, Aug. 5, 16, Sept. 13, 1856.
43. *Ibid.*, June 7, Aug. 1, 7, 16, Sept. 13, 1856.
44. *Ibid.*, Oct. 29, 1856.
45. *Ibid.*, Oct. 27, 1856.

46. *Ibid.,* Oct. 2, 1856. Anti-Irish editorials all but disappeared in the summer of 1856 and were exceptional thereafter.

47. *Ibid.,* July 4–Nov. 4, 1856, *passim.*

48. *Ibid.,* Oct. 2, 1856.

49. *Ibid.,* Aug. 4, 6, 7, Sept. 1, 3, 17, 23, 24, 1856.

50. *Ibid.,* July 30, 31, Aug. 2, 30, 1856.

51. *Ibid.,* June 24, July 31, 1856.

52. *Ibid.,* Aug. 4, 1856.

53. *Ibid.,* Nov. 4, 1856.

54. *Ibid.,* Nov. 18, 26, 1856; Feb. 12, 1857.

55. *Ibid.,* Mar. 10, 12, 14, 16, 17, 26, 30, 1857.

56. *Ibid.,* Dec. 29, 1857.

57. *Ibid.,* Jan. 14, Mar. 27, 29, 1858.

58. *Ibid.* Jan. 2, Nov. 15, 1858.

59. *Ibid.,* Mar. 3, 1858.

60. *Ibid.,* May 7, 1858.

61. *Ibid.,* Aug. 26–Oct. 28, 1857, *passim;* Dec. 21, 26, 1857; Jan. 12, Feb. 27, May 1, 15, July 9, Sept. 24, Oct. 20, 1858.

62. *Ibid.,* Sept. 21, 1859.

63. *Ibid.,* Aug. 6, Nov. 13, 14, 25, 1857.

64. *Ibid.,* Mar. 14, 1860.

65. *Ibid.,* Oct. 6, 1858; Mar. 10, 1859; Mar. 7, 1860.

66. *Ibid.,* Mar. 21, 1857.

67. *Ibid.,* Oct. 22, Nov. 8, 1859.

68. *Ibid.,* Oct. 31, Nov. 3–5, Dec. 16, 1859.

69. *Ibid.,* Nov. 9, 11, 19, 29, Dec. 16, 1859.

70. *Ibid.,* Dec. 2, 1859.

71. *Ibid.,* Dec. 10, 13, 15, 16, 1859.

72. *Ibid.,* Nov. 8, Dec. 2, 1859.

73. *Ibid.,* Nov. 15, 1859; Jan. 17, 21, 24, Feb. 27, 1860.

74. *Ibid.,* Mar. 6, 1860.

75. *Ibid.,* May 19, 23, 24, 30, 1860.

76. *Ibid.,* Apr. 8, 1857; Apr. 6, 1858; Apr. 5, 1859; Apr. 3, 1860.

77. *Ibid.,* Jan. 27, May 29, Aug. 28, Oct. 8, 30, 1858; Jan. 18, Mar. 25, 1859.

78. *Ibid.,* Jan. 26–Nov. 7, 1860, *passim.*

79. *Ibid.,* Dec. 16, 17, 26, 29, 1859; Jan. 5, 10, 18, 25, Feb. 1, Mar. 24, 1860; and scattered issues following.

80. *Ibid.,* Sept. 26, 1860.

81. *Ibid.,* Nov. 6, 1860.

82. *Ibid.,* Jan. 5, Nov. 2, 1860.

83. *Ibid.,* Nov. 2, 1860.

84. *Ibid.,* Dec. 17, 1859; July 27, Sept. 7, Oct. 31, 1860.

85. *Ibid.,* June 27, 1860.

86. *Ibid.,* Sept. 25, 1860.

87. *Ibid.,* June 27, July 9, Sept. 25, 27, 1860. In 1858 the *Courant* thought the Illinois Republicans had made a mistake by not endorsing Douglas for the Senate. Day believed that this would have detached the anti-Lecompton Democrats from the administration party, hence eliminating Douglas' chances for the presidency. *Ibid.,* Oct. 8, 15, 1858.

88. *Ibid.,* May 11, June 27, Oct. 1, 1860.

89. *Ibid.,* Aug. 30, Sept. 8, 1860.

90. *Ibid.,* Sept. 11, Oct. 10, 11, 1860.

91. *Ibid.,* Oct. 10, 30, 1860.

92. *Ibid.,* July 10, 12, 28, Sept. 17, Nov. 1, 7, 1860.

93. *Ibid.,* Sept. 29–Nov. 7, 1860.

94. *Ibid.,* May 1–Nov. 7, 1860, *passim.*
95. *Ibid.,* July 17, 1860.
96. *Ibid.,* Nov. 7, 15, 1860.
97. *Ibid.,* Nov. 10, 17, 1860.
98. *Ibid.,* Jan. 9, 12, 16, 21, 1861.
99. *Ibid.,* Feb. 9, 19, 22, 23, 1861.
100. *Ibid.,* Mar. 2, 15, 1861. The day before the *Courant* announced the attack on Fort Sumter, an editorial spoke favorably of a growing sentiment to avoid civil war by recognizing the Confederacy. *Ibid.,* Apr. 12, 1861.

CHAPTER XIV

RAILROADS, INDUSTRY, AND CULTURE

1. John Warner Barber, *Connecticut Historical Collections, Containing a General Collection of Interesting Facts, Traditions, Biographical Sketches, Anecdotes, &c. Relating to the History and Antiquities of Every Town in Connecticut, with Geographical Descriptions* (New Haven, 1836), pp. 32–33.
2. Cf. *ante,* pp. 169–174.
3. *Connecticut Courant,* May 13, 1837.
4. *Ibid.,* Dec. 21, 1839.
5. *Ibid.,* Dec. 5, 12, 26, 1840; Mar. 6, Oct. 2, 9, 1841.
6. *Hartford Daily Courant,* Dec. 3, 1844.
7. *Conn. Cour.,* May 10–Dec. 20, 1845, *passim.*
8. *Ibid.,* May 24, June 14, 28, July 5, 12, 19, 26, 1845.
9. *Ibid.,* June 14, 1845.
10. *Ibid.,* June 27, 1846.
11. *Ibid.,* July 4, 1846; *Hart. Daily,* July 10, 1847.
12. *Conn. Cour.,* June 13–July 7, 1846. *Hart. Daily,* Jan. 13, 19, 22, June 1–July 23, 1847, *passim;* June 3, 22, July 7, 11, 1848; Apr. 19, 1850.
13. *Conn. Cour.,* June 13, 1846.
14. *Ibid.,* June 13, 27, July 4, 1846; *Hart. Daily,* July 1, 1847.
15. *Hart. Daily,* June 22, July 11, 1848.
16. *Conn. Cour.,* Nov. 4, 1843.
17. *Idem.*
18. *Hart. Daily,* Feb. 3, 1844.
19. Cf. *ante,* pp. 4–5, 18–19, 169–174.
20. *Conn. Cour.,* Nov. 4, 1843; Jan. 1, July 12, 19, 1845. *Hart. Daily,* May 17, 1844; Jan. 11, 1845.
21. *Conn. Cour.,* July 19, 1845.
22. *Ibid.,* July 5, 19, 1845.
23. Letter by "A Steam Cotton Mill." *Ibid.,* Feb. 21, 1846.
24. *Ibid.,* July 5, 1845.
25. *Hart. Daily,* Oct. 23, 1847.
26. *Conn. Cour.,* July 12, 19, 26, 1845; Feb. 21, 28, Mar. 7, 14, 1846.
27. *Ibid.,* July 5, 1845.
28. *Ibid.,* Mar. 7, 1846.
29. *Hart. Daily,* Jan. 23, 1847.
30. *Ibid.,* Feb. 2, 1847.
31. *Ibid.,* Sept. 28, 1849. Editorial comment on local "prosperity" is in daily issues of Aug. 28, Oct. 10, 20, Nov. 6, 1849; Jan. 4, Mar. 6, 1850.
32. *Ibid.,* Nov. 13, 1849.
33. *Ibid.,* Dec. 22, 1849; Dec. 15, 1850.
34. *Ibid.,* May 13, 1850.
35. *Ibid.,* May 22, 25, June 1, 1850.

36. *Ibid.*, May 25, 1850.
37. *Ibid.*, Sept. 15, 1849, May 25, 1850.
38. *Ibid.*, July 17, 1850.
39. *Ibid.*, Dec. 16, 1850.
40. *Ibid.*, Nov. 27, 1848; Sept. 28, 1849; Sept. 4, 1851.
41. *Ibid.*, Sept. 28, Nov. 14, 1849; Mar. 11, 1850; Sept. 4, 1851; Apr. 28, 1853.
42. *Ibid.*, Dec. 12, 18, 1848.
43. *Ibid.*, Dec. 9, 1848; July 9, 1859; Jan. 31, 1861.
44. Colt established a factory at Hartford in 1847, reclaimed an extensive tract of meadow along the Connecticut River in the 1850's and built his armory there. *Ibid.*, Aug. 25, 1847; Sept. 28, 1849; Sept. 4, Dec. 1, 15, 1851; Sept. 18, 1852; Aug. 11, 1854; Nov. 19, Dec. 12, 13, 1857; May 29, Sept. 15, 1858; Mar. 23, 1859. Sharp's industry began in 1852. *Ibid.*, Aug. 10, Sept. 18, 1852; Aug. 11, 1854; Jan. 9, 1855.
45. *Ibid.*, Sept. 18, 1852.
46. *Ibid.*, Nov. 6, 1850.
47. *Conn. Cour.*, Dec. 19, 1846; *Hart. Daily,* June 3, 1847; Nov. 7, 1849; Jan. 31, 1850.
48. *Hart. Daily,* Nov. 6, 1850.
49. *Conn. Cour.*, Nov. 16, 1839; Dec. 17, 1842; Nov. 11, 1843.
50. *Ibid.*, Dec. 20, 1845; July 4, 1846.
51. *Ibid.*, Nov. 18, 1843; *Hart. Daily,* Nov. 11, 1850; Nov. 1, 1853; Aug. 2, 1854.
52. *Hart. Daily,* June 5, 1852; Sept. 6, 1854.
53. *Ibid.*, Sept. 14, 1849; May 1, 19, 1856; Nov. 23, 1857.
54. *Ibid.*, Dec. 5, 1848.
55. *Ibid.*, Aug. 4, Nov. 9, 14, 1849; Jan. 1, 1850.
56. *Ibid.*, Feb. 3, 1851; Mar. 17, 19, Apr. 30, May 5, 1852.
57. *Ibid.*, Mar. 5, 1852; Dec. 8, 1856; Mar. 9, May 29, Dec. 7, 1857; Mar. 9, 10, 12, May 23, 1859.
58. *Ibid.*, Aug. 16, 1852.
59. *Ibid.*, July 18, 19, 1853.
60. *Ibid.*, July 21, 23, 1853; Aug. 19, 22, 24, 28, 1854.
61. *Ibid.*, July 4, 1856.
62. *Ibid.*, Mar. 26, 1861.
63. *Ibid.*, Nov. 15, 18, Dec. 10, 1850; Jan. 17, 18, Feb. 6, 1851.
64. *Ibid.*, Mar. 26, 1851.
65. *Ibid.*, Apr. 22, June 8, 1858; July 13, 1859.
66. *Ibid.*, Sept. 6, 1854.
67. *Ibid.*, May 1, 1844; Sept. 6, 1854.
68. *Ibid.*, May 19, 1852; May 18, 1859.
69. *Ibid.*, Jan. 19, Feb. 4, 1852.
70. *Ibid.*, Sept. 6, 1854; Aug. 1, 1856; July 18, 1857; Oct. 19, 1859.
71. *Ibid.*, Jan. 6, 1855.
72. *Ibid.*, Sept. 25, 1860; June 3, 1861.
73. *Ibid.*, Aug. 31, 1853; Nov. 27, 1854; May 27, Sept. 16, 1859. Material on the Horticultural Society is in scattered issues throughout the period.
74. *Ibid.*, Aug. 31, 1853.
75. *Idem.*
76. *Ibid.*, Oct. 7, 1853.
77. *Ibid.*, July 27, 1853.
78. *Ibid.*, Oct. 7, 1853.
79. *Ibid.*, Oct. 7, Nov. 12, Dec. 27, 1853; Jan. 3, 5, 6, 1854.
80. *Ibid.*, May 27, July 27, Sept. 2, 4, 6, 1858; May 9, June 7, Oct. 27, 1859; June 3, 1861.
81. *Ibid.*, June 3, 1861.
82. *Ibid.*, Aug. 10, 1863.

83. *Ibid.*, Feb. 12, 15, 17, 1851; June 15, 1853; June 18, Sept. 5, 1859; Mar. 23, 1861.

84. *Ibid.*, Oct. 22, 1851.

85. *Ibid.*, Aug. 22, Oct. 29, 1860; July 18, 1864.

86. *Ibid.*, Dec. 28, 1849; Mar. 26, 1851.

87. *Ibid.*, Mar. 3, 1861.

88. *Conn. Cour.*, Oct. 27, 1838; June 25, 1842. *Hart. Daily*, Dec. 6, 1849; Oct. 11, 1851; Apr. 4, Oct. 22, Nov. 22, 1853; Nov. 29, 1859.

89. *Hart. Daily*, Dec. 11, 1848; Sept. 27, 28, Oct. 27, 1855.

90. *Ibid.*, Oct. 22, 1851.

91. *Daily Courant*, Nov. 10, 1837. *Conn. Cour.*, Dec. 1, 1838; Feb. 23, Apr. 6, July 27, Aug. 17, 1839; May 24, Aug. 2, 1845.

92. *Hart. Daily*, Sept. 6, 1854.

93. *Ibid.*, Mar. 16, 1861.

94. *Daily Cour.*, Feb. 16, 1838; *Conn. Cour.*, Jan. 1, 1839.

95. *Conn. Cour.*, Dec. 12, 1846; *Hart. Daily*, Mar. 24, 1852. Wells's early advertisements are in *Conn. Cour.*, Oct. 28, 1837; Apr. 27, May 11, 18, 25, June 8, 1839.

96. *Hart. Daily*, July 2–Sept. 4, 1849, *passim*.

97. *Ibid.*, June 1, 1852; Mar. 3–27, Apr. 17, 1854.

98. *Ibid.*, July 28, 1856.

99. *Ibid.*, May 18, 1859; Feb. 2, 1861.

100. *Ibid.*, Dec. 2, 1847.

101. Articles and editorials on the common schools are in the following issues: *Conn. Cour.*, Apr. 28, June 2, Aug. 11, Oct. 20, 27, Nov. 3, Dec. 1, 1838; Jan. 5, 26, Feb. 2, Apr. 20, May 18, July 6, Sept. 7, 1839; Nov. 28, Dec. 19, 1840; Jan. 2, 1841; May 10, July 12, 19, 26, Aug. 30, 1845; Jan. 3, May 30, Oct. 31, Nov. 21, 28, 1846. *Hart. Daily*, July 30–Aug. 24, 1844; Jan. 2, 4, Mar. 1, 1847; Jan. 29, June 17, Nov. 7, 8, 1850; Nov. 26, 1853.

102. *Conn. Cour.*, Aug. 11, 1838; Feb. 2, July 20, Sept. 7, 1839.

103. *Ibid.*, Sept. 7, Oct. 19, 1839; Feb. 1, Aug. 8, 1840.

104. *Hart. Daily*, Jan. 29, 1850.

105. *Ibid.*, Aug. 31, 1847; *Conn. Cour.*, Nov. 28, Dec. 19, 1840; Jan. 2, 1841.

106. *Hart. Daily*, Apr. 22, 1856.

107. *Ibid.*, Mar. 23, 1861.

108. *Ibid.*, Mar. 5, 1853.

109. *Ibid.*, Feb. 9, 1857.

110. The first city mission school was established in 1851. *Ibid.*, Sept. 26, 1860.

111. *Ibid.*, Feb. 22, Mar. 16, 20, Apr. 6, May 6, 14, 19, Oct. 11, 1858; Feb. 23, 1859.

112. *Conn. Cour.*, Dec. 11, 1841; July 9, 1842; Sept. 16, 1843.

113. *Ibid.*, July 7, Oct. 6, 1838; Jan. 12, 1839; July 12, 1845. *Hart. Daily*, Jan. 8, Nov. 9, 1848; Mar. 17, 1864.

114. *Hart. Daily*, Nov. 22, 1849; Dec. 28, 1850.

115. *Conn. Cour.*, Feb. 11, 1843; *Hart. Daily*, June 12, 1854.

116. *Conn. Cour.*, Dec. 1, 1838; Nov. 21, 1840. *Hart. Daily*, Oct. 22, 1853.

117. *Conn. Cour.*, Nov. 21, 1840; Dec. 4, 1841; *Hart. Daily*, Jan. 3, 1850; Dec. 12, 1851; Feb. 1, 1853; Oct. 28, Dec. 18, 1854; Dec. 23, 1856; Nov. 4, 1858.

118. *Hart. Daily*, Nov. 28, 1849; Dec. 28, 1850; Oct. 22, Nov. 2, 1853; Nov. 2, 1854; Oct. 17, 1855; Sept. 9, 1859.

119. They were not all reported regularly or in detail after the winter of 1850–1851.

120. *Ibid.*, Mar. 20, 1848.

121. *Conn. Cour.*, Nov. 19, 1842; *Hart. Daily*, July 24–26, 1844.

122. *Hart. Daily*, Aug. 16, 1860.

123. *Daily Cour.*, Dec. 13, 1837; *Conn. Cour.*, June 6, 1840. *Hart. Daily*, Jan. 16, 1847; July 19, Oct. 17, 1850; Aug. 9, 1851; Jan. 17, 18, 1853.

124. *Hart. Daily*, Sept. 21, 1858.

125. *Daily Cour.,* Oct. 27, 1837. *Conn. Cour.,* Feb. 16, 1839; Feb. 29, 1840.

126. *Conn. Cour.,* July 14, 1858; Mar. 20, 27, 1861.

127. *Ibid.,* Oct. 22, 1855; Feb. 21, 1857; Aug. 21, 1858; July 8, 1859.

128. *Ibid.,* May 13, 1837; July 5, 1845. *Daily Cour.,* Sept. 29, Nov. 14, 1837. *Hart. Daily,* Mar. 8, Sept. 12, Dec. 6, 1844; Jan. 10, June 24, 1856; Dec. 8, 1858; Mar. 10, 1859; Oct. 10, 1860.

129. *Hart. Daily,* Jan. 11, 18, 28, Feb. 21, 1854; May 4, 1856; Mar. 2, 1857.

130. *Ibid.,* June 1, Sept. 8, 1852; May 31–June 3, Sept. 29, Oct. 31, Nov. 30, 1853; Oct. 1, 1855; Nov. 13, 1856.

131. *Ibid.,* Aug. 21, Oct. 23, Nov. 15, 1850; May 24, 1851.

132. *Ibid.,* Aug. 21, 1850.

133. *Ibid.,* July 2, 7–9, 1851.

134. *Conn. Cour.,* May 20, 27, 1837; Dec. 4, 1841.

135. *Hart. Daily,* July 27, 1851; Nov. 16, 22, 25, 1852.

136. *Ibid.,* May 21, 22, Nov. 20, 1851; Nov. 16, 22, 25, 1852; Apr. 20, 1853.

137. *Ibid.,* Oct. 16, 29, 1855; Mar. 5, 14, June 14, 18, Sept. 15, 16, Nov. 18, 25, 1846; June 11, 15, July 2, 1857; Feb. 25, 1861.

138. *Ibid.,* Oct. 16, 1855.

139. *Daily Cour.,* Sept. 14, 1837; *Hart. Daily,* Dec. 15, 1848.

140. *Conn. Cour.,* Sept. 24, 1842; *Hart. Daily,* Oct. 29, 1858.

141. *Hart. Daily,* Apr. 30, 1859.

142. *Ibid.,* Aug. 30, 1860.

143. *Ibid.,* Sept. 18, 1849.

144. *Ibid.,* Oct. 22, 1855.

145. *Ibid.,* Oct. 27, Nov. 16, 1855.

146. *Ibid.,* Nov. 10, 1858.

147. *Ibid.,* July 9, 22, Aug. 14, 21, 1858; July 30, Oct. 6, 1859; Oct. 6, 27, 1860.

148. *Ibid.,* July 8, Oct. 26, 1858; June 4, 6, July 22, Sept. 27, 1859; Aug. 23, Sept. 27, 1860.

149. *Ibid.,* May 21, 1844; Dec. 2, 10, 18, 25, 30, 1850; July 4, Nov. 30, 1859.

150. *Ibid.,* Aug. 17, 1857.

151. *Ibid.,* Sept. 2, 1857; Jan. 19, 1858; Oct. 2, 1860.

152. *Ibid.,* July 31, 1844; July 4, 8, 12, 1853; Nov. 7, 8, 1855; Dec. 19, 1857.

153. *Ibid.,* July 29, 1856.

154. *Ibid.,* Feb. 3, 23, 1859; Jan. 2, 1861; Jan. 1, 1862.

155. *Ibid.,* Jan. 26, 1861.

156. Examples are in daily issues of Oct. 10, 1850; Dec. 7, 1854; June 17, Aug. 6, 1857; Sept. 6, 1859.

157. *Ibid.,* July 4, 1860.

158. *Conn. Cour.,* May 5, Oct. 6, 1838; Sept. 10, 1842. *Hart. Daily,* Aug. 6, Sept. 3, Nov. 27, 1847; July 18, 1850; Apr. 29, 1853; Apr. 30, July 9, Sept. 27, 1858; June 26, 1859.

159. *Daily Cour.,* Dec. 13, 1837; *Conn. Cour.,* June 6, 1840. *Hart. Daily,* Jan. 16, 1847; July 19, Oct. 17, 1850; Aug. 9, 1851; Jan. 17, 18, 1853.

160. *Hart. Daily,* July 18, 1856; Aug. 9, 1859; Feb. 25, 1861.

161. *Ibid.,* May 30, June 23, 24, 1851. Bailey's circus visited Hartford in 1860. *Ibid.,* Oct. 13, 1860.

162. *Ibid.,* May 30, 1853.

163. *Ibid.,* Aug. 25, 26, Sept. 9, 18, 1856.

164. *Ibid.,* Aug. 22, 1856.

165. *Ibid.,* May 23, 1857; Feb. 6, Dec. 4, 1858.

166. *Ibid.,* Oct. 30, 1850; May 26, 1851; Feb. 3, 1852. Boswell favored women doctors for women. *Ibid.,* Feb. 3, 1852. Day doubted the moral merits of coeducation on the college level. *Ibid.,* Oct. 27, 1858.

167. *Ibid.,* Sept. 13, 1853; May 21, 1857.

168. *Ibid.,* July 26, 1844; *Conn. Cour.,* Jan. 11, 1845.

169. *Conn. Cour.,* Jan. 11, 1845.

170. *Ibid.,* Jan. 18, May 17, July 12, 1845. *Hart. Daily,* Aug. 28, Oct. 24, 1849; Jan. 19, 1852; Aug. 9, 1853; Sept. 27, 1858; May 17, Oct. 21, 1859.

171. *Conn. Cour.,* Feb. 11, 1843. *Hart. Daily,* Aug. 12, 17, 1850; Jan. 15, 18, 28, Feb. 1, July 8, Sept. 25, 1851; Dec. 29, 1852; May 19, 1853; Mar. 9, 1855; Dec. 17, 18, 1856; Jan. 5, 1857; Aug. 16, 1858.

172. *Hart. Daily,* July 8, 1851.

173. *Ibid.,* Aug. 16, 1858.

174. *Ibid.,* Feb. 6, 7, 9, 26, 1855.

175. *Ibid.,* Aug. 17, 1857; June 30, 1858; Aug. 27, 1860.

176. *Conn. Cour.,* Feb. 12, 1842.

177. *Ibid.,* Aug. 26, 1843. Sour comments were in previous issues. *Ibid.,* Jan. 7, July 29, 1843.

178. *Ibid.,* Jan. 21, 1843; Feb. 22, 1845. *Hart. Daily,* May 17, 1844; May 2, 1850; June 26, 1851; Feb. 23, May 27, June 2, 3, 1852.

179. *Conn. Cour.,* June 19, 1841. *Hart. Daily,* Nov. 19, 1850; Jan. 21, 1851.

180. *Conn. Cour.,* June 18, 25, July 26, Oct. 18, Nov. 22, 1845; July 25, 1846. *Hart. Daily,* May 17, 1851.

181. *Conn. Cour.,* June 19, 1841; June 4, 1842.

182. *Ibid.,* July 31, 1841; June 4, 1842; Feb. 4, May 27, June 3, Nov. 11, 1843.

183. *Ibid.,* May 29, 1841; May 17, 1845. *Hart. Daily,* Sept. 21, 1844; Mar. 16, 1848.

184. *Conn. Cour.,* Feb. 4, July 22, 1843; *Hart. Daily,* July 17, 1851.

185. *Hart. Daily,* Dec. 11, 1844.

186. *Ibid.,* July 3, 26, Aug. 1, 7, 1854.

187. *Ibid.,* Aug. 1, 10, 15, 1854.

188. *Ibid.,* July 29, 31, 1854.

189. *Ibid.,* Aug. 3, 4, 31, Sept. 1, 1854.

190. *Ibid.,* Jan. 30, 1855.

191. *Ibid.,* Sept. 18, 1855.

192. *Ibid.,* Dec. 20, 1856; July 8, Aug. 18, 19, 21, Dec. 21, 1857.

193. *Ibid.,* Sept. 30, Oct. 1, 5, 19, 24, Dec. 2, 17, 21, 1857; Feb. 22, May 3, July 21, Sept. 15, 1858; Oct. 1, 1860.

194. *Ibid.,* Mar. 23, 1861.

CHAPTER XV

THE COURANT *IN THE CIVIL WAR*

1. *Hartford Daily Courant,* Apr. 13, 1861.

2. *Ibid.,* Apr. 22, 1861.

3. *Ibid.,* Apr. 24, 26, 1861.

4. *Ibid.,* Apr. 26, 1861.

5. *Ibid.,* June 18–Aug. 27, 1862, *passim.*

6. *Ibid.,* June 18, 1862.

7. *Ibid.,* May 11, June 11, 1861. Hartford's four daily papers took subscriptions for a fund for families of volunteers. *Ibid.,* Apr. 19, 22, 1861.

8. *Ibid.,* July 14, 1862.

9. *Ibid.,* July 8, 1862.

10. *Ibid.,* Aug. 22, 1862.

11. *Ibid.,* July 10, Aug. 6, 1862.

12. *Ibid.,* Aug. 4, 1862.

13. *Ibid.,* Aug. 11, 15, 1862.

14. *Ibid.,* Sept. 11, 12, Dec. 10, 1862.

15. *Ibid.,* Feb. 7, 1863.

16. *Ibid.,* Feb. 7, July 15, Dec. 16, 1863; June 21, 1864.

17. *Ibid.,* July 15, 24, 1863; July 11, Aug. 22, 1864.

18. *Ibid.,* Aug. 19, 1863; Aug. 8, Nov. 15, 1864.

19. *Ibid.,* Aug. 25, 31, 1864.

20. *Ibid.,* Nov. 2, 1861.

21. *Ibid.,* Oct. 27, 1862; June 15, 1863.

22. *Ibid.,* May 18, Oct. 11, Nov. 2, 1861; Feb. 4, Mar. 11, 28, May 17, July 25, Sept. 9, 29, Dec. 8, 10, 1862; May 19, June 15, 1863; June 27, 1864.

23. *Ibid.,* Apr. 15, June 27, 1864.

24. *Ibid.,* Oct. 4, 1861; Jan. 1, 6, 25, 31, Mar. 5, Oct. 25, 1862; Apr. 21, Nov. 17, 1864.

25. *Ibid.,* Jan. 6, 15, 25, Nov. 26, 1862; Mar. 2, 1863; July 28, 1864.

26. *Ibid.,* Mar. 2, 1863.

27. *Ibid.,* Jan. 25, Mar. 5, 1862.

28. *Ibid.,* Feb. 9, 1863; Jan. 11, 1864.

29. *Ibid.,* Apr. 20, 1864.

30. *Ibid.,* Feb. 4, 1862.

31. *Ibid.,* May 29, July 18, 1861; Jan. 26, 28, 31, Feb. 2, 14, 1863; Jan. 26, Apr. 14, 1864.

32. *Ibid.,* July 8, Oct. 29, 1861; Feb. 17, July 14, 15, 1862; Mar. 4, 1863.

33. *Ibid.,* Feb. 17, 1862.

34. *Ibid.,* Apr. 15, May 21, June 12, 17, Aug. 19, 1861; June 12, 16, 1862.

35. *Ibid.,* Mar. 24, 1864.

36. *Ibid.,* May 30, Oct. 12, 1861; Jan. 3, June 28, Aug. 4, Oct. 22, 1862.

37. *Ibid.,* May 23, 1861.

38. *Ibid.,* Nov. 18–20, Dec. 12, 16, 21, 30, 1861.

39. *Ibid.,* Oct. 22, Nov. 3, 1862.

40. *Ibid.,* Oct. 29, 1862; Apr. 25, Aug. 22, Sept. 3, 1863; July 14, 1864.

41. *Ibid.,* May 22, June 28, 1862.

42. *Ibid.,* May 22, Nov. 26, 1862.

43. *Ibid.,* Nov. 26, Dec. 11, 1862.

44. *Ibid.,* Oct. 25, 1861; Aug. 18, 1862.

45. *Ibid.,* May 22, June 15, July 27, 1861.

46. *Ibid.,* Oct. 11, 1861.

47. *Ibid.,* Dec. 6, 1861; Apr. 1, 15, 17, May 5, 16, 28, July 15, 16, Aug. 1, 1862.

48. *Ibid.,* Jan. 1, 2, Mar. 31, 1863; Feb. 27, 1864.

49. *Ibid.,* Apr. 15, Aug. 27, Dec. 3, 1862; Jan. 1, June 23, 1864.

50. *Ibid.,* July 24, 1861; Feb. 5, May 28, 1862.

51. *Ibid.,* Jan. 4, Feb. 6, 13, 15, June 23, July 11, 24, 1862.

52. *Ibid.,* June 23, Sept. 5, 6, Dec. 18, 20, 1862; Apr. 9, 1863.

53. *Ibid.,* July 7, Aug. 22, 1862; May 14, June 4, 1863. Cf. *ante,* p. 202.

54. *Hart. Daily,* July 24, Sept. 13, Oct. 28, Nov. 10, 11, 1862; Jan. 27, June 30, Nov. 7, 1863.

55. *Ibid.,* Aug. 16, Sept. 6, 1862; Jan. 7, 1863.

56. *Ibid.,* Feb. 2, 1863.

57. *Ibid.,* Aug. 16, 30, 1861; June 11, 23, July 24, Dec. 30, 1862.

58. *Ibid.,* Apr. 2, 1861; Apr. 8, 1862; Apr. 7, 1863; Apr. 5, 1864; Apr. 4, 1865.

59. *Ibid.,* Aug. 20, 1861.

60. *Ibid.,* July 9, 1864.

61. *Ibid.,* Jan. 20, Feb. 17, 25, 27, 1864.

62. *Ibid.,* Sept. 10, 21, 28, Nov. 7, 1864.

63. *Ibid.,* Sept. 3–Nov. 9, 1864, *passim.*

64. *Ibid.,* Feb. 6, Mar. 6, 1865.

65. *Ibid.,* Mar. 6, 1865.

66. *Ibid.,* July 22–24, 1861.

67. *Ibid.,* Feb. 13, 15, 28, Apr. 22, May 5, June 21, 30, 1862.

68. *Ibid.*, July 8, 1862 ff.
69. *Ibid.*, Jan. 27, Feb. 2, May 9, June 30, July 6–8, 1863.
70. *Ibid.*, July 23, 1861; July 8, 10, 28, 29, 31, Aug. 5, 6, Dec. 23, 24, 1862; Jan. 1, 14, 1863.
71. *Ibid.*, Sept. 23, 1861; Dec. 11, 1862; June 4, Dec. 30, 1863; Jan. 12, 1864.
72. *Ibid.*, Aug. 12, 1862; Apr. 8, Nov. 11, 1863; Mar. 15, May 25, June 30, Nov. 29, 1864.
73. *Ibid.*, May 9, 31, June 2, Sept. 25, 26, 1862; Apr. 29, May 5, 7, July 17, 28; Aug. 12, 1863; May 24, Sept. 29, Oct. 5, Nov. 1, 1864.
74. Letters and editorial comment are in daily issues of Aug. 6, 20, 21, 1861; Apr. 29, 1862; Apr. 24, May 15, Dec. 3, 1863; Mar. 12, Apr. 26, 1864; Feb. 25, 1865.
75. *Ibid.*, Apr. 17, May 27, Aug. 6, 1861; May 10, 1864.
76. *Ibid.*, Aug. 13, 1861.
77. *Ibid.*, Aug. 1, 1861.
78. *Ibid.*, Dec. 21, 1863; Jan. 23, June 18, 1864.
79. *Ibid.*, Oct. 10, 1864.
80. *Ibid.*, July 17, 1861; July 16, 1862; Aug. 13, 1863.
81. *Ibid.*, July 18, Aug. 9, 1864.
82. *Ibid.*, Feb. 6, 9, 10, July 18, Sept. 8, Oct. 11, 1864.
83. *Ibid.*, Feb. 2, 3, Dec. 15, 1864; Jan. 3, 1865.
84. *Ibid.*, May 20, 1862; May 26, Nov. 14, 23, 1864.
85. *Ibid.*, Dec. 15, 1862.
86. *Ibid.*, Dec. 30, 1862; Feb. 9, June 27, Oct. 16, 1863.
87. *Ibid.*, May 3, 1862; Jan. 27, Aug. 11, 1863.
88. *Ibid.*, Dec. 18, 27, 1862; Oct. 21, 1863.
89. *Ibid.*, Oct. 10, 1861; Oct. 15, 1862; Sept. 8, 1863; Sept. 13, 1864.
90. *Ibid.*, Aug. 16, Nov. 10, 1864; Feb. 20, 1865.
91. *Ibid.*, June 9, 1862; Sept. 23, 1863.
92. *Ibid.*, June 27, 1863.
93. *Ibid.*, Apr. 24, 1863.
94. *Ibid.*, Apr. 10, 1865.
95. *Ibid.*, Apr. 12, 1865.
96. *Ibid.*, Apr. 19, 1865.

BIBLIOGRAPHY

PRIMARY SOURCES

Connecticut Courant, 1764–1865. For the earlier years, the more complete volumes are in the Connecticut Historical Society Library; and for the later years, in the office of the Hartford Courant Company.

Daily Courant, 1837–1839. In the Connecticut Historical Society Library and in the office of the Hartford Courant Company.

George Goodwin & Sons. Letter Books, Vols. II–VII, 1815–1836. In the Connecticut Historical Society Library.

Hartford Daily Courant, 1840–1865. In the Connecticut Historical Society Library and in the office of the Hartford Courant Company. Except for the first six months of 1849, few daily issues are missing.

The Hudson & Goodwin Letters, 1787–1788. In the Connecticut Historical Society Library.

Supplement to the Connecticut Courant, 1825–1829, 1832–1859, 1861–1865. In the Connecticut Historical Society Library.

Webster, Noah. Letters to Hudson & Goodwin, 1786–1789. In the Ford Collection, New York Public Library.

SECONDARY WORKS

Baker, Daniel. *Platen Printing Presses, A Primer of Information Regarding the History & Mechanical Construction of Platen Printing Presses, From the Original Hand Press to the Modern Job Press, to Which is Added a Chapter on Automatic Presses of Small Size.* Chicago, 1918.

Barber, John Warner, comp. *Connecticut Historical Collections, Containing a General Collection of Interesting Facts, Traditions, Biographical Sketches, Anecdotes, &c. Relating to the History and Antiquities of Every Town in Connecticut, with Geographical Descriptions.* New Haven, 1836.

Bates, Albert Carlos. *Supplementary List of Books Printed in Connecticut 1709–1800.* Hartford, 1938.

Bates, Albert Carlos. *The Work of Hartford's First Printer.* Cambridge, 1925.

Brown, William Garrott. *The Life of Oliver Ellsworth.* New York, 1905.

Clark, Charles Hopkins. "The Press, Newspapers, Publishing Houses, Etc.," *The Memorial History of Hartford County Connecticut 1633–1884,* I, 605–627. J. Hammond Trumbull, ed. Boston, 1886.

Cowie, Alexander. *John Trumbull, Connecticut Wit.* Chapel Hill, 1936.

Ford, Emily Ellsworth Fowler. *Notes on the Life of Noah Webster.* Emily Ellsworth Ford Skeel, ed. New York, 1912. 2 vols.

Goodrich, S. G. *Recollections of A Lifetime or Men and Things I Have*

Seen: in a Series of Familiar Letters to A Friend, Historical, Biographical, Anecdotical, and Descriptive, Vol. I. New York, 1856.

Goodwin, James Junius. *The Goodwins of Hartford, Connecticut.* Hartford, 1891.

Goodwin, Joseph O. *East Hartford: Its History and Traditions.* Hartford, 1879.

Hamilton, Frederick W. *Type and Presses in America, A Brief Historical Sketch of the Development of Type Casting and Press Building in the United States.* Chicago, 1918.

Harlow, Thompson R. *Early Hartford Printers.* Hartford, 1940.

The Hartford Courant, October 25, 1914. One hundred and fiftieth anniversary issue.

Love, William DeLoss. *The Colonial History of Hartford Gathered from the Original Sources.* Hartford, 1914.

Marble, Annie Russel. *The Hartford Wits.* New Haven, 1936.

Miner, Louie M. *Our Rude Forefathers, American Political Verse 1783–1788.* Cedar Rapids, 1937.

Morse, Jarvis Means. *Connecticut Newspapers in the Eighteenth Century.* New Haven, 1935.

North, S. N. D. *History and Present Condition of the Newspapers and Periodical Press of the United States, with a Catalogue of the Publications of the Census Year.* Washington, 1884.

Parker, Edwin Pond. *History of the Second Church of Christ in Hartford.* Hartford, 1892.

Pell, John. *Ethan Allen.* Boston, 1929.

Thomas, Isaiah. *The History of Printing in America, with a Biography of Printers, and an Account of Newspapers,* Vol. I. 2d ed. Albany, 1874.

Trumbull, James Hammond. *List of Books Printed in Connecticut 1709–1800.* Hartford, 1904.

Walker, George Leon. "The Historical Address," *Commemorative Exercises of the First Church of Christ in Hartford, at its Two Hundred and Fiftieth Anniversary, October 11 and 12, 1883,* pp. 37–99. Hartford, 1883.

Walker, George Leon. *History of the First Church in Hartford, 1633–1883.* Hartford, 1884.

Warfel, Harry R. *Noah Webster, Schoolmaster to America.* New York, 1936.

Webster, Noah (Hampden, *pseud.*). *A Letter to the President of the United States, Touching the Prosecutions, Under his Patronage, Before the Circuit Court in the District of Connecticut: Containing a Faithful Narrative of the Extraordinary Measures Pursued, and of the Incidents Both Serious and Laughable, That Occurred, During the Pendency of These Abortive Prosecutions.* New Haven, 1808.

Zunder, Theodore Albert. *The Early Days of Joel Barlow, A Connecticut Wit.* New Haven, 1934.

INDEX

Abolitionists, 214, 230; development of movement, 166–167; editorial policy toward, 167, 217, 224

Adams, John, 72, 76, 80, 89, 111

Adams, John Quincy, 153, 168, 249; administration of supported by *Courant*, 143, 144; campaign for re-election, 145–146

Adams, Samuel, 69, 71

Advertisements, variety of before 1800, 6, 7, 16, 38, 45, 47, 104, 106–110, 114, 132; increased importance of under later editors, 166, 169, 177, 182, 183, 184, 185, 186, 198–199, 201, 204, 206

Advertisers, increased patronage of *Courant* by, 128, 184, 206; list of early, 114; publication of *Daily Courant* sponsored by, 193

Advertising rates, 128, 185, 194, 198–199, 204

Air Line Road, 236–237, 238

Alien and Sedition Laws, 73, 74, 128

Allen, Ethan, "Bible" of, 134

Alsop, Richard, 130

American Asylum for the Deaf and Dumb (Hartford), 159, 234, 244

American Mercury (Hartford), 65, 74, 75, 79, 80, 84, 85, 125, 140, 179; first issue of, 117

American Party. *See* Know-Nothings

American System, principles of endorsed by *Courant*, 143, 146; *see also* Tariff

Anarchiad, 63, 120–122

Antimasons, 150–151, 152

Antislavery: *Courant*'s sentiments in colonial times, 112; *see also* Slavery

Athenaeum (Hartford), 162, 248–249

Babcock, Elisha editor of *American Mercury*, 74, 75, 117, 131

Barber, John Warner, 234

Barlow, Joel, 77, 117, 119, 121, 123, 130, 131, 132, 135

Bates, Edward, of Missouri, 230–231

Bee (New London), 74, 75

Bell, John, of Tennessee, 232

Benton, Thomas H., 249; land-distribution program of, 208–209, 210

Birney, James G., 214

Boston Port Act, colonial opposition to, 27

Boston Tea Party, 25, 26–27

Boswell, John L., owner, editor, and partner of *Courant*, 1836–54: purchased *Courant*, Sept. 12, 1836, 156, 186, 188; apprenticeship and early years, 193; prospectus of *Daily Courant*, Aug. 29, 1837, 194; personal reaction to increased news tempo, 196; partnership with William Faxon, Jan. 1, 1850, 199; member of railroad investment committee, 235; died July 30, 1854, 200

Brace, John P., editor under Boswell and Day, 199, 205

Brainard, John G. C., 179

Breckinridge, John C., 232

Brown, John, raid on Harper's Ferry by, 230

Buchanan, James, election campaign of, 227–228; policies of administration opposed by *Courant*, 228–229

Buckingham, William A., Civil War Governor of Connecticut, 231, 264

Bunce, Hannah. *See* Mrs. Ebenezer Watson

Burke, Edmund, 66

"Burleigh" letters, 76–78

Burr, Aaron, 78, 81, 89, 123

Burr, Alfred E., owner and editor of *Hartford Times*, 199, 203; offered *Courant* by Goodwin, 187–188

Burr, Warren H., city reporter under Day, 201, 202

Bushnell, Horace, 245–246

Business. *See* Connecticut; Hartford

Buy American. *See* Politics, 1764–83

Calhoun, John C., 211; views on slavery, 151, 153, 218, 219, 228

California, 220; admission of as free state, 218, 219

"Carrier's Address," annual New Year's poems in *Courant*, 122–123; revived under Goodwins, 182; continued under Boswell, 197

Cass, Lewis, of Michigan, 217–218

Charter Oak, fall of described in *Courant*, 252

Chase, Samuel, impeachment and trial of, 82

Chesapeake affair, 87, 90

Churches, in Hartford, 112, 163, 234, 248; state support of, 54, 84, 112, 140

Circuit Court Act of 1801, repeal of, 81

Civil War, outbreak of, 202, 256; appeasers and Copperheads stigmatized, 202, 257, 260–261, 264, 265; Republican policies criticized, 256–257, 264; enlistment encouraged, 257–258; conscription, 258–259; civilian war work, 257, 259–260; federal taxation in, 257, 260; intervention and the southern blockade, 261–263; editorial policy on emancipation, 263–264; conduct of war favorably reviewed, 265–266; wartime prosperity, 266–267; victory celebration in Hartford, 267

Clap, Thomas, president of Yale College, 44, 50–51

Clark, Abel N., business manager under Boswell, 199; business partner of Day, Jan. 1, 1857, 204, 205; purchased Day's share in *Courant*, Dec. 1864, 204

Clay, Henry, as presidential candidate, 142, 152, 214, 217; political principles of endorsed by *Courant*, 151, 193, 211; tariff proposals of, 153; plan for disposal of public lands, 208; member of Congress, 218; attitude toward slavery, 218–219; death of, 221

Clergy, Anglican and Episcopal, 28, 54–55; monopoly of Yale Corporation by, 49; rights of defended by *Courant*, 84, 140

Colonization Society, program of endorsed by *Courant*, 166, 167

Colt, Samuel, arms manufacturer, 242, 255, 266–267

Commutation Act, *Courant*'s policy toward, 59–61

Compromise of 1850, opposed by *Courant*, 218, 220, 221, 222, 223

Connecticut, state of: commercial future of, following the Revolution, 102–104; Democratic party in, 155, 156, 209, 213, 221, 222, 224, 225, 232; economic position of in Revolutionary period, 18, 22, 25, 34–35, 101–102; Federalist party in, 78, 85, 86, 87, 88, 141; first American Episcopal Bishop of, 54; first state banks in, 102–103, 160; interest in distribution of public lands, 62–63, 209, 211; Know-Nothing party in, 225; prohibition in, 254; protective tariff favored by, 147, 148; Republican party in, 225–226, 232–233, 264; Statehouse, 115, 234, 246; state support of churches, 54, 84, 112, 140; Whig party in, 155, 156, 193, 209, 214, 219, 222–223, 224; *see also* General Assembly

Connecticut Courant. See Courant (Hartford) under Hudson & Goodwin, Goodwin & Sons, John L. Boswell, Thomas M. Day

Connecticut Courant and Daily Intelligencer. See Courant (Hartford) under Thomas Green, Ebenezer Watson, George Goodwin

Connecticut Gazette (New Haven), oldest paper in Connecticut, 3, 4, 21

Connecticut Mirror (Hartford), 179

Connecticut Mutual Life Insurance Company, 242

Connecticut River, bridges over, 115, 175, 236–237, 244; importance of to business, 102, 114, 169, 238; improved navigation of, 102, 170–171, 172

Connecticut Toleration Act of 1791, 112

Connecticut Valley, canal and river projects in, 102, 169–172; railroad plans for, 236; resources of, 4, 102, 169

Connecticut Whig (Hartford), 199

Constitution (U.S.): framing and ratification of supported by *Courant*, 63–66, 125; Jefferson's disrespect for, 75–76; repeal of Circuit Court Act an assault upon, 81; Twelfth Amendment to opposed, 82

Continental Congress, 27–28; local committees of, 30; proceedings of published by Watson, 8

Copperheads. *See* (Democrats, northern)

Courant (Hartford)

Under Thomas Green, 1764–70: first prospectus, Oct. 29, 1764, 3, 5, 6; early format, 5–6, 205; treatment of local and foreign news, 6–7, 101; circulation, 7; essay writers featured, 7; increase of paid advertisements, 7; no editorials, 7; political viewpoint, 17–23; suspension of publication under Stamp Act, 21; *see also* Politics, 1764–83

Under Ebenezer Watson, 1767–77: move to larger quarters, 8; publishing and other activities, 8; difficulties of newsgathering during Revolution, 8–9, 32–33, 128; changes in format, 9–10; personal tone of journalism, 10, 15, 36; patriotic bias of news, 10, 15, 27, 33–34; circulation and price, 10–11, 11–12; difficulties of procuring paper, 11, 12, 128; paper mill established, 1775, 11; difficulties of procuring type, 12, 128; Green's political viewpoint continued, 23–35; *see also* Politics, 1764–83

Under George Goodwin, 1778–79: partnership with Mrs. Watson, 1778, 14; burning and rebuilding of paper mill, 14; seal dropped, 15; circulation and price increased, 15; partnership with Barzillai Hudson, Mar. 1779, 15–16

Under Hudson & Goodwin, 1779–1815: paper making expanded, 16, 128; development of editorials, 36, 124–125, 126–127; political viewpoint, 36–37, 68, 73–74, 78, 92–93, 123, 124, 126–127; price reduction, 1783, 117; first legislative reporting, 117–118; letters and essays featured, 118–120; characteristic verse, 120–123; agricultural column, 125–126; owners indicted for criminal libel, 1806, 127; improvement in appearance, 127–128; circulation increased, 128; name shortened to *Connecticut Courant,* 128; newsgathering more dependable, 128; new members of the firm, 135; *see also* Hudson & Goodwin, booksellers and publishers; Politics, 1783–1800, 1800–15

Under Goodwin & Sons, 1815–36: dissolution of partnership with Hudson, Nov. 15, 1815, 135–136; political news featured, 152, 181, 184; new members of firm, 177–178; restriction of bookselling, 178; publishing business, 179; competition with local papers, 179–180; varied content of newspaper, 180–183; publication of literary *Supplement,* 183–184; increased patronage of advertisers, 184; appearance improved, 184–185; improve-ment in typographical processes, 185; circulation enlarged, 185–186, 188; *see also* Politics, 1815–36

Under John L. Boswell, 1836–54: Whig party supported, 155, 156, 193, 207–224; publication of *Daily Courant,* 1837, 193–194; preponderance of political news, 194, 197; appearance and size, 194, 199; circulation and price, 194, 199; increased efficiency of newsgathering, 194–196, 197, 203; increased coverage of local news, 196–197; business interests featured in 1840's, 197; major portion of space devoted to advertising, 198–199; prosperity of paper, 199; *see also* Politics, 1837–54

Under Thomas M. Day, 1855–64: connection with Whig party severed, 200, 225; increase in news content and coverage, 200, 201; changes in appearance, 200, 201, 204, 205; increased efficiency in newsgathering, 200, 201, 202–203, 205; Know-Nothing party supported, 200, 224–228, 253; Republican party supported, 200, 225–226, 227–233, 256–266, 267, 268; caliber of editorials improved, 200–201; city news featured, 201; marked improvement in typography, 201; first fashion reporting, 202; competition with local papers, 203; increase in circulation and price, 203, 204, 206; description of office, 204–205; celebration of 100th anniversary of the paper, 205, 267; *see also* Politics, 1855–56, 1856–64

Courant, circulation and price of, 7, 10–11, 11–12, 15, 128, 185–186, 188, 194; price reduction, 1783, 117; price of *Daily* and weekly, 1854, 199, 213, 204, 206

Courant, format of, 5–6, 9–10, 127–128, 184–185, 194, 199, 200, 201, 204, 205; largest daily paper in Connecticut, 1854, 199; facsimile of first issue, 205

Courant, paper mills owned and operated by: early difficulties in procuring paper 11, 12, 128; establishment of paper mill under Watson, 1775, 11; burning and rebuilding of paper mill by public lottery, 14; additional mills acquired under Hudson & Goodwin, 16; mills destroyed by fire and flood

Courant, paper mills (*cont.*)
under Hudson & Goodwin, 128; paper-making enterprises continued, 128; division of mills between Hudsons and Goodwins, 1815, 135–136; competition with local mills after 1815, 178; promotion and expansion of business under Goodwin & Sons, 186; mills taken over by sons of George Goodwin, 1836, 186

Courant Supplement, established under Goodwin & Sons, 183–184; continued under Boswell, 198; increased size of under Day, 205

Crime, causes of discussed in *Courant,* 246–247, 254; in colonial Connecticut, 45–47; court coverage by *Courant,* 107, 181, 196, 201; founding of city court advocated by *Courant,* 1851, 246

Cuba, invasion of, disapproved by *Courant,* 220

Currency, regulation of in Connecticut, 22, 34–35; cheap-money movement in Rhode Island, 62; control of by United States Bank, 148, 208, 210; lack of confidence in under Jackson, 154, 155, 207; Independent Treasury, 207–208, 210, 212, 214; Van Buren's policies on, 208–209; as an issue in Whig politics, 210, 214; problems of in Civil War, 260

Daily Courant. See Courant (Hartford), under John L. Boswell, Thomas M. Day

Dartmouth College, commencement celebration, 1772, described in *Courant,* 49

Davis, Jefferson, 202, 226, 260, 261, 262

Day, Thomas M., owner, editor, and partner of *Courant,* 1855–64: purchase of *Courant,* Jan. 1, 1855, 200; personal qualifications, 200; partnership with Abel N. Clark, Jan. 1, 1857, 204; share in paper sold to Clark, Dec., 1864, 204; retirement of, 205–206; patriotism during Civil War, 256

Declaraton of Independence, published in *Courant,* July 15, 1776, 32

Democrats, northern: victories in Connecticut, 155, 156, 221; support of Van Buren, 156; party press criticized by *Courant,* 202, 222, 260–261; in favor of Independent Treasury, 208, 214; enemies of Connecticut Whigs, 209, 213, 224; party platform of 1844, 214; presidential candidates supported by, 217–218, 222, 228, 232, 265; accused of soliciting foreign votes, 224, 225; stigmatized as appeasers and Copperheads during Civil War, 257, 260–261, 264, 265

Democrats, southern: in favor of slavery and secession, 214; Lecompton constitution endorsed in Kansas, 229; defeat of Lecompton forces in Congress, 229; sectional split of party threatened, 229, 230, 232; support of John C. Breckinridge as presidential candidate, 1860, 232

"Democrats," Jeffersonian: rise of "Jacobin" or "Democratic" clubs, 68, 69, 71; influence of in foreign relations, 69–70, 72–73; political methods of, 75, 76, 84–85; immorality of, 76–78, 83–84, 113, 123, 142; *see also* Republicans ("democrats")

Depressions: economic dislocation following Revolution, 101; following War of 1812, 100, 177, 178; "derangement of business," 1834, 154–155; in 1837, 174, 207–208, 235; in 1857, 229–230, 248

Dickens, Charles, visit of to Hartford, 1842, 253

Disease: care and cure of, 106–107, 175, 247; epidemics, 43, 105–106, 134, 174–175, 247; medical societies, 44–45, 106, 159–160; prescriptions and nostrums, 43–44, 107, 247; prevalence of deplored by *Courant,* 43, 106

Doolittle, Enos, clock foundry of, 103

Douglas, Stephen A., sponsorship of Kansas-Nebraska Act by, 222, 223, 229; as presidential candidate, 230, 232

Dred Scott decision, reversal of demanded by *Courant,* 228–229

Dwight, Theodore, 123, 130, 179

Dwight, Timothy, defense of the clergy by, 84; hatred of Napoleon, 97; president of Yale College, 130; *Psalms* published by Hudson & Goodwin, 135, 179; school taught by, 48, 49

Editorial form, development of in *Courant:* none in early issues, 7; "incipient" in Revolutionary period, 25, 36, 124–125; as a means of political expression after 1800, 125, 126–127; character of under later editors, 177, 182, 193, 197, 200–201; *see also* Politics

Education, cause of supported by *Courant*, 160–161, 163, 247–248; first local high school, 247; first state convention of teachers, 161; first state normal school, 247; for girls, 48–49, 161; institutions of higher learning, 49, 160; public and private schools, 47–49, 107–108, 160–161, 247–248

Edwards, Henry W., Governor of Connecticut, 156

Election Day, annual dinner for clergy on, 84, 140; traditional celebration of in Hartford, 42, 55, 111, 140

Eliot, Jared, 52

Ellsworth, Oliver, 76; agricultural column in *Courant*, 125–126; steamboat named for, 168, 169–170

Embargo Act of 1807, unpopularity of, 87–88; results of, 91–92

Essay writers, contributors to *Courant* in Revolutionary period, 7; increased importance of under Hudson & Goodwin, 118–119; diminished importance of under Boswell, 197

Farmington Canal, 170, 171, 172

Fashions, in colonial period, 39–41; women's, 169; first spring reporting in *Courant*, 202; "Bloomerism," 253

Faxon, William, partnership of in *Courant*, Jan. 1, 1850, 199

Federalism. *See* Federalists

Federalists: campaigns against Jefferson, 71, 75–79, 85; activities of party in Connecticut, 78, 85, 86, 87, 88, 141; popularity in New England, 80, 88; resurgence under Madison, 89; Hartford Convention a gathering of, 99; concerned with moral principles, 110, 113; foes of satirized in verse, 123; waning spirit of after War of 1812, 139, 141–143; ceased to participate in elections, 139, 143; "Independent Ticket" supported by, 150

Field, Cyrus W., 203

Fillmore, Millard, vice-presidential candidate of Whigs, 217, 221; presidential candidate of Know-Nothings, 225, 228

Fire protection, advocated by *Courant*, 104–105, 174, 247, 266–267; *see also* Insurance

Fitch, Thomas, Governor of Connecticut, 20, 22

France, declaration of war against by British, 67; Jefferson sympathetic toward, 67, 71, 72, 75–76; Madison pro-French, 71, 89, 90–91, 96–97; relations with under Adams, 71–72; naval warfare with Americans, 1798–99, 72; XYZ affair, 72–73; commercial intercourse with under Jefferson and Madison, 90–91; claims to Mexico by, 262; threatened intervention in Civil War, 262–263

Franklin, Benjamin, 4, 160; electrical findings of, 50, 52

Freeman's Chronicle (Hartford), 60, 117

Frémont, John C., presidential candidacy of endorsed by Day, 227, 228

French Revolution, 66, 118, 124; condemned by *Courant*, 66–67, 68; Jefferson sympathetic with ideas of, 67, 76, 139; opposed by Federalists, 113

Gallatin, Albert, 71, 72, 80

Gallaudet, Thomas H., 159, 161

Garrison, William Lloyd, 167

General Assembly (Connecticut): rebuilding of *Courant*'s paper mill authorized by, 14; petitioned for repeal of Stamp Act, 21; opposition to the king, 31–32; control of Yale College by, 49; grain tax of 1780, 53; petitioned by Episcopalians, 54; protest against Commutation Act by, 59; Republican bloc in, 84–85, 86; Embargo Act declared unconstitutional by, 88; refusal to furnish militia in War of 1812, 98; attempt to stimulate commercial prosperity, 101; restriction of theatrical exhibits by, 110, 164; legislative methods of criticized in *Courant*, 117–118, 141–142; proceedings of legislature reported by *Courant*, 117–118, 181, 194–195, 200; statutes of published by Hudson & Goodwin, 129; action taken against abolitionists, 166; prohibition enacted by, 254

Genêt, Edmond Charles, Minister from France, 1793, 67, 69, 71, 72

Georgia, state of, disputes with Cherokee Indians, 149–150
Gerry, Elbridge, 64, 71; involved in XYZ affair, 72
Goodrich, Chauncey A., 161
Goodrich, Samuel G. ("Peter Parley"), 115–116, 136
Goodrich, William H., printer under Day, 199, 205
Goodwin, George, partner, owner, and editor of *Courant,* 1778–1836: early years under Green and Watson, 14, 187; partnership with Watson's widow, 1778, 14; first printer of *Courant* to call himself an editor, 15; partnership with Barzillai Hudson, Mar., 1779, 15–16; sons assisting in business, 135, 177–178, 186; partnership dissolved Nov. 15, 1815, 135–136; local reputation and activities, 135, 136, 166, 186–187; description of personal appearance in later years, 187; last days with *Courant,* 187–190; sale of paper to John L. Boswell, Sept. 12, 1836, 156, 186, 188; died May 13, 1844, 189
Goodwin, George, sons of active in *Courant* enterprises: charitable and business activities of, 135, 187; Richard, editor, 135, 177; Henry, foreman of press, 177; George, Jr., in charge of paper mills, 177, 186; Charles, in charge of bookselling, 177–178, 186; Edward, editorial assistant, 177–178; paper mill taken over by, 186
Gough, John B., temperance reformer, 254, 255
Granger, Gideon, Postmaster General under Jefferson, 75, 80, 85
Great Britain: claims on Mexico, 262; Orders in Council, 87, 90, 95; threats of intervention in Civil War, 261–263; *see also* Politics, 1764–83, 1800–15
Green, Samuel, great-grandfather of Thomas Green, 3
Green, Samuel, brother of Thomas Green, 8
Green, Thomas, founder, owner and partner of *Courant,* 1764–70: previous journalistic experience, 3; printing a family tradition, 3–4; business activities in connection with *Courant,* 5, 8; partnership with Ebenezer

Watson, *ca.* Dec. 1767, 8; move to New Haven, 8; severed connection with *Courant,* Dec. 1770, 8
Green, Timothy, grandfather of Thomas Green, died 1757, 3–4
Green, Timothy, brother of Thomas Green, 4
Grenville, George. *See* Stamp Act of 1765

Hamilton, Alexander, fiscal policies of endorsed by *Courant,* 66, 67
Hancock, John, 69
Harrison, William Henry, presidential candidacy of endorsed by Whigs, 1836, 156; campaign supported by *Courant,* 156, 209–210
Hartford (Connecticut)
Appearance and location: advantages as location for *Courant,* 4–5, 18–19, 194; characteristics of in Revolutionary period, 101; descriptions of in nineteenth century, 115–116, 175–176, 234–235, 244–245; location a factor in commercial and political importance, 4–5, 18–19, 238; map of in 1640 published by *Courant,* 197
Business and commercial activities: banking, 102–103, 115, 160, 169, 235, 242; canal and river projects, 102, 169–172, 235, 237, 240; decline in business, 237, 238–239, 240; food marketing, 103–104; hotels, 162, 243; importance of river navigation to, 5, 18–19, 102, 114, 169, 238; insurance interests, 104, 169, 197, 242, 266; manufacturing interests, 103, 169, 197, 237–238, 239–240, 241–242; prosperity of, 4, 18, 235, 240–243, 255, 266–267; railroad activities, 172–174, 235–237; retail trade, 103, 111, 113–114, 197; stimulation of by legislative measures, 101
Cultural and social interests: educational institutions, 160–161, 247–248; fashions and social customs, 38–42, 169, 202, 251–252, 253, 267; libraries and museums, 108, 109, 135, 161, 162, 248–249; lyceums and lectures, 162–163, 249; music, 108, 162, 249–250; recreation, 42, 109–111, 163–164, 250–252, 267
Municipal and civic affairs: condition and appearance of streets, 115,

175, 243, 244–245, 255; courts and prisons, 47, 107, 196, 246; fire department, 105, 174, 246, 266; health regulations, 106, 174–175; municipal organization of, 101, 246; park, 245–246; police force, 246, 266; schools, 47–48, 161, 247–248; 200th anniversary celebration, 1835, 186; water supply, 106, 243–244

Political importance: county seat, 4–5; Election Day celebrations, 42, 55, 111, 140; seat of General Assembly, 4, 19, 140, 194; Statehouse, 115, 234, 246

Religious and charitable activities: charitable and fraternal organizations, 111, 158–159, 248; churches, 112, 163, 234, 248; humanitarian institutions, 112, 163, 234; temperance societies, 166, 253–254, 254–255

Hartford Convention, 99, 128, 147, 150; secret journal of, 179

Hartford Fire Insurance Company, 104, 135

Hartford Hospital, first annual report of, 1856, 247

Hartford Journal, 199

Hartford Library, 135, 162

Hartford Museum, 161; establishment of, 1797, 109

Hartford and New Haven road, 235–236

Hartford Times. See Times (Hartford)

Hartford Wits, 63, 123, 134; *see also Anarchiad*

Harvard College: student boycott of British imports, 23

Hawley, Joseph R., editorial writer under Day, 203

Heart & Crown, printer's emblem of *Courant*, 3, 5; dropped by George Goodwin, 15

Hemans, Felicia, 184

Holt, Charles, printer of the *Bee*, 74

Holt, John, printer of *Connecticut Gazette*, 3, 4

Hopkins, Joseph, 120, 121

Hopkins, Lemuel, 121, 130

Hotchkiss, A. S., city reporter under Day, 201, 205

Howard, Chauncey, associate editor under Boswell, 199

Hubbard, Stephen A., editor under Day, 203

Hudson, Barzillai, partner in *Courant,*

1779–1815: marriage to Watson's widow, Feb. 11, 1779, 15; partnership with George Goodwin, Mar., 1779, 15–16; background and local activities, 15–16, 101, 103, 135, 136; son, Henry, admitted to the firm, 135; partnership dissolved, Nov. 15, 1815, 135–136

Hudson & Goodwin, booksellers and publishers: beginning of firm, 16, 128; publication of Trumbull's *M'Fingal*, 16, 130–131; publication of Webster's spelling book, 16, 132–134, 136; expansion of business, 128–130; publication of Strong's almanac, 131–132; publication of *Children's Magazine*, 134; first Bible in Connecticut published by, 134, 135, 136; religious publications of, 135; restriction of bookselling under Goodwin & Sons, 178, 186; publishing activities continued, 179; original publications discontinued after 1823, 179

Humphreys, David, 121, 130

Independent Treasury, opposed by *Courant,* 207–208, 210, 212, 214

Ingersoll, Jared, forced to resign as Connecticut Stamp Distributor, 20–21

Insurance, editorials in favor of, 104, 169, 197, 242; various types of, 104, 242, 266

Inventions, colonial interest in, 51–53

Jackson, Andrew, personal criticism of in *Courant*, 142, 144–145, 151–152, 153, 154–155, 156, 157, 207, 212; inaugural address, 146; appointees criticized, 146; hostility to administration's policies, 146–150, 151–152, 153–155, 208–209; first message to Congress, 148

"Jacobins." *See* "Democrats"

Jay, John, 76

Jay Treaty, 69–71, 72, 91

Jefferson, Thomas, accused of pro-French leanings by *Courant,* 67, 71, 72, 75–76; election campaigns of, 71, 75–79, 85; appointments criticized, 75, 80–81; lack of respect for Constitution, 75–76; personnel and methods of followers condemned, 75–79, 83–85, 86, 113, 142; Jeffersonian newspapers, 76–77; inauguration, 80; op-

Jefferson, Thomas (*cont.*)
position to foreign policy of, 86–88, 90; small-navy policy criticized, 87, 90; retirement of, 89

Kansas-Nebraska Act of 1854, 197, 254; introduction of by Douglas, 222; editorial policy on, 222, 223–224, 226–227, 229; signature of by Pierce, 223; issue side-stepped by Know-Nothing party, 225; defeat of Lecompton forces, 229
Know-Nothings, party policies supported by *Courant,* 1856–57, 200, 224–228, 253; split on Kansas-Nebraska issue, 225; nomination of Fillmore, 225; activities of Connecticut party, 225–226; principles held in common with Republicans, 226, 227; party repudiated by *Courant,* 228
Kossuth, Louis, 195, 220

Lafayette, gala reception in Hartford, 111, 176; grand tour of America in 1824, 168, 220
Land distribution: Connecticut's interest in, 62–63, 209, 211; in connection with westward migration and Indian problems, 148, 149; editorial policy on, 149–150, 208–209, 214, 220–221; relation to tariff issue, 211; Whig program of enacted, 1841, 211
Ledyard, Austin, partner in Watson's paper mill, 11; died 1776, 14; widow inherits share in mill, 14
Ledyard, John, author of first "Carrier's Address," 122–123
Libraries (Hartford): Athenaeum, 162, 248, 249; "City Library," 108; Library Association, 248; Library Company, 162
Lincoln, Abraham, administration of supported by *Courant,* 200, 257–264, 265–266; speeches and proclamations by, 203, 256, 263; election campaigns of, 230–233, 264–265; praise of statesmanship, 233, 265; criticism of war policies, 256–257, 264; editorial on death of, 268
Lind, Jenny, concert in Hartford, 1851, 249–250
Locofocos, attacked in *Courant,* 209, 213; *see also* Democrats, northern

Louisiana Purchase, 222; opposed by *Courant,* 82–83
Lyceums, popularity of, 162–163, 249; lectures sponsored by Young Men's Institute reported in detail by *Courant,* 249
Lyon, Matthew, 73, 74; conviction of under Sedition Law, 128

Madison, James, pro-French sentiments of, 71, 89, 90–91, 96–97; resignation rumored under Jefferson, 81; election to presidency, 88; policies of administration opposed by *Courant,* 89, 91–92, 93–94, 94–96, 99, 142; conduct of War of 1812 criticized, 94–100
Maine, state of, 208, 228; prohibition law of adopted in Connecticut, 254
Manifest Destiny, doctrine of condemned by *Courant,* 216, 220
Marshall, John, 72
Massachusetts, state of: "Circular Letter" reprinted in *Courant,* 24; delegates to Continental Congress entertained in Hartford, 27; economic dependence of Connecticut on, 18, 102; Farmington Canal approved by legislature, 172; opposition to Commutation Act in, 59
Massachusetts Emigrant Aid Society, activities of endorsed by *Courant,* 223
Mecom, Benjamin, publisher of *Connecticut Gazette,* 4, 8
Mercury. See American Mercury
Mexico, relations with, 213, 214; Polk's conduct of war with condemned in *Courant,* 215–216; foreign claims to disputed, 262
Middletown (Connecticut), political gatherings held in, 24, 59–60, 260; railroad competition with Hartford, 236–237, 238; smallpox epidemic in, 43
Missouri Compromise, supported by *Courant,* 216, 218, 222, 223
Monroe, James, as Minister to France, 70; administration of favored by *Courant,* 142, 143; profanation of Sabbath by, 168
Monroe Doctrine, 142, 262
Music, in connection with religion, 108, 162; local musical events covered by *Courant,* 162, 249–250

Napoleon (Bonaparte), influence in precipitating War of 1812, 87, 89–91, 127; condemned editorially, 96–97; downfall of, 97, 99

Napoleon (Louis Napoleon), claims to Mexico, 262; threats of intervention in Civil War by, 262–263

New England: dependence on protective tariff, 143, 146–147; industrialization of, 237; railroad mania in, 156; sectional feeling in War of 1812, 94, 97, 99; support of Federalism, 80, 88

New Haven, appearance of compared with Hartford, 1835, 175; attacked during Revolution, 53; canal project of opposed by *Courant,* 170; legislative sessions in, 140, 193; railroad projects of, 172–174

New Haven Gazette, 121

New London (Connecticut), "Marine List" covered in *Courant,* 118, 182; port of, 53, 98; Union Bank of, 102

New London Gazette, 4, 21

New York, state of: economic dependence of Connecticut on, 18, 102; illicit traffic with Connecticut, 35–36, 54

New York City, abolitionist meetings held in, 166–167; Stamp Act Congress held in, 20

New Year's poems. *See* "Carrier's Address"

Newsgathering, in earlier issues, 6–7, 101; during Revolutionary period, 8–9, 32–33, 128; increased speed of under later editors, 194–196, 197, 200, 201, 203, 205

News coverage, agricultural, 125–126, 181, 197; crime, 45–47, 107, 174, 181, 196, 201; local, 6, 101, 182, 196–197, 200, 201; political, 9–10, 32–33, 34, 117–118, 124, 152, 181, 184, 194–195, 197, 200; war, 8–9, 15, 32–34, 36–37, 117, 201, 202–203, 266

Niles, John M., 203, 248; political activities of, 146, 156, 209, 222; writer for *Hartford Times,* 145, 179

Order of the Cincinnati, 59–61, 111–112, 120

Orders in Council, British, 87, 90, 95

Paine, Thomas, friendship with Jefferson, 71, 84; writings of, 8, 32, 34, 69, 77

Parker & Company (New York), publishers of *Connecticut Gazette,* 3, 4

Patten, Nathaniel, copyright controversies with Hudson & Goodwin, 130–131, 133–134

"Pelham" letters, 77

Pennsylvania, state of: land grant disputes with Connecticut, 62–63

Philadelphia, abolition meetings held in, 166–167; political gatherings held in, 27–28, 63

Philadelphia Congress. *See* Continental Congress

Philadelphia Convention. *See* Constitution

Pickering, Timothy, 87

Pierce, Franklin, 221, 223, 226; administration of criticized by *Courant,* 225

Pinckney, Charles C., 71–72

Politics (*Courant*)

    Anti-British, 1764–83: influence of location on political viewpoint, 17–19; opposition to Stamp Act, 19–22; Buy American movement, 22–24; smuggling encouraged, 25–26; opposition to Boston Port Act, 27; support of Continental Congress, 27–28; stimulation of war morale, 27, 33–34, 36; persecution of loyalists, 29–31, 36; in favor of independence, 31–32, 36; illicit traffic with British condemned, 35–36; account of peace celebration in Hartford, 37

    Federalist, 1783–1800: in favor of Commutation Act, 59–61; support of federal union and the Constitution, 61–65; French Revolution condemned, 66–67; opposition to Jeffersonian "democrats," 67–69, 71–72, 73; in favor of Jay Treaty, 69–71; hostility toward French, 71–72; XYZ affair, 72–73; support of Alien and Sedition Laws, 73, 74; "nonpartisan" before 1800, 126

    Federalist, 1800–15: campaign against Jefferson, 1800, 71, 75–79; principles of Federalism upheld against Jefferson, 80–88; Madison's administration opposed, 89; prewar attitude pro-British, 89–91, 93–94;

Politics (*cont.*)
    criticism of Madison and Jefferson, 91–92, 92–93; conduct of War of 1812 opposed, 94–100; official organ of Federalist party, 1801, 126–127; *see also* Federalists

    Federalist sympathies, 1815–36: waning spirit of Federalism supported, 139, 141–143, 150; political indifference in 1820's, 142; support of Monroe's administration, 142, 143; support of John Q. Adams' administration, 143, 144; protective tariff advocated, 143–144; opposition to Jackson, 146–150, 151–152, 153–155; *see also* Federalists

    Whig, 1837–54: organ of Whig party under Boswell, 155, 156, 193; connection with Whig party severed, 200, 225; support of party candidates and principles, 207–224, 264; *see also* Whigs

    Know-Nothing, 1855–56: organ of Know-Nothing party, 200, 225; support of party candidates and principles, 224–228, 253; party repudiated, 228; *see also* Know-Nothings

    Republican, 1856–64: drift toward Republican party, 200, 225–226; party policies and candidates endorsed, 226, 227–233, 256–266, 267, 268; *see also* Republicans

Polk, James K., campaign of 1844, 213–214; policies of administration opposed by *Courant,* 214–215; conduct of Mexican War criticized, 215–216

Post (Hartford), 203, 232

Press (Hartford), 203

Railroads, building of subsidized by Congress, 148, 221; competing interests, 235–237; enthusiasm for, 156, 172–174, 235; growth of, 240–241; promotion of local investment, 197, 235, 241

Recreation, varied forms of, 42, 109–111, 163–164, 250–252, 267; changing policy on the theater, 42, 109–110, 164, 250–251; circus condemned by *Courant,* 110–111, 164, 197, 252; sports encouraged, 251–252, 267

Religion, *Courant*'s interest in, 54–55, 112, 158, 180, 253; charitable and humanitarian activities, 111–112, 158–160, 248, 253; clergy, 28, 49, 54–55, 84, 140; local churches, 112, 163, 234, 248; music in connection with, 108, 162; Sabbath observance, 113, 163, 168–169, 253; state support of, 54, 84, 112, 140

Republicans ("democrats"), political methods of, 75, 76, 84–85; accused of immorality, 76–78, 83–84; repeal of Circuit Court Act advocated by, 81; first Republican Congress, 82; opposition to Federalists in Connecticut, 84–85, 86, 88, 139–140

Republicans (Lincoln's party): support of Lincoln's administration, 1860–64, 200, 257–264, 265–266, 268; appearance of new party, 224, 225–226; campaigns in Connecticut, 226, 227–228, 230–233, 264–265; party policies, 228–230, 231–232, 233, 256, 264; Frémont's candidacy endorsed, 227, 228; Lincoln's candidacy endorsed, 230–232, 264–265; Wide-Awakes, 232–233; *see also* Civil War; Slavery

Retreat for the Insane (Hartford), 160, 234

Revenue Act of 1764, colonial oposition to, 17

Revolutionary War. *See* Politics, 1764–83

Rhode Island, state of, 65; cheap-money movements in, 62

Rivington's *Gazetteer* (New York), 33; loyalism of, 29–30

Rush, Benjamin, antiliquor sentiments of, 112

Sampson, Ezra, "Brief Remarker" letters, 180; editorial assistant under Hudson & Goodwin, 125

Seabury, Reverend Samuel, first American Episcopal bishop, 54

Secession, Democrats in favor of, 214; editorial policy toward, 231–232, 233; growth of disunion sentiment, 219–220; threats of, 228, 232

Seymour, Thomas, first mayor of Hartford, 1784, 101

Seymour, Thomas H., editor of *Jeffersonian,* 180

Sigourney, Lydia, 184, 198; poem on death of George Goodwin, 190

Slavery, annexation of Texas in relation to, 213, 214, 215, 218; Compromise of 1850, 218, 220, 221, 222, 223; Dred Scott decision, 228–229; emancipation, 263–264; expansion of into federal territories opposed by *Courant,* 193, 216–223, 226–227, 229, 233; John Brown's raid, 230; Kansas-Nebraska Act, 222, 223–224; Missouri Compromise, 216, 218, 222, 223; perpetuation of favored by Democrats, 214; recovery of fugitive slaves, 45, 218, 223; system condemned by *Courant,* 112, 217, 222–223, 226, 228, 265–266; Whig policies on, 219, 264; Wilmot Proviso, 216–217, 218

Smith, Lucius E., associate editor under Boswell, 199

Social customs, family life in colonial period, 38; place of women in society, 38–39, 253; fashions for women, 39–41, 202, 253; "town ways" in rural Connecticut, 41–42; social life of 1860's, 251–252, 267; fads and manners of, 1850's, 252–253

South Carolina, state of: tariff nullification movement in opposed by *Courant,* 147, 153, 210

Stagecoaches, travel by, 114–115, 128, 168, 169

Stamp Act of 1765, colonial opposition to, 19–22

Stanton, Edwin M., incompetence of, 264

Steamboats, beginning of local interest in, 114; interference of schedules with Sabbath observance, 168; first advertisement of in *Courant,* 169; canal and river projects in connection with, 169–172; decline in river traffic, 237, 238, 240

Strong, Nathan, 134

Strong, Nehemiah, *Courant's* authority on celestial mechanics, 51; author of almanac published by Hudson & Goodwin, 131–132

Stuart, Isaac W., ("Scaeva"), 197

Suffrage, Republican policies on opposed by *Courant,* 85, 139–140; women's rights movement disapproved, 253

Supplement to the Connecticut Courant. See Courant (Hartford)

Tariff, protective: compromise of 1833, 153–154, 210; connection with land distribution, 148, 211; demand for in Connecticut, 147, 148; editorial policy on, 143–144, 153–154, 156, 193, 211–212, 220; favored by New England, 143, 146–147; issue in Whig politics, 211–212, 214, 221; nullification movement, 147, 153, 210; Walker tariff of 1846, 214, 220

Taxes, federal, 61–62, 81, 211, 257, 260; increase of advocated by *Courant,* 161, 257, 260

Temperance movement, support of by *Courant:* antiliquor sentiments, 1786, 112; major issue in 1820's, 164–166, 197; editorial endorsing total abstinence, 165–166; liquor advertisements refused after 1832, 166; support of Washington movement, 253–255; "Maine law" enacted, 1854, 254

Texas, annexation of opposed by *Courant,* 212–213, 215; favored by Democrats, 214; admission of as slave state, 215, 218

Thayer, Eli, 226

Times (Hartford), founding of by Frederick D. Bolles, 1817, 179; politically in opposition to *Courant,* 140, 145, 150, 193, 203, 209, 222, 230, 232, 254, 260

Toucey, Isaac, Democratic senator from Connecticut, 209, 222, 249

Transportation. *See* Railroads; Stagecoaches; Steamboats

Travel, facilities for increased by government appropriation, 148, 221; improvement of road conditions, 104, 128, 169; *see also* Connecticut River

Travelers Insurance Company, 266

Trumbull, Benjamin, *History of Connecticut,* 134

Trumbull, John, 119, 121, 130; *M'Fingal,* 16, 130–131

Trumbull, Jonathan, Governor of Connecticut, 35, 119, 120

Trumbull, Jonathan, son of preceding, 73, 83, 88

Turner, Jacob A., compositor under Day, 204

Tyler, John, presidency of, 210, 211–212; editorial attack upon, 212

United States Bank: approved by *Courant,* 148, 208, 210; manipulation of by Jackson, 154, 155, 207

Van Buren, Martin: presidential candidacy of supported by Democrats, 156; personal criticism of in *Courant,* 207, 209; creation of Independent Treasury by, 207–208; land policies of, 208–209
Virginia, state of: Resolves of 1767, 24; undue political influence of, 81, 82, 91

War of 1812: Napoleon's connection with, 87, 89–91, 96–97, 127; editorial policy in prewar years, 89–94; antiwar feeling in New England, 94, 97, 99; Madison personally blamed for, 94–96; obstruction of war program encouraged by *Courant,* 97–99; close of, 99–100; depression following, 100, 177, 178
Warner, Charles Dudley, assistant editor under Day, 203
Washington, George, 71, 76, 103, 109, 111, 134, 217; Federalist principles of, 73, 78, 92; first administration of, 66; naval policy of, 89–90, 98–99; neutrality proclamation by, 67
Washington College (Hartford), 160, 234
Watson, Ebenezer, partner and owner of *Courant,* 1767–77: partnership with Thomas Green, *ca.* Dec., 1767, 8; in complete charge of *Courant,* 1767–70, 8; sole owner, Dec., 1770, 8; early training under Green, 8; business activities in connection with *Courant,* 8; personal viewpoint in journalism, 10, 15, 36; establishment of paper mill undertaken by, 1775, 11; partnership with Austin Ledyard, 11; projected journey to procure type, 12; died Sept. 22, 1777, 13; inventory of estate, 13
Watson, Mrs. Ebenezer (Hannah Bunce): inheritance of paper mill, 14; partnership with Ledyard's widow, 14; partnership with George Goodwin, 1778, 14; authorized to raise funds by public lottery to re-build paper mill, 14; marriage to Barzillai Hudson, Feb. 11, 1779, 15
Webster, Daniel, debates and speeches, 147, 148, 152, 153; as presidential candidate, 156, 217; settlement of Maine boundary dispute by, 213; support of Compromise of 1850 by, 218–219; death of, 221
Webster, Noah, *American Spelling Book,* 16, 129, 132–134; dictionary compiled by, 129, 179, 242; "Honorius Letters," 119; letters in favor of federal taxation, 61–62; letters on land-grant disputes, 62–63; miscellaneous publications, 130, 134; prolific contributor to *Courant,* 118–120, 121, 123; teaching activities of, 47–48, 49, 161
Welles, Gideon, 203, 248; political activities of, 146, 209, 264; writer for Hartford *Times,* 145, 180
Wells, Horace, 197; claims to discovery of anesthesia by, 247
Whigs, appearance of new party, 155; activities of party in Connecticut, 155, 156, 193, 209, 214, 219, 222–223, 224; presidential campaigns, 1836–52, 156, 207, 209–210, 213–214, 217–218, 221; currency and tariff as major issues, 208, 210, 211–212, 214, 220, 221; political program of 1840, 210; land-distribution program enacted 1841, 211; opposition to Mexican War, 215–216; fusion with Know-Nothing party, 224–225; *see also* Slavery
Whiskey Rebellion, 70
Whittier, John Greenleaf, 179
Williams, William, 120, 121
Wilmot Proviso, fought for by *Courant,* 216–217, 218
Wimble War, 120–122
Winthrop, John, of Harvard College, 52
Wolcott, Oliver, Jr., political sympathies of, 119, 120; elected Republican Governor of Connecticut, 1817, 139

XYZ correspondence, 72–73, 128

Yale Medical School, opening of in 1810, 106
Yale College, commencement news in *Courant,* 6, 55; criticism of curriculum, 49; students of, 23, 48